True Crime

CLASSIC, RARE AND UNSEEN

True Crime

CLASSIC, RARE AND UNSEEN

Tim Hill

Photographs from the

Daily Mail

Welcome Rain Publishers   New York

This Edition Published by Welcome Rain Publishers LLC in 2009

First published by
Transatlantic Press
38 Copthorne Road
Croxley Green
Hertfordshire, WD3 4AQ, UK

ISBN 1-56649-994-1/ 978-1-56649-994-1

Printed in Singapore

Contents

Dr Hawley Harvey Crippen:
Murder at Hilldrop Crecent — 10

The Assassination of
Archduke Franz Ferdinand — 18

Henri Desire Landru:
The French Bluebeard — 20

Roscoe 'Fatty' Arbuckle — 24

Al Capone:
Chicago's gangland overlord — 28

Bonnie and Clyde — 34

The kidnapping of
Charles Lindbergh Jnr — 38

John Dillinger:
Public Enemy No. 1 — 48

John Christie:
10 Rillington Place — 52

Marcel Petiot:
The Butcher of Paris — 64

The Black Dahlia:
Elizabeth Short — 68

Geraghty and Jenkins:
Charlotte Street, 1947 — 70

John George Haigh:
The Acid Bath Murders — 76

Lloyds Bank Raid:
The Murder of George Black — 90

Double Jeopardy:
The murder of Stanley Setty — 92

Derek Bentley:
'Let him have it' — 96

Contents

Drummond Murders 110

Teddington
Towpath Murders 114

Ruth Ellis: The last woman
to be hanged in Britain 118

Arthur Albert Jones 122

James Hanratty:
The A6 murders 124

Albert Henry DeSalvo:
The Boston Strangler 132

The Great Train Robbery 134

Dallas: November 22, 1963 148

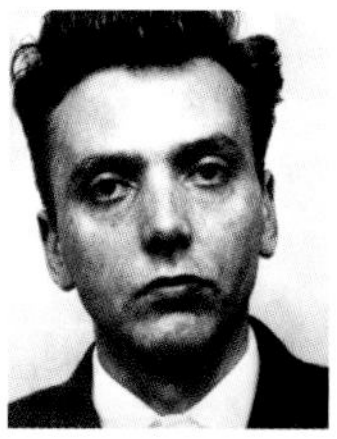

Moors Murders:
Ian Brady and 154
Myra Hindley

The Profumo Affair 166

The Krays 174

Harry Roberts:
The Braybrook Street massacre 184

John Gotti 194

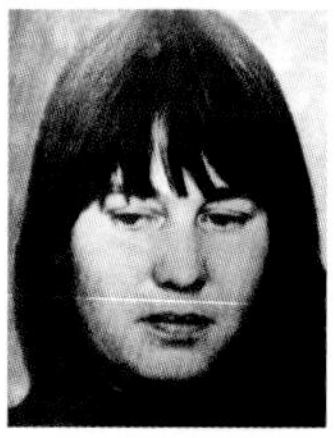

Baader-Meinhof 196

John Wayne Gacy:
The killer clown 198

Charles Manson:
The Sharon Tate murders 200

Contents

Ted Bundy 204

Lord Lucan:
The murder of Sandra Rivett 206

Patty Hearst:
Kidnapped heiress 212

Mayfair Bank robbery 214

Donald Neilson:
The Black Panther 216

Peter Sutcliffe:
The Yorkshire Ripper 224

Australia's trial of the
century 236

Wayne Williams:
The Atlanta murders 238

Jeffrey Dahmer 242

Brinks-Mat robbery:
22 million gold haul 244

Dennis Nilsen 248

Michael Ryan:
The Hungerford Massacre 256

O.J Simpson: Murder case 262

The Wests:
House of Horrors 268

Harold Shipman:
Doctor Death 276

Introduction

Crime fascinates us endlessly, perhaps because we can readily identify with the common motives – greed, fear, sex, anger, hatred, jealousy, a craving for self-esteem. Adults find criminals and their monstrous acts as ghoulishly compelling as any child immersed in a fairy tale. The fact that Rillington Place, where the remains of Christie's victims were discovered, had to be renamed Rushton Close to throw sightseers off the scent, demonstrates that gruesome deeds have the capacity to attract as well as repel.

True Crime: Classic, Rare and Unseen examines the lives and deeds of some of the most notorious criminals of the past century through contemporaneous reports and many previously unseen photographs from the Daily Mail, archives which vividly recreate the impact of some of the greatest causes célèbres in legal history. There are murders, gangland killings, kidnappings, scandals and robberies, with an unsavoury cast that includes Crippen, Dillinger, Bonnie and Clyde, Gacy, Brady, Manson and Sutcliffe. Some crimes are more commonly known by place or modus operandi, such as The Boston Strangler and The Acid Bath Murders while others, for instance the assassinations of John F. Kennedy and Arch Duke Ferdinand, and acts of terrorism, like those perpetrated by the notorious urban guerrillas Baader-Meinhof, have made an impact on the course of history.

Dr Hawley Harvey Crippen:
Murder at Hilldrop Crecent

The case of Hawley Harvey Crippen has gone down in the annals of the criminal justice system for the part that cutting-edge communications technology played in the arrest. It was the first time that wireless telegraphy had been used to relay information regarding the whereabouts of a murder suspect, information that led to a dramatic chase on the high seas and the apprehension of both the wanted man and his mistress. Less well remembered are the gruesome events that occurred seven months earlier, in January 1910, which precipitated the flight.

ABOVE RIGHT: Dr Crippen, the Camden Town murderer. Crippen went down in history because of the part cutting-edge communications technology played in his arrest.

ABOVE: Crippen's house at number 39 Hilldrop Crescent. He and his second wife Cora took in lodgers to supplement Crippen's meager income.

Medical training

Crippen was born in Coldwater, Michigan in 1862. He undertook medical training at Cleveland Homeopathic Hospital, taking a sabbatical to gain experience at Bethlehem Royal Hospital in London before graduating in 1885. He would become an eye and ear specialist, but the edges of the medical profession were blurred during that period, and Crippen devoted a considerable amount of his professional career to dispensing patent medicines. He wasn't above penning hard-sell missives extolling the benefits of some miracle cure in an unregulated market that was notorious for the number of quacks it attracted.

Crippen takes a second wife

In September 1892, Crippen married 18-year-old Cora Turner, the daughter of Eastern European immigrants, whose real name was Kunigunde Mackamotzki. He had buried his first wife just eight months earlier, consigning the son from that union, Hawley Otto, to the care of grandparents in California. In 1894 Crippen took up employment with Munyon's Remedies, a patent medicine company that specialised in homeopathic treatments. Around the turn of the century, he was dispatched across the Atlantic to oversee the running of a new Munyon's office in London. That field held little attraction for Cora, who was far more interested in the capital's theatrical set. She soon cultivated many friends from that milieu, and as well as getting some work as a performer, using the stage name Belle Elmore, she also became treasurer of the Music Hall Ladies' Guild, an organisation formed to support female artistes who had fallen on hard times.

39 Hilldrop Crescent

Accounts of Crippen's second marriage vary, from tender to combustible. The doctor was, by all accounts, docile and indulgent, traits that came in very handy when dealing with an ill-tempered wife who had extravagant tastes and lofty theatrical ambitions. Cora was too lacking in refinement to make the impression she craved on the operatic world, despite the image she sought to project. The couple appeared to drift towards a status quo in which they put up a reasonably harmonious public front, while pursuing their separate agendas in private. A house move in 1905 was part of the charade. The Crippens took up residence at 39 Hilldrop Crescent in Camden Town, a property large enough for them not to be under each other's feet, and indeed, large enough to obviate the need for them to share a marital bed.

Clandestine affair

The care and expense Cora lavished on her own appearance did not extend to the rest of the household. She was happy to leave 39 Hilldrop Crescent a dirty, chaotic mess, but her housekeeping skills – or lack thereof – appeared not to ruffle her husband. When they took in paying guests to supplement their income, it was Crippen who took on most of the domestic chores. It needed more than slatternliness to drive Dr Crippen to murder; namely, the appearance on the scene of a lover.

There is evidence to suggest that Cora was unfaithful many times over, whereas Crippen had but a single grand passion. Ethel Le Neve was the latter's secretary at Munyon's, the two conducting a clandestine affair over several years. Matters came to a head in January 1910, when Ethel celebrated her 27th birthday. Having seen her sister marry at nineteen and produce two children, Ethel yearned to put the mistress's tag behind her and gain the respectability that would attend becoming the wife of respected medical practitioner and businessman Hawley Harvey Crippen. Who knows whether she brought any pressure to bear on the doctor, but what is clear is that they both willed the same end: that Cora Crippen should be an obstruction no longer.

There is a suggestion that Cora discovered the affair and demanded its termination, something Crippen could not countenance. In December 1909, Cora gave the Crippens' bank the required 12-months notice for the withdrawal of their funds, some £600. Was this part of a threat to her husband or, as was also suggested, merely the action of a supportive wife seeking to raise capital to fund his various business ventures? At Crippen's trial, the prosecuting counsel would highlight this as a motive for murder, though it appears a somewhat meagre reward for such drastic action.

> The Crippens took up residence at 39 Hilldrop Crescent in Camden Town, a property large enough for them not to be under each other's feet.

TOP: Miss Ethel Le Neve, Crippens lover. Crippen claimed that Cora had returned to the United States and had died in California. Le Neve moved into Hilldrop Crescent and began openly wearing Cora's clothes and jewellery.

ABOVE: Mrs Cora Crippen, also known as variety actress Belle Elmore.

LEFT: Miss Smythson and Miss Fawkes, witnesses in the Crippen trial.

Meticulous planning

If Crippen considered taking the more natural option of pressing for a divorce, amicable or otherwise, he obviously soon discounted it. In mid-January he used his professional position to place an order for five grains of hyoscine hydrobromide, which in minute quantities – one-hundredth of a grain - could be used as a sedative. The quantity acquired by Crippen was enough to kill several times over. The fact that the drug was not recorded in any Munyon's ledger was a damning piece of evidence, as was the fact that he obtained it two weeks before Cora's death. This was to be no crime passionel, carried out in a fit of rage. Rather, it was the result of meticulous planning on the part of a man desperate to be rid of a slovenly, shrewish wife so that he could make an honest woman of his long-time mistress.

Murder in mind

On 31 January 1910 Crippen invited friends Paul and Clara Martinetti round to Hilldrop Crescent for dinner and a game of cards. He had murder in mind but wanted witnesses who would be able to attest to a convivial evening, should they be required to do so. Indeed, Paul Martinetti had felt unwell that day, yet Crippen made no offer to release him from the engagement, even though it was a cold winter night. It was around 1.30 am when the party broke up, but Crippen's work was only just beginning. After the hyoscine took its deadly effect on Cora, he dismembered her body, removing all means of identification. Or so he thought.

Many of the body parts, including the head and all the bones, were never found. The likelihood is that some were incinerated – neighbours recalled much waste-burning activity in the back garden – or else deposited in some watery depths. But unaccountably, Crippen chose to bury some tissue in the cellar, covering it in quicklime to hasten the decomposition process. His next task was to account for Cora's sudden disappearance, and that required putting pen to paper.

Crippen wrote to the Music Hall Ladies' Guild – of which Clara Martinetti was also a member – informing them that it might be some time before they saw their treasurer again. 'Please forgive me a hasty letter and any inconvenience I may cause you, but I have just had news of the illness of a near relative and at only a few hours' notice I am obliged to go to America.' It was signed Belle Ellmore, Cora's stage name. It soon emerged that Crippen was behind the letter, for he had misspelt his wife's theatrical moniker, which was written with a single L. He waved that away by saying that he had acted as scribe while Cora was preparing for her hasty departure. It was all very odd, though not unduly suspicious.

JULY 15, 1910

Absconding couple

Yesterday Scotland Yard made a new departure of a most interesting character in their method of crime investigation. The authorities for the first time in their history took the Press into their confidence and issued the following official statement relating to the crime and the steps which led to its discovery:-

Mrs. Cora Crippen, otherwise Belle Elmore, or Belle Mackamotski, an American lady and music-hall artiste, was married some years ago in New York to an American doctor named Hawley Harvey Crippen, alias Peter Crippen, alias Franckel, who for some years represented Munyon's remedies in London, was connected with the Drouet Institute, and has latterly carried on a dental business at Albion House, New Oxford-street, as the Yale Tooth Specialist. Mrs. Crippen was a very charming lady, and was very popular in the music-hall world, and was honorary secretary to the Music-hall Ladies' Guild. They have been in England for some years, and for the past four years they have resided, apparently very happily, at 39, Hilldrop Crescent, Camden Road.

TOP RIGHT: Crippen's house, where police found the remains of a human body buried under the brick floor of the basement. Traces of scopolamine, a calming drug, were also found. The corpse had to be identified from a piece of skin from its abdomen because the head, limbs and skeleton were never recovered. The body was that of Cora Crippen.

FAR LEFT: Witnesses Miss Lil Hawthorne and Mrs Stallon attend the trial.

ABOVE: Chief inspector Walter Dew. Crippen and his lover Ethel Le Neve fled to Brussels after police inquired into Cora's disappearance. Even though detectives had been satisfied with their story, their disappearance led to searches of the house on Hilldrop Crescent.

> Many of the body parts, including the head and all the bones, were never found. The likelihood is that some were incinerated.

Series of lies

Crippen wasted little time before cashing in some of Cora's jewellery at a pawnbroker's, though first he picked out some pieces for his beloved Ethel. The unseemly speed with which Crippen and Ethel were seen about town, the latter attired in Cora's clothes as well as jewellery, raised eyebrows. Crippen even had the nerve to take her to a ball organised by the Music Hall Ladies' Guild less than three weeks after Cora's sudden departure. In doing so he flaunted his mistress in front of some of his wife's dearest friends. It was a month later, mid-March, that those friends became truly alarmed. Crippen reported that Cora had become dangerously ill with pneumonia, but he showed no inclination to listen to their entreaties and take the next available crossing. On 23 March, the stage publication *The Era* carried the news that Belle Elmore had succumbed to the infection. Crippen packed his bags now, though not for America; he took himself off to France with Ethel. The latter claimed to know nothing of Cora's death at this point, though bizarrely, she spoke of her engagement to Crippen back in January, and now wrote to her family saying that she was a married woman. No wedding took place, but she and Crippen regarded themselves as 'hubby' and 'wifey', as they affectionately called each other.

Cora's friends raise the alarm

Cora's friends, meanwhile, were reeling with the kind of shock that evidently was not afflicting Crippen. They wanted further details of the tragedy but found Crippen vague on the subject. First he said she had died at his son's house in Los Angeles, but a letter from Hawley Otto Crippen said that he was as much in the dark as anyone. All he knew was what his father had told him, namely, that Cora had died in San Francisco. Crippen claimed it was an error born of confusion. He was asked what boat Cora had taken. Crippen blustered. There was no record of Cora, or Belle, on any passenger list. This, along with the evidence of their own eyes watching Ethel Le Neve disporting herself around town with Crippen wearing Cora's finery, was enough to persuade the missing woman's friends to take their concerns to the police.

On 6 July 1910 Chief Inspector Walter Dew paid Crippen a visit, to be informed that Cora had left him, and that the story of the sick relative in America had been fabricated as a face-saving exercise. Ethel was there at the time, introduced to Dew as the housekeeper. Crippen invited the policeman to search the premises, even though he had no warrant to do so, and Dew appeared to be satisfied. The mild-mannered, co-operative physician might have appeared unflappable, but the visit obviously spooked him, for he and Ethel soon hatched their plan for a daring transatlantic escape. First they went to Antwerp, where they boarded the Canada-bound SS Montrose.

THE ARREST.

COLLAPSE OF MISS LE NEVE.

INSPECTOR DEW'S DISGUISE.

DRAMATIC SCENE.

CAPTAIN KENDALL'S FULL NARRATIVE.

Dr. H. H. Crippen and Miss Ethel Le Neve were arrested in the Montrose at 9.30 yesterday morning (2.30 p.m. Greenwich time). They were described in the police notice as, "Wanted for murder and mutilation."

Scotland Yard at 4.5 p.m. received the following message from Inspector Dew, who had formally identified them:—

Crippen and Le Neve arrested. Will wire later.—Dew.

This wireless pursuit of Crippen is due alone to the acumen, astuteness, and ability of Captain Kendall, of the Montrose, whose exclusive messages to the "Daily Mail" have been a triumph of detective journalism.

Inspector Dew and the Canadian police were disguised as pilots when they boarded the vessel. Crippen betrayed anxiety as the boat approached, but was taken quite unawares when the police accosted him. Miss Le Neve almost collapsed.

Both were subjected to a lengthy examination by Mr. Dew, and it is understood that Crippen admitted his identity, and said that he was glad that the suspense was over. Several diamond rings were found in his possession.

He is charged with the murder and mutilation of his second wife, Mrs. Cora Crippen, known as Belle Elmore on the music-hall stage. The circumstances of the case are fully told on the next page. The Montrose carried him and the police on to Quebec yesterday. According to cablegrams, he will be sent back immediately.

BELOW: Inspector Dew and C. Denis, disguised as pilots, in a boat. They boarded the S S Montrose as it entered the St Lawrence River. At the time Canada was a British dominion so Inspector Dew could act without limitation.

Grisly Secret

Meanwhile, police had discovered that Crippen and his accomplice had flown and were swarming over 39 Hilldrop Crescent. The cellar's shallow grave soon gave up its grisly secret. While forensics experts got to work on the remains, Dew was in hot pursuit of the fleeing couple. Their descriptions had been widely circulated, and Crippen must have thought himself clever to have Ethel decked out in boy's clothes so that they might travel as father and child. The disguise didn't fool the Montrose's captain Henry Kendall for long. There was something not quite right about the 'child's' demeanour or his attitude towards the adult accompanying him. He tested his suspicions by calling out to Crippen by his assumed name, Robinson, and saw that he had to be prompted by his 'son' to respond. Kendall's vessel was fitted with radio communication, then a fledgling technology, and he sent a message to London expressing the belief that the Mr and Master Robinson on his passenger list were in fact Crippen and Le Neve. He had more than half an eye on the £250 reward on offer for information leading to the capture of the two absconders.

Police and press give chase

The police had already learned that Crippen had sent dental technician William Long to purchase a suit of boy's clothes, so the communication from the Montrose represented another piece of the jigsaw slotting into place. Dew gave chase aboard a faster ship, the Laurentic, which overhauled the Montrose a day before the latter docked. A large press pack was in attendance, for the paths of the two vessels had been plotted in the newspapers, which gave acres of space to the gruesome Camden Town murder. Dew wrong-footed the reporters by boarding the Montrose via a tugboat on 31 July, and when he bade Crippen good morning by his real name, there was no attempt at dissembling. 'I am more than satisfied,' said Crippen, when asked for an assurance that he wouldn't jump overboard, 'the anxiety has been too awful.' His immediate concern was to protect Ethel, saying she was a complete innocent, and the latter professed to be shocked when told what had been unearthed in the cellar of 39 Hilldrop Crescent.

LEFT: Dr Crippen returns to England to face trial. He was tried at the Old Bailey and was found guilty after just 27 minutes of deliberation.

LEFT: Mr Arthur Newton preparing the evidence at his office. During the trial there was a forensic evidence battle over the remains that were found in Crippen's home.

BELOW: Superintendent Frost attending court.

BOTTOM: Witnesses gather at the courtroom. Initially Crippen had told his wife's friends that she had died at his son's house in Los Angeles, but a letter from Hawley Otto Crippen said that he was as much in the dark as anyone. All he knew was that his father had told him that Cora had died in San Francisco.

Experts battle over forensic evidence

Crippen was charged with murder, Ethel with being an accessory after the fact. It was against the husband that the prosecution trained their weapons; they were much less concerned about what Ethel knew and when. The defence counsel contended that there was doubt over the sex of the cellar tissue, let alone that it was the remains of Cora Crippen. One particular piece of skin became the main battleground for rival experts. Eminent pathologists Augustus Pepper and Bernard Spilsbury said it came from the abdomen, and bore a scar of the kind that Cora would have been left with following an ovariectomy some fifteen years earlier. The defence tried to suggest that it was thigh tissue, and a fold in the skin rather than a scar, but Pepper and Spilsbury were imperious in their pronouncements and the experts lined up to oppose them crumbled.

Prosecution toxicologists also won the day, countering the defence's argument that the poison might have been the result of the putrefaction process. They convinced the jury that the deadly hyoscine had to have been ingested by the victim. Crippen had made a vital error in using quicklime to destroy the body, for it acted as a preservative for the hyoscine; without it, the toxicologists would have been unable to pinpoint the cause of death.

The defence tried another tack. Perhaps the remains had been there several years, pre-dating the Crippens' arrival in Hilldrop Crescent? Again the prosecution experts spiked the defence's guns: the remains had been there eight months at most.

The scientific evidence aside, much weight was attached to Cora's supposed decision to leave Crippen for good without taking all her furs, clothes and jewellery, something barely conceivable to members of her class. Crippen's lawyer was left to focus on his client's good character, and the preposterousness of the suggestion that he should have turned into 'a fiend incarnate' on the night of 31 January. The jury believed exactly that, returning a unanimous guilty verdict in barely half an hour.

A week later, Ethel pleaded Not Guilty at her trial, which lasted less than a day and ended in an acquittal. Having nailed Crippen, the prosecution seemed to have no appetite for the battle to prove Ethel's complicity.

> **Having nailed Crippen, the prosecution seemed to have no appetite for the battle to prove Ethel's complicity.**

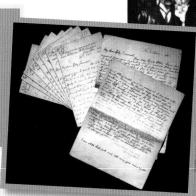

Her suit is anything but a good fit. Her trousers are very tight about the hips and are split a bit down the back and secured with large safety pins.

JULY 30, 1910

Captain's telegram: life of the couple in the Montrose'

The man on board the Montrose supposed to be Crippen answers all the descriptions given in the police report, as does also his companion that of Miss Le Neve. I discovered them two hours after leaving Antwerp, but did not telegraph to my owners until I had found out good clues. I conversed with both, and at the same time took keen observations of all points, and felt quite confident as to their identity.

They booked their passage in Brussels as Mr. John Robinson and Master Robinson, and came on board at Antwerp in brown suits, soft grey hats, and white canvas shoes. They had no baggage except a small handbag bought on the Continent. My suspicion was aroused by seeing them on the deck beside a boat. Le Neve squeezed Crippen's hand. It seemed to me unnatural for two males, so I suspected them at once.

Suspicious circumstances

I was well posted as to the crime, so got on the scent at once. I said nothing to the officers till the following morning, when I took my chief officer into my confidence. During lunch I examined both their hats. Crippen's was stamped "Jackson, Boulevard du Nord." Le Neve's hat bore no name, but it was packed around the rim with paper to make it fit. Le Neve has the manner and appearance of a very refined, modest girl. She does not speak much, but always wears a pleasant smile. She seems thoroughly under his thumb, and he will not leave her for a moment. Her suit is anything but a good fit. Her trousers are very tight about the hips and are split a bit down the back and secured with large safety pins.

Revolver in hip pocket

They have been under strict observation all the voyage, as, if they smelt a rat, he might do something rash. I have noticed a revolver in his hip pocket. He sits about on the deck reading or pretending to read, and both seem to be thoroughly enjoying all their meals. They have not been seasick, and I have discussed various parts of the world with him. He knows Toronto, Detroit, and California well, and says he is going to take his boy to California for his health, meaning Miss Le Neve.

Crippen says that when the ship arrives he will go to Detroit by boat if possible, as he prefers it. The book he has been most interested in has been "Pickwick Papers," and he is now busy reading "Four Just Men," which is all about a murder in London and a £1,000 reward.

When my suspicions were aroused as to Crippen's identity I quietly collected all the English papers on board the ship which mentioned anything of the murder, and I warned the chief officer to collect any he might see.

Captain Kendall's ruse

This being done, I considered the way was clear. I told Crippen a story to make him laugh heartily to see if he would open his mouth wide enough for me to ascertain if he had false teeth. This ruse was successful. All the "boy's" manners at the table when I was watching him were most ladylike, handling knife and fork and taking fruit off dishes with two fingers. Crippen kept cracking nuts for her and giving her half his salad, and was always paying most marked attention.

Watching the wireless

He would often sit on deck and look up aloft at the wireless "aerial," and listen to the cracking electric spark messages being sent by the Marconi operator. He said "what a wonderful invention it was." He said one day that according to our present rate of steaming he ought to be in Detroit on Tuesday, August 2. At times both would sit and appear to be in deep thought.

Though Le Neve does not show signs of distress and is perhaps ignorant of the crime committed, she appears to be a girl with a very weak will. She has to follow him everywhere. If he looks at her she gives him an endearing smile, as though she were under his hypnotic influence.

Crippen was very restless on sighting Belle Isle, and asked where we stopped for the pilot, how he came off, how far from the pilot-station to Quebec, and said he would be glad when we arrived. He was anxious to get to Detroit.

Condemned to death

Hawley Harvey Crippen was hanged at Pentonville Prison on 23 November 1910. In one of his last letters, Crippen gave Ethel his blessing to marry, and she did so in 1915, when she was going by the name of Harvey. For forty-five years, until his death in 1960, Stanley Smith remained unaware that his wife was none other than Ethel Le Neve, mistress of Dr Crippen. Ethel died seven years later, aged 84. Some believe she was an inveterate liar who profited from Crippen's selfless insistence that she was innocent of all wrongdoing, and that the prosecution could have made a much stronger case against her. But almost a century on, it seems that the precise role Ethel Le Neve played in the events at 39 Hilldrop Crescent on the night of 31 January 1910 will never be known.

OCTOBER 24, 1910

Crippen's fate

The jury were out of the box considering their verdict half an hour. It was a quarter-past two when the Lord Chief Justice concluded his powerful and lucid analysis of the grim facts of the trial. The jury took away with them to their deliberations the pyjama trousers belonging to the prisoner, and the pyjama jacket of corresponding pattern and material found among the buried remains of what had been Belle Elmore. At a quarter to three they came back.

The game was up

In the tones in which the twelve answered to the roll call of their names there was the note of consciousness of stern duty done. "Have you agreed upon your verdict?" asked the clerk. "We have," the foreman said. The Lord Chief Justice, in his scarlet and ermine robes, had returned to the Bench, but the prisoner was still in the cells to which when the jury retired he had descended. There was a pause of a moment or two until he reappeared.

"Guilty"

"Have you agreed upon your verdict?" the Clerk of Arraigns asked again. "We have," the foreman said. A silence of death fell, in which the question was put: "Do you find the prisoner guilty or not guilty?" With emphasis the foreman's answer came: "We find the prisoner guilty of wilful murder."

The little man's intertwined fingers tightened in the effort to preserve his self-command. A pallor spread over his forehead and cheeks. The bald patch at the back of his little, flat head became a dull white. His ears, placed so low that they seem to belong to the neck instead of the head, became transparent as the blood receded. The face showed no expression of emotion, but its look of concentrated attention and purpose ceased now that purpose and effort were no more of value.

Protests of innocence

The question whether he had anything to say why sentence should not be passed upon him received no answer. He stood looking at nothing, his mind blankly revolving. The clerk put the question again. Then, recalling his self-control by a supreme effort, he answered in a perfectly firm, even voice, "Only that I still protest my innocence."

The judge fitted the black cap upon his head and spoke the words of doom; to be hanged by the neck, and the body to be buried within the precincts of the prison, just as Belle Elmore's body had been buried in the house where he had killed her.

He stood motionless, with his clasped hands resting on the ledge of the dock, his head bowed a little and his hairless brows knitted. But no thought came to him to bring back purpose and intelligence to the colourless features till one of the warders touched him on the shoulder. He looked up and realised his position. He could do no more.

NOVEMBER 24, 1910

Execution of Crippen

Dr. Hawley Harvey Crippen was executed in Pentonville Prison at nine o'clock yesterday morning.

The execution was expeditiously carried out, the time which elapsed from the entrance of Ellis, the executioner, into the condemned cell for the process of pinioning until the complete fulfilment of the sentence being exactly sixty seconds. Crippen had passed a restless night, and he left untouched the frugal breakfast which had been provided for him. He paid the greatest attention to the ministrations of the Rev. Thomas Carey, the rector of the Roman Catholic Church in Eden-grove, Holloway, who was with him from shortly after six o'clock, and went to the scaffold calmly and resignedly, fortified by the last rites of his faith.

No knowledge of any confession

It was officially stated yesterday that the Home Office has no knowledge of any confession having been made by Crippen. The only persons, in addition to the prison authorities, to visit Crippen since his incarceration in Pentonville Prison have been Miss Le Neve, Mr. Arthur Newton (his solicitor), and three Roman Catholic priests connected with the Church of the Sacred Heart, Eden Grove, Holloway.

OPPOSITE TOP LEFT TOP LEFT & RIGHT: In recent years letters written by Crippen have been sold at auction. These include letters written in his cell whilst he was awaiting trial, a letter to a doctor that was sent shortly after Crippen had murdered his wife and correspondence with Lady Somerset.

OPPOSITE PAGE TOP RIGHT: Dr Marshall attending the inquest to give forensic evidence.

OPPOSITE PAGE LEFT: Superintendent Frost and Mr Williamson from the Treasury discuss the case.

OPPOSITE PAGE RIGHT: Inspector Dew gives evidence at Crippen's trial. He led the operation that had captured Crippen aboard the S. S. Montrose.

The assassination of Archduke Franz Ferdinand
Sarajevo, 28 June, 1914 - the tinder-box is ignited

Flashpoint

The tensions across Europe in the early years of the twentieth century made national security a key issue and many tried to anticipate the flashpoint which would be the precursor to a major conflict. Some eagerly awaited it. The continent had not seen war for forty years, denying states and individuals the opportunity to cover themselves in military glory, to test might and mettle. Those who felt it would be a relief for the waiting to end almost got their wish in 1911, when France and Germany clashed over their respective interests in Morocco. But although sabres were rattled, the Powers chose peace over escalation. Restraint was also shown in 1912-13, when two Balkan wars were fought. Then, on 28 June 1914, the tinder-box was ignited.

Heir to the Hapsburg throne

Archduke Franz Ferdinand, the 51-year-old nephew of Franz Josef and heir to the Habsburg throne, was well aware of the potential danger of his visit to Sarajevo. There had been previous assassination attempts by disaffected Bosnian Serbs, and for his well-publicised trip through the streets of the capital that June day he wore a jacket of a specially woven fabric that was thought to be bullet-proof. Franz Ferdinand had a reforming zeal for this part of the Austro-Hungarian Empire. Oppression of the Serb population would end under his leadership, but that was a future prospect; for now his intention was to win over the people - but to take suitable precautions just in case. Ironically, the Archduke's moderation helped to galvanise the secret society committed to the formation of a greater Serbian state (the Black Hand) into action. If oppression had fanned the flames of Serbian nationalism, a more tolerant incumbent of the Austro-Hungarian throne might dampen the ardent desire of those committed to see a Greater Serbia established. From the moment the Archduke's visit to Sarajevo had been announced, the Black Hand had got to work in earnest.

> *From the moment the Archduke's visit to Sarajevo had been announced, the Black Hand had got to work in earnest.*

Assassination in Sarajevo

In the event, the seven-strong assassination squad had fortune on their side. After a failed attempt to blow up the car carrying the Archduke and his consort Sophie, it seemed that the gang had lost their chance. But as one of their number, 19-year-old Gavrilo Princip, was pondering his next move, he was confronted by his target. The driver of the Archduke's car had taken a wrong turn, and Princip turned his 22-calibre Browning pistol on its occupants. Franz Ferdinand was struck in the neck; Sophie, who was pregnant with their fourth child, took a bullet to the stomach. Both were soon declared dead.

> *The Archduke deflected the bomb with his arm. It fell to the ground and exploded.*

> *Franz Ferdinand was struck in the neck; Sophie, who was pregnant with their fourth child, took a bullet to the stomach.*

OPPOSITE ABOVE: Archduke Franz Ferdinand and his family. His marriage was morganatic, which meant his children could not inherit the throne of Austria-Hungary.

OPPOSITE BELOW: Archduke Ferdinand and his wife alight from their car at Sarajevo city hall after the first failed assassination attempt.

ABOVE RIGHT: The Archduke and his wife leave a reception at city hall. A wrong turn on the way to their next engagement resulted in their assassination.

ABOVE: Crowds try to attack the assassin, Gavrilo Princip as police lead him away.

JUNE 29, 1914

Murder of the Austrian heir and his wife

We regret to state that the Archduke Francis Ferdinand, the heir to the throne of Austria-Hungary, and his morganatic wife, the Duchess of Hohenberg, were assassinated yesterday.

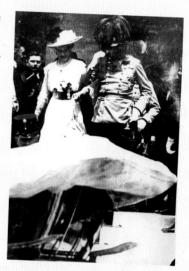

The assassination took place at Sarajevo, the capital of Bosnia, which State, together with Herzegovina, was annexed by Austria-Hungary from Turkey in 1908. Bosnia, which is bounded on the south by Montenegro and Servia, has a large Slav population that is discontented with Austrian rule.

The Archduke had paid no heed to warnings to him not to go to Bosnia on account of the disturbed state of the province. Anti-Austrian demonstrations were made before his arrival at Sarajevo on Saturday. Two attempts were made to kill the Archduke and his wife at Sarajevo yesterday. The first failed; the second was only too successful.

A twenty-one-year-old printer of Servian nationality living in Herzegovina threw a bomb at the Archduke's motor-car in the street. The Archduke deflected the bomb with his arm. It fell to the ground and exploded. The heir to the throne and his wife escaped, but a number of other people were injured, six of them seriously.

A little while later the Archduke and his wife were driving to see the victims of the bomb explosion, when a schoolboy aged nineteen, apparently also of Servian nationality, threw at them a bomb which, however, did not explode, and then fired at them with a Browning automatic pistol. Both were wounded and both died shortly afterwards. An unexploded bomb which was evidently to have been used if the other attempts failed, was found on the ground near the scene of the second attempt.

The Archduke, who was aged fifty, was the nephew of and heir to the Emperor Francis Joseph, who is aged eighty-three. His wife was formerly a Czech countess, Sophie Chotek. Both of them came to England on a visit to the King last November. They leave three young children, two boys and a girl.

Last angry speech about the bomb thrower

The authors of both attempts are born Bosnians. Gabrinovitch, the man who threw the bomb, is a compositor and worked for a few weeks in the Government printing works at Belgrade, the Servian capital. He returned to Sarajevo a Servian Chauvinist and made no concealment of his sympathies with the King of Servia. Both he and the actual murderer of the Archduke and the Duchess expressed themselves to the police in most cynical fashion about their crimes.

It appears that after the first attempt the Duchess did not want the Archduke to enter the motor-car again, but the Governor of Bosnia, General Potiorek, said: "It's all over now. We have not got more than one murderer in Sarajevo." On this the Archduke decided to enter the car again.

Before their departure for Sarajevo the Archduke and the Duchess went to the chapel of their Vienna palace and spent a long time in prayer before the altar. Of recent times the Archduke has declared more than once his conviction that he would not die a natural death.

Henri Desire Landru:
'The French Bluebeard'

Henri Désiré Landru was born in Paris on April 12, 1869, the son of a fireman at an ironworks. After leaving school, where he was regarded as being of average intelligence, he enlisted in the French army, serving four years before being discharged with the rank of sergeant.

Fraud conviction

While in the army Landru began an affair with his cousin, Mademoiselle Remy, which resulted in the birth of a daughter, and soon afterwards the couple married and eventually had another three children. Landru's life might had remained uneventful, but around 1894 his new employer absconded with a large amount of his money and this seems to have led him to begin preying financially on others, usually rich older widows. In 1900 he was charged with and convicted of fraud, which led to his spending two years in prison. While in prison this first time he attempted suicide, but over the next few years he was convicted of fraud again several times. By 1914 he was estranged from his wife, and although he had previously been penniless he had set up a business in Paris dealing in second-hand furniture and cars.

ABOVE: Landru served in the French army for four years before being discharged with the rank of sergeant. He was convicted of fraud on many occasions after leaving the army and spent time in prison.

LEFT: Landru with his wife and cousin, Mademoiselle Remy. The two had four children together but they were estranged by 1914.

BELOW AND OPPOSITE BELOW: At the trial it was alleged that Landru killed his victims after taking over their assets.

Forty years on: 'I did it. I burned their bodies in the kitchen stove.'

War widows

By this time the First World War had begun and the carnage in the trenches had resulted in many new widows but a shortage of eligible men. Landru had come up with a new scheme; he put a series of advertisements in newspapers in cities across France, most of them with very similar wording: he was a widower with two children, earning a secure income and of a high standing in society, and he wanted to meet a widow since he wished to marry again. Not surprisingly, he had a very good response.

Suitable victims

Landru would select several suitable victims from the replies and would correspond with them all until he was able to assess their individual assets and prospects. He would then charm and seduce the chosen lady, eventually proposing marriage and inviting her to come and live with him. While he was courting the lady Landru would make sure that he discovered the relevant details about all her assets, so that after she moved in with him he could quietly take control of all the money, selling any furniture or personal effects through his second-hand business. Meanwhile the lady would vanish without trace – although friends and relatives would often receive messages at first to convince them that she had moved on elsewhere. With war raging and people going missing all the time it was not unusual for someone to disappear without notice and there were no bodies, which might have raised an alarm. As an extra precaution, Landru used a wide range of aliases – so many that he had to keep a careful record of which name he used to communicate with each woman to avoid making a mistake.

With war raging it was not unusual for someone to disappear without notice.

TOP LEFT: Landru's villa was known by the local villagers as 'The Secluded'. Every inch of the grounds was dug up by the police.

TOP RIGHT: Police pictured digging in Landru's garden. Fragments of bone, a tooth and a hairpin were among the findings.

ABOVE: Landru's victims: Madame Collomb, Madame Laborde, Madame Buisson, Mademoiselle Pascal and Madame Jaume.

ABOVE LEFT: Monsieur Godefroy making his speech for the prosecution during which he drew on Landru's criminal background and described him as a monster fit only to be guillotined.

> After more than two years of investigation it became apparent that between 1914 and 1918 Landru had killed 11 people.

Criminal record

In 1916 Landru bought the Villa Ermitage, just outside the small town of Gambais twenty miles west of Paris, moving in that December. From this new base he continued his activities, now inviting his affianced ladies to come and live in the villa with him. However, in 1919 the sister of a Madame Anna Collomb, who had vanished at the beginning of 1917, began to look for her sibling in earnest. Although she did not know Landru's real name, she did know what he looked like and that Madame Collomb had travelled to Gambais, so she contacted the local mayor asking for help. He put her in touch with the sister of Madame Celestine Buisson, Madame Lacoste, who was also searching for a mysterious man that her sibling had travelled to Gambais to visit in mid-1917. The two ladies compared notes, soon realized t hat they were searching for the same man and gave his description to the local police. With his previous convictions for fraud Landru already had a criminal record so he was quickly identified as the mysterious stranger, but since he was not currently living at the Villa Ermitage at the time all the authorities could do was issue a warrant for his arrest. At this point Landru's luck ran out – Madame Lacoste happened to see him by chance in the streets of Paris and alerted the local police. He was living with yet another woman in an apartment in the city and it was not long before he was found and arrested.

Bluebeard's black notebook

Throughout his interrogation, Landru remained uncooperative and insisted he was innocent of any crime. Despite digging up the garden of the Villa Ermitage the authorities could not find any bodies, so initially he was only charged with fraud and swindling after the accounts of his second-hand business came under close scrutiny. However, a black notebook he was carrying at the time of his arrest proved to contain cryptic notes about all his victims and his assessments of their financial prospects, while the villa contained a great deal of legal paperwork belonging to them as well as some of their clothing. After more than two years of investigation it became apparent that between 1914 and 1918 Landru had killed 11 people – 10 women as well as the young son of one of them – and he was finally charged with murder. Since he had a heavy black beard, he quickly came to be known as the French Bluebeard in the popular Press, after the story by Charles Perrault (1697) in *The Tales of Mother Goose*.

TOP LEFT: Witnesses in the case against Landru were summoned by the police to identify exhibits believed to have belonged to his victims. Among the items were underwear, shoes and trinkets. Witnesses were also asked to examine hair found in the house.

ABOVE LEFT: The President of the Versailles Assize Court, Monsieur Gilbert.

ABOVE AND LEFT: The crowd in the Versailles Assize Court listen intently as Landru promises to divulge the address of one of the women with whose murder he was charged.

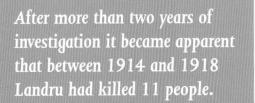

Bone fragments

At the trial it was alleged that after taking over their assets Landru had killed his victims, possibly by strangulation, then dismembered the bodies and burnt the parts in the extra-large kitchen stove of the villa. The ashes taken from the stove proved to contain many small fragments of bone, although forensic science was not advanced enough in this period to prove without any doubt that these were human. Neighbours testified that voluminous clouds of putrid black smoke had often been seen issuing from the chimney of the villa, although at the time they had thought nothing of it. Other evidence presented at the trial showed that on the occasions when Landru had bought tickets for himself and his fiancé to travel to Gambais, he had purchased only one return ticket – the other was invariably a single. Throughout the trial Landru continued to protest his innocence, claiming that he had the legal paperwork only because the women were business clients – and demanding to know why the prosecuting lawyer was not mentioning his many male business clients as well. Despite the lack of any bodies he was convicted of murder in November 1921 and sentenced to death on the guillotine, even though his defence lawyer made a moving last-minute plea for clemency.

Revealing drawing

Landru was executed in prison in Versailles on February 25, 1922. No trace was ever found of any of his victims, and their money and other assets had all vanished too. Some forty years later, the daughter of the defence lawyer took down a drawing that was believed to have been made by Landru, which he had given to his defence lawyer just before his execution and which had been hanging on the office wall ever since. On the back she is said to have found a scribbled note:

"I did it. I burned their bodies in the kitchen stove."

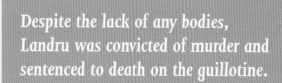

Despite the lack of any bodies, Landru was convicted of murder and sentenced to death on the guillotine.

ABOVE LEFT AND OPPOSITE MIDDLE: Maitre de Moro Giaferri begins Landru's defence at the trial. In his speech Maitre Gaiferri made a strong case for the fact there was an absence of bodies to be used as evidence in the case against Landru.

ABOVE RIGHT: Landru making his statement to the court with the characteristic calm that he maintained throughout the trial. He was answering the judges questioning as to why he had signed a lease under a false name.

MIDDLE RIGHT: Mademoiselle Fernande Segret, Landru's surviving fiancée. She described the happy hours she had spent with the accused at his villa.

RIGHT: The kitchen at the Villa Gambine. In the corner is the furnace in which Landru burnt the remains of his victims after cutting them into pieces.

TOP RIGHT: Landru pictured in his cell as he waits for the jury to decide his fate. Despite the lack of any body, the jury reached a guilty verdict and on November 1921 he was sentenced to the death on the guillotine.

Roscoe 'Fatty' Arbuckle

SEPTEMBER 12, 1921

'Fatty' Arbuckle: charge of murdering a film actress

Mr. "Fatty" Arbuckle, the popular rotund film comedian, has been questioned by the San Francisco police following the death of a young film actress, Virginia Rappe, in an hotel where Mr. Arbuckle was staying. The girl's death, it is stated, took place shortly after she had attended an entertainment in the comedian's room.

Roscoe 'Fatty' Arbuckle was a hugely popular comedian of the silent screen era, his drawing power putting him in the same league as Chaplin and Keaton. At the height of his fame Arbuckle was earning $3000 a day, working on multiple projects as the studios couldn't get his films into the movie theatres fast enough. His good fortune ran out in 1921, when he became embroiled in a scandal that ruined his career. Arbuckle was cleared, yet he became a pariah in the industry he had served so well, for the incident occurred at the worst possible time: when America got onto its moral high horse and decided that Hollywood had to clean up its disreputable act.

Slapstick routines

Roscoe Conkling Arbuckle was born in Kansas on 24 March 1887, tipping the scales at fourteen pounds. The rotundity that would earn him his celebrated moniker was there from the start. He hated the 'Fatty' tag, though undoubtedly his distinctive shape helped single him out from the acting pack and propel him to stardom. That was still some way off, though, for Arbuckle served a long apprenticeship in the entertainment business. He made a decent living as a singer in San Francisco, the city to which his family relocated when Roscoe was a toddler, and later he went on the road in a vaudeville show.

Arbuckle turned to movie-making in 1909, when he joined the Selig Polyscope Company, a pioneering studio which also launched the career of Tom Mix. Mix would become the hero of countless Westerns, while Arbuckle's forte on the silver screen would be comedy. To that end, 1913 was a watershed year, for it marked his move to Mack Sennett's newly founded Keystone studio. Sennett had learned his directorial trade working under the legendary D W Griffith, but his mentor wanted to make epic dramas, whereas Sennett's interest lay in comedy. It was a marriage made in heaven, though when Sennett unleashed his intrepid crime-fighting force the Keystone Cops, Arbuckle was just one of the uniformed ensemble, earning less than five dollars a day. It was during this period that the 'Fatty' tag stuck. His bulk didn't stop him from joining in the Keystone Cops' madcap chases, for Arbuckle was extremely nimble for a man of his size. If his distinctive appearance was one trademark, Arbuckle soon had another to single him out from his peers, for he became the undisputed king of the custard pie fights. These slapstick routines became a staple in many a comic feature, allowing Arbuckle to show off another party piece: the ability to hurl two pies in different directions at the same time with impressive accuracy.

His bulk didn't stop him from joining in the Keystone Cops' madcap chases, for Arbuckle was extremely nimble for a man of his size.

Financial request

At the time the ill-fated party took place, Fatty Arbuckle was thirteen years into his first marriage. His relationship with actress Minta Durfee was all but over by then, yet it had an instructive bearing on the tragic events that were about to unfold. Both in public and in private, Arbuckle was quite puritanical regarding matters of the flesh. It took him a week to consummate his marriage to 'Minty', and although he had effectively rejoined the bachelor ranks by 1921, he was said to have remained faithful to his estranged wife. Arbuckle also eschewed the use of bad language, while any off-colour gags in a 'Fatty' feature were liable to find themselves excised with a red pen or on the cutting-room floor. Thus, while he would have heartily sanctioned the raucous alcohol-fuelled roistering that was going on at the St Francis Hotel, Arbuckle would have frowned upon anything bordering on the sleazy. However, that adjective was readily applicable to the lifestyle of one of the guests, Virginia Rappe, whose attendance at that Labor Day weekend party would lead to Arbuckle being ostracized in Hollywood and vilified throughout the land.

Virginia Rapp – she amended her surname to make it sound more refined and exotic - was a small-time actress and model whose career had never really taken off. She was well known on the studio circuit, though not so much for her meagre achievements in the industry as her licentiousness. She had had five abortions by the age of sixteen and gave birth to another child whom she had adopted. Rappe was riddled with venereal disease and by all accounts had little compunction about turning to prostitution in lean times. When she went along to join the fun at the St Francis Hotel she was carrying yet another unwanted baby, or else had just had a termination. She asked Arbuckle for financial assistance, either to pay for an abortion or settle with whoever had carried out the procedure. He counselled her to talk the situation over with her partner Henry Lehrman, who had directed Arbuckle in a number of the Keystone features. From Rappe's horrified reaction Arbuckle deduced that her current beau may not have been the father. Or maybe the baby was Lehrman's but the stormy nature of their relationship left her disinclined to involve him in the decision-making process.

> Events would destroy Arbuckle's hard-earned reputation, casting him in the role of predatory sex fiend.

Lavish party

In 1916 Arbuckle moved to Paramount, who also poached Sennett's star comedienne Mabel Normand. The Fatty and Mabel series was hugely popular with audiences, a golden goose that allowed Paramount to pay the male star a $1000 a day and give him total artistic control of Comique Film Corporation, the production company formed to showcase his talents. Arbuckle's career appeared to be on an ever upward curve. He had worked his way up from one-reelers to two-reelers, taken the directorial tiller and seen his earnings rocket. By 1919 Paramount boss Adolph Zukor was keen to tie him in to an even more lucrative 22-picture contract, focusing on full-length features. The mogul and the star had shaken hands on the deal, though the paperwork wasn't signed until 1921.

It was partly to celebrate his new $3000-a-day contract that Arbuckle threw a lavish party on 5 September. He had also just become the proud owner of a $25,000 Pierce-Arrow motor car, and felt he had earned a break from his punishing schedule. This was no tepid wine and cheese affair; the revellers took over three suites at San Francisco's swish St Francis Hotel and embarked on a marathon three-day binge. Booze flowed like water, despite the fact that the 18th Amendment had been passed the year before, ushering in thirteen years of Prohibition. Arbuckle was a party animal. He had a reputation as a hard drinker but he was also amiable and generous, an inveterate practical joker. Most importantly, women of his acquaintance were as one in lauding his polite, respectful manner. Events at this sybaritic bash would destroy Arbuckle's hard-earned reputation, casting him in the role of predatory sex fiend.

OPPOSITE: Arbuckle was a hugely popular comedian of the silent screen era, earning $3,000 a day at the height of his career.

RIGHT: 30 May 1925: Arbuckle (born William B Goodrich) and Doris Deane on their wedding day in Los Angeles.

ABOVE: Vibrant San Francisco in the 1920s. It was here, at the St Francis Hotel, that Arbuckle hosted a three-day lavish party.

Vindictive

Rappe consoled herself by getting blind drunk. She became ill and managed to stagger into one of the spare suites, which happened to be Arbuckle's. She promptly threw up in the bathroom, where she was found when Arbuckle left the party to get changed. He laid her on the bed, gave her some water and cleaned up the mess. He summoned Rappe's friend Bambina Maude Delmont to help tend to her, and the hotel doctor was also called. He diagnosed nothing more than severe intoxication, and was happy to leave her to sleep it off. That, it seemed, was that. The party could now continue minus one guest who had over-indulged.

Bambina Maude Delmont had other ideas. She had ever an eye for the main chance, her various scams having earned her a lengthy rap sheet with the local police department. A favourite money-making exercise was acting as a hired co-respondent, providing incriminating evidence in divorce cases. Another was using compromising photographs to indulge in a spot of blackmail. With her friend lying prostrate on a top movie star's bed, moaning that she was in pain and dying, Delmont couldn't help thinking that a big payday lay within her grasp if she marshalled – and massaged - the facts in a certain way. At one point during Rappe's delirious, histrionic ranting, she had shouted to her friend: 'What did he do to me, Maudie? Roscoe did this to me.' Those words set Maude Delmont thinking. And if she was already harbouring vindictive thoughts towards Arbuckle, the fact that the star had her thrown out of the hotel for doing an impromptu striptease would have helped the crystallisation process.

> There was not a shred of evidence to support such allegations, but the press had a field day.

SEPTEMBER 15, 1921

Arbuckle films hooted

The San Francisco grand jury yesterday returned a bill charging Mr. Roscoe ("Fatty") Arbuckle, the Cinema comedian, with the manslaughter at Miss Virginia Rappe, a film actress. Apart from the failure of the prosecution to sustain the change of murder, the outstanding development in the case is the allegation of the District Attorney that attempts have been made to tamper with witnesses for the prosecution. "In a nut-shell", says the official, "there is too much money in sight."

The result of the publication throughout the country of the sordid details and circumstances surrounding the death of Miss Rappe is that the whole cinema industry is under fire. In Pittsburg, Kansas City and other large cities the clergy are demanding that the entire industry shall be closed down for a period while complete changes of management are carried out. Films showing Mr. Arbuckle are greeted by hostile demonstrations at a great many theatres in various parts of the country. Even bills and photographs of the comedian outside the theatres are being torn down by angry audiences.

Bowing to the storm of public opinion, cinema theatre owners have passed a resolution excluding Arbuckle films from 600 New York cinemas.

Wild speculation

The next day Delmont told the police that Fatty Arbuckle had sexually assaulted Virginia Rappe, while at the same time contacting lawyers and informing them she had the wealthy movie star over a barrel. Rappe herself would play no part in the lengthy legal battle that ensued: she died four days later. The cause of death was peritonitis, brought on by a ruptured bladder. That injury would fuel wild speculation, notably lurid tales of Arbuckle taking a bottle to her during a frenzied attack. There was not a shred of evidence to support such allegations, but the press had a field day. Scandal made excellent copy, particularly when the details were embellished by the hacks. Moreover, the papers didn't want a blurred picture so Virginia Rappe was cast as the virtuous ingénue, Arbuckle the rapacious violator.

Arbuckle was arrested and charged under the section of the Criminal Code which decreed that a life taken during a rape or attempted rape should be deemed murder. It was later reduced to a manslaughter charge, possibly because the chief prosecution witness was proving to be so unreliable. San Francisco District Attorney Matthew Brady got a different version every time Delmont told her story, and was so concerned at the mass of contradictions that he didn't dare call her to testify in court.

ABOVE: Arbuckle's films were immediately withdrawn from movie theatres pending the outcome of legal proceedings.

False testimony

Fatty Arbuckle's films were immediately withdrawn from movie theatres pending the outcome of legal proceedings. Paramount's top executives moved quickly to distance the studio from its erstwhile main asset. The timing couldn't have been worse for Arbuckle. Hollywood was widely regarded as a repository of hedonistic excess and moral turpitude. It was high time the film industry cleaned up its act, and the studio movers and shakers decided to jump before they were pushed. The outrage that the Arbuckle case provoked, particularly among women's groups, led to the formation of a new watchdog body, the Motion Picture Producers and Distributors of America. William Hays, a former lawyer and US postmaster general, was drafted in on a $100,000 salary to head the MPPDA. Hays would draw up the censorship code that would keep Hollywood – or, at least, the product that appeared on the screen – on the straight and narrow for the next forty years.

> 'Even bills and photographs of the comedian outside the theatres are being torn down by angry audiences'.

Hays took up his appointment in March 1922. By then, Arbuckle had already gone through two trials, both resulting in a hung jury. Even the prosecution's medical expert admitted that Rappe's chronically inflamed bladder had not been ruptured by external force, thus giving the lie to the lurid tales doing the rounds of a bottle attack. It also came to light that certain prosecution witnesses had been railroaded into giving false testimony. The defence argued that Roscoe Arbuckle had been the victim of a smear campaign, and the defendant's straightforward account of how he tried to help a sick, distressed, hysterical woman played well in court. But after almost two days' deliberation, two members of the jury were still holding out for a guilty verdict and refused to budge.

That result seemed to lull the defence into thinking that the retrial was a foregone conclusion. With so many holes in the prosecution's case, and the continued deafening silence of Bambina Maude Delmont, Arbuckle's lawyers took their eye off the ball. The defendant wasn't called, despite the fact that his lucid, measured testimony had won over many doubters at the previous hearing. Defence counsel even waived the right to a summation, hence the jury retired with no impassioned argument as to why they ought to acquit ringing in their ears. They also returned a 10-2

Acquittal

At the third trial, which opened on 13 March 1922 and lasted five weeks, the defence pulled out all the stops. The jury took just five minutes to return a Not Guilty verdict, and decided that an acquittal was not of itself enough. A statement was added to express their profound sympathy for the ordeal Arbuckle had been forced to endure. There was, they said, 'not the slightest proof adduced to connect Arbuckle with the commission of the crime'. They wished him success, and hoped the American people would take their cue from those who had heard the evidence and concluded that 'Roscoe Arbuckle is entirely innocent and free from all blame'. If there was such a thing as a triumphant exoneration, this was it.

Industry closed ranks

Adolf Zukor announced plans for the release of a new Fatty Arbuckle film, though he wanted to test the waters of public opinion before agreeing a new contract with the comedian. The picture became clearer within a matter of days, when William Hays slapped a moratorium on the distribution of all Arbuckle's films and suspending him from entering into any contractual agreement. The MPPDA president's first intervention in his new job disabused Arbuckle of any notion that winning the legal battle meant an end to all his troubles. He had violated the liquor laws, for which he incurred a separate fine, but that hardly warranted the savage treatment meted out. Arbuckle just wanted to get back to what he did best, not least to enable him to pay off legal debts of around $750,000, but the industry closed ranks against him.

Fatty Arbuckle did work in films again, but with a much lower profile and under a different name. He turned to directing as William Goodrich, his father's two Christian names. As his father was cold and abusive towards him, it seems unlikely that the pseudonym was chosen for honorary reasons. Some say that the idea came from Buster Keaton, who had been given his big break by Arbuckle and remained loyal when others turned their backs. Perhaps Keaton's suggestion, 'Will B Good', was an act of contrition, whether it was needed or not.

Roscoe 'Fatty' Arbuckle died 29 June 1933, aged 46. His death came just as it seemed he had paid his dues, for he had started work on a new Warner Brothers film, this time in front of the camera, and there were several more projects in the pipeline. Today, most film historians subscribe to the view that Arbuckle got an extremely raw deal. He was in the wrong place at the wrong time, and the prevailing antipathy towards Hollywood demanded that a sacrificial lamb be offered up. More than eighty years on, Fatty Arbuckle is still best remembered not as a great slapstick comedian of the silent era but as the first victim in the crusade to clean up Tinseltown.

> At the third trial, which opened on 13 March 1922 and lasted five weeks, the defence pulled out all the stops.

LEFT: Arbuckle arrives in Cleveland in 1932, just one year before he died at the age of 46. By this time he had started work on a new film and there were several more projects in the pipeline.

Al Capone:
Chicago's gangland overlord

The Chicago police believe that the recent cold-blooded murder of seven men who were placed in a row and riddled to death with machine-gun bullets was the work of Al Capone's gunmen, and that vengeance has been sworn against the murderers.

29 May 1928

Mob rule

Al Capone was Chicago's gangland overlord in the 1920s, his name synonymous with mob rule during the Prohibition era. It was estimated that Capone made over $100 million from illegal booze alone, while gambling, vice and protection swelled the coffers still further. That kind of money bought a lot of influence, and Capone had police, members of the judiciary and politicians in his pocket. By the end of the decade he appeared to be as bulletproof as the car that ferried him round the Windy City. But his reign was almost over, and it wasn't murder raps or rival mobsters that brought him down; it was the work of forensic accountants.

He was born 17 January 1899 in Brooklyn, the fourth of Italian immigrants Gabriele and Teresina Capone's nine children. His father was a hard-working barber, the family unit conventional and law-abiding. Al took the first step on his chosen career path when he was expelled from school at 14 after assaulting a teacher. He started running with street gangs, running errands for Johnny Torrio, one of New York's top racketeers. Torrio was one of a new breed of gangsters, operating his criminal empire along corporate lines. The young Capone would learn many lessons by watching his mentor at work.

LEFT: Capone didn't like his left profile because of the unsightly scar that disfigured that side of his face. When posing for photographs he would try to hide the scar which was inflicted on him by gangster Gallucio.

ABOVE: Al Capone (left) after his release from Philadelphia jail. With him is Mr John Stage, the chief of Chicago city detectives. After disappearing for several days, Capone emerged in Stage's office.

OPPOSITE TOP LEFT: It was estimated that Al Capone made over $100 million from illegal liquor alone. In order to achieve this Capone had many of Chicago's authority figures in his pocket, paying them to look the other way.

Scarface

Through his underworld contacts Capone got a job as a bartender on Coney Island. One night he had a run-in with gangster Frank Gallucio, who took exception to a personal comment Capone made to his sister. Gallucio pulled a knife and slashed him across the face, little knowing that in settling a difference he was playing a part in the building of a legend. Capone was prickly about the 'Scarface' tag. When he ruled the roost, no one who valued his health used the nickname within his earshot. And after 1921, when he moved to Chicago, the rise to the top was swift and dramatic.

By then Capone had married Mae Coughlin, who bore him a son, named after his father but known as Sonny. For a while Capone tried to go straight, but when his father died suddenly in 1920 it signalled the end of his legitimate career, as though he was now free of the shackles of respectability. He went to Chicago at the behest of Johnny Torrio, who told him it was fertile ground for enterprising criminals. Capone eventually became Torrio's right-hand man and protégé, but they weren't the only men looking to milk Chicago illegitimately.

Rivals gunned down

The first obstacle to be overcome was Torrio's uncle 'Diamond Jim' Colosimo, who founded his empire on the vice trade and was slow to see the potential for profit in Prohibition. He was gunned down in May 1920. Their next run-in was with Dion O'Bannion, head of the Chicago's North Side gang. Until 1924 Torrio and O'Bannion both prospered during the territorial carve-up of the city. Then O'Bannion announced he was getting out of the bootlegging business and sold his brewery interests to his rival for $500,000. O'Bannion double-crossed Torrio and Capone by tipping off the police, leading to a raid on the brewery. Retribution followed swiftly as O'Bannion was gunned down in the florist shop he used to front his operations. Torrio himself was badly wounded in a reprisal attack the following year, taking a bullet in the neck on the orders of O'Bannion's successor, Hymie Weiss. He decided to retire to Sicily, leaving the Chicago operation in Capone's hands.

JUNE 11, 1929

Like a rabbit warren

Many picturesque raids have been made on his Cicero headquarters. It was revealed as a stronghold burrowed like a rabbit warren, with so many exits and entrances that a stranger would be lost hopelessly in the maze of concealed panels, stairways and winding passages. Incidentally, 5,000 rounds of rifle bullets were uncovered in this rendezvous of crime.

In 1925 he visited his birthplace. It was Christmas-time, and another notorious gangster "Peg-leg" Lonergan, was shot to death in New York. Capone was arrested, but the New York police were no more successful than their Chicago allies in holding him.

But if Capone has been immune from undue legal zeal, he himself has confessed that his associates led him a life of terror. Early in 1927 he was driving his car across the mountains from Hot Springs, Arkansas, when bullets from a passing car poured in upon him. He escaped only by slipping out of the car and rolling down a steep incline that edged the road.

His wealth has never been known, but "Scarface" has always spent money freely, and he remarked when arrested in Philadelphia that he wanted nothing but to seek the quietude of his "beautiful" Florida home. He is a dollar millionaire, although not worth a million in sterling. His fortune has been made in the exercise of gambling rights and the sale of "bootleg" liquor.

He went to Chicago at the behest of Johnny Torrio, who told him it was fertile ground for enterprising criminals.

TOP RIGHT: Al Capone pictured fishing from a yacht in Biscayne Bay, Florida, shortly after he was released from prison where he served one year for carrying a concealed weapon.

RIGHT AND MIDDLE RIGHT: Al Capone photographed in the grounds of his palatial home in Florida.

St Valentine's Day Massacre

Capone inherited a powder-keg situation with rival gangs vying for control. Weiss was dealt with, dispatched by a Capone henchman in October 1926, but that merely pushed George 'Bugs' Moran up the pecking order in the North Side gang. There was a short-lived uneasy truce, but the feud soon reignited. Many law-abiding citizens shrugged their shoulders as the gangsters waged an internecine war. Their hostility was directed at the Prohibition laws themselves, which were widely reviled as puritanical and an infringement of civil liberties. But the mood of the city changed after a bloodbath that took place on 14 February 1929, the day Capone vowed to shut the North Side outfit down once and for all. That morning, six of Moran's men assembled at 2122 North Clark Street, a garage used by the gang as a distribution point for booze shipments. A seventh man, optician Reinhardt Schwimmer, was a hanger-on who chose the wrong day to flirt with the criminal fraternity.

> The mood of the city changed after a bloodbath that took place on 14 February 1929, the day Capone vowed to shut the North Side outfit.

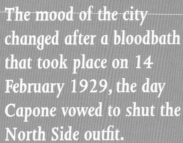

DECEMBER 10, 1929

Rugs in his cell

Scarface Al Capone, Chicago's most picturesque gunman, who is serving a year's sentence in Philadelphia penitentiary for illegally carrying arms, spends his time in prison reading Balzac and Victor Hugo. It was reported at the time of his arrest that Capone - he likes his name to be pronounced as two syllables - sought prison as an escape from greater dangers outside. If so, he must have regretted his decision for he has made six unsuccessful attempts through his lawyers to secure release.

For exercise Capone plays handball. His wife is allowed to visit him. She leaves their young son behind, for the Chicago war lord says: "I wouldn't have him come to the prison for anything. My boy thinks that I am in Europe. Whenever he sees a picture of a big boat he asks his mother if that boat is bringing Daddy home."

'Get Capone'

The Moran mob were expecting a liquor consignment from Detroit; what they got instead was a raid by police officers carrying Thompson sub-machine guns. The North Siders weren't unduly alarmed, thinking it was a routine shakedown when they lined up against the wall. They were mown down mercilessly, for the 'officers' were out-of-town hitmen hired by Capone, who made sure he was sunning himself in Florida when the bullets started flying. Moran escaped the carnage by a whisker but it hardly mattered; it was the end of the North Side gang and Capone now ruled Chicago unopposed. Police knew who had carried out the St Valentine's Day Massacre but had no evidence to bring a case.

The events of 14 February 1929 galvanised the city's power-brokers into action. They included a group of businessmen determined to do something about Chicago's reputation as a city of lawlessness and anarchy. The Secret Six, as they were called, petitioned President Herbert Hoover, whose approval rating was on the floor thanks to the parlous state of the country's economy. He saw political salvation in cleaning up Chicago and gave a terse instruction to his Attorney-General: 'Get Capone'.

TOP RIGHT: Capone pictured at the Chicago Muncipal Court when he appeared on charges of 'common vagrandy' in March 1931. At the time Capone was already under a federal sentence for contempt of court and facing trial for income tax evasions. Also pictured are (from left) Assistant State's Attorney E.A. Ferrari, Defence Attorney Michael Ahern and Assistant State's Attorney Frank Mast.

ABOVE: Capone's sister, Mafalda, leaving with her bridegroom, John Maritote, after their wedding ceremony.

LEFT: Following his part in the Valentine's Day Massacre, Capone began to fear for his life. He went so far as to seek a sentence behind bars in order to ensure his safety.

OPPOSITE TOP RIGHT: Al Capone in court with his attorney Michael Ahern. Frank Wilson had built up a case that would prove that Capone had made $1,038,000 between 1924 and 1929.

OPPOSITE LEFT AND RIGHT: Scarface sitting next to his son at a charity baseball match while a player obliges him with his autograph. Such a picture is rare since Al Capone was seldom seen at public events.

The Untouchables

The attack on Capone's empire was two-pronged. The high-profile, glamorous arm of the operation was led by Eliot Ness, a 26-year-old enforcement officer who had joined the Bureau of Prohibition in 1928. That department was itself rife with corruption, so Ness led a small hand-picked team that was hugely successful in hitting Capone's bootlegging activities. Capone tried to buy him off, but Ness turned down an offer of $2000 per week to look the other way, as so many other officials did. He held a press conference to affirm his team's incorruptibility, and the media dubbed them The Untouchables. Decades later, when the story of the era was adapted for both the small and large screen, the producers had a ready-made title.

> Ness held a press conference to affirm his team's incorruptibility, and the media dubbed them The Untouchables.

Illegal gambling den

Wilson had plenty of ledgers to study, books seized during raids, but linking the profits to Capone was a different matter. He dealt in cash, and left no paper trail to follow. A breakthrough came when Wilson spotted an entry of $17,500 for 'Al' in the 1926 accounts of Hawthorne Smoke Shop, an illegal gambling den. He tracked down the book-kepper and got him to testify that 'Al' referred to Capone. Witnesses who clammed up over a drive-by shooting weren't so reticent when it came to discussing ledger entries. Capone himself underestimated the seriousness of the situation, even though his brother Ralph had been indicted on similar charges and was left facing a 20-year jail term.

Wilson established that from 1924-29 Capone had received $1,038,000 plus change. That was obviously not his total income; but it was income Wilson could prove had ended up in Capone's pocket. His lawyers, who weren't tax experts, advised him that in the worst-case scenario he would have to stump up the unpaid tax, around $215,000. That wasn't enough to tempt the prosecution, so Capone's counsel offered a guilty plea in return for a two-and-a-half-year jail term. Wilson thought that acceptable when weighed against the inherent risk of going to trial and facing the vagaries of the courtroom. Capone thought he was off the hook, bragging that he could do such a stretch with ease. But both sides reckoned without Judge James Wilkerson, who refused to sanction the deal, which in turn led Capone to withdraw his guilty plea. Both sides would have to take their chances in court.

Tax liability

Ness's efforts put a large dent in Capone's economic juggernaut, yet it could also be seen as window dressing, a morale-boosting PR job that gave ordinary people hope that organised crime could be beaten. It was in the parallel covert operation where the vital work was being done. Behind the scenes, accountants embarked on a painstaking investigation of Capone's tax affairs. The gangster's lavish lifestyle told them that he must have fallen foul of the 'Sullivan Law', passed by the Supreme Court in May 1927, which stated that profits from illegal alcohol sales were liable for tax. It was a clever piece of legislation which put bootleggers in a double bind: if they didn't file a return disclosing their ill-gotten gains, they ran the risk of going to jail; if they did, they incriminated themselves. Tax evasion was more prosaic than the dashing raids that Ness and his men were carrying out, but it was potentially far more effective. In May 1929, Capone received a year's jail sentence for carrying a concealed weapon, and even that was said to be the work of crime bosses from other cities, who wanted to cut him down to size because of the bad press the St Valentine's Day Massacre had generated. The team of accountants, led by the tenacious, indefatigable Frank Wilson, was looking for evidence that would put Capone away for a lot longer than that.

JUNE 8, 1931

Al Capone's income tax

Mr. Robert E. Neely, Inland Revenue collector, announced tonight that steps will shortly be taken to sell up the property of "Scarface" Al Capone, the gangster chief, in order to obtain 215,083 dollars (£43,016) stated to be owing for income tax. Among property to be sold will be Capone's eight-ton armoured limousine car, an arm-chair fitted with a machine-gun and a bullet-proof back, his breweries, distilleries, stocks, bonds, with his luxurious country homes with their armouries of machine-guns, revolvers and ammunition.

In the meantime Capone, who is out on bail of £10,000, spent the weekend in hiding. He will probably appear early this week in court to stand his trial on 22 charges of defrauding the Federal Government. If he is found guilty he faces a maximum sentence of 32 years' imprisonment and a fine of 90,000 dollars (£16,000).

He served his time at Atlanta State Penitentiary, transferring to Alcatraz when 'The Rock' opened its doors.

Concerns over juror intimidation led Wilkerson to switch the jury at the last minute.

Capone's 12-day trial

Capone's trial opened 6 October 1931. Concerns over juror intimidation led Wilkerson to switch the jury at the last minute, swearing in men and women from rural communities who had a track record for convicting in bootlegging trials. The indictment included 5,000 violations of the Volstead Act – the legislation that ushered in the Prohibition era – but the prosecution focused exclusively on financial irregularities. Eliot Ness was not even called to testify. At the end of the 11-day trial the jury returned a guilty verdict on five counts: failing to file a return in 1928 and 1929, a misdemeanour, and evading tax for the years 1925-27, a felony. Capone was given 11 years in jail and fined $80,000. He served his time at Atlanta State Penitentiary, transferring to Alcatraz when 'The Rock' opened its doors as a federal prison in August 1934.

Capone was released on health grounds in November 1939 suffering from mental impairment. It was a symptom of tertiary syphilis, a disease he had contracted in his youth. He retired to his luxurious Florida estate, where he died 25 Jan 1947 after suffering a heart attack.

TOP LEFT: D'Andrea, Capone's bodyguard, (left) and Capone leaving the Detective Bureau.

TOP RIGHT: Capone winks at photographers as he leaves court in Chicago. His trial lasted 11 days before the jury returned the guilty verdict.

ABOVE: A cheque paying off part of Capone's fine. He owed $57,692.29 in total.

OPPOSITE TOP LEFT AND OPPOSITE TOP RIGHT: Capone and United States Marshal, Laubenheimer, in a compartment of the train that took Capone to federal prison in Atlanta, Georgia, where he was to serve 11 years for tax evasion.

OCTOBER 19, 1931

Capone found guilty

"Scarface" Al Capone, the notorious gang chief, after 12 days' trial, replete with bizarre testimony regarding his sartorial and other expenditures, has been found guilty at Chicago – not of murder or any other of a thousand crimes he is credited with organising – but of cheating the United States Government on income taxes.

His counsel grandiloquently compared him to Cato, idealised by the Romans as a model republican, as well as to Sinbad the Sailor, and referred to the Punic wars in which Rome battered Carthage into subjection, in an endeavour to bring home to the jury the full extent to which the cruel Government was persecuting the arch-gangster. Capone listened to all this oratory with a constant grin. He was dressed in a screaming green suit and with his huge bulk towering over everyone else in court, looked as one observer remarked "like an elephant at a convention of ants."

A jury of farmers took eight hours and ten minutes to bring in its verdict, which enables the judge to sentence him to a maximum of 17 years' imprisonment and a £10,000 fine. Capone will be brought up for sentence on Tuesday, when his counsel will seek to have the verdict set aside on technical grounds.

OCTOBER 26, 1931

Al Capone furious

"How are the mighty fallen!" is the comment of Chicago citizens as they contemplate the downfall of "Scarface" Al Capone, the erstwhile lord of their underworld. Sentenced to eleven years imprisonment for evasion of income-tax payments, Capone's name will be forgotten by the time he emerges from Leavensworth Gaol. He must pay a £10,000 fine and £20,000 for the cost of his prosecution which, together with income-tax payments, brings the total amount demanded from him by the Federal Government to £57,447. Faced with the loss of all his power and fortune, Capone took the sentence furiously. Standing before stern Judge Wilkerson, he tried to smile, but it was a pitiful effort. His fingers, locked behind his back, were twitching and twisting.

Outside the court he tried to vent his rage on a photographer by seizing a bucket of water to throw over the man but his guards held him back. Arriving at the door of his cell, the gangster chief threw his hat and coat inside with a savage gesture. Then his mood changed, and Capone became benevolent. His cell companion is being held for non-payment of a fine. In the presence of reporters, Capone drew a bunch of dollar bills from his pocket and handed some to his awestruck mate, saying, "I'm going help him out." As his rage lessened Capone remarked: "It was a bit below the belt, but if we have to do it we can do it. I have never heard of anyone getting more than five years for income tax trouble, but they are prejudiced against me. I never had a chance."

Judge Wilkerson refused to admit Capone to bail pending an appeal. The gangster is spending the weekend in Cook County Gaol. To-morrow his lawyers will file an application for bail with the circuit court of appeals. If this is granted Capone will be at liberty while a legal fight is waged against the sentence.

In the streets everyone expressed astonishment at the conviction, the impression being that Capone had too much money and influence not to beat the law.

A jury of farmers took eight hours and ten minutes to bring in its verdict.

ABOVE: Capone pictured leaving a federal building in Miami, Florida, with his attorney, Abe Teitelbaum, following a meeting about Capone's assets. He had just been released from Alcatraz owing to health problems.

ABOVE RIGHT: Arthur Madden – the man who built up the income tax evasion cases that sent Capone to prison.

RIGHT INSET: Al Capone with U.S. Marshal Harry Laubenheimer who escorted him to his Atlanta prison. Capone was later transferred to Alcatraz when it became a federal prison in 1934.

Bonnie and Clyde:

'Bonnie's' boast was, 'They'll never take me alive.' She made good her boast.

It was love at first sight when Clyde Barrow and Bonnie Parker met in January 1930. Clyde had long since decided on a life of crime, and already had a string of transgressions to his name, but that merely increased the attraction for Bonnie, who was drawn to dangerous types.

Live fast, die young

Clyde Barrow was the perfect replacement for the husband she'd taken at the age of sixteen, who was serving time for murder. Bonnie and Clyde knew that theirs would be a shooting-star existence and readily bought into the idea of living fast and dying young.

Bonnie Parker was born 1 October 1910 in Rowena, Texas. She was a pretty, waif-like creature who excelled at school, but she was also wilful, rebellious and passionate, as she demonstrated by marrying local bad boy Ray Thornton in 1926. Bonnie had their intertwined names tattooed on her thigh, but excitement gave way to drudgery when Ray was jailed and she had to take a job waiting tables to make ends meet. By 1929, the marriage was over in all but name and Bonnie was looking for a new source of excitement. She was about to get all the drama she could handle.

Clyde Chestnut Barrow was a year older than Bonnie, and he, too, grew up in Texas, the son of an impoverished sharecropper who swapped the cotton fields for running a gas station. Clyde had a chip on his shoulder, burning with resentment for the straitened circumstances in which he and his family had grown up. At an early age he decided that scholarship wasn't the route to the lifestyle he wanted, turning to petty crime with his older brother Buck both for kicks and for profit.

Clyde had reservations about putting Bonnie in the firing line, but she proved that she was made of stern stuff.

ABOVE: Gangsters Bonnie and Clyde. The pair were inseparable from the moment they met.

OPPOSITE ABOVE: The parents of gangster Clyde Barrow pictured at home. Both Clyde and their other son, Buck, turned to petty crime from an early age.

OPPOSITE BELOW: Clyde Barrow crouching in front of a car with a handgun hanging from the hood ornament, two handguns in the front grill and three rifles laid against the front fender. Barrow and his gang enjoyed recording their adventures in stylised poses with their weapons on show.

Prison stretch

The nascent gangsters received a setback when Buck Barrow was apprehended during one of their escapades and given a prison stretch. Clyde joined him behind bars in 1930, but his new girlfriend came to the rescue. Bonnie smuggled a gun into the prison and Barrow escaped with another felon awaiting trial, but both were soon recaptured. The escape increased the severity of Clyde's sentence; he now faced 14 years hard labour. With nothing to look forward to except heavy toil in the fields under a broiling sun, he went to drastic lengths to get off that duty. He had a fellow inmate 'slip' with an axe and chop off two of his toes. Unbeknown to him, his mother's intercessions with the prison authorities had borne fruit and he was about to be paroled. Clyde hobbled out of Texas State Penitentiary on crutches in February 1932.

Inseparable lovers

He put together a gang, including Bonnie, who had no intention of being parted from her lover. Clyde had reservations about putting her in the firing line, but she proved that she was made of stern stuff. Apart from a short spell that spring, when Bonnie herself served a jail term, the two were inseparable.

In April 1932, while Bonnie was out of commission, Clyde and fellow gang member Ray Hamilton hit a store run by John and Martha Bucher. Bucher was killed during the raid and his wife identified Barrow. It was a watershed moment. Now wanted for murder, he resolved to enjoy the ride until such times as the 'laws' caught up with him, as they surely would. That was good enough for Bonnie, too.

The crime spree continued apace when Bonnie was released. They often hit outlets in border towns, crossing state lines to thwart their pursuers. They stole cars at a dizzying rate, switching plates regularly to keep one step ahead of the law. And if the police got too close, they, too, risked cold-blooded execution. On 5 August 1932, the gang were approached by two officers when they stopped off to unwind at a dance in Stringtown, Oklahoma. Both were shot; one died from his wounds.

A shoot-out left two officers dead, the gang managing to smash their way through the police cordon.

Shoot-out in Missouri

Ray Hamilton decided to go his own way and the Barrow Gang recruited three new members. In came William Daniel 'WD' Jones, Buck Barrow, who was released from jail in March 1933, and Buck's wife, Blanche. The five met up in Joplin, Missouri, where they rented an apartment to enjoy some downtime. Local police became suspicious of the newcomers, found that their car had stolen plates and staked the place out. On 13 April they made their move. A shoot-out left two officers dead, the gang managing to smash their way through the police cordon. Inside the bullet-ridden apartment police found plenty of tell-tale signs to identify the killers. The evidence included undeveloped film featuring the gang members, who obviously enjoyed recording their adventures in stylised poses with their weapons on show. Other pictures were more intimate portraits of the leader and his moll, leaving no doubt that they were deeply in love. Bonnie was shown with a cigar clamped in her mouth, perhaps to illustrate that she was the equal of the male members of the gang. It was a mere prop, but it was an image that would forever be associated with her.

Following a hunch that the duo might pay a home visit to celebrate the birthday of Clyde's mother, the police lay in wait.

Suspicions aroused

In June 1933, Bonnie sustained serious leg injuries when the gang's car overturned at a bridge under construction. To help her recover they rented cabins at a holiday complex in Platte City, Missouri. Once again, their presence aroused suspicions which brought the police to their door. Buck took a bullet in the head, Blanche was hit in the eye by a shard of flying glass and WD was also wounded. They managed to escape, but three days later, they were cornered once more in woodland near Dexter, Iowa. Buck was hit again; he succumbed to his injuries five days later. Blanche was arrested and handed a 10-year jail term. WD Jones soon wanted out, leaving Bonnie and Clyde to carry on alone. Following a hunch that the duo might pay a home visit to celebrate the birthday of Clyde's mother on 21 November, the police lay in wait. The outlaws arrived right on cue, but when challenged and invited to give themselves up, they responded by jumping into their car and fleeing. It was a salutary lesson for the police; next time they would shoot first and read them their rights afterwards.

Jailbreak

In January 1934, the Barrow Gang sprang Ray Hamilton and several other inmates from the notorious Eastham Prison Farm in Huntsville, Texas. The breakout witnessed the death of the yet another law enforcement officer, Joe Crowson. Hamilton and another escapee, Henry Methvin, temporarily swelled the ranks of the gang back up to four, but the former soon departed. He was later arrested and given the electric chair for his part in Crowson's murder.

The jailbreak was the final straw for both the Texas and federal authorities. Former Texas Ranger Frank Hamer was given the task of ending the Barrow Gang's crime spree, a commission he readily accepted. Hamer was a step behind them in early April, when three more police officer were killed in two separate incidents. Then, when Henry Methvin started to get cold feet, Hamer was handed the break he was looking for.

Posse ambush

Methvin's father cut a deal with the police: a pardon for Henry in exchange for Bonnie and Clyde, offered up on a plate. On the morning of 23 May 1934, Hamer and a hand-picked posse lay in wait on Highway 154, near Sailes, Louisiana. They were expecting Bonnie and Clyde to pass that way en route to the Methvins' house in Bienville Parish, and at around 9.15 am their quarry came into view. A few weeks earlier, the gang had stolen a Ford sedan V8, hailed as the fastest production car on the road. Clyde was a speed merchant even when not being pursued, but he slowed down when he saw Henry Methvin's father's truck, which had been stationed in the ambush zone for that very purpose. This time there was no police warning. On Hamer's signal, over a hundred steel-jacketed bullets from high-powered Browning rifles ripped into the target. Many bullets passed right through the car, hitting both bodies on the way. Around fifty struck flesh.

Shortly before the fateful day, Bonnie had visited her mother, seeming to realise that the end was near. She had penned a poetic account of the duo's exploits, The Story of Bonnie and Clyde, a tale that was printed in many newspapers after their death. The final, prophetic, verse ran:

> Some day they'll go down together
> They'll bury them side by side
> To few it'll be grief
> To the law a relief
> But it's death for Bonnie and Clyde.

On Hamer's signal, over a hundred steel-jacketed bullets from high-powered Browning rifles ripped into the target.

Ruthless felons

The prophecy failed in one respect, however, the Parker family refusing to allow Bonnie to be laid to rest with Clyde. Henry Methvin did get his Texas pardon, but there was no deal with Oklahoma, where he was still a wanted man. He was eventually arrested and given the death sentence, commuted to life imprisonment. He served 12 years.

> Bonnie and Clyde were ruthless felons who held life cheap, including their own.

The ghoulish fascination with Bonnie and Clyde — and the commercial exploitation that sprang therefrom — began immediately. There were reports of souvenir hunters trying to cut off pieces of the couple's clothing, and even hack off body parts. The car in particular became a magnet for morbid sightseers, who were charged 25c for the privilege. It gave the owners a nice return in 1940 when it sold for $3,500, around four times what they paid for it six years earlier. Over the decades it changed hands for ever-increasing sums and is currently on display in a Nevada casino.

The hardships of the Depression led many to hold a sneaking admiration for anyone who kicked against a system that was the perceived source of their grinding poverty. Banks and the law were bulwarks of that system, which explains why the Barrow Gang were seen as champions of the downtrodden, striking at the heart of discredited, uncaring capitalism. That the gang was led by young lovers merely increased the romantic appeal of their exploits, masking the fact that Bonnie and Clyde were ruthless felons who held life cheap, including their own.

MAY 24, 1934

Woman bandit shot at sight

Bonnie Parker, the notorious cigar-smoking woman outlaw, and her highwayman lover Clyde Barrow, known as Public Enemy No. 2, who since January have terrorised Texas with a record series of crimes, were shot at sight today by Texas police, who had tracked them to their hiding-place near Gibson, Texas. Barrow and his gunwoman friend were shot in their motor car. They saw a group of police officers concealed behind a clump of trees and drew their guns. Before they could pull the triggers a burst of gun fire put an end for ever to their careers.

The pair were known as "wild human rats," and their murderous exploits equal, if they do not exceed for desperate daring and ruthlessness, those of Dillinger.

Barrow and his gunwoman companion were driving at 85 miles an hour when they were shot down. Both of them crumpled up in their seats as the car turned over in a ditch. The officers found Barrow's body twisted behind the steering wheel with a revolver still clutched in his right hand. In the lap of "Bonnie" Parker was a machine gun. Both bodies, as well as the car, were riddled with bullets.

Many victims of the couple describe "Bonnie" Parker as a marvellously expert markswoman. She liked corn whisky as much as her cigars and was adept with a machine gun, with which she invariably covered Barrow's retreat when his arms were full of loot. In the house which the police surrounded after the couple had shot their way out some weeks ago they found a poem in the gunwoman's handwriting entitled "Suicide Girl," and testified to her exultant pride in her life of crime.

"Bonnie's" boast was, "They'll never take me alive." She made good her boast.

OPPOSITE ABOVE: Bonnie Parker poses with a gun. She killed her first man in 1932. Bonnie came from a poor background but was an honour roll student in high school, where she excelled in creative writing. She even gave introductory speeches for local politicians.

OPPOSITE BOTTOM: The Ford V-8 in which Clyde and Bonnie were shot dead.

TOP LEFT: The coat worn by Clyde Barrow when he was shot and killed by police.

ABOVE: Bonnie and Clyde were killed in an ambush on 23 May 1934. Some accounts indicate that neither was given a chance to surrender.

The kidnapping of Charles Lindbergh Jr

'Baby safe. Wait instructions later. Act accordingly.'

In 1927 Charles Lindbergh became an instant all-American hero for his aeronautical derring-do, the first man to fly solo across the Atlantic. The pioneering feat captured the public imagination, and Lindbergh's name would be cemented into the country's folklore when his intrepid story was told in the 1957 film *Spirit of St Louis*, with James Stewart in the title role.

All-American hero

The film took its name from the aircraft that carried Lindbergh from New York to Le Bourget Airport on the outskirts of Paris, where he landed on May 21, 1927. He picked up the $25,000 prize money on offer to the first man who managed to complete the 3,600-mile journey non-stop, and thereafter was feted wherever he went, home or abroad, basking in the celebrity of being the world's best-known aviator.

One of Lindbergh's last engagements of the year of his epic flight was to visit the US Embassy in Mexico City. There he met Ambassador Dwight Morrow's three daughters, Elisabeth, Anne and Constance, creating an understandable stir as one of the country's most eligible bachelors. It was Anne who took his eye, and after a brief courtship the couple married.

ABOVE: Colonel Charles Lindbergh met Anne Morrow on a visit to Mexico City, where her father worked as a U.S ambassador. After a brief courtship they were married.

RIGHT: Lindbergh was the first man to fly solo across the Atlantic. He completed the 3,600 mile journey and picked up $25,000 prize money.

LEFT: The Ryan Monoplane, *Spirit of St Louis* It was piloted by Lindbergh before his non-stop flight to Paris from New York.

Charles Jr abducted

For two years the Lindberghs lived something of a nomadic lifestyle, Anne falling in with her husband's hectic work schedule as an aviation consultant, which took him to all corners of the globe. They decided to put down roots when Charles Jr arrived in June 1930, and built a house on a 400-acre estate in Hopewell, New Jersey. Insulated against the hardships of the Depression, the Lindberghs appeared to have an enviable lifestyle. All that came crashing down around their ears on the night of March 1, 1932, when Charles Jr was abducted from his bedroom. Nurse Betty Gow looked in on her charge around 8 pm. When she checked again two hours later, she discovered that an intruder had entered the house and committed what would go down as one of the crimes of the century.

A window had been left open to air the nursery, and a crudely constructed broken ladder was found outside, so there was no mystery regarding access. The motive also soon became evident as a ransom note had been left. It was error-strewn but the import was clear enough: the perpetrator wanted 'mony', $50,000 in exchange for the safe return of Charles Jr.

MIDDLE LEFT: Lindbergh taking things easily after his transatlantic flight. Strolling with him through the grounds of the American embassy are Mr Houghton (left), the Ambassador and Lieut. Colonel Joyce, Military Attaché.

LEFT: Mrs Charles Lindbergh addresses audience about their experience in the Chinese floods, in which they nearly lost their lives while on an aerial tour of the orient.

BOTTOM LEFT AND BELOW: *Spirit of St Louis* in a test flight over San Diego.

BOTTOM: Conquering hero: massive celebrations after the pioneering feat that captured the imagination of the American public.

FAR LEFT: Charles Augustus Jr, the Lindbergh's baby, who was abducted from their home on March 1, 1932.

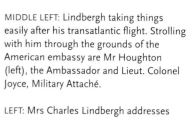

MARCH 3, 1932

Resembles his father

Descriptions broadcast throughout the country of the kidnapped baby have set all hearts beating with sympathy and the determination, if possible, to restore the boy to his parents and punish the authors of the most sensational crime of recent years.

The descriptions read simply: He is 20 months old. At the time of the kidnapping, between 7.30 and 10 p.m. yesterday, he was dressed in a white sleeping suit. His eyes are blue, his hair is fair and curly, his complexion is fair. He is able to walk a little and talk, though as yet he uses only a few simple words such as a child just beginning to talk would know. He is of average weight and height for his age, which is to say, 30lb. and 2ft.9in. He is said to resemble his father, allowing for the chubbiness of his baby face.

The home of the Lindberghs is situated at Hopewell, New Jersey, in an estate of 550 acres, chosen for its loneliness and inaccessibility.

£10,000 house

The house is a two-storey building of ten rooms, and was built at a cost of £10,000, while Col. Lindbergh and his wife were in China last year. Besides Col. and Mrs. Lindbergh, there were in the house last night three other adults, Betty Gow, a young English nurse, and Ollie Wheatley, the butler, and his wife. The baby was put to bed in the nursery on the second floor at 7.30. He had been ill with a cold for

several days and was fretful, but went to sleep in a few minutes, and Mrs. Lindbergh and the nurse went downstairs. The nurse returned to the nursery at about 10 o'clock. The sight that met her eyes set her screaming with alarm. The baby's cot was empty and one of the two windows was open. Col. Lindbergh and his wife hastened upstairs. There was no trace of the baby, but on the windowsill was an ominous scrap of paper. What was written on it they still refuse to divulge, except to say that it contained a demand for £10,000 and the statement that: "We shall be back to-morrow to talk business."

Footprints

Col. Lindbergh dashed downstairs into the garden. On the wall leading to the nursery window were dirt marks made by a ladder. The ground showed footprints. Thirty yards away was a discarded ladder. Col. Lindbergh rushed to the telephone and 20 minutes later the county chief of police and his assistants arrived. They found the famous airman pale but calm. His wife was wringing her hands in agony, seeking by the utmost effort of will to regain control of herself but unable to speak.

Armed with searchlights, Col. Lindbergh and the police took up the trail of footsteps, which led through a dirty lane to the main highway. There the footprints were lost. As the searchers reached the highway a body of 50 mounted police arrived. It was evident that the kidnappers had made their escape in a motorcar.

The alarm was flashed to New York, Philadelphia, and to every police station in the two States. At the Hudson Tunnel, leading under the river in the metropolis, a strong guard was placed. Every truck and motorcar was searched. All approaches to Philadelphia were rigidly guarded. Every village and town in a wide radius was awakened and ordered to stop and search all passing vehicles.

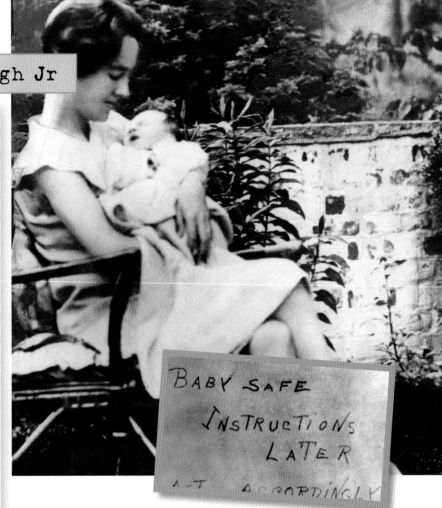

Condon acts as intermediary

A massive police search of the surrounding area turned up nothing. There was little to go on, but the authorities were determined to leave no stone unturned to find the kidnapper and return the son of a national hero to his family. The Lindberghs' loss also hit home with families across the land. A wave of sympathy and outrage swept the country; even Al Capone was moved to offer a $10,000 reward from his Chicago jail cell. America demanded retribution, but as yet there was no one against whom to direct their anger.

The Lindberghs' sole focus was the safe return of Charles Jr, and they were willing to pay the agreed price. Retired schoolteacher John Condon wrote an open letter to the Bronx Home News offering his services as an intermediary, an offer accepted by both parties. Contact was made with a representative of the kidnappers, a man known as 'John', and arrangements were made for the drop to take place at St Raymond's Cemetery in the Bronx. Charles Jr's nightclothes were posted to Condon to prove it wasn't a hoax. A note received by the go-between said: 'After we have the mony in hand we will tell you where to find your boy. You may have a airplain ready it is about 150 miesl away.'

> 'We shall be back tomorrow to talk business.'

TOP LEFT: Descriptions and photographs of the baby were issued immediately and a wave of sympathy and outrage swept across the country. Even gangster Al Capone offered a reward of $10,000 from his jail cell.

LEFT: The Lindbergh baby photographed with his nurse in the grounds of the summer estate of his Grandfather, Mr Dwight Morrow at North Haven, Maine.

TOP: Mrs Lindbergh with her son. A massive police search of the surrounding area drew a blank.

ABOVE: A copy of one of the notes received by Colonel Lindbergh from the supposed kidnappers, after which he paid the ransom, in the belief that his child would be returned.

MARCH 3, 1932

Hunt for a man

Late this afternoon a general alarm was sent out for the apprehension of a man at Newark, New Jersey, described as wearing a grey hat and a blue overcoat, and as being about 40 years of age. He bought a postcard shortly before noon at a small shop near a post office in Newark. A second postcard was bought by a woman soon afterwards. At noon the post office authorities spotted a postcard addressed to "Charles Linberg, Princeton, New Jersey." It bore this message written in pencil in block letters: "Baby safe. Wait instructions later. Act accordingly."

The police are now making a house-to-house search in the neighbourhood of the post office. Meanwhile, Mrs. Lindbergh has issued a public appeal "to the kidnapper of the Lindbergh baby." The appeal reads: Here is a heartbroken appeal direct from the mother of the child you stole. The baby has been ill and his recovery may depend on the treatment he gets from you. You must be especially careful about his diet.

Mrs Lindbergh has issued to the Press a strict diet she has been following since the baby fell ill. She did this in the hope that you might read this story and that there is some spark of humanity even in the heart of a baby-thief

The diet

Here is the diet, accompanied by the fervent prayer of a grieving mother:

One quart of milk during the day;
   Three tablespoons of cooked cereal morning and night;
   Two tablespoons of cooked vegetables once a day;
   One yolk of egg daily;
   Two tablespoons of stewed fruit daily;
   Half a cup of orange juice on waking;
   Half a cup of prune juice after afternoon nap; and
   14 drops of medicine called Viosterol during the day.

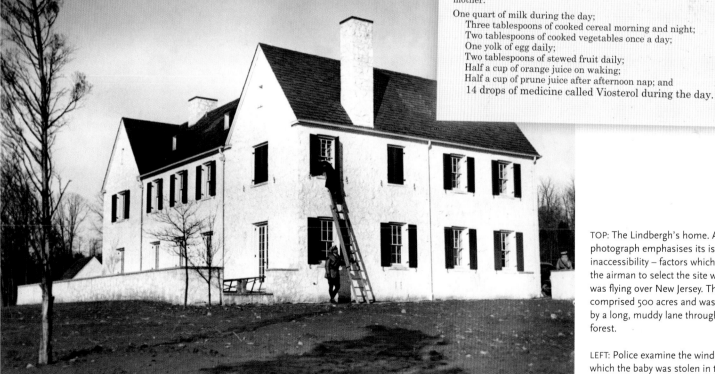

TOP: The Lindbergh's home. An aerial photograph emphasises its isolation and inaccessibility – factors which induced the airman to select the site when he was flying over New Jersey. The estate comprised 500 acres and was approached by a long, muddy lane through a thick forest.

LEFT: Police examine the window from which the baby was stolen in the hope of finding fingerprints.

The kidnapping of Charles Lindbergh Jr

Ransom money handed over

On 2 April Lindbergh and Condon drove to the cemetery to keep the appointment, the former remaining in the vehicle while the latter went to meet 'John' again, this time carrying the ransom money. Against the kidnappers' demands, a record had been made of the serial numbers on the bills, and as extra insurance the bulk of the money was paid in gold certificate bills. These bills, soon to be withdrawn as US currency, were pegged to the gold standard and, crucially, easier to trace.

The money was handed over and 'John' disappeared into the shadows whence he came, leaving Condon with a note. It read: 'The boy is on the Boad Nelly. It is a small boad 28 feet long. Two persons are on the boad. The are innosent. You will find the Boad between Horseneck Brach and gay Head near Elizabeth Island.'

Child's body found

The following day, Lindbergh flew over the waters between the mainland and Martha's Vineyard, finding no vessel matching the description. Five weeks later, 12 May 1932, a trucker in need of relieving himself pulled up by some woods just four miles from the Lindbergh home. He found the badly decomposed body of Charles Jr lying in a shallow grave, partly dismembered and with some of the internal organs removed. The autopsy revealed cause of death to be a blow to the head, the police surmising it may have been delivered in the bedroom itself, or perhaps the result of being dropped when the rickety homemade ladder gave way.

> The money was handed over and 'John' disappeared into the shadows whence he came.

TOP, AND BELOW LEFT: A happy, playful, Charles Augustus Lindbergh Junior.

LEFT: Copies of the ransom notes sent to the Lindberghs. On 2 April, they handed over the demanded ransom and were given instructions as to where the baby was to be found.

BELOW: The man who found the Lindbergh baby's body points to the spot where he discovered it, 4 miles from the Lindbergh home. The badly decomposed body was in a shallow grave, partly dismembered and with some of its internal organs missing.

A green car

One man came forward with the information that two men in a green car at seven o'clock had asked him the way to the Lindbergh home. Hours later a green car stolen the previous night was found several miles from Hopewell. Its cushions reeked of chloroform. Soon the alarm was sounded at Albany and Washington. All railway stations were put on the alert. Bridges across the Hudson and the Peace Bridge leading into Canada at Buffalo were placed under guard. The whole nation was aroused. It is realised this afternoon that the criminals have pitted their brains against those of more than 100,000,000 people.

Experts, after a prolonged examination of the footprints outside the window, believe that the actual kidnapping was done by one man. The chisel with which he forced open the window was found near the ladder. Ellis Parker, chief of the local police, declares the criminals must be "drug fiends" since no men in their senses would attempt an outrage calculated to mobilise against them every man, woman, and child throughout the world.

Nation's anger

But Colonel Lindbergh is indifferent to all these theories. His conviction is that "it is a hard cash proposition," and he has allowed it to become known that he is anxious to pay the ransom "if means and occasion" for doing so are made known to him. At his request the New Jersey State Legislature has withdrawn for the time being a reward of £5,000 it offered for the capture of the kidnappers. Colonel Lindbergh fears that such reward may endanger the child's life.

When the child was born 20 months ago his father in one day received 300,000 letters of congratulation and advice. Never in history was the advent of a baby greeted with such fervent acclaim, never in history has the disappearance of a baby caused such universal sorrow and indignation. The child was snatched from his cot without even a blanket to cover him. Apart from the possibility of murder, the health of the sick child cannot but be seriously jeopardised by his being carried in a chill night dressed only in his sleeping clothes.

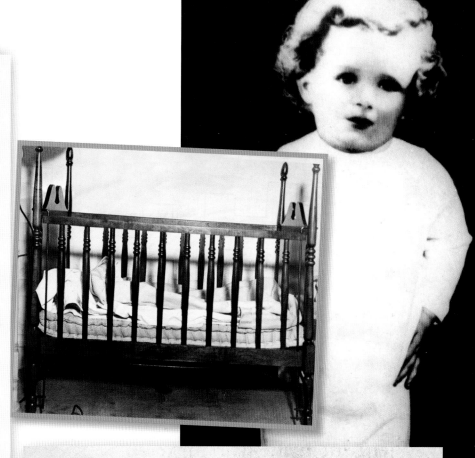

If the kidnappers of our child are unwilling to deal direct we fully authorize "Salvy" Spitale and Irving Bitz to act as our go-between. We will also follow any other method suggested by the kidnappers that we can be sure will bring the return of our child

Charles A. Lindbergh
Anne Lindbergh

JEFATURA DE POLICIA
CIUDAD DE MEXICO.

SE suplica cualesquiera información relativa al paradero del niño

CHAS. A. LINDBERGH, Jr.

quien fué secuestrado de su hogar el primero de marzo del presente año.

SEÑAS:

Edad 20 meses; peso 27 a 30 libras; altura 73 centímetros; pelo rubio, ensortijado; ojos azul oscuro; tez blanca; frente grande, ancha; nariz ligeramente remangada; tiene un hoyuelo en la barbilla.

Todo informe se tratará confidencialmente.

Director del Laboratorio
Criminalística e Identificación.
Prof. Benjamin A. Martinez.

El Jefe de la Policía.
Manuel Rubio Oviedo.

LEFT: Mexico published information about the Lindbergh baby, causing almost as much comment there as in America. Anne Lindbergh's father was the U.S. ambassador to Mexico at the time.

RIGHT: The baby's thumbguard found by his nurse, Miss Betty Gow, 100 yards from the Lindbergh's home a month after the kidnapping.

ABOVE: The note, signed by the Lindbergh's, informing the kidnappers that they had authorised two gangsters to act as a go-between.

TOP LEFT: The empty crib of the Lindbergh baby. The nurse, Betty Gow, screamed when she realised what had happened, causing the Lindberghs to run upstairs to the baby's second-floor room.

TOP RIGHT: The baby was found dead in May 1932. An autopsy revealed that he had been killed by a blow to the head. Police believed this may have happened in the bedroom or that he was dropped when the rickety ladder that the kidnapper used gave way.

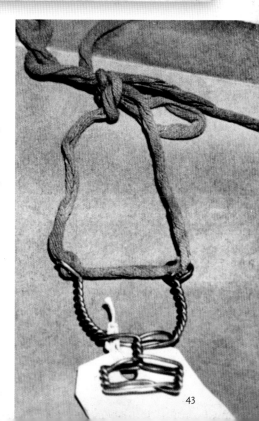

Inside job suspected

President Hoover said that the forces of law and order would be galvanised to bring those responsible to book, and Congress rushed through a law making kidnapping a federal offence. But there was little to go on. Condon drew a blank trying to identify 'John' from police mugshots, and the investigating team began to come round to the idea that it was an inside job. For one thing, the intruders had known which bedroom to target, and the fact that the family should have been visiting family on the night of 1 March, belatedly changing their plans when Charles Jr came down with a cold, also suggested a degree of knowledge close to home.

Suspicion fell on Violet Sharpe, a maid at the Morrow estate. Her account of her whereabouts on the night in question was extremely hazy, and she became agitated under questioning. But she was to become the second victim of the crime, taking poison when she could bear the interrogation no longer. It transpired that she had not wanted to name the people she was out drinking with, fearing it would be regarded as unseemly behaviour that might cost her her job. Instead it claimed her life.

Ransom money begins to surface

The police's best hope lay in the spending of the ransom money, and it started to appear. The pressure on the kidnappers increased in the spring of 1933, following the newly elected President Roosevelt's decree limiting holdings of gold certificates to $100. None of the bills could be traced back to the person who passed them until 15 September 1934, when an astute gas station attendant took down the licence plate of a man who had just paid using a $10 gold certificate. He was more concerned as to whether the proffered bill was legal tender, but his actions led police to the door of Bruno Richard Hauptmann.

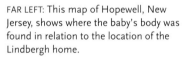

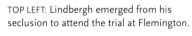

FAR LEFT: This map of Hopewell, New Jersey, shows where the baby's body was found in relation to the location of the Lindbergh home.

LEFT: Charles Jr came down with a cold around the time he was abducted, changing the Lindbergh's plans to go to visit family the evening of the kidnapping. It was this fact that turned investigators to the idea that it was an inside job since few had known their plans had changed.

TOP LEFT: Lindbergh emerged from his seclusion to attend the trial at Flemington.

TOP RIGHT: Lindbergh gave evidence in the Court at Flemington, New Jersey, in the case against Bruno Hauptmann, a German ex-convict, who was on trial for kidnapping and killing his son.

Bruno Hauptmann

Linguistics experts who examined the ransom notes, which contained expressions such as 'The child is in gute care' thought that the author might have Germanic origins. And now it was found that their chief suspect hailed from a town near Dresden.

Hauptmann had a history of petty crime in his native country, though it was born of desperation in the post-war period, when jobs and food were in short supply. Vowing to put his criminal past behind him, Hauptmann stowed away on a boat bound for America and a new life. He found work as a carpenter, a trade he had learned at home, and also a wife, Anna, whom he married in 1925. The Hauptmanns lived a frugal lifestyle and were well liked. They worked hard, saving much of what they earned, which helped them survive the economic woes of the early 1930s better than many.

On 1 March 1932, the day that Charles Lindbergh Jr was kidnapped, Bruno Hauptmann was hard at work on a new maintenance job at a large apartment block. Anna was working late that day and he picked her up from the bakery where she was employed, as was his custom. The next day, they, like the rest of America, seemed to have but one topic of conversation as news of the abduction hit the airwaves and newsstands.

Isidor Fisch

Hauptmann quickly became frustrated at the low-skill, low-wage nature of his new employment, leaving after a month to start up as a stockbroker, a field he had already dabbled in with some success. Soon he had acquired a business partner, Isidor Fisch, whose acquaintance he had made through mutual friends. Unbeknown to Hauptmann, Fisch was a rogue and a conman. One of the many shady schemes he involved himself in was dealing in 'hot' money, bought at around half the face value. The Lindbergh ransom money would find its way into his grubby hands.

TREASURY DEPARTMENT

WASHINGTON

OFFICE OF
TREASURER OF THE UNITED STATES

April 6, 1932.

To the President of
the Banking Institution addressed.

Sir:

There is inclosed a list of the serial numbers of certain United States Notes of the $5 denomination, United States Gold Certificates of the $10 denomination, and United States Gold Certificates and Federal Reserve Notes of the $20 denomination.

If any of the currency so listed is received by your bank, it will be appreciated if you will take note of the source from which you received it and immediately notify the Treasurer of the United States, Washington, D. C., by telegraph.

Very truly yours,

W O WOODS.
Treasurer of the United States.

> One of the many shady schemes he involved himself in was dealing in 'hot' money, bought at around half the face value.

TOP: A circular issued to banks during the search for the $50,000 paid by Lindbergh for the return of his son.

LEFT: Lindbergh in the courtroom at Flemington where he gave a damning testimony that identified Hauptmann as the man who had taken the ransom money.

ABOVE: Bruno Hauptmann who was executed for the kidnap and murder of Charles Lindbergh Jnr.

Damning evidence manufactured

When FBI started crawling over his house and it dawned on him that he was in possession of the Lindbergh ransom money, Hauptmann knew he was in trouble and panicked. He told them he had a small amount of the gold certificate bills, acquired from banks, an untruth that lasted for as long as it took the police to take the garage apart. Handwriting experts said there were certain similarities between Hauptmann's style and that on the ransom notes. The police were convinced that they had their man, despite the prisoner's steadfast refusal to have a confession beaten out of him.

The trial took place in Flemington, New Jersey, opening 2 January 1935. There was more heat than light in the proceedings, the prosecuting counsel David Wilentz launching a tirade of abuse instead of reasoned argument. When evidence was required, it was manufactured, several witnesses suborned into placing Hauptmann near the scene of the crime at the crucial time. One of those, Amandus Hochsmuth, had such poor eyesight that he mistook a filing cabinet with a vase on top for a woman wearing a hat at a distance of just ten feet. Another witness, Millard Whited, was a known liar who changed his statement to one that was helpful to the prosecution when told that a share of the reward money would come his way. He eventually received $1,000 of the $25,000 on offer.

By contrast, evidence that put the accused many miles away that evening was suppressed. Hauptmann lived a two-hour drive from Hopewell, and the time sheets alone for the job he had just started should have been enough to clear him. They disappeared.

Hauptmann had willingly copied out random words from the mistake-filled ransom notes, hoping the differences would help clear him. Instead, these were used against him. Hauptmann, the jury was told, had made the same spelling errors as those contained in the ransom demand. The prosecution said that part of the ladder had been made with lumber cut from the attic trusses at the Hauptmann's rented house, another tawdry attempt by the police to nail their man.

Stash of gold certificates found

In December 1933 Fisch departed for Germany, putatively to set up the overseas arm of a fur-trading enterprise. Before leaving, Fisch committed a package into his partner's care for safekeeping, and Hauptmann absently stashed it away at the back of a kitchen cupboard. Spring 1934 brought news that Fisch had succumbed to tuberculosis, a disease that had long afflicted him. A routine investigation into the deceased's affairs revealed to Hauptmann the true nature of the man he had been dealing with.

He went back to his old way of life, dividing his time between carpentry jobs and stock market dealing. Then, in August, he came across the package Fisch had given him, having forgotten about it for the past nine months. When he saw the contents – over $14,000 in gold certificates – Hauptmann thought serendipity had provided him with the opportunity to recoup the money he was owed by Fisch. It was morally justifiable, he reasoned, but, knowing the limits imposed on private holdings of such bills, he secreted them in his garage, transferring a few bills into his wallet for petty cash. It was one of these that he used at the gas station, and that brought the police to his door on 15 September 1934.

> The police were convinced that they had their man, despite the prisoner's steadfast refusal to have a confession beaten out of him.

RIGHT: Lindbergh at the trial. Hauptmann was found guilty and an appeal was dismissed. Despite the fact that evidence was found that could have blown the case wide open, the request for a retrial was denied and Hauptmann was executed.

ABOVE: Colonel Lindbergh, his wife and their second son stayed at Brynderwen, Llendaff, Cardiff, as the guests of Mr. J. Llewellyn Morgan following the death of their first son.

Final testimonies

Under duress, Condon testified that Hauptmann was the man he had met in the cemetery, contradicting an earlier statement. Perhaps the most damning testimony of all came from the bereaved father. When Condon met 'John', the latter had attracted the academic's attention by calling out 'Hey Doc'. Lindbergh, who was over fifty yards away at the time, had already gone on record to say that he could not positively identify the speaker. Now, almost two years on, he testified that the two words were uttered by Bruno Hauptmann. In truth, the all-American hero had allowed himself to be subverted by police officers, who assured him of Hauptmann's guilt. It was justifiable chicanery to guarantee that a murderer did not walk free.

Inept defence and failed appeal

The multiple fabrications had the desired effect, helped in no small measure by the inept performance of defence counsel Edward Reilly. The Lindberghs' paediatrician said he could not be absolutely sure that the decomposed and mutilated corpse was that of Charles Jr, yet Reilly willingly conceded the point, throwing away the opportunity to demand an acquittal on grounds of habeas corpus. A member of his own team said that Reilly had condemned Hauptmann to the electric chair, and at the end of the six-week trial, that was indeed the outcome.

Hauptmann's last chance of escaping death row rested with the Appeals Board, whose chairman, New Jersey governor Harold Hoffmann, already had misgivings about the handling of the case. Unfortunately, his was a lone voice and the best he could do was to secure a 60-day stay of execution. By the end of that period, Hoffmann had found hard evidence to blow the prosecution's trumped-up case wide open, yet his request for a retrial was denied. The sentence was carried out on 3 April 1936.

Heroic victim

Over the years the roles of Lindbergh and Hauptmann would be somewhat reversed. Lindbergh's star waned when he positioned himself as a Nazi appeaser and isolationist, a man who allowed himself to be decorated by Luftwaffe chief Hermann Goering. By contrast, Hauptmann was transmuted into heroic victim, a man who faced wrongful conviction with dignified stoicism. Not, however, in the eyes of the US establishment, which cleaved to the blinkered view that the guilty man had gone to the electric chair. But a host of independent investigations into the case, most notably that conducted by journalist and broadcaster Ludovic Kennedy in the 1980s, provided ample evidence to suggest that whoever kidnapped and killed the Lindbergh baby, it was not Bruno Hauptmann.

ABOVE: Anne Morrow Lindbergh was an author of many books. Among them were *North to the Orient* and *Listen! The Wind*. She received numerous awards for her contribution to literature and aviation.

FAR LEFT: Lindbergh received the Wright Brothers Memorial Trophy for his service to aviation in 1949. By this time the roles of Lindbergh and Hauptmann had reversed. Lindbergh was known to be a Nazi appeaser and Hauptmann a man who was executed because of a wrongful conviction.

LEFT: The first picture of John, the second child of Charles and Anne Lindbergh.

John Dillinger: Public Enemy No.1

Against the backdrop of the Great Depression John Herbert Dillinger came to evoke the gangster era and stirred the emotions of an American public who followed the trail of devastion across the mid-west like a modern-day soap opera.

Terrorising the mid-west

When Al Capone was put out of commission in 1931, the man who would inherit his Public Enemy No. 1 tag was languishing in Michigan State Penitentiary. John Dillinger was a small-time hoodlum serving a 10 to 20-year sentence for robbing a grocery store in Mooresville, Indiana. His accomplice had pleaded not guilty and received a two-year stretch. Dillinger, who had been persuaded that it would go better for him if he admitted the charge, was shocked and embittered at the severity of his term. The man who was paroled in May 1933, after serving nine years behind bars, was a hardened criminal. Far from returning Dillinger to the straight and narrow, his time in jail had been spent consorting with seasoned offenders and putting together a gang that would terrorise the Midwestern states.

Teenage tearaway

John Dillinger was born in Indianapolis on 22 June 1903. His father ran a thriving grocery store and the family had a comfortable middle-class lifestyle. The only blight on John's early life was the loss of his mother to a stroke when he was three years old. He was a teenage tearaway who ran with street gangs, and John Snr thought the answer to his son's waywardness was a move to the country. He swapped the grocery business for a farm in Mooresville, but the rural lifestyle didn't have the desired calming effect on John. Nor did a spell in the navy, for he enlisted only to evade the consequences of his latest misdemeanour; within a matter of months he had deserted and was back on the streets of Mooresville. There was a brief marriage, but Dillinger was never going to settle for a life of domesticity. It was at this point, in September 1924, that the law caught up with him; for the next nine years the Midwest was safe from John Dillinger's nefarious designs.

Jailbreak

Following his release from jail in May 1933, Dillinger hit five banks in as many months, and also plotted to spring some of his cronies from jail, a group including John 'Red' Hamilton and Harry Pierpont. Although he was back in custody by the time the plan was carried out, the eight men he had helped escape were quick to return the favour. Posing as policemen, they marched into the jailhouse at Lima, Ohio, and freed Dillinger, shooting dead the sheriff in the process. The gang's crime spree continued apace, and during one escape another officer was killed, this time by Dillinger's hand.

On 23 January 1934, the bandits were holed up in a Tucson hotel, but their cover was blown when a fire broke out and one of the firemen informed the police that they might be interested in the guest list. Dillinger faced only robbery charges in Arizona so he was flown to Indiana, where he was wanted for murder. There was a good-humoured photo-call as the captors posed with the captive outside Indiana's 'escape-proof' Crown Point county jail. Warden Lillian Holley was confident of holding Dillinger, but her words rang hollow as the prisoner mounted a daring escape on 3 March. The guards capitulated when Dillinger brandished a weapon, only later to discover that he had fashioned the gun from scraps of wood and blackened it with boot polish. To compound the ignominy, Dillinger made off in Holley's car. She was soon relieved of her post.

> 'Six of Dillinger's associates have bitten the dust and six policemen have been mown down by machine-gun fire.'

Baby Face Nelson

Crossing a state boundary in a stolen vehicle made Dillinger an FBI target, and Bureau boss J Edgar Hoover assigned agent Melvin Purvis the task of bringing him to book. Dillinger, meanwhile, formed a new gang, including Lester Gillis, aka Baby Face Nelson, and continued as before, criss-crossing state lines and pulling off a string of bank raids. The nearest police came to apprehending their man was a shoot-out at St Paul, Minnesota, where Dillinger was hit in the leg before making good his escape.

The gang decided to lie low and headed for Little Bohemia, a resort on the shores of Star Lake, Wisconsin. Owner Emil Wanatka became suspicious of his arrivals and managed to get a message through to the police, but Dillinger again proved too slippery. One FBI agent was killed in the ensuing gun battle, while another shot an innocent bystander. To cap a PR disaster for the Bureau, the gang slipped out of the back window and got clean away.

APRIL 25, 1934

Hunting down Dillinger

"Kill Dillinger at sight" is the order issued today to the army of Federal and State police who, in the wilds of Wisconsin and its neighbouring states, are hunting the most desperate and successful outlaw in the recent history of the United States. The death-roll so far in the fight between Public Enemy No. 1 and the forces of law has been evenly divided. Six of Dillinger's associates have bitten the dust and six policemen have been mown down by machine-gun fire. Innocent bystanders who by chance found themselves between the opposing sides account for the remainder of the 15 fatalities caused by the fugitive's ruthless fight for liberty.

Once more Dillinger has gone into hiding, either in the city of St. Paul, Minnesota, or in the trackless wastes of Wisconsin and Upper Michigan. One crumb of comfort remains to the authorities. They believe that the arch-criminal is short of weapons and ammunition, and that his small band of followers has been forced to separate.

Prolonged search

Dillinger and five of his men early this morning visited Park Falls, Wisconsin, 50 miles from the scene of yesterday's fierce battle at Mercer, where the gangsters escaped after police had surrounded them in the Bohemia Hotel. The men appeared at Park Falls shortly after midnight. They departed in the direction of St. Paul and off the main highway leading to Chicago. Meanwhile police near the Chicago highway had fired several shots at the stolen motorcar, wounding, they believe, one of the bandits.

If, as the authorities fear, Dillinger and his remaining companions have fled into the trackless waste of Wisconsin, a prolonged search awaits the police, for the land there is dotted with scores of lakes and tiny islands, on any one of which the outlaws may have had the foresight to stock provisions.

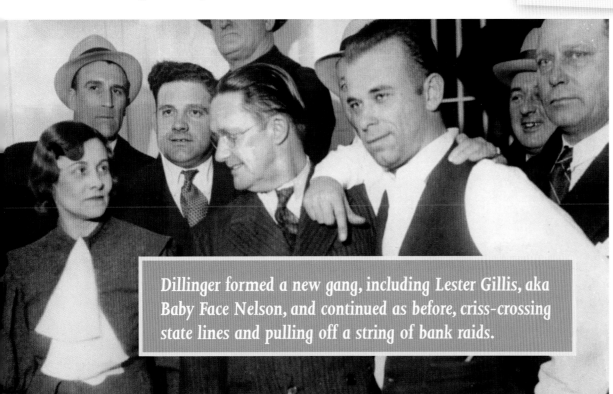

> Dillinger formed a new gang, including Lester Gillis, aka Baby Face Nelson, and continued as before, criss-crossing state lines and pulling off a string of bank raids.

OPPOSITE RIGHT: Dillinger was never a man for domesticity. He attempted a rural life, had a brief marriage and a spell in the navy but these all failed to have a calming effect on him.

OPPOSITE TOP LEFT: Police hold up a car in the search for Dillinger following another escape from jail in 1934. After the demise of Al Capone, Dillinger inherited his Public Enemy No.1 tag.

OPPOSITE BELOW: A man posts a Dilllinger wanted sign. The government offered a $10,000 reward for his capture.

ABOVE: Dillinger pictured sitting in between guards in court where he faced charges of killing a policeman. He had been flown to Indiana from Arizona after his capture in order to be tried for murder.

LEFT: Dillinger pictured with Mrs Lillian Holley, warden of the prison in which he was held. In March 1934 he escaped from the prison in a sensational break-out.

MAY 5, 1934

Dillinger shoots his way out again

The daredevil gangster, John Dillinger, wanted by six States for murder, has robbed another bank. Descending with a companion on Fostoria, Ohio, he has escaped with £3,000, leaving the chief of police, Mr. Frank Culp, severely wounded and three citizens injured after a gun battle between himself and the police.

Adopting a ruse often used by less desperate criminals, Dillinger escaped by using a man and a girl as shields from the rain of bullets threatening him from the police squad, but not until 100 shots had been exchanged during the looting of the bank Determined to get out of what seemed a certain death trap, the two gunmen seized a bookkeeper, Miss Ruth Harris, and the assistant cashier, Mr. William Daub, forcing Mr. Daub to carry the stolen currency.

With the bag, containing the £3,000, safely placed on the back seat of a motorcar Dillinger and his companion compelled their hostages to ride on the running boards of the car as it sped away. From behind the girl and the man loomed machine guns ready to blaze away at any pursuers venturesome enough to attempt a capture.

Crude plastic surgery

Handicapped by having one of the most recognisable faces in the land, Dillinger underwent plastic surgery in an attempt to alter his appearance. It was a crude procedure which had little effect and almost cost him his life. He benefited little from the operation, for the net was finally about to ensnare the country's most wanted outlaw. On 30 June 1934, Dillinger pulled one last bank job, hitting Merchants National Bank in South Bend, Indiana and making off with $28,000. Three weeks later, 22 July 1934, Dillinger had a night out in Chicago in the company of two women. This was purely pleasure, a visit to the Biograph Theatre to watch Clark Gable in Manhattan Melodrama. The final reel of the gangster film also signalled the end of the line for John Dillinger.

Betrayed by the 'Lady in Red'

The women accompanying him were new girlfriend Polly Hamilton, a waitress and sometime call-girl, and her madame, Rumanian immigrant Anna Sage. The latter was deemed an undesirable alien for her brothel-keeping activities and had the threat of deportation hanging over her head. Sage cut a deal with the FBI: she would lead them to Dillinger in exchange for having her right to remain in the country assured. She wore a red dress on the night in question to make identification easier, and as the three spilled out of the theatre at 10.30 pm, Purvis gave his G-men the agreed signal. Dillinger was hit before he could draw his gun, managing to stagger into an adjacent alley before more bullets found their mark and he fell to the ground, fatally wounded.

There was a carnival atmosphere as people thronged to the spot where John Dillinger was slain. It was reported that the first in a long line of souvenir hunters dipped handkerchiefs in the blood of the fallen folk-hero. For although Dillinger and his mob were responsible for a string of murders, the gang leader still managed to surround his misdeeds with an aura of Robin Hood-style romanticism. Many focused on the success he had in relieving banks of their cash, institutions that were rock bottom in the popularity stakes for enforcing foreclosures during the Depression era strictures. One person who may have had mixed feelings about Dillinger's death was Anna Sage. She received $5,000 for her part in his downfall, but her public-spiritedness didn't save her from being deported.

As befitting a celebrity outlaw, Dillinger's story had one final twist. The autopsy revealed discrepancies that called into question whether the FBI had got their man after all. Dillinger had blue-grey eyes; those of the dead man were brown. There were indications that the deceased had suffered a bout of rheumatic fever, a disease that Dillinger never contracted. There also appeared to be a mismatch between the dental profiles of the two men. These anomalies led some to speculate that Dillinger may have turned the tables on his pursuers, setting up a fall-guy to take the hit while he slipped off the stage to enjoy a long and comfortable retirement.

Dillinger was hit before he could draw his gun, managing to stagger into an adjacent alley before more bullets found their mark.

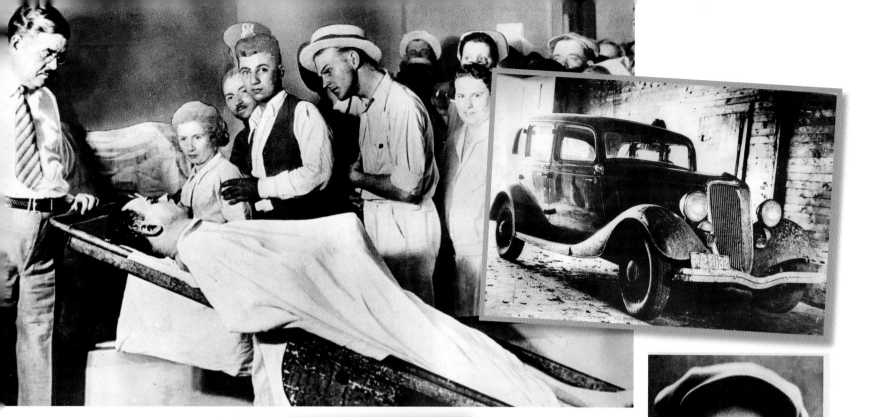

Drama of Dillinger's death

John Dillinger, known to all the world as the United States' most dangerous killer, is dead. Four bullets from the pistols of Federal Government agents sent Public Enemy No. 1 into eternity amid scenes of intense drama.

The gangster spent Sunday evening at the Biograph Cinema, two miles from Chicago's famous Loop (business quarter). The film "Manhattan Melodrama," featuring Clark Gable and William Powell, was a picture after Dillinger's own heart. He believed that the gangster scenes, with their hair-breadth escapes, reflected his own sensational doings in the past year. He passed two hours and a half in the cinema, accompanied, according to a city policeman on the spot, by two women.

While Dillinger was enjoying shadow thrills, events of tremendous moment for the wily killer were quietly hatching. Mr. Melvin Purvis, chief of the detective force of the Department of Justice here, had received a "tip off" that Dillinger went nightly to the Biograph Cinema. He chose 15 men, watched the gangster enter the theatre, and laid plans for his capture when the show was over.

Dillinger came out. He went towards an alley where his Ford was parked. His keen eyes darted to right and left, but not a whisper had reached him of his impending doom. One of the Federal agents drew close to him. In tones husky with emotion and excitement he murmured in the gangster's ear: "Hallo, John." The gangster whipped round as though shot. His hand sped towards his automatic. Pistols rang out and Dillinger fell with three bullets in his chest and one in his neck. In the trouser pockets were £10 in dollar notes, and a gold watch containing inside the case a photograph of a girl. She was identified as Evelyn Freschetti, the young Indian girl now in prison, who had shared with the gangster his Wisconsin hiding-place.

An examination of the body revealed the extraordinary lengths to which Dillinger had gone in an effort to disguise himself. All that plastic surgery could do to change a man had been done. A mole between his eyes had been removed; his nose, originally puggy, had been straightened; a cleft in his chin had been flattened out. His hair, originally sandy, was black, and the gangster wore gold-rimmed spectacles to hide those piercing eyes, described by crime experts as "the eyes of a born killer." "His fingertips had been scarred with acid in an effort to remove ever-telltale fingerprints. A scar on the left side of his nose had been carefully treated.

The gangster spent Sunday evening at the Biograph Cinema. The film 'Manhattan Melodrama,' featuring Clark Gable and William Powell, was a picture after Dillinger's own heart.

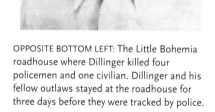

OPPOSITE BOTTOM LEFT: The Little Bohemia roadhouse where Dillinger killed four policemen and one civilian. Dillinger and his fellow outlaws stayed at the roadhouse for three days before they were tracked by police.

OPPOSITE TOP LEFT: The upper window at the rear of the roadhouse from which Dillinger and his gang leapt to escape.

TOP RIGHT: The car which Dillinger and his companion, John Hamilton left behind after spending the night at the home of Hamilton's sister. She was subsequently arrested for habouring a fugitive from justice.

ABOVE LEFT: The body of Dillinger lies on the floor of a police patrol car as he was taken to the mortuary. He was shot by police as he was leaving the Biograph Cinema in Chicago in July 1934.

LEFT: The bullet-riddled body of Dillinger was placed on view to the public. He had undergone plastic surgery in order to disguise his infamous face but this had little effect.

ABOVE: George 'Baby Face' Nelson was part of Dillinger's gang. He was wanted for jail break, bank robbery and for his part in the roadhouse killing.

John Christie: 10 Rillington Place

John Reginald Halliday Christie will forever be associated with the murderous spree he embarked upon between 1943 and 1953, crimes so heinous that the infamous address where they occurred, 10 Rillington Place, was expunged from the record, renamed Ruston Mews when the row of unprepossessing three-storey houses in Notting Hill was demolished.

ABOVE LEFT: This picture of John Christie, issued by Scotland Yard on March 27, 1953, started a nationwide man-hunt. Christie was educated at Halifax Secondary school, where he excelled at mathematics. He was skilled with his hands and had a high IQ. He sang in the choir and became a Scout, but he was never popular with his classmates.

BELOW: Crowds gathering in Rillington Place. Despite a change of street name the address would never lose its sinister associations.

An impotent loner

Christie was born in Halifax on 8 April 1898. His father was authoritarian and abusive, while his mother and sisters were overprotective and bossy. The young Christie was a good scholar, a choirboy and Boy Scout, though something of a loner and given to flights of hypochondria. He cast himself as something of a ladies' man, yet he was taunted following a disastrous early sexual liaison. It was an unsympathetic response to the impotence that would afflict him throughout his life. Scarred and humiliated by the experience, he would find nefarious ways to demonstrate his potency in the years ahead.

By 1920, aged 22, Christie recovered confidence enough to marry Ethel Waddington, a homely type of woman who would be less likely to undermine his performance. The marriage endured sexual failure and a lengthy separation, during which time Christie moved among the seedy strata of London society. He had a number of brushes with the law that led to custodial sentences, his transgressions including petty theft and a violent attack on a prostitute. The latter incident was a portent of what lay ahead, and an indication of his ambivalent attitude towards women.

In 1933 Christie attempted to put his dubious past behind him by taking a position as a clerk and seeking a reconciliation with Ethel. The couple moved into the cramped ground floor flat at 10 Rillington Place in 1938, and Christie's credentials for respectability received a further boost the following year, when he was appointed a special constable, the vicissitudes of war causing his criminal record to be overlooked.

> Christie had a number of brushes with the law that led to custodial sentences, his transgressions including petty theft and violence.

TOP LEFT: Christie on Brighton pier. During the 1920s Christie was convicted for petty criminal offences. These included three months' imprisonment for stealing postal orders while working as a postman in 1921. He served another three months in 1933 for stealing a car from a priest who had befriended him.

ABOVE: Ethel Waddington from Sheffield married Christie on May 10, 1920 in Halifax. She separated from her husband after four years and Christie moved to London while Ethel went to live with relatives. They were reconciled after his release from prison in November 1933.

LEFT: Police guard the entrance to the house where the bodies had been found. They had been dead between four days and three months.

John Christie: 10 Rillington Place

LEFT AND OPPOSITE BELOW RIGHT: Mothers push their babies in prams in Rillington Place. Timothy Evans and his pregnant wife, Beryl, moved into the top-floor flat of 10 Rillington Place in April 1948.

BELOW LEFT: Muriel Amelia Eady was Christie's second victim. He promised to cure her bronchitis with a 'special mixture' he had concocted. He used domestic gas, which contained carbon monoxide that would render a person unconscious. Once Eady was knocked out, Christie choked her to death.

BELOW RIGHT: Christie murdered his wife in bed on the morning of December 14, 1952. She was last seen alive two days earlier.

BOTTOM: Three of Christie's eight victims: Rita Elizabeth Nelson and Kathleen Maloney were both killed in January 1953 and Hectorina McKay MacLennan was murdered on or about February 27.

Modus operandi established

It was during a tour of duty in 1943 that Christie met Ruth Fuerst, a 21-year-old munitions worker and part-time prostitute. He lured her back to 10 Rillington Place, safe in the knowledge that Ethel was away visiting her parents. Fuerst became his first victim, raped and strangled to death. Sex and strangulation would be his modus operandi, which next accounted for Muriel Eady, whom he met in the factory where both were employed. She met her end in October 1944, Christie later bragging about the ingenious way in which he drew her into his web with the offer of an efficacious inhaler that would benefit her bronchial condition. The tubing was linked to the gas supply, which rendered his victim semi-conscious and unable to resist his sexual and physical assault. He would say that the lifeless naked bodies of Fuerst and Eady thrilled him; he exerted power over them, with no threat of rebuke. Both women were buried in the tiny back garden of 10 Rillington Place.

Christie claims a mother and her daughter as his next victim

Christie's murderous proclivities were held in check for four years, until Timothy John Evans and his teenage wife Beryl took possession of the second-floor flat in the spring of 1948. Evans, who came from Merthyr Vale, was an illiterate, feeble-minded fantasist who just about managed to hold down a job as a delivery driver. Christie ingratiated himself with his new neighbours, focusing his attention on Beryl, who was heavily pregnant with their first child. Baby Geraldine was born in October, but not into a happy home. Her parents were struggling financially, and the arguments over money threatened to worsen when Beryl found herself pregnant once again. She was adamant that she did not want another child, which was music to the ears of John Christie when news of the predicament filtered down two floors. He had little trouble passing himself off as a one-time medical student who had experience of terminating unwanted pregnancies.

The date set for the proposed procedure was Tuesday, 8 November. Christie primed the hapless Evans for the bad news that would follow by spelling out the chances of the mother dying during the operation. Christie later described his failed attempt to have intercourse with the unconscious Beryl. He then strangled her and waited to give Evans the bad news.

Christie suggested concealing Beryl's body in one of the outside drains and having the motherless infant adopted by acquaintances of his. Evans went along with it. No doubt the confused, distraught simpleton, faced with the consequences of abetting a criminal act, was easily persuaded to take on the role of co-conspirator. He was also fearful of Christie, who would boast of his ability to manipulate his intellectually impaired neighbour.

Two days later, Evans arrived home to find that his daughter had departed to her new family. In reality, she, too, had been strangled and the body put with that of her mother in an outhouse. Evans believed that his wife had died during an abortion and that his daughter had been taken in by another family. He was soon to learn the terrible truth.

Guilt forces Evans to confess go to the police

On Monday 14 November, a furniture dealer cleared out Evans's flat, and Evans himself took a train to his home in South Wales, where he spent the next two weeks visiting relatives. He would give differing accounts of his wife and child's whereabouts, at one time saying they were holidaying on the south coast; at another that they had relocated to Bristol, where he was to join them; and even that the marriage had foundered over Beryl's infidelity.

On 30 November Evans could bear the guilt no longer. He walked into the Merthyr Tydfil police station and confessed to murdering his wife, telling officers he had put her body into the drain outside 10 Rillington Place. In his initial statement Evans said that Beryl had been depressed at becoming pregnant again and told her husband she wanted an abortion. Evans had procured the necessary medication, and when he arrived home from work on Tuesday 8 November, he found his wife's lifeless body and disposed of it in the property's drainage system.

Evans's story unravelled as soon as police examined the drains of the London property and found no body. He then changed his story, saying that his original statement had been tailored to protect his neighbour, John Christie. This time he related the truthful tale of Christie's offer to perform the abortion, and his arrival home on the night of 8 November to be informed that the procedure had gone wrong. The two men had hidden the body, Christie telling Evans he would dispose of it in the drains at a later date. A more thorough search of 10 Rillington Place was conducted, and the bodies of Beryl and 14-month-old Geraldine were found in the outside washhouse. Both had been strangled.

In yet another statement, Evans confessed to both murders. This was the first time that he had mentioned the death of the child, and it was that crime on which the police decided to proceed. In their view, Evans was guilty of a callous double murder, but a conviction for killing his young daughter was all that was needed to send him to the gallows. And the confession meant that he was damned by his own hand, an open and shut case.

Protests of innocence go unheard

But there was a problem. Some of the language used in the confession was far too sophisticated for its illiterate author, and it was also said that the use of numbers in the subscript to indicate the time and date of the statement would have been beyond his capabilities. In short, there were strong grounds for thinking that Evans had been manipulated by the presiding officers, just as he had been manipulated by Christie. Indeed, he retracted the confession, implicating Christie in Geraldine's death, the only possible perpetrator. But this was an amendment too far for the jury, who decided it was a desperate effort to shift the blame elsewhere. During the trial, Evans insisted that Christie had committed both crimes, and that the confession had been gained through intimidation. It was to no avail. The jury believed the star Crown witness, John Christie, a man who had received commendations for his wartime service as a special constable. What possible motive could he have for killing Geraldine? As well as giving a bravura performance in denying all knowledge of the abortion and Evans's version of subsequent events, Christie ensured that Evans remained firmly in the frame by highlighting the couple's stormy relationship.

The jury took just forty-five minutes to return a guilty verdict, and Timothy Evans went to the gallows at Pentonville Prison on 9 March 1950, protesting his innocence to the last.

> **Evans's story unravelled as soon as police examined the drains of the London property and found no body.**

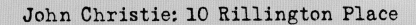

MARCH 25, 1953

Three women die in murder house

The boarded-up bodies of three women were found last night hidden behind gay, new wallpaper in the scullery of the ground-floor flat at 10, Rillington Place, Notting Hill, West London. So triple murder came to the tall Georgian house which had already been the scene of a double murder in 1949.

Mr. Beresford Brown, a Jamaican, uncovered the secret. He was moving from the top floor flat to the vacant ground floor flat, and began to examine the scullery. He wanted to install a bath, noticed that a part of the wall looked different. He tapped, and there was a hollow echo. When he pulled the wallpaper off he found a cavity, roughly boarded up. Behind the boards were the remains of the three women.

Last night Chief Superintendent Beveridge, of Scotland Yard, put out a country-wide request for the previous tenants of the flat, Mr. John Christie and his middle-aged wife, Ethel, to come forward, in the hope that they might be able to help with the inquiry.

TOP: Chief Superintendent Peter Beveridge entering 10 Rillington Place where the new tenant, Beresford Dubois Brown, discovered bodies hidden in a wallpapered-over coal cellar in the kitchen. Pathology tests later revealed carbon monoxide in their bodies. A nationwide manhunt for Christie ensued on March 25, 1953.

LEFT: Holes in the ground of the garden at 10 Rillington Place. Following the discovery of the bodies inside the house, the search was extended to the garden. Detectives drove steaks into the earth in order to search for more bodies.

ABOVE AND OPPOSITE PAGE: Police search through weeds, rubbish and neglected shrubs for clues in the derelict garden behind number 10. The bones of Fuerst and Eady were discovered, taking the body count to six.

MARCH 25, 1953

Riddle of identity

With Dr. F. E. Camps, Home Office pathologist, and Chief Inspector Low, of the finger-print department, he was working until the early hours today, to identify the dead women and form an opinion of the probable dates of their deaths. It was established that the tragedy has no link with the murder of 19-year-old Mrs. Beryl Evans and her 14-month-old daughter Geraldine, who were found strangled at the same address in 1949. Mrs. Evans's husband, Timothy Evans was hanged for the murder of his child.

Mr. Christie, a British Road Transport clerk, employed at the Shepherd's Bush depot, had lived for about 15 years in the ground-floor flat with his wife. About two months ago, said Mrs Doreen Lawrence, a neighbour, Mrs. Christie disappeared. Mr. Christie stayed on alone with his dog, but was not seen much. "He said his wife had gone to her sister's at Birmingham," Mrs. Lawrence added.

Flat sub-let

"Last Thursday Mr. Christie left the flat. Before going he sub-let to a young Irish couple without the knowledge of the landlord. He did not give them the key and when they arrived they had to put their furniture in through the window. But on Saturday the landlord made them leave because he had arranged to let Mr. Brown have the flat."

Mr. Christie was last seen having a meal at a fish and chip bar at the top of the road. He said then that he was going to have his dog "done away with." Mr. Christie was a special constable at Harrow Road police station during the war, and police in the Notting Hill area know him well. Recently he had visited the local police station to lodge complaints about coloured residents in Rillington Place. He was one of the principal witnesses at the murder trial of Timothy Evans.

'Last Thursday Mr Christie left the flat. Before going he sub-let to a young Irish couple without the knowledge of the landlord.'

57

John Christie: 10 Rillington Place

The net finally closes in on Christie

There the matter rested for the next three years, until 10 Rillington Place's ground-floor flat had a change of tenant. In clearing out the apartment prior to occupation, the new occupant discovered a deep alcove that had been papered over. There he found a woman's body, and the subsequent police search uncovered two more cadavers in the alcove, another under the floorboards, and bones enough to form two skeletons buried in the garden – the remains of Fuerst and Eady.

The hunt was on for Christie, who appeared to realise the net was closing in when he quit his job, sold his possessions and papered over the alcove before illegally sub-letting his flat. He made little effort to flee, however. On 31 March 1953, he was apprehended by police on Putney Bridge, near the embankment where he had been sleeping rough. Under questioning he related the details of his ten-year killing spree.

Christie had murdered Ethel in December 1952, placing her body under the floorboards, and in his final months of freedom claimed three more victims, those whose bodies were hidden in the alcove. Prostitutes Kathleen Maloney and Rita Nelson were each subjected to the same gassing treatment, their unconscious or lifeless bodies subjected to a sexual assault. His last victim, Hectorina MacLennan, represented a departure from his usual choice of target. She was searching for accommodation when the two struck up a conversation at Ladbroke Grove Station in March 1953. Christie offered to help, but his plans were thwarted when MacLennan arrived at 10 Rillington Place with a boyfriend in tow. He allowed them to stay for three nights before asking them to leave. He followed the couple and caught MacLennan alone, inviting her to return home with him. She met the same fate as the others, and Christie coolly dealt with the concerned boyfriend who turned up at the door in search of a partner who appeared to have vanished into thin air.

John Christie was tried and convicted for the murder of Ethel, the jury rejecting his plea of insanity as they reached a guilty verdict after barely an hour's deliberation. He was executed at Pentonville Prison on 15 July 1953.

TOP LEFT: A copper boiler from the scullery of 10 Rillington Place is placed in a police car and taken to Scotland Yard.

ABOVE LEFT AND BELOW LEFT: The spot, near Putney Bridge, where Christie was found by P.C. Thomas Ledger. The constable had stopped Christie and asked him who he was. Subsequently Christie was taken away to be questioned and the manhunt for the Rillington Place murderer came to an end.

ABOVE: The police station where Christie was detained. After word got out about his capture, crowds gathered outside the building.

OPPOSITE: Christie was driven from Notting Hill Police Station to West London Magistrates' Court to appear on charges of murdering his wife. From there, as crowds began to gather, he was taken to Brixton Prison.

APRIL 1, 1953

Christie charged with murder of his wife

Behind the drawn blinds of a ground floor room in Notting Hill police station, West London, last night, John Reginald Halliday Christie, 55-year-old haulage clerk, was charged with the murder of his wife, Ethel Christie, of 10, Rillington Place, Notting Hill. He was charged by Detective-Inspector Griffin, who since Tuesday has been investigating the mystery of the house.

The charge as read to Christie was "that on or about December 14 at 10, Rillington Place you murdered your wife, Ethel Christie, aged 54." Christie was brought to Notting Hill police station from Putney, where he was arrested at 9 o'clock yesterday morning. He was to remain at Notting Hill police station overnight and appear at West London Magistrates' Court today.

'Excuse me, but who are you?'

Police Constable Thomas Ledger, of Putney, is 6ft. 3in., aged 43, and holds a Long Service Medal, a Good Conduct Medal, and a Commendation. He gained these awards in years of dutiful but rather uneventful service.

At nine o'clock yesterday morning he was patrolling near the point where Lower Richmond-road joins the embankment at Putney. There, leaning on the embankment railings, watching men unload some barges, he saw a dishevelled-looking man. In the memory and in the notebook of every policeman in the country was the description of John Reginald Halliday Christie. P.C. Ledger had also a photograph and this he took out of his pocket.

Challenge

Then, as Christie turned and was about to walk away, he found Ledger barring his path. The policeman gave the challenge that has been repeated all over the country during the week that Christie was sought for interview - a challenge which has seriously embarrassed many hundreds of men with thinning hair and spectacles, and an air of gentility.

P.C. Ledger asked: "Excuse me, but who are you?"

He was answered. Then he invited the bespectacled man with three days' growth of beard to walk with him to a police call-box. There the officer telephoned Putney Police Station and stood waiting until a van arrived with two other policemen. Christie was driven to Putney Police Station. Deputy Commander Rawlings hurried there from Scotland Yard and Chief Superintendent Barratt and Chief Inspector Griffin went from Notting Hill five miles away, where they been working on the Rillington Place murders.

Then Chief Superintendent Barratt sent an official message to Scotland Yard calling off the nation-wide search for Christie. Shortly afterwards he sent another message announcing that Christie had been charged with the murder of his wife, and would appear at West London Magistrates' Court. Hundreds of men, women, and children gathered outside the police station at Putney, and later at Notting Hill Police station, in the hope of catching a glimpse of Christie.

> The charge as read to Christie was 'that on or about December 14 at 10 Rillington Place you murdered your wife, Ethel Christie.'

John Christie: 10 Rillington Place

Evans case reopens

Christie's confession inevitably cast doubt on the conviction of Timothy Evans, not least because he included Beryl Evans in his list of victims, though he vehemently denied any culpability regarding the fate of Geraldine. The Howard League for Penal Reform pressed for the case to be reopened, and Labour MP George Rogers took up the issue. Home Secretary Sir David Maxwell Fyfe acceded, and the events of November 1949 were re-examined, in camera, in an inquiry headed by Mr John Scott Henderson QC. Remarkably, that inquiry found the case against Evans to be overwhelming, and that no miscarriage of justice had taken place. Christie's inclusion of Beryl Evans in his confession was discounted as a device to help his own defence. This meant that according to the official version of events, there were two unconnected stranglers operating out of 10 Rillington Place in the autumn of 1949. Many thought such a coincidence stretched credulity to breaking point, but another twelve years would pass before the recently elected Labour Government ordered yet another re-examination of the Evans case.

ABOVE: The crowds outside Putney Police Station try to catch a glimpse of Christie. Elaborate police precautions prevented them from doing so.

TOP RIGHT: Dr Nickolls, head of the Science Laboratory (wearing a hat) attempts to make his way through the crowds queueing outside Clerkenwell Magistrates' Court. They were hoping for seats at Christie's hearing.

ABOVE RIGHT: People queueing outside the Old Bailey the day before the Christie trial opened. Miss Joan Elton was the first to arrive – she had prepared food and brought a blanket for her overnight wait.

OPPOSITE BOTTOM RIGHT: A deck chair is carried into the Old Bailey as evidence in Christie's trial.

RIGHT: Crowds outside the Old Bailey after the verdict. Christie's attempt to plead insanity failed and he was sentenced to death after not even an hour's worth of deliberation.

OPPOSITE BOTTOM LEFT: The sentence notice that was put up outside Pentonville Prison on 4 July 1953.

Two MPs and mother of hanged man demand new inquiry

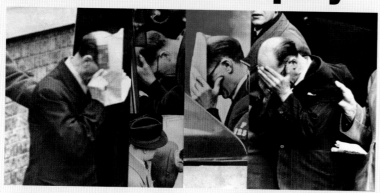

Immediately after John Christie was sentenced to death last night, the mother of Timothy John Evans, hanged in Pentonville three years and three months ago, called on the Home Secretary, Sir David Maxwell Fyfe, to reopen her son's case and hold a public inquiry. She charged that her son had been hanged for a murder he did not commit - the strangling of his baby daughter, 14-month-old Geraldine, found dead at 10, Rillington Place, the Christie death-house, with her mother.

Christie, who appeared to be weeping as he left the Old Bailey dock for a condemned cell at Pentonville, said during his trial that he strangled Mrs. Evans. But he strenuously denied killing Geraldine. Backing up Evans's mother in her demand are two M.Ps - Mr. George Rogers, North Kensington, and Mr. Sydney Silverman, who are trying to table questions in the House - and the Howard League for Penal Reform. Mr. Rogers wants to ask: Was there a miscarriage of justice; will the Home Secretary order an inquiry?

The League wants a public inquiry too, and in a letter to the Home Secretary, says: "Although Evans was only charged with the murder of his child, evidence regarding the murder of his wife was part of the case for the Crown. Within the last few days, however, statements have been made which throw doubt on that evidence. The whole of the evidence then available must have been considered by the Home Secretary [then Mr. Chuter Ede] in deciding how to advise his late Majesty on the exercise of the royal prerogative of mercy. There is, therefore, a possibility that such advice may have been based on incorrect information."

What is there now to help the Home Secretary make his decision on whether or not to reopen the case?

Baby's bottle still Half-full

First, there are the Evans family - his mother, Mrs. Probert, and his sister, Mrs. Eleanor Ashby, who live in St. Mark's Road, a few hundred yards from 10, Rillington Place, where Timothy Evans had a flat. Mrs. Ashby said last night of her 25-year-old lorry-driver brother: "Tim did not know his baby was dead until he arrived at the police station in Notting Hill. He told me that after he was charged. We now know that when the police searched at Rillington Place they found all Geraldine's belongings hidden in a cupboard in Christie's front room Her clothes, her pram, and even her feeding bottle, half-filled with milk, were there. No one has mentioned these facts before."

Devoted to his daughter

Now for Evans's aunt - Mrs. Violet Lynch of Mount Pleasant, near Merthyr Tydfil. He went to her home after leaving Rillington Place. Of those days she said: "His life was devoted to Geraldine and he would not have harmed a hair on her head. When on trial Timmy swore to me over and over again that a man named Christie had promised to take the child to a safe home. What a terrible man he was to have sat there after murdering Beryl, Timmy's wife, and yet saying nothing as he watched Timmy being sent to the gallows."

There will also be before the Home Secretary the report of the Evans trial, where it was first alleged that Christie knew something about the deaths of Mrs. Evans and the baby. Then there are Christie's admissions at his own trial, and the questioning there of Chief Inspector Albert Griffin.

Sir Lionel Heald, the Attorney-General asked the inspector: "Have you any ground for believing that the wrong man was hanged in the Evans case?" Inspector Griffin: "None."

'It is possible'

Sir Lionel; "Is one possibility that two men were concerned with the death of Mrs. Evans?" Inspector Griffin: "It is possible. I do not know." And, yesterday, the judge said of the Evans murder: "It is foolish for us to pretend it may not be a matter of disturbing interest."

There is, too, the view of the Home Secretary at the time, Mr. Chuter Ede. He said last night: "I am making no comment on this matter. Whether more is heard of it rests with his successor, Sir David Maxwell Fyfe, who will have before him today these final words from the Penal Reform League: It is imperative that public confidence in justice be maintained."

'Have you any ground for believing that the wrong man was hanged in the Evans case?' Inspector Griffin: 'None'.

Crowds Wait As Christie Dies

Two hundred people outside Pentonville Prison yesterday watched the posting of the notice announcing the execution of John Reginald Halliday Christie, the mass murderer of Rillington Place. The crowd which included women and children, surged across the road to read the notice which was posted at 9.06 a.m.

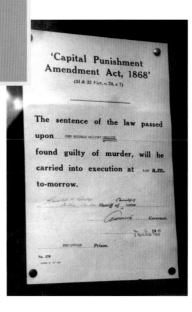

'Capital Punishment Amendment Act, 1868'
(31 & 32 Vict. c. 24, s. 7)

The sentence of the law passed upon JOHN REGINALD HALLIDAY CHRISTIE found guilty of murder, will be carried into execution at 9 a.m. to-morrow.

Posthumous free pardon for Evans

In October 1966, High Court judge Sir Daniel Brabin delivered a report which endorsed the findings of the Scott Henderson inquiry. Like his predecessor, Brabin found the thought of an egregious miscarriage of British justice an unconscionable proposition. In his view, the balance of probability suggested that Christie killed Geraldine Evans, and the child's father, therefore, was hanged for a crime he didn't commit. But the inquiry also concluded that Evans's confession regarding the death of his wife was genuine, not the misguided gesture of a remorseful husband who had allowed her to die at the hands of an illegal abortionist. In other words, the charge sheet may have been wrong but Evans was still a murderer who had received the appropriate come-uppance. Brabin subscribed to the fanciful view that two men, each responsible for killing women by means of a ligature, were living under the same roof. The report's author met the charge head on, commenting: 'It is no solution to the problem of the coincidence to ignore the evidence which points to the coincidence being a fact.'

Within a week, Home Secretary Roy Jenkins gave his verdict on the coincidence theory, eliciting cheers from the benches of the House of Commons when he granted Timothy John Evans a posthumous free pardon. Evans's remains were exhumed from Pentonville Prison and reinterred on consecrated ground, and the case was instrumental in the decision to abolish the death penalty, but it didn't quite represent the closing of an unseemly chapter in British legal history. The pardon exonerated Evans only from the charge on which he was convicted, that of killing his daughter. In 2004 family members failed in their bid to have the case referred to the Court of Appeal, and although it is widely accepted that Evans was innocent of all wrongdoing, the findings of the two official inquiries have left a cloud hanging over his name.

ABOVE: The front cover of Ludovic Kennedy's book. Sir Hugh Lucas-Tooth, Under-Secretary at the Home Office at the time, was of the opinion that the book contained no fresh evidence and had misled a great number of M.P.s: 'The book provides a flattering picture of Evans and damns Christie on every possible occasion.'

OCTOBER 13, 1966

'Speculative'

Mr. Ludovic Kennedy, author of a book about the Evans case, described Mr. Justice Brabin's findings as "speculative." He was surprised, he said, that the judge should have treated the murders of the wife and baby as separate transactions, whereas they had previously been treated as one transaction.

Mr. Kennedy said that he thought Mr. Justice Brabin had said three fairly significant things. "One is that no jury would have convicted Evans, in his opinion, if they had known what we know now. The second is that he is not satisfied of Evans's guilt beyond reasonable doubt. The third is that he thinks it improbable that Evans killed the baby. All these things taken together make it in my view possible for the Home Secretary to grant a free pardon. If people say that there is no precedent for this, I would say that this case is entirely without precedent."

Evans's remains were exhumed from Pentonville Prison and reinterred on consecrated ground, and the case was instrumental in the decision to abolish the death penalty.

ABOVE: Justice Brabin said that he wasn't satisfied of Evans's guilt beyond reasonable doubt while his mother said: 'I don't believe my son did either of these murders. Christie did them both'.

TOP: The grave of Mrs Beryl Evans and her baby Geraldine in Gunnersbury Cemetery. Their bodies were found in the wash house of 10 Rillington Place.

OPPOSITE TOP AND MIDDLE: Rillington Place, where the remains Christie's victims were discovered, had to be renamed Rushton Close to throw sightseers off the scent. After the road had been demolished a new housing complex was built around Bartle Road.

OPPOSITE BOTTOM: Christie and Ethel.

Evans 'hanged for the wrong murder'

Timothy Evans was probably hanged for the wrong murder. That is the main conclusion in Mr. Justice Brabin's 156-page report on his inquiry into the murders at 10, Rillington Place, Notting Hill, 16 years ago. Evans, a 25-year-old illiterate van driver, was hanged at Pentonville Prison, London, in 1950 for killing his 14-month-old daughter, Geraldine.

That killing, the judge says, was probably done by John Reginald Christie, Evans's landlord at Rillington Place, who three years later, was revealed as a mass-murderer. Evans was also accused of killing his wife, Beryl, but never stood trial for it. That killing, the judge concluded, probably was done by Evans. The inquiry was commissioned by the Government after intense pressure on the then Home Secretary, Sir Frank Soskice, to clear up the question of Evans's guilt or innocence.

For almost a year, Mr. Justice Brabin studied and heard more than a million words given in evidence. The time lag, blurred memories, the tangle of lies, confessions and denials from both Evans and Christie made it impossible for him to nail down the complete truth of whether there were one or two killers living in the same house. But the judge's personal view is that there were.

He says: "It is a coincidence which it is claimed cannot be accepted in fact," but adds: "In human affairs few things are surprising." He sees events at Rillington Place like this:

Evans killed his wife after a violent row. He may have confided in Christie, who promised to dispose of the body, then fled to Wales. Christie, with two undetected war-time murders already committed, then killed Geraldine. Evans, in giving himself up, confessed to the murder of his wife. But, for some unknown reason, Christie managed to persuade Evans not to implicate him in the killing of Geraldine.

Mr. Justice Brabin's report completely overturns the ruling of the Scott Henderson inquiry, which was set up after the murders of Christie came to light. This inquiry reported that there had been no miscarriage of justice in the Evans case. But the true story will never be known, as the judge makes clear in an explanation of the difficulties he faced in making the investigation.

Findings

He says: "One fact which is not in dispute, and which has hampered all efforts to find the truth, is that both Evans and Christie were liars. They lied about each other. They lied about themselves."

The report points to differences in the killing of Mrs. Evans and Christie's victims. Evans had a violent temper and had struck his wife on various occasions. A pathologist's findings showed injuries to her head caused by hand or fist blows about 20 minutes before her death. But none of Christie's victims showed any sign of violence other than strangulation.

The report says: "If Christie was to strangle for the sake of strangling, it would be likely that he would do so immediately after striking her and not wait for 20 minutes or five minutes when screams might be heard."

In 1953 Christie had sexual intercourse with three women - later found in the house - and gassed them. But there was no evidence of this murder pattern in the murder of Beryl Evans. It goes on: "The evidence further satisfies me that the only person who mentioned that Beryl Evans had been strangled with a rope was Evans himself. "He could only have known this because he used a rope or because he saw a rope used or saw one on his wife's neck or because Christie told him that a rope had been used. "speculative ."

Mr. Justice Brabin found Geraldine's death "more perplexing." He says: "I do not believe that he who killed Beryl Evans must necessarily have killed Geraldine. They were separate killings done.

I think, for different reasons. The wife was killed in anger. Her daughter died because her crying might have got on the nerves of her father." Geraldine is believed to have been murdered 48 hours after her mother.

"It is not possible to know how Christie became aware of the killing of Beryl Evans. Whether he discovered it after hearing yet another row, or whether Evans sought his help after he had killed his wife, cannot be known."

Clever

"In any event with Beryl Evans dead, Christie, who was staying at home, would have become aware that Geraldine was alone in the flat and thereby would learn that her mother was at least missing and might well have discovered her death. Christie knew everything that went on in that small house. He was known to creep about the stairs and landings."

Mr. Justice Brabin says he is sure that Christie would never have allowed two bodies to remain in his home "unless he was himself involved in the killing of one or both persons." He describes the killing of Geraldine as "in cold blood" and says Christie would be more likely to do it. "Christie denied that he killed Geraldine until the end of his own trial because he was clever enough to know that to admit killing her would have inflamed any jury against him - first because Evans had been hanged for her death and secondly because it was the deliberate killing of a baby in cold blood."

His mother says: I'll fight on

Mrs. Thomasina Probert, Evans's 65-year-old mother, said last night: "I don't believe my son did either of these murders. Christie did them both. I want to continue the fight until I clear my son's name."

'No jury would have convicted Evans if they had known what we know now'.

Marcel Petiot: The Butcher of Paris

Dr Marcel Petiot, also known as the 'Butcher of Paris' and the 'French Bluebeard', was born in Auxerre on January 17, 1897. Details of his early years are uncertain, but he was certainly expelled from school several times and diagnosed as mentally ill in 1914.

A qualified doctor

He was drafted during the First World War, but after having been wounded and gassed he began to show signs of more serious mental disorder and was eventually discharged on disability grounds. After the war he entered a special training programme for war veterans and qualified as a doctor. However, his early medical career was rather chequered – he was suspected of performing illegal abortions and not only supplying narcotics but also taking them himself. Despite this he ran for mayor of Villeneuve-sur-Yonne in 1928 and was elected, but soon became involved in shady financial deals and was suspected of embezzling from town funds. He resigned as mayor in 1931 and moved to Paris soon afterwards, where he set up his own successful medical practice at 66 Rue Caumartin.

ABOVE: Marcel petiot, a wild-eyed French doctor accused of scientifically killing 63 of his countrymen.

RIGHT: Petiot sneered, gibed and laughed as he answered the questions of the prosecutor and the judge. Piled up behind the dock are suitcases containing the clothes and other effects of those whom he is accused of murdering.

False medical certificates

After Paris fell into German hands during the Second World War, Petiot developed a lucrative sideline supplying false medical certificates – but also set up an 'escape route' for those wishing to leave France, which was supposed to guarantee safe passage via Portugal to South America. Those who took advantage of the offer were never seen again, and in March 1944 neighbours in his apartment building at 21 Rue le Sueur began to complain that the building's furnace was producing copious amounts of greasy black smoke. The police found that the chimney was on fire and called the fire brigade, who soon discovered the source of the problem: bodies were being burnt in the furnace. Petiot was questioned, but claimed that the bodies were those of Nazis who had been executed by the French resistance, so he was set free and quickly disappeared for several months. However, in October 1944 the newspaper Resistance published an article that denounced Petiot as a Nazi collaborator, and he couldn't resist responding. Police traced his letter and quickly arrested him for the murders.

MARCH 3, 1932

The trial: Petiot storms: 'I killed, but you will acquit me.'

Standing accused before the Paris Assize Court, of murdering 27 people, the hypnotic-eyed Dr. Marcel Petiot completely lost his temper on the first day of his trial today and bellowed at the judge. 'Yes, it is true, it is true – I killed them!' he cried. 'But I killed them to help the Resistance Movement. You will acquit me for these killings, and when I have been acquitted for them I will give you the names of other victims for whose deaths you will also acquit me...'

Piled up in the courtroom, forming a background in this fantastic trial, were great cabin trunks, hat boxes, little brown-paper parcels with clothes bulging from them, wooden crates, wicker baskets. These were the property of the 27 dead identified by the police. In a long glass case were scores of macabre gadgets which, it is alleged, Petiot used to wipe out his victims or dispose of their remains – pulley wheels, petrol tins, medical instruments, bits of rope and wire. Petiot had shaved off his black beard and came into court smartly dressed in a mauve pin-stripe suit with bow tie and a tweed overcoat.

'Yes, it is true, it is true – I killed them!' he cried. 'But I killed them to help the Resistance Movement. You will acquit me for these killings.'

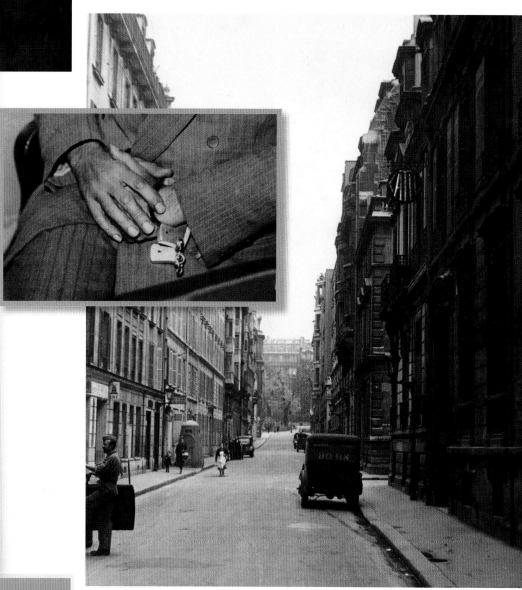

TOP LEFT AND MIDDLE: Handcuffed, Dr Marcel Petiot is led away after preliminary questioning in a Paris court.

ABOVE: A view of the Petiot house. The van in the picture is parked outside the entrance.

MARCH 19, 1946

Traitors!

At one point Petiot had an argument with the Public Prosecutor over the number of his victims, insisting that there were 63. During three hours of questioning by the judge he declared: 'I was concerned in the Resistance from the very time that the Germans arrived in Paris.'

The Judge (President Leser): 'Do you consider there was a Resistance organization in Paris in the first days of the German occupation?'

Petiot: 'I think there were certainly some men of the Resistance in Paris even in those early days.'

The Judge: 'There were none.'

This declaration by the judge was greeted with shouts of protest from many parts of the court. 'Well, if you were a member of the Resistance, and if you were a hero of the Maquis, give us the names of the men you fought with,' the judge said sarcastically. The Public Prosecutor joined with the judge in shouting, for minutes on end: 'Give us names! Give us names!'

Petiot for a time ignored their questions. Then, crouching in the dock, looking, with his blazing eyes and strange twisted face, like an animal, he shouted: 'No, no! I will not give you the names! I will not betray the men with whom I fought! The purge in France has not yet ended. There are too many followers of Petain, too many traitors still at liberty in my country.'

Secret group

The accusation against Petiot, which took more than an hour to read, alleged that he used the Maquis as a cloak for a gigantic murder racket, by means of which he made a fortune of many millions of francs. He is accused of pretending to be able to help people escape from France during the German occupation. To each victim he said: 'Bring all your valuables.' When they arrived at his house, it is alleged, he told them they needed inoculations for the journey, but proceeded to administer cyanide instead and then stole his victims' belongings. The bodies were initially dumped in the Seine or buried in a pit of quicklime to dissolve them, but after realizing that the quicklime was not acting as quickly as expected he began burning bodies instead.

In his defence, Petiot went into considerable detail about his Resistance activities. He said he belonged to a Maquis group, the 'Fly Spray' group, formed to wipe out Gestapo agents, and that he was trained by 'a Resistance agent from Britain.'

The Judge: 'You say you invented a secret weapon with which you killed Germans at a distance of a hundred feet. Where is this famous weapon? Tell us about it.'

Petiot: 'I will only disclose the details of this weapon when I am satisfied that to disclose them publicly would be in the interests of France.' He said he offered a plan of the weapon to a Mr. Thompson and a Mr. Miller of the United States Embassy in Paris. When the judge ordered the session suspended until tomorrow Petiot leaned towards him and muttered defiantly: 'I'm not tired yet!'

> 'France will not behead a man who killed nine German agents. I put my trust in my country.'

LEFT: Dr Petiot looks at the trap door through which he was alleged to have dropped his victims.

ABOVE: Marcel Petiot at police headquarters after his arrest. He had an evening meal of one piece of bread with cheese and a pint of water in an old wine bottle.

OPPOSITE TOP RIGHT: Petiot returns to the house of death where he was alleged to have murdered 63 people. Great crowds shouted 'murderer' and shook their fists.

OPPOSITE TOP LEFT: Dr Marcel Petiot in the dock, 19 March 1946.

The verdict

The judge and jury were absent for two and a half hours, but they apparently reached a unanimous verdict on the 165 questions they had to answer. Before the jury retired, after a five-hour speech by Petiot's counsel, Petiot had turned to his guards with a look of triumph in his eyes. 'I shall not die on the guillotine,' he cried. 'France will not behead a man who killed nine German agents. I put my trust in my country. I shall not die... I shall not die.'

Late on April 5, 1946, Petiot was found guilty of 24 of the 27 murders with which he was accused, and condemned to death on the guillotine. The other three murders were found to be 'not proven'. He was also condemned for robbing 24 out of the 27 victims. The verdict came a few minutes before midnight amid scenes of confusion extraordinary even for a French court. At one point it was impossible for the judge to see the man he was sentencing to death, and he mumbled the decision so much that it was some time before Petiot realized his fate. Then, his eyes blazing with fury, he turned to the public gallery and shouted: 'I must be avenged.' He addressed the words to his brother and to a fair woman sitting next to him in the gallery.

Handcuffed and chained

Petiot signed an appeal against the death sentence within a few minutes of sentence being read, which his counsel, Maitre Floriot, said would be lodged within the next three days. After being sentenced Petiot was kept in the dock for ten minutes while counsel representing the families of his victims began arguments with the judge about how much money should be awarded to them as compensation for the thefts. He was then taken to the condemned cell at the Sante Prison, where he was kept handcuffed and with chains on his feet. Although Petiot was only convicted of 24 murders, it is believed that he may have killed between 63 and 150 people – and that the 86 dissected bodies pulled out of the Seine between 1941 and 1943 may also have been down to him. He was guillotined on May 26, 1946 in the Paris Sante Prison.

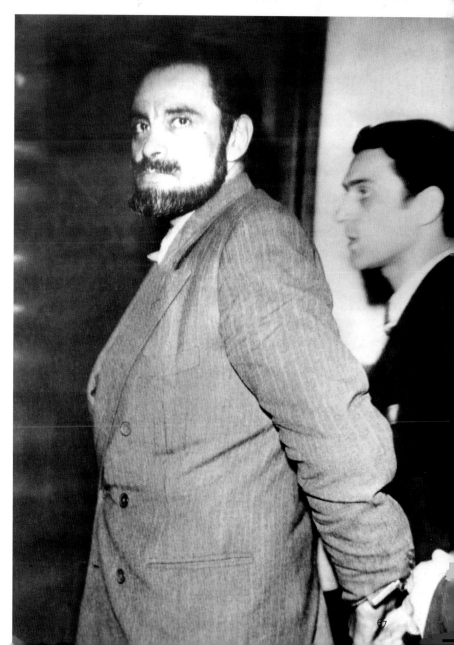

The Black Dahlia: Elizabeth Short

Jet black hair, striking features and a liking for dark attire, earned her the name 'The Black Dahlia'. Her murder remains one of the most infamous and unsolved crimes in American history.

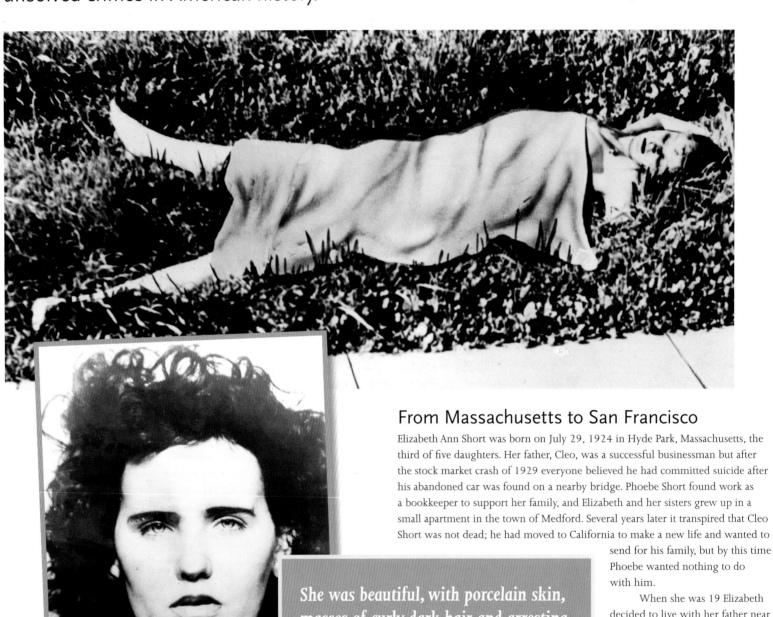

From Massachusetts to San Francisco

Elizabeth Ann Short was born on July 29, 1924 in Hyde Park, Massachusetts, the third of five daughters. Her father, Cleo, was a successful businessman but after the stock market crash of 1929 everyone believed he had committed suicide after his abandoned car was found on a nearby bridge. Phoebe Short found work as a bookkeeper to support her family, and Elizabeth and her sisters grew up in a small apartment in the town of Medford. Several years later it transpired that Cleo Short was not dead; he had moved to California to make a new life and wanted to send for his family, but by this time Phoebe wanted nothing to do with him.

She was beautiful, with porcelain skin, masses of curly dark hair and arresting light blue eyes.

When she was 19 Elizabeth decided to live with her father near San Francisco. She was beautiful, with porcelain skin, masses of curly dark hair and arresting light blue eyes and she hoped that in California she would be able to break into the movies. However, she and her father didn't get on and Elizabeth soon moved out and found a job in the mailroom at Camp Cooke (now Vandenberg Air Force Base), near Los Angeles. Here she was surrounded by hundreds of soldiers vying for her attention – but soon she was arrested for underage drinking and sent back to Medford.

Fiancé killed

Over the next years Elizabeth drifted around, earning money by waitressing, and dancing the night away, but on New Year's Eve 1944 she met Major Matt Gordon and the two of them became engaged. That summer Gordon was sent to the Philippines to fight and Elizabeth returned to Medford to prepare for the wedding, but in August 1945 Gordon was killed – tragically on his way home after hostilities had ceased. For the rest of her short life Elizabeth carried Gordon's obituary in her purse, but meanwhile she returned to her drifting life. She stayed with acquaintances when possible, or in the cheapest rooms – most of the money she earned was used to buy clothes. She knew the effect her beauty had on men; they whistled as she passed, they offered to buy her dinner – and frequently she accepted, although she always made it clear she wasn't interested in a physical relationship. Perhaps she still hoped that someone important would notice her and make her a movie star.

Mutilated

On January 15, 1947, a housewife walking down a street in Los Angeles saw what she thought was a broken display dummy on a vacant lot. As she drew nearer she realized it was the body of a woman who had been cut completely in half, lying on grass near the path. The arms were raised over the head, the lower half of the body was a foot away and the legs were spread wide open. The face and body were horribly slashed and rope marks on wrists and ankles indicated the woman had been restrained, and possibly tortured. From the lack of blood the police soon decided that the victim had been murdered elsewhere and other evidence suggested the body might have been kept on ice.

It wasn't long before the body was identified as that of Elizabeth Short. Ten days later her purse and one of her shoes were discovered several miles from where her body was found, adding weight to the theory that she had been murdered elsewhere. The contents of her purse – including Major Gordon's obituary – were mailed to the offices of the *Examiner*, perhaps by the murderer. The last time Elizabeth had been seen alive was a week before her body was found, leaving the luxurious Biltmore hotel alone, but there was no clue as to where she had been during the missing period.

The case caused a sensation in the Press; a beautiful young victim, horribly murdered, possibly with a sexual motive. They soon dubbed Elizabeth the Black Dahlia – perhaps after the film *The Blue Dahlia*, perhaps because in many photos she wears flowers in her hair and had a penchant for black clothes. The murder investigation involved hundreds of police officers interviewing thousands of people who knew or had met the victim. Despite many possible suspects – both at the time and those who have been put forward subsequently – no one has ever been brought to justice for the murder of the Black Dahlia.

> The contents of her purse – including Major Gordon's obituary – were mailed to the offices of the Examiner, perhaps by the murderer.

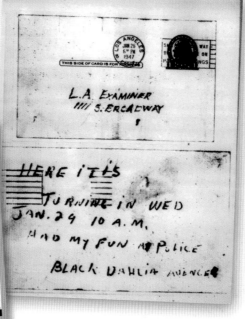

OPPOSITE ABOVE: The body of Elizabeth Ann Short was discovered by a housewife walking down the street who thought it was a broken display dummy. On closer inspection she realised it was the body of a woman that had been cut completely in half.

OPPOSITE BELOW: Elizabeth Short. After her fiancé Major Matt Gordon was killed, Short returned to her drifting lifestyle. She knew the effect her beauty had on men and frequently accepted when they offered to buy her dinner.

ABOVE: Short had dreams of becoming a movie star and was known by friends as 'Black Dahlia.' The nickname crossed over into the press following her grim murder.

LEFT: Letters sent to the L A Examiner. The case of the Black Dahlia has never been solved.

Geraghty and Jenkins:
Charlotte Street, London, 1947

'I did my best,' said the dying man, who had a history of stepping into the breach to help others, heedless of the risk to himself.

Too young to hang

Many will recall the infamous Bentley-Craig case of 1952, in which Christopher Craig's age saved him from the rope, leaving Derek Bentley to answer for the murder of PC Sidney Miles, killed during a rooftop showdown following a bungled robbery. It was not a unique case. Five years earlier, three young men were convicted of murder following a botched raid on a jeweller's shop. Two hanged for their part in the crime, while the third member of the gang, a 17-year-old youth, escaped with a custodial sentence.

Jeweller's shops targeted

On Friday 25 April 1947, three men robbed a jeweller's shop next to Queensway Tube station, Bayswater, and made off with goods worth £4,500. Guns were trained on staff during the raid, though it was clear that their sole purpose was to deter any heroic act, for manager Stanley Coleman reported that one of the masked raiders specifically instructed his accomplices not to shoot.

BELOW: A police car leaves Marlborough Street police station on 21 May 1947, as the crowds push forward to try to catch a glimpse of the men charged with the murder of Alec de Antiquis. The father of six was shot whilst trying to prevent the escape of three men who had attempted to rob a jeweller's.

ABOVE: A few days earlier one of the accused, his face covered by the jacket of one of the accompanying detectives, had attended a hearing at Tottenham Court Road police station.

Three perpetrators

The police inquiry was still ongoing when another London jeweller's, Jay's in Charlotte Street, W1, was hit four days later. Once again there were three perpetrators, masked and armed, but any similarity to the previous week's crime ended there. For the trio who burst into Jay's on the afternoon of 29 April 1947 it was all about to go horribly wrong. Firstly, managing director Alfred Stock had the presence of mind to slam shut the open door of the safe. A scuffle ensued between Stock and one of the raiders, who used the butt of his pistol to reinforce his demand that the safe be opened. The shop manager then weighed in, hurling a chair in the direction of the other attackers. It missed, but provoked a retaliatory burst of gunfire that left a bullet embedded in the woodwork. The commotion brought other backroom staff running and the alarm was sounded. The raiders panicked and fled empty handed, piling into a Vauxhall saloon parked outside. The alarm was raised on the streets, too, and the cry went up to stop the car and apprehend its occupants. A van driver responded to the rallying call by blocking the vehicle's path. The three men clearly thought their best chance of escape was on foot, for they abandoned the car and took flight.

> The raiders panicked and fled empty handed, piling into a Vauxhall saloon parked outside.

Father of six shot dead

The hue and cry attracted the attention of motorcyclist Alec de Antiquis, a 34-year-old garage owner and father of six, who rode his machine onto the pavement and blocked the thoroughfare. It was a brave gesture, but should have been no more than that, for it was no difficult task for the fugitives to sidestep the obstruction. Indeed, two of the men did just that, but the third chose to vent his fury at this latest effort to thwart his intentions. He raised his weapon and shot at Mr de Antiquis, who sustained a fatal head wound. 'I did my best,' said the dying man, who had a history of stepping into the breach to help others, heedless of the risk to himself.

There followed a further struggle with another have-a-go hero, this time without a firearm being discharged. The men then melted into the afternoon throng, with nothing to show for their efforts other than the fact that they had avoided capture.

> The hue and cry attracted the attention of motorcyclist Alec de Antiquis who rode his machine onto the pavement and blocked the thoroughfare.

TOP: Passers-by try to comfort 34-year-old mechanic Alec de Antiquis as he lies dying on the pavement. De Antiquis was on his way to collect some parts he needed for his small repair shop when he came face to face with three armed men running directly towards him. (Copyright G H Higgins).

ABOVE AND LEFT: The broken goggles, split glove and bloodstained army haversack of the brave have-a-go hero were picked up from the gutter in Charlotte Street and piled onto the saddle of his motorcycle before it was wheeled away by a local bobby.

No clues

Leading the police investigation was Chief Inspector Robert Fabian, who had spent a quarter of a century cleaning up the streets of the capital and would be immortalised in the 1950s TV series Fabian of Scotland Yard. Fabian's detection rate was legendary, and it looked as if the Charlotte Street robbery would tax his powers to the limit. The Vauxhall, stolen shortly before the robbery, provided no clues. A .32 calibre bullet had killed Alec de Antiquis, while the one recovered from the shop's woodwork came from a .455 calibre revolver. A third gun dropped at the scene had a set of fingerprints on it, but these failed to match any on police files. The amateurishness with which the job was carried out suggested it was the work of young tearaways, and there were plenty of those who had yet to acquire a rap sheet. There were a number of eyewitnesses, but with handkerchiefs covering the men's faces that proved to be a fruitless line of inquiry. There were even wild discrepancies over the visible features, such as height, build and the apparel they were wearing.

> There were a number of eyewitnesses, but with handkerchiefs covering the thieves' faces that proved to be a fruitless line of inquiry.

Breakthrough

A breakthrough came after three days, when taxi driver Albert Grubb reported a contretemps with a man who jumped onto the running board of his cab and tried to force his way into vehicle. Grubb got the better of the exchange and he watched as the man and a companion entered Brook House, an office building in Tottenham Court Road. When the pair emerged a few minutes later, one was minus the raincoat he'd been wearing. A sweep of the building turned up not only that garment - stuffed at the back of a janitor's cupboard – but also a knotted scarf that had been used as a facemask. A key that fitted the stolen car was also found.

The Montague Burton coat was common enough and held no clues other than the batch number. Records kept by the well-known firm of gents' outfitters showed that it would have been sold at one of their London shops. Fabian and his team were helped by the fact that clothing was still subject to rationing. As a hedge against the use of counterfeit coupons, retailers logged sales against the name on the ration card supplied by the purchaser. That gave police a long list to work through, and they set about the painstaking task of eliminating possible suspects one by one. Eventually, they lighted upon Thomas Kemp, who had bought a raincoat of the required type from the Deptford High Street store the previous December. Kemp had no convictions but he was related by marriage to some unsavoury characters well known to the police. These were his wife's brothers, Tommy and Harry Jenkins.

ABOVE: The published sketches played a significant role in apprehending the criminals – particularly the raincoat which proved pivotal in solving the crime. After a tip off from a local taxi driver, the police were eventually able to trace the raincoat to Thomas Kemp, the brother-in-law of 23-year-old Charles Henry 'Harry' Jenkins who was already known to the police.

Two of Jenkins' associates, Christopher James Geraghty (aged 20) and Terence John Peter Rolt (aged 17) were then also brought in for questioning and detained.

RIGHT: One of the suspects is pictured arriving at Tottenham Court Road police station on 17 May, following his arrest in Plumstead the previous day.

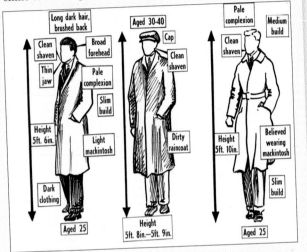

APRIL 30, 1947

The amateur killer

The minutes went by. Gunman No. 3, in the Vauxhall outside - right opposite a poster advertising "Odd Man Out" - became scared. He ran - and took the ignition keys of the car with him. Then out came Gunmen Nos. 1 and 2. They could not start the car, so they, too, ran. At that moment Mr. de Antiquis came along Charlotte Street on his big, red Indian motor cycle. He was wearing a leather jerkin and a crash helmet. He tried with his powerful machine to intercept the running pair.

[Diagram of three figures with labels:]
- Long dark hair, brushed back
- Clean shaven
- Broad forehead
- Thin jaw
- Pale complexion
- Height 5ft. 6in.
- Light mackintosh
- Dark clothing
- Aged 25
- Aged 30-40
- Cap
- Clean shaven
- Slim build
- Dirty raincoat
- Height 5ft. 8in.–5ft. 9in.
- Pale complexion
- Medium build
- Clean shaven
- Height 5ft. 10in.
- Believed wearing mackintosh
- Slim build
- Aged 25

The watchers

One of the men stopped, aimed and fired a shot which hit Mr. de Antiquis in his left temple. He fell dying on the corner. It was here last night, in the dusty road, that a woman dressed in black placed a rough cross and an arum lily. Round this wreath gathered all the black men, the yellow men, and the seedy white men who make up the street boys in this crowded corner of London. Strange crowds - and strange names on the shops along the street. Barba-Yanny, the restaurant, for example; Mr. Tong, the barber; Chinese signs on a cafe; Jinghi, the fur dealer; Mystic, the woman who reads your hands.

Inside Jay's, the police were working late. Chief Inspector Rob-ert Fabian, ex-chief of the Flying Squad, was there in charge. With him were Divisional Detective-Inspector "Bob" Higgins, and fingerprint experts, Superintendent F. Cherrill, with his assistant, Chief Inspector S. Birch.

In their search for clues, walls were stripped, counters and fittings unscrewed, or sawn off. There will be no business at Jay's today.

It was motor bikes, and his unceasing hunt for spare parts for them, that led Alec de Antiquis to the back streets of Tottenham Court Road yesterday. To earn a living for himself, his wife, and their six children in his little repair shop in High Street, Colliers Wood, Alec had to find spares where he could.

Suspects hauled in

Tommy Jenkins was serving time for a smash-and-grab raid on a jeweller's in 1944, a robbery in which a naval officer who tried to intervene was run over and killed by the getaway car. The driver, Ronald Hedley, was given the death sentence, later commuted to life imprisonment. Jenkins was found guilty of manslaughter and given eight years. Police strongly suspected that his younger brother Harry was also involved in the heist but couldn't prove it. Harry had since had a spell at Borstal, released just a week prior to the Charlotte Street raid.

Fabian's first port of call was the home of Thomas and Vera Kemp. Thomas Kemp wasn't in so Fabian questioned his wife about the raincoat. She said it looked similar to one her husband had lost. Fabian left, but the house was kept under surveillance and Mrs Kemp was soon on the move. She led the police straight to the Jenkins' abode and Fabian knew he was onto something.

> **Thomas Kemp admitted that the raincoat had not been lost but lent to his brother-in-law Harry Jenkins.**

Under questioning Thomas Kemp admitted that the raincoat had not been lost but lent to his brother-in-law Harry Jenkins. That was enough to haul Jenkins in, and the police also rounded up some of his known confederates. They included 20-year-old Christopher Geraghty and 17-year-old Terence Rolt, both of whom claimed to have been at home ill on the day of the robbery. Jenkins also denied involvement, though he refused to disclose his alibi. Even at 23 he was well versed enough in police procedure to know that they had to prove he was involved; he didn't have to prove he wasn't. Jenkins remained ice cool when Fabian put him in an identity parade in front of 27 eyewitnesses, including four who had seen the unmasked visages of two of the gang when they ducked inside the office block. None pointed Jenkins out. It later came to light that he pulled a classic trick to throw the witnesses off the scent. Before the parade he had idly asked for a copy of the morning paper, which he stuffed into his pocket when he took his place in the line-up. It gave the impression that he had been out on the streets mid-morning, hauled in at the police's request to make up the numbers and therefore not the prime suspect.

TOP RIGHT: 23-year-old lighterman Harry Jenkins from Bermondsey is pictured travelling in a police car from Tottenham Court Road police station on his way to Marlborough Street Court.

LEFT: Jenkins was remanded in custody for a week with 20-year-old labourer Christopher Geraghty (pictured) and 17-year-old warehouseman Terence John Peter Rolt. The three Londoners were charged with 'being concerned with intent to commit an armed robbery and also being concerned in the murder of Alec de Antiquis'.

TOP LEFT AND ABOVE: As Harry Jenkins leaves Tottenham Court Road police station in an open-necked shirt, he is surrounded by some of the detectives who had been involved in the investigation. The leading detective was Chief Inspector Robert Fabian, who would later be immortalised in the TV series 'Fabian of Scotland Yard'.

Confessions

Jenkins was off the hook for the time being, and even tossed the police a lead. He said he had given the raincoat to another career criminal, Bill Walsh, whose name was in the frame for the Bayswater robbery on 25 April. The hunt for Walsh ended on Plumstead Common on 16 May. Visibly shaken at the prospect of being implicated in a murder inquiry, Walsh readily confessed to participating in the Queensway raid. His role had been lookout, he insisted; the actual robbery was carried out by Jenkins, Geraghty and a third man later identified as Michael Gillam. Walsh also admitted to 'casing' the Charlotte Street jeweller's on behalf of Jenkins, Geraghty and Rolt. There was obviously crossing and double-crossing going on between the band of thieves, but Walsh had a solid alibi for the Charlotte Street robbery and Fabian was inclined to believe his version of events.

Rolt was picked up again and this time the youngest member of the gang cracked under pressure. He admitted driving the stolen vehicle for the Charlotte Street raid and named Geraghty and Jenkins as his accomplices. Geraghty later admitted he fired the shot that killed Alec de Antiquis, disposing of his gun in the Thames. It was found by some children playing on the river bank, ballistics experts confirming it as the murder weapon. Harry Jenkins continued to maintain that he was elsewhere at the time the crime was committed.

JULY 29, 1947

Antiquis: 2 will hang

Ninety days after Alec de Antiquis was shot dead after a daylight "hold-up" in a crowded Soho street - a crime which shocked Britain - three men were found Guilty at the Old Bailey last night of his murder. Two were sentenced to death - Christopher James Geraghty, 20-year-old labourer, who fired the shot, and Charles Henry Jenkins, 23-year-old lighterman. The third, 17-year-old Terence John Peter Rolt, warehouseman, was saved by his youth; the death sentence cannot be passed on anyone under 18. Mr. Justice James Hallett ordered that Rolt should be detained during the King's pleasure, and gave the opinion that he should not be released for at least five years.

The jury of nine men and three women returned just before 6 p.m., after an absence of 50 minutes. There was deathly quiet as they returned their verdicts of Guilty against all three.

As the tension in the famous court eased slightly, the judge instructed a warder to send Rolt below.

'Their duty'

Geraghty and Jenkins stood impassive. Then Mr. Justice Hallett, wearing the black cap, passed sentence of death on them both. "The jury have in my judgment merely done their duty." he said, "a duty which they owe to the community whose representatives they were. For the crime of which you have been found Guilty there is only one sentence known to law."

Jenkins and Geraghty turned smartly about and, silent, hurried down the steps to the cells below. As Jenkins disappeared he gave a quick glance round and smiled at relatives.

In his summing-up, Mr. Justice Hallett said: "It is not every day, thank God, that innocent people are shot down in the streets of London in circumstances such as occurred here. It is not every day even that hold-ups by three men, armed with guns, occur in London, though naturally this case has attracted a great deal of public notice. I described this affair as an outrage. I do not know whether you were surprised when Mr. Russell Vick (K.C. who defended Jenkins) protested against that description but I shall continue to so describe it."

TOP LEFT: Harry Jenkins arrives back at court for the resumed hearing of the murder charges in May 1947. He had completed a spell in borstal just one week before the Charlotte Street robbery took place.

LEFT: Once again a large crowd gathers to see the notorious felons Jenkins, Geraghaty and Rolt, as they leave Marlborough Street Police Station.

Murder charge upheld

On 21 July 1947 the three men took their place in the dock at the Old Bailey, each pleading not guilty to the murder charge they faced. The fact that each of them was carrying a loaded weapon ensured that their fates were intertwined, and any hopes that the shooting might be downgraded to manslaughter owing to a lack of premeditation were soon dashed. Trial judge Mr Justice Hallett said that citizens doing their duty in trying to apprehend fleeing felons were accorded special protection in the eyes of the law, a tradition dating back almost three hundred years. If the felon meted out violence resulting in the death of the citizen, he was liable to a murder charge even if the outcome was unintended. That statement alone was enough to counter Geraghty's claim that he had meant only to scare Mr de Antiquis, and the defendants' prospects were dealt another blow when it was pointed out that firing at the head at close range could hardly be construed as a warning shot.

Neither Geraghty nor Rolt took the stand but Jenkins did testify. He finally provided the long-awaited alibi, which family members and acquaintances endorsed, but to the jury it had the hollow ring of fabrication. After a week-long trial, it took them less than an hour to find all three guilty. Jenkins and Geraghty were given the death sentence, and after all appeals failed the two were hanged at Pentonville Prison on 19 September 1947. Rolt, being aged under 18 at the time of the crime, was detained at His Majesty's pleasure with a recommendation that he serve a minimum term of five years. In fact, he served nine years, released in June 1956.

The case formed the basis of the plot for the 1949 film *The Blue Lamp*, with a youthful Dirk Bogarde playing the callow hoodlum who guns down a man standing in the way of his escape following a robbery. Some details were changed, notably that the murder victim was not a passing motorcyclist but a serving police officer, PC George Dixon. Actor Jack Warner famously came back from the dead to reprise the role in a long-running TV series *Dixon Of Dock Green*.

> **The case formed the basis of the plot for film**
> **The Blue Lamp, with a youthful Dirk Bogarde.**

TOP LEFT, BOTTOM LEFT AND ABOVE: There were many court appearances before the case finally reached the Old Bailey in July 1947, when the trio of perpetrators were charged with the murder of Alec de Antiquis. After a week-long trial the jury needed less than an hour to find all three men guilty. As Rolt was under 18 at the time of the crime, he was ordered to be detained at His Majesty's pleasure for a minimum of five years. Jenkins and Geraghty (seen getting into a police car) were both sentenced to death by hanging. Christopher James Geraghty and Charles Henry Jenkins were hanged in a double execution at London's Pentonville Prison on 19 September 1947. Terence Rolt was released from prison on licence in June 1956 after spending nine years in jail.

John George Haigh: The acid bath murders

Habeas Corpus has been enshrined in English law for centuries as a means of protecting the individual from unwarranted detention by the state. It is incumbent upon the state to 'produce the body' if it wishes to incarcerate a person, whereupon the accused can weigh and counter the evidence against him and due process can take place. Habeas corpus is not restricted to capital crimes, but in 1949 John George Haigh took this vital guarantor of individual freedom quite literally when he was tried for murder. He took great pains to eradicate all traces of his victim's body, then openly defied the police to secure a conviction, fully expecting the ancient writ to come to his rescue.

TOP LEFT: Haigh, handcuffed to a police officer, smiles broadly for the cameraman as he arrives at the Horsham Court for his second hearing.

ABOVE: Crowds gather to catch a glimpse of Haigh and the witnesses as they arrive. The noise from the crowd outside the court drowned out the voice of a witness and police were sent outside to block the road if necessary.

Expensive lifestyle

John Haigh was a conman, forger and fraudster who had killed at least five times before he was brought to book. When he was casting around for a new target early in 1949, he had every reason to believe the modus operandi that had served him so well would prove successful again. It involved murdering the chosen individual, destroying all traces of the body and using his considerable forgery skills to appropriate the deceased's worldly goods. It was a lucrative career, but Haigh had an expensive lifestyle to maintain. There was the cost of his permanent residence at a South Kensington hotel and the running of a sleek Alvis motor car, plus a weakness for gambling. By February 1949 he was running perilously short of funds. His bank account was £80 in the red and he was coming under pressure from the Onslow Court Hotel to settle arrears of £50. Salvation seemed to present itself in the shape of 69-year-old Olive Durand-Deacon, a fellow guest at the hotel and, more importantly, a wealthy widow. She would be his next victim.

RIGHT: Haigh's family home in Ledger Lane, Wakefield. His parents were members of the Plymouth Brethren and so Haigh was confined to living within a 10ft fence that his father put up around their garden to lock out the outside world.

> By February 1949 Haigh was running perilously short of funds. Salvation seemed to present itself in the shape of 69-year-old Olive Durand-Deacon, a wealthy widow. She would be his next victim.

Business proposition

The pair were observed deep in conversation on 14 February 1949.

Mrs Durand-Deacon had a proposition for the urbane John Haigh, who suavely promoted himself as a successful businessman. She had come up with the idea of manufacturing false fingernails and needed advice on how to go about bringing the idea to market. Who better to ask than a fellow guest who owned a light engineering firm in Crawley? This latter statement was stretching a point somewhat. The enterprise referred to was Hurstlea Products, and although Haigh knew the owner of the company and had at one time been invited to become a director, that offer had never come to fruition. The extent of Haigh's connection with Hurstlea Products was the use of a small workshop facility and storeroom in Leopold Road, though that didn't stop him from portraying himself in a grander light if it suited his needs.

Clock now ticking

The following day Haigh borrowed £50 from the managing director of Hurstlea Products, Edward Jones, promising to repay the principal five days later. That wouldn't be a problem, for Haigh said he was in talks with someone over the manufacture of plastic nails. Haigh used the funds to settle his hotel bill. The clock was now ticking towards 20 February, the date that the loan was due to be repaid.

TOP RIGHT, TOP RIGHT(INSET), ABOVE AND RIGHT: Haigh's expensive Alvis car helped to exaggerate his status but it also provided clues for the police. Following the disappearance of Olivia Durand-Deacon, Haigh is referred to in the media, as a 'friend of the missing widow'. Once police discovered his record of theft they searched his Crawley workshop and he became the prime suspect.

TOP LEFT: By February 1949 Haigh had little money left. His bank account was £80 in the red and he was coming under pressure from the Onslow Court Hotel to settle arrears of £50.

Police informed

Haigh arranged to take Olive Durand-Deacon to the Crawley workshop on 18 February, ostensibly to meet one of his business associates. At around 4 pm he was seen with a woman answering Mrs Durand-Deacon's description at a nearby hotel, the George, though he later claimed she failed to keep the appointment. The following morning, he played the part of the concerned friend, asking another of the Onslow Court Hotel's long-standing residents if she could shed light on Mrs Durand-Deacon's whereabouts. Constance Lane was far less enamoured with Haigh than her friend, and after finding that Olive's room had not been slept in, she felt uneasy. It went against the grain for the methodical, punctilious Mrs Durand-Deacon to go away without telling anyone at the hotel. When another twenty-four hours passed with no news, Mrs Lane resolved to inform the police. The unflappable Haigh even offered to drive her to the station, which was coolness personified considering he had already sold Mrs Durand-Deacon's watch and put her Persian lambskin coat in for cleaning.

TOP LEFT, AND LEFT: A wrecked Lagona car was found at the foot of Beachy Head, Sussex, having crashed over the cliffs in June 1948. No occupants were found, but an unidentified torso was discovered near the scene three months later. A mile from the crash is the Birlington Gap Hotel where Dr Archibald Henderson and his wife had booked rooms. The booking was later cancelled by letter, apparently by Dr Henderson.

TOP RIGHT: Miss Kirkwood (left) and Miss Robbie, manageress and book keeper at the Onslow Court Hotel, where Olive Durand-Deacon lived for two years before her murder.

ABOVE: Letters sent to Madge Mohan at the Onslow Court Hotel from Haigh.

Sinister motive suspected

A major Scotland Yard missing persons investigation was soon under way. Haigh was questioned, sticking to his story that Mrs Durand-Deacon hadn't kept their 18 February appointment. The police felt that something wasn't quite right, and when they discovered the true nature of Haigh's relationship with Hurstlea Products, it begged the question: was he a mere self-publicist who liked to exaggerate his status, or did he have a more sinister motive for wanting Olive Durand-Deacon to believe he was a successful businessman? After a third interview, Haigh complained of harassment, but the police had unearthed elements in his past that encouraged them to think it was a line of inquiry that was worth pursuing. Here was a man who had a long history as a confidence trickster, a man whose transgressions had earned him three spells behind bars.

Enfield .38 revolver found

On 26 February the police conducted a thorough search of the Leopold Street premises. Among the expected workshop paraphernalia were several items that gave cause for concern, including a gas mask, oildrums, heavy-duty gloves and an Enfield .38 revolver that had recently been fired. There was also a dry-cleaning ticket for Mrs Durand-Deacon's lambskin coat.

TOP RIGHT AND TOP MIDDLE: Barbara Stephens, one of Haigh's few friends.

ABOVE: Mr Stephens, father of Barbara Stephens and business partner of Haigh.

RIGHT: A police photographer emerges from the small two storey factory used by Hurst Lea Products Ltd in Crawley, where police found the remains of Olive Durand-Deacon after her body had been decomposed in acid. Haigh was a director of the factory.

79

'Destroyed her with acid'

Haigh was questioned once again by the chief investigating officer Inspector Shelley Symes, and now he was forced to play what he thought was his trump card. He told Symes: 'Mrs Durand-Deacon no longer exists. She has disappeared completely and no trace of her can ever be found again. I have destroyed her with acid. You will find the sludge that remains at Leopold Road.' There was no remorse, merely a cocksure confidence that an admission of guilt was worthless if the body could not be produced. Haigh went further, describing how he slit his victim's throat and drank her blood before consigning her body to the acid bath. It wasn't long before such gory details reached the public domain. When the Daily Mirror published material deemed to be prejudicial to the case, describing Haigh as a vampire and referring to other individuals who had died by his hand, it earned the paper a £10,000 fine and its editor Silvester Bolam a three-month stay in Brixton Prison. The court frowned upon the sensational nature of the revelations aimed at increasing circulation, with no thought to the judicial process. Notwithstanding the severe penalty imposed on the national daily, it was impossible to keep the lid on the case of the 'vampire killer'.

> 'She has disappeared completely and no trace of her can ever be found again. I have destroyed her with acid.'

LEFT: While detectives searched the Hurst Lea factory, they repeatedly brought Haigh in for questioning. Among the items they found in the workshop that were cause for concern were a gas mask, oil drums, heavy-duty gloves and an Enfield .38 revolver that had recently been fired.

TOP RIGHT: Haigh eventually boasted to the police that no trace of Mrs Durand-Deacon would be found since he had dissolved her in acid. However, pathologist Dr Keith Simpson recovered three human gallstones, more than ten kilograms of melted body fat and a number of bone fragments. It was enough to prove the sex of the victim. It was the survival of her acrylic dentures that allowed police to trace their origin back to Mrs Durand-Deacon.

ABOVE: Chief of West Sussex CID leaving the Crawley workshop.

Carboy of sulphuric acid

The full details of the events leading up to Mrs Durand-Deacon's death on 18 February began to emerge. Police found a shopping list in Haigh's hotel room, detailing his requirements for disposing of the body. On 16 February he collected a carboy of sulphuric acid from the chemical suppliers White and Sons, and the next day obtained a 45-gallon oil-drum, making sure its interior was acid-resistant. Haigh then paid another visit to Jones, not to redeem the debt or discuss plastic fingernails but to ask him to make adjustments to the stirrup pump he'd bought. The reason was simple: the leg of the pump prevented it from being inserted into the neck of the acid container.

> He drained the drum in the yard and refilled it with fresh acid to finish the job.

Body place in acid

Haigh admitted driving Mrs Durand-Deacon to Crawley on the afternoon of 18 February, first to the George Hotel and thence to the workshop. He then shot her in the head and set about covering up the crime. He removed her lambskin coat and jewellery, took a small amount of cash and a set of keys from her handbag, then let the acid get to work. The following day, as well as playing the role of worried neighbour and selling off the first tranche of the victim's jewellery, he went to check on progress at Leopold Road. There remained some pieces of fat and bone, and the acid had had little effect on the handbag. He drained the drum in the yard and refilled it with fresh acid to finish the job. By Tuesday 22 February he thought that all traces of organic matter had been obliterated and he was in the clear. Hence his swaggering, defiant demeanour when he made his statement to the police. Eminent pathologist Dr Keith Simpson was about to prick that ill-judged hubris.

ABOVE LEFT: The interior of the factory in Crawley where Mrs Durand-Deacon was killed. She had mentioned to Haigh an idea that she had for artificial fingernails. He invited her down to the Crawley workshop on February 18, 1949, and once inside he shot her in the back of the head, stripped her of her valuables, including a Persian lamb coat, and put her into the acid bath. She was reported missing two days later by her friend Constance Lane.

RIGHT: Scotland Yard forensic expert, H.B. Holden, searches the Crawley workshop on Leopold Road for remains of the widow.

TOP RIGHT: Dr George Furfitt of Police Laboratory and H. B. Holden, Scotland Yard forensic expert.

Body fat and bone fragments found

Simpson found bloodstains of Mrs Durand-Deacon's type, and from the sludge recovered three human gallstones. There was more than ten kilograms of melted body fat and a number of bone fragments; these proved the sex of the victim. The presence of arthritis in the joints suggested that she had been in late adulthood. But the most damning physical evidence was a set of acrylic dentures which had survived intact and could be traced back to the London dental surgeon who had fitted them for Mrs Durand-Deacon two years earlier.

> **Haigh had become fascinated with the idea of committing the perfect murder, and now he planned to turn theory into practice.**

Plea of insanity

The trial opened at Sussex Assizes in Lewes on 18 July 1949. Haigh entered a Not Guilty plea, which on the surface looked to be somewhat odd as chief prosecuting counsel Sir Hartley Shawcross introduced as evidence the uncontested statement detailing the murder of Olive Durand-Deacon and the attempted disposal of her body. Those facts were not in doubt; and they left the defence with just one available weapon: an insanity plea. To help his cause, defence counsel Sir David Maxwell Fyfe wanted the full details of Haigh's grisly past aired in court. Haigh was being tried only for the murder of Mrs Durand-Deacon, but he had admitted to several similar crimes. They could hardly make matters worse for the defence, and indeed could help support the contention that Haigh was insane at the time of their commission.

TOP LEFT: An early picture of Mrs McSwann with her son in 1917. They were both victims of Haigh.

FAR LEFT: The house in Grand Drive, Raynes Park, South West London, where Donald McSwann had once lived. He lived there alone for two years, his parents having moved to Pimlico.

LEFT: A fanfare outside the County Hall at Lewes as the trial of John George Haigh opens.

TOP RIGHT: Haigh is smiling as he is brought to the Horsham Police Court for the opening of the trial.

McSwann family: his first victims

Haigh's first victims had been three members of the same family, the McSwanns. He had at one time worked for William McSwann in the amusement arcade business. They lost touch when Haigh was forced to go on the run but met up again in wartime London. During one of his stints in prison Haigh had become fascinated with the idea of committing the perfect murder, and now he planned to turn theory into practice. William McSwann was lured to a basement flat in Gloucester Road, bludgeoned to death and placed in an acid bath. Haigh said he tapped the body for blood before destroying it, and after the acid had done its work he poured the remaining sludge down a manhole. He repeated the exercise with McSwann's parents, using his forgery skills to gain control of the family assets.

His next victims

When the proceeds of those crimes ran out, Haigh looked around for a new source of funds, lighting upon Dr Archibald Henderson and his glamorous wife Rosalie. Haigh met the Hendersons when he responded to an advertisement for the sale of their Ladbroke Square property. He wasn't interested in buying the house, but in cultivating the friendship of the owners. In February 1948 he took Mr Henderson to the Crawley workshop and dispatched him using his tried and trusted method. Rosalie Henderson was then summoned, told that her husband had been taken ill. She suffered the same fate and Haigh once again turned a tidy profit. He even managed to get his hands on the Hendersons' new house in Fulham by forging a deed of transfer.

Unsound mind?

Haigh said there were others, too, though he was hazier about the details of those crimes, apart from the fact that the victims were all impoverished. It was suggested that these belated additions to his statement were fabrications intended to balance the fact that his six known victims were all murdered for gain. It was in Haigh's – and Maxwell Fyfe's - interest to assert that some had died not for profit but as a result of the tortured childhood dreams of Christ's stigmata that Haigh claimed had haunted him. If the sole motive in those additional cases was the desire to slake his thirst for blood, then surely the perpetrator had to be of unsound mind?

In February 1948 Haigh took Mr Henderson to the Crawley workshop and dispatched him using his tried and trusted method.

RIGHT: The entrance to the basement of 79, Glouscester Road, Kensington, where police found the remains of Mr and Mrs McSwann and their son. Haigh had once worked for William McSwann in the amusement arcade business.

FAR RIGHT: Mrs McSwann: her husband and her son had been Haigh's first victims. After they were killed and their bodies dissolved in acid, Haigh used his forgery skills to obtain control of the family assets.

ABOVE: A workman emerges from 79 Gloucester Road with a pick and a shovel. Haigh had been obsessed with committing the perfect murder and with the McSwanns he managed to put this theory into practice.

Delusional and egocentric

Maxwell Fyfe called just one witness, the eminent Harley Street practitioner Dr Henry Yellowlees. The jury heard an account of Haigh's severe and austere upbringing. His parents had been religious zealots, members of the fundamentalist Christian sect the Plymouth Brethren. All forms of entertainment, even newspapers and radio, were regarded as sinful and banned from the house. John and Emily Haigh preached hellfire and damnation to their son, who was harshly dealt with for the slightest misdemeanour.

Dr Yellowlees said that Haigh was delusional and egocentric. The fact that he was forbidden from having childhood friends would have had a profound effect on his development. Yellowlees asserted: 'The disorder of mind which I submit has affected the reason of the accused is that rare but quite well known type of mental aberration which is called in psychological medicine pure paranoia'. One of the ways that the disorder manifested itself was the sufferer's belief that he was in a mystical union with a controlling external power. When Haigh had been in his mid-teens, that power had instructed him to drink his own urine, a practice he had continued ever since. All of this Dr Yellowlees had gleaned from three interviews totalling around two hours; and he was placing a medical interpretation on information exclusively supplied by Haigh himself: a practised liar whose life was in the balance.

TOP (INSET): In 1938 Dr Archibald Henderson, a Jermyn street Physician, and Mrs Rosalie Mercy Erren were married. A decade later they fell victim to Haigh's acid bath.

TOP: Dr Henderson (left) with his wife at a dinner party at a casino in Blackpool with Mr and Mrs Burlin. When the proceeds of the McSwann murders ran out, Haigh looked for an new source of funds and so his attention turned to the Hendersons.

ABOVE: The Dolls Hospital on Dawes Road in Fulham, owned by Henderson.

LEFT: Mr J. Davies supplied Haigh's acid and invented the rocking horse that Haigh used to lure Henderson to his death.

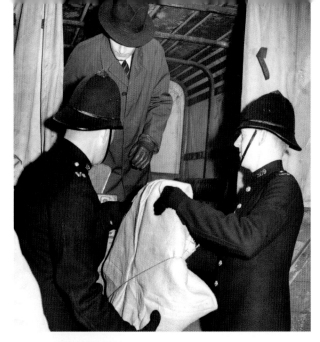

'Dreams led him to kill nine'

Sir David Maxwell Fyfe, great lawyer and interpreter of the human mind, this afternoon sought to initiate a Sussex jury of 11 normal men and one normal woman into the strange and horrifying world of fantasy in which, he contends, his client, John George Haigh, has confessed to destroying nine human lives. He told them of dreams which have haunted Haigh since childhood, dreams in which crucifixes turn into trees and drip first rain and then blood; dreams in which the Cross figures, dreams which culminate in an overmastering desire to have blood.

ABOVE: Exhibits used in the case against Haigh. Among these was the metal drum he filled with acid in order to eliminate any trace of his victims' bodies.

RIGHT: The child's motor-car invented by Haigh. This electrically driven car could do 12 miles an hour for 50 miles without the battery being re-charged and was valued at £15. This picture was taken at the Dolls Hospital, Dawes Road, Fulham, where police searched the coal cellar.

TOP RIGHT: Sergeant Patrick Heslin, Divisional Inspector Shelley Symes and Inspector Mahon, Chief Inspector of the Missing Persons Bureau, arriving at the court for Haigh's trial.

ABOVE RIGHT: Doctor Henderson's former maid, Mrs Daisy Rowntree, is interviewed by Detective Sergeant Aspinall at the Dolls Hospital in Dawes Road.

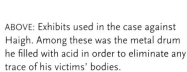

JULY 19, 1949

'Three others'

Another statement read by Inspector Webb spoke of three others Haigh claims to have murdered. Haigh's descriptions of them were in themselves almost in the form of police "Missing Persons" circulars.

The first, he said, was: Woman, aged 35, 5ft. 9in., well built, dark hair, no hat, dark cloth coat; carrying an envelope-type of blackish handbag. In his alleged statement he said he had met her between Hammersmith Bridge and the Broadway about two months after he killed young McSwann - that is, about April 1944. He took her to the Gloucester Road flat, hit her with a cosh, and "tapped her for blood." He dissolved her body in acid. There was "next to nothing in her handbag."

He said further that in the following autumn he had murdered a man he met in the Goat public house, High Street, Kensington. The description: About 35, "same height and build as myself." (which could be interpreted as well built but shortish), brownish wavy hair; wearing dark double-breasted suit, believed blue.

'Same thing'

Haigh bought him a drink and took him to the Gloucester Road flat, where "the same thing happened... He had no jewellery and no more than a pound in money." No mention of blood in this case.

In autumn last year it had been a woman at Eastbourne. The description: Christian name Mary, surname unknown; probably Welsh. Wearing white and green summer dress, white beach shoes, carrying light-coloured handbag. They had a meal together in the old part of Hastings. He drove her to Crawley, hit her with a cosh, "tapped her for blood, put her in the tub, and left her there until the next morning." She had little property except a bottle of scent in her handbag.

Superintendent Guy Mahon said that there was no evidence in confirmation of Haigh's statement relating to the three unknown people.

At 3.40 p.m. the Attorney-General completed the case against Haigh, and Sir David Maxwell Fyfe rose to tell the jury he would ask from them the special verdict of "Guilty of the acts charged, but insane at the time they were committed." Haigh, he said, was a victim of what was known to psychological medicine as 'pure paranoia' Sir David explained: "The badge of this disorder is that the victim knows his secret life of fantasy must be lived alongside the ordinary life of the world. He is, therefore, lucid, astute, shrewd when not actually acting under the influence of his fantasy. He takes steps to avoid trouble to do the best he can for himself."

LEFT, ABOVE AND TOP: A metal drum, covered in sacking, is brought to the court in Horsham for Haigh's hearing. Haigh devloped the idea of using acid when conducting experiments with mice during a stint in prison.

Profit as the primary motive

Shawcross anticipated the insanity plea and was ready to counter. He focused on the sale of the ill-gotten goods, wanting to stress that these were cynical crimes with profit as the primary motive. Also, the fact that Haigh had already enquired about the chances of getting out of Broadmoor suggested a degree of reasoning. The elaborate planning aimed at avoiding detection, and, thus, punishment, also indicated that Haigh knew all too well what he was about. Shawcross invited Dr Yellowlees to agree that Haigh's word could not be trusted, then pointed out that the witness's assessment of the accused's state of mind had been based entirely upon utterances from that same unreliable source. The doctor was further invited to admit the possibility that a man so well practised in the arts of deceit might have fooled him. Yellowlees was forced to answer in the affirmative. Shawcross also pointed out that as the Hendersons had been murdered hours apart on the same day, wasn't it likely that the second crime was committed, not in response to some dream or inner voice but to silence Mrs Henderson? Dr Yellowlees had to concede that possibility, too. It was game, set and match to the Attorney-General.

JULY 20, 1948

'Divine course'

Haigh's "dream-ridden existence" was traceable to his mother and the strength of her belief in the effect of dreams on the future. Brought up in severe surroundings of strict Plymouth Brethren parents, he left that influence and the formative years of his adolescence were associated with Wakefield Cathedral, then very High Church. What he saw, thought, and experience there had penetrated "the cloudy recesses of his abnormal mind and personality" Thus, said Sir David, "when he came to do these dreadful deeds he thought himself to be following a divinely appointed course that had been set for him."

Sir David Maxwell Fyfe rose to tell the jury he would ask from them the special verdict of 'Guilty of the acts charged, but insane at the time they were committed.'

TOP: Sightseers crowd every vantage point in the narrow street to watch the arrival of the personalities attending Haigh's trial.

LEFT: Following a stint in prison Haigh moved into Barbra Stephen's house, which she shared with her father. Despite being 20 years his junior, Stephens was intent on becoming the next Mrs Haigh.

BELOW: Five women witnesses in the Haigh trial at Lewes Assizes drink coffee after lunch. Left to right: Mrs Hilda Kirkwood, Miss Alicia Robbie, Mrs Constance Lane, Miss Esme Fargus and Mrs Birin.

JULY 20, 1949

'To the last he smiled'

Stepping from the dock with a faint but unshaken smile, John George Haigh this afternoon joined the ranks of the most extraordinary criminals of history. All through the hot afternoon his sleek round head had rested easily against the panelled door behind him. Occasionally the door threatened to swing open and he turned round to refasten it. Otherwise he seldom changed his position. He, at least, seemed perfectly composed, and quite content to leave anxiety to the array of learned counsel.

Meanwhile the pace of the trial was rapidly accelerating. Earlier in the day the defence had produced its single witness, and the expert testimony of Dr. Yellowlees had very soon run into somewhat heavy crossfire. For the scientific mind, with its habit of qualification, and the legal mind, with its liking for precise unqualified statements, have few common terms of reference.

Fantasy

No further witnesses were called, and from that moment the drama of the trial became the drama of three different personalities.

The solid dignity and robust realism of Sir David Maxwell Fyfe's appearances were in curious contrast as he spoke of the fantastic and mysterious character of the subject that concerned him - dreams and manias and sadistic delusions, crimes that were perhaps real, perhaps more than half imaginary. At times he reminded me of a fully armed gladiator, courageously attempting to hack his way through a world of ghosts and cobwebs.

Sir Hartley Shawcross had the easier task. Sir David now and then rose to vehemence. The Attorney-General kept his speech quiet and clear and low-tone, allowing himself now and then some telling strokes of sarcasm. But for the most part the voice he employed was that of unemphatic commonsense.

Finally came the Judge's summing up. Mr. Justice Humphreys has a delivery that many younger men might envy. He speaks quietly, almost casually, but every word is distinct, every period well-shaped. His analysis of the mass of evidence was as fascinating to observe as a piece of skilled dissection. He seemed to remove irrelevances with a flick of the fingers.

Gravely paternal towards members of the jury - 11 men and one motherly woman who bore the name Mary English and an exceedingly English-looking brown and yellow straw hat - he was merciless in his elimination of any hint of muddled thinking.

ABOVE: Mrs Constance Lane (right) and Mis Elizabeth Robbie. Lane reported Mrs Durand-Deacon missing. When her friend was not at her usual seat for dinner or breakfast the following morning, Lane new something was amiss and reported it to the police.

LEFT AND FAR LEFT: Helen Mayo, a dental surgeon and a witness in the trial of John Haigh. She stated that she had made a set of dentures for the woman whom Haigh is alleged to have murdered. She was a crucial witness since the dentures were all that could be used to identify the remains of Olivia Durand-Deacon's body.

Fifteen minutes to reach verdict of Guilty

Presiding judge Sir Travers Humphreys passed comment on the defence's decision to call a single expert witness, when others who could have commented on Haigh's alleged mental infirmity might have been produced. The judge also made disparaging reference to Dr Yellowlees's response when asked whether the accused knew what he was doing when he murdered Olive Durand-Deacon. A psychiatrist would have to live with that person for years to form an accurate opinion, came the doctor's reply. If the jury knew what to make of that, said Humphreys, then they had greater understanding than him. The jury took just fifteen minutes to decide that there was no divine guidance at work, and no grounds for returning a verdict of Guilty but insane.

John George Haigh was hanged on 10 August 1949. Realizing that he would soon be joining the ghoulish line-up of convicted murderers at Madame Tussaud's, he even donated a suit of clothes to ensure that the waxwork effigy would look as dapper as the original.

JULY 20, 1949

Little emotion

The jury retired, but returned to the court in 15 minutes. Their verdict was a unanimous "Guilty," but Haigh, standing in the front of the dock, a neat upright figure - hair smooth, suit unwrinkled, his hands behind his back - received it with as little emotion as though he were being fined for an incorrectly parked car. Asked by the clerk of the court if he had anything to say, he replied: "None at all" - meaning obviously "Nothing at all," the only suggestion he gave of any hidden feeling - in his rather high and cynical Kensingtonian accent.

Sentence of death was pronounced - the dreadful formula made more dreadful by the ceremony of the black cap. Haigh immediately turned to go, and as he descended the stairs one could see that he was smiling.

Grotesque and hideous series of crimes

He has left behind him a considerable question mark. In the whole history of English criminal trials I doubt if any murderer has been condemned of whom the future criminologist may decide he knows so little.

Those who had been watching him for the past two days came out into the freedom of Lewes High Street exhausted and bewildered. It was still impossible to connect that neat, commonplace figure in the dock with the grotesque and hideous series of crimes of which he had accused himself.

Impossible to find any clue to the mind that lay beneath them, or to the expression of unruffled composure with which he had heard his death sentence.

By comparison, Crippen was a sentimentalist, and Landru a boastful playboy.

> Sentence of death was pronounced - the dreadful formula made more dreadful by the ceremony of the black cap. Haigh immediately turned to go, and as he descended the stairs one could see that he was smiling.

TOP RIGHT: John George Haigh (seated at rear of car, centre) is driven away by police. Barbara Stephens (standing left with arms folded) looks on.

RIGHT AND ABOVE RIGHT: Spectators await the verdict in the Haigh trial. Some had waited all night in anticipation.

OPPOSITE TOP: Haigh is watched by crowds as he is escorted by police. He received the verdict with little emotion. When he was taken out of the court room and down the stairs he was seen to be smiling.

Lloyds Bank raid:
The unsolved murder of George Black

George Black, 50-year-old bank manager, often said to his wife: 'If anyone ever tries to rob my bank I'll fight them.' Yesterday afternoon he was shot dead as he grappled with a spectacled gunman who stole £1,000.

'This is a stick up!'

Up to no good

At around 2.00pm on January 7, 1949, a young man walked into a small branch of Lloyds Bank on the corner of Broad Walk and Wells Road in Bristol. He told staff he was meeting a man called Murray at the bank and sat down to wait at one of the tables. He was there most of the afternoon and was noticed by one of the other customers, John Rowe, a trainer at the nearby Greyhound stadium who had come into the bank to deposit some takings. Rowe decided the man was up to no good – although he seemed quite respectably dressed – and after he left the bank he went to a nearby phone box and called 999, leaving a message about a man loitering suspiciously in the bank. Meanwhile the bank staff began preparing to close up, but the man suddenly jumped up, slammed the front door shut and announced, 'This is a stick up!'

ABOVE AND OPPOSITE ABOVE RIGHT: Lloyds Bank on the corner of Broad Walk and Wells Road in Bristol, where bank manager George Black was shot twice.

ABOVE LEFT: A police photographer enters the bank.

OPPOSITE TOP LEFT: The gunman's stolen 16 h.p. Austin, which was abandoned at Temple Mead's Station.

OPPOSITE BELOW: The superintendent arrives at the bank. Police had little success in finding out who had robbed the bank and the trail soon ran cold. The crime that claimed Black's life was never solved.

Getaway car

The bank manager – George Black, a 50-year-old man who lived with his family in nearby Clifton – tried to restrain the robber but without hesitation the man shot him twice. The shocked cashier, 17-year-old Donald Twitt, was forced into a cloakroom and locked in while the thief opened the till and shoved £1,430 in £5, £1 and 10-shilling notes (approximately £30,000 today) into his briefcase. He then left the bank, jumping into a car parked outside. Rowe saw him leave and jumped onto the running board of the car to stop him getting away, but was punched and fell off into the road. Despite his injuries he ran back into the telephone box to call the police again, telling them: 'A rough-looking man has just rushed out of the bank and driven towards the city in an Austin 16 car, registration number JHY 812.'

> *George Black, a 50-year-old man who lived with his family in nearby Clifton – tried to restrain the robber but without hesitation the man shot him twice.*

Detailed description

Auker Hewlett, a nearby chemist, tried to resuscitate the manager but he was already dead. Several people had seen the killer quite clearly during his long wait at the bank and the police were able to issue a very detailed description: he was aged about 26, five feet six or seven inches tall, with a pale round face, and was wearing a dark overcoat and trilby and carrying a black leather briefcase. He also wore glasses, although these may have been intended as a disguise. He not only left fingerprints in the bank but also a scribbled note, which said: 'See you Monday. Missed you today. Joe' – but this may also have been an attempt to throw police off the trail. The car was soon found abandoned in Totterdown area of Bristol, but proved to have been stolen earlier that day.

Cold trail

A murder hunt was launched in Bristol, but soon police in Birmingham were also involved since the killer's description matched that of a man wanted there. Then a grocer in Bodmin reported that a man answering the killer's description had tried to cash a bogus cheque, so the search was widened even more. Thousands of leaflets were distributed across the country with the suspect's description, stressing that he was probably not an experienced criminal because he had drawn so much attention to himself in the bank.

Although many leads were followed, and Lloyds Bank offered a reward of £1000 (approximately £18,000 in today's money), the trail soon ran cold. Even today the crime remains unsolved.

Donald Hume:
Double jeopardy - The murder of Stanley Setty

Hume had hired a plane and had been seen to load a large parcel before taking off.

In October 1949, a farm worker walking across the Essex marches in eastern Britain saw a large parcel half-submerged in the water. He fished it out and was horrified to find that it contained the torso of a man, missing the head and legs, who had been brutally stabbed.

It was not long before the body was identified as that of Stanley Setty, a 46-year-old car dealer who traded in Warren Street in central London. Setty had recently been reported missing and although his car had later been found empty and abandoned, no trace had been discovered of the one thousand pounds in cash that he had been carrying.

The gruesome nature of the crime soon caught the attention of the nation, and the Press followed developments in the case closely. Not long after the body was found, the United Services Flying Club at Elstree, on the outskirts of London, contacted the police. They reported that one of their members, Donald Hume, had hired a plane and had been seen to load a large parcel before taking off. However, when he arrived at his destination – Southend, which would have taken him over the Essex marshes – the parcel was no longer in the plane, and the mechanic checking everything over had noticed some damage to one of the windows. The police made further enquiries and soon also established that Hume had taken a taxi from Southend and had paid for it with cash taken from a large roll of bank notes, so they brought him in for questioning.

OPPOSITE: Police officers examine marshland near the Essex village of Tillingham. A farm worker had found a large parcel in the marshes which contained the torso of Stanley Setty.

OPPOSITE (INSET): Hume was an illegitimate child whose mother refused to acknowledge him. He drifted into a life of petty crime.

BELOW: Police inspect Stanley Setty's car for fingerprints outside Setty's garage in Cambridge Mews, Regents Park, London.

LEFT: Donald Hume's second floor flat in Finchley Road.

BOTTOM: Detectives pictured taking up the floorboards in Hume's flat on Finchley Road. They found blood under the floorboards of the hall and living room.

Forensic evidence

Brian Donald Hume had been born illegitimate in 1920 and his mother had always refused to acknowledge him as her son, instead pretending that she was his aunt. Hume always felt resentful and hard done by and grew up feeling unwanted and unloved. He drifted into the life of petty crime and lies, often telling associates that he was an RAF officer who had been discharged when he contracted meningitis. By 1949 he was married to Cynthia Mary, lived in a flat in Finchley Road, Golders Green and was describing himself as a company director. He told the police that the parcel had contained forged petrol coupons, which he had been asked to dump out at sea by a smuggler and that the cash had merely been payment for the job. However, when they searched Hume's flat forensic scientists found traces of blood under the floorboards in both the hallway and the living room. At this point Hume changed his story slightly, saying he had returned home to find blood everywhere and that he had cleaned it up, assuming that the smuggler had killed Setty. The police did not believe Hume's account of events and on October 28, 1949, he was formally charged with murder. His trial began on November 26, but the jury could not agree on a verdict so a new trial date was set for January 18, 1950, at Bow Street Magistrates' Court. This time Hume pleaded guilty to the lesser charge of being an accessory after the fact for dumping Setty's body and was sentenced to just eight years in prison, which he spent in Dartmoor.

> Hume changed his story saying he had returned home to find blood everywhere.

Jealous frenzy

However, this was by no means the end of the story. Four months after his release in February 1958, Hume sold his story to London's *Sunday Pictorial* newspaper for an estimated £3,600 – and sensationally revealed to the paper's five-and-a-half million readers that he had committed the murder. According to the published account he had suspected Setty of making moves on his wife, Cynthia, so in a jealous frenzy he had grabbed a knife and stabbed him to death. Despite this revelation Hume could not be re-arrested – under the rules of double jeopardy no one could be charged twice for the same murder, and if he had been charged with perjury he could just say he had lied to the newspaper for money and restate his original trial testimony.

Escape to Switzerland

Despite the scandal being well aired in the Press, nothing could be done – but the influx of funds did not last Hume long. By the end of 1958 he had turned to armed robbery to raise more money, hitting a branch of the Midland Bank in Brentford twice. When the authorities came close to apprehending him he fled to Zurich in Switzerland, where he met an attractive brunette called Trudi Sommer who owned her own beauty parlour. Hume told her he was Canadian test pilot Johnny Bird and soon she invited him to move into her apartment. By January 1959 Hume was running short of cash again, so fortified by communion wine stolen from a local church he walked into a branch of Zurich's Gewerbebank brandishing a pistol and demanding money. The bank teller refused to hand it over, so Hume shot and wounded him, then scooped up a mere $45. As the alarm went off he ran into the street, killing a taxi driver who tried to stop him, but was soon brought down by a young pastry cook.

> **Under the rules of double jeopardy Hume couldn't be charged twice for the same murder.**

Moved to Broadmoor

On trial in Switzerland in September 1959, Hume grandly confessed all – including the robberies in Britain, where he had shot and wounded the bank manager who tried to stop him. He was found guilty on five counts – from murder to violating the Swiss resident alien laws – and sentenced to hard labour for life. Amazingly, the Swiss judge allowed him to sell his story to the Sunday Pictorial again, with some money going to the family of the murdered taxi driver but the rest to Hume 'to buy cigarettes or something in jail'. Hume was imprisoned in Regensdorf cantonal penitentiary, but later moved to Broadmoor in Britain.

OPPOSITE TOP RIGHT: Hume with his wife Cynthia in 1949. He pleaded guilty to a lesser charge of being an accessory after the fact to the murder of Setty but later admitted to the crime in a newspaper. He claimed to have acted in a jealous rage over the advances Setty had made towards his wife.

OPPOSITE TOP LEFT: People wait for the bus outside the building in which Hume lived. Inside, ten men and two women jurors studied the lay-out to help them with future evidence.

OPPOSITE BOTTOM LEFT: The plane Hume used to dump the parcel containing Setty's body. After the gruesome crime attracted the attention of the press, United Services Flying Club at Elstree contacted the police saying that Hume had hired a plane and loaded a large parcel.

LEFT: A Scotland Yard camera takes a look at the fingerprints found on Setty's car. It had been found abandoned after his disappearance.

BELOW: A large crowd watches as a van with Hume inside leaves Bow Street following the first hearing of the murder charge. Convicted of a lesser charge, he served just eight years in Dartmoor Prison. After his release he admitted to a newspaper that he had killed Setty but the law of double jeopardy meant he could not be tried again.

Swiss judge: you can sell your story.

Derek Bentley: 'Let him have it, Chris!'

'That night I was out to kill, because I had so much hate inside me for what they had done to my brother.' Those words were spoken by 16-year-old Christopher Craig on 2 November 1952, the night he shot PC Sidney Miles during a botched raid on a warehouse with his 19-year-old accomplice Derek Bentley. The crime resulted in a murder conviction and an execution, but it was not Craig who went to the gallows. Derek William Bentley, who was already in custody when the fatal shot was fired, was hanged for the killing of PC Miles.

Officers on the scene

The Derek Bentley case sparked a campaign for justice that lasted over 40 years; it also marked a watershed moment in legal history for the part it played in removing capital punishment from the statute book.

On the night of 2 November at around 9.15 pm Croydon police station received a telephone call from a woman stating that she had witnessed a break-in. She reported seeing two men climb the gateway entrance to the premises of Barlow & Parker, a confectionery warehouse situated in Tamworth Road, Croydon. Several officers were dispatched to investigate, arriving in two squad cars. By the time they reached the scene, the would-be thieves had made it onto the building's flat roof.

LEFT: Barlow & Parker, the confectionery warehouse in Croydon which was the scene of the shooting.

ABOVE: PC Sidney Miles, the officer shot dead during the break-in.

A knife and a knuckleduster

PC Frederick Fairfax was the first to challenge them, having reached the roof via a drainpipe. A disembodied voice gave a belligerent reply: if he wanted them, he'd have to come and get them. Fairfax ran to the lift stack behind which they had taken cover and grabbed one of the men, whom he later discovered to be Derek Bentley. Still maintaining his hold on Bentley, the officer rounded the stack, hoping to apprehend the accomplice, Christopher Craig. Fairfax and Craig came face to face, and Bentley seized the opportunity to break away, shouting, 'Let him have it, Chris.' There was a flash and a report, and Fairfax fell to the ground with a gunshot wound to the shoulder.

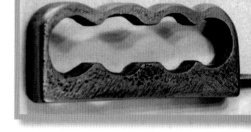

Bentley and Craig ran off in different directions, and Fairfax had to choose which of them to pursue. He collared Bentley for the second time, at which point a second shot rang out. Fairfax took cover behind a skylight, pulling Bentley down beside him. A search revealed that Bentley was in possession of a knife and a knuckleduster, but no gun.

Another officer, PC Norman Harrison, had been trying to reach the scene by edging his way along a sloping roof that abutted the flat roof, but Craig spotted him and fired off two shots, forcing Harrison to retreat. Further reinforcement arrived in the shape of PC James Macdonald, who had taken the same drainpipe route as Fairfax, and he joined his fellow officer in restraining Bentley. They asked the detainee about Craig's firearm, to be told that it was a Colt 45 and that he had plenty of ammunition.

RIGHT AND BOTTOM RIGHT: Nine-year-old Edith Ware and her mother who lived in Tamworth Road, Croydon. Edith had been looking out of her bedroom window when she saw two men climbing over the warehouse gates. Her father rushed to the nearest phone box to alert the local police.

BELOW: DC Fairfax (second from left) was the first officer to arrive on the scene. He challenged the two men, apprehending Derek Bentley on the roof.

TOP RIGHT: Despite being shot, DC Fairfax was able to continue chasing Bentley and after apprehending him found a knife and a vicious spiked knuckleduster but no firearms.

ABOVE: Christopher Craig was 16-years old at the time of the shooting and still a minor. After Craig had shot Fairfax, PC Sidney Miles, who had obtained keys to the building, tried to gain access to the roof using the stairs but as soon as the door was opened Craig shot him between the eyes, instantly killing the officer.

ABOVE (INSET): Derek Bentley was 19 years old. He had suffered a serious head injury after an accident during the Second World War and this had left him with permanent brain damage. He suffered from epilepsy and had a very low IQ.

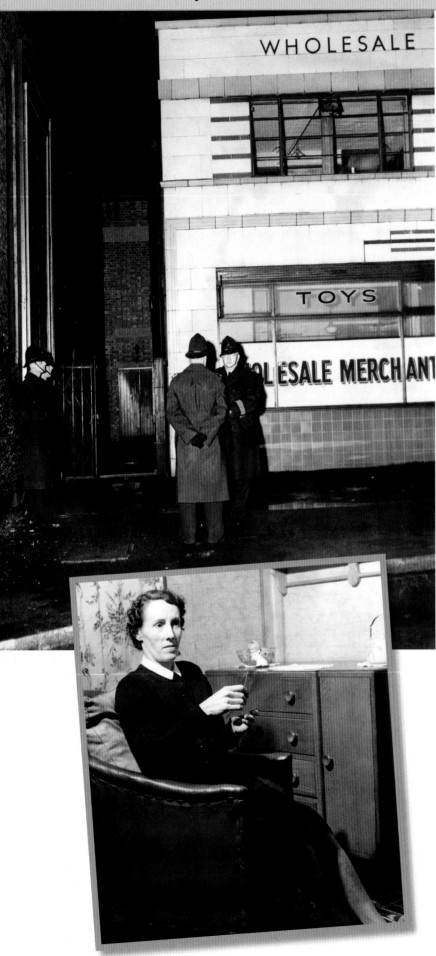

'Come on coppers, I'm only sixteen'

Keys to the premises had been obtained, and officers who had taken the internal staircase could now be heard on the other side of the door that led out onto the roof. One was PC Sidney Miles, the other PC Harrison, who had taken the stairs after his abortive attempt to reach the scene via the adjoining roof. Fairfax shouted to his colleagues to advise them on the position of the gunman, to the left of the door. It made little difference, for as soon as Miles burst through the opening he fell to the ground, shot between the eyes.

Harrison hurled his truncheon, a bottle and a block of wood in Craig's direction and managed to join Fairfax and Macdonald. A fourth officer, PC Robert Jaggs, had also made his way up the drainpipe.

Craig was now ranting, making reference to his elder brother Niven, who had just been sent down for a 12-year stretch for armed robbery. He apparently wanted to take that conviction out on those before him, for he taunted them by yelling out: 'Come on, coppers! I'm only sixteen!'

Much would be made of that remark. Was it a sneering jibe, that a group of police officers oughtn't to have much trouble arresting one youth in his mid-teens? Or was Craig telling them that he was too young to hang, and could therefore act with impunity?

LEFT: Police guard the entrance to the factory after the shooting. During the chase on the factory roof, Craig had jumped 20 feet into a neighbouring garden, sustaining multiple injuries.

BELOW LEFT: Mrs Miles, widow of the murdered policeman. PC Miles was posthumously awarded the King's Police and Fire Service Medal.

Multiple injuries

Bentley was ushered down the stairs, informing Craig of what was happening by calling out: 'They are taking me down.' When Fairfax returned from handing over the prisoner, he was now armed with a revolver. He told Craig to put down his weapon, but the latter was in no mood to go quietly. 'Come on, copper, let's have it out,' came the reply, accompanied by another shot. Fairfax launched an assault on Craig, making an arcing run and discharging two covering shots as he ran. Craig's weapon clicked, later found to have misfired, for there were two live cartridges still in the chamber. To evade capture Craig dived headlong into a garden 20 feet below. He sustained multiple injuries but remained conscious during his arrest, and lucid enough to express the wish that he was dead and that he had taken the officers with him.

While Craig was being transported to Croydon Hospital for medical attention, Bentley was taken to the local police station. He told officers he knew Craig had a gun but didn't think he would use it. As far as he was concerned, robbery was to have been the extent of their illicit deeds that night.

Both Illiterate

The history of the two youths then emerged. Bentley and Craig had attended the same school, Norbury Secondary Modern, though the three-year age gap meant that their paths didn't cross much during that period. When they did begin hanging around together, it was Craig who assumed the dominant role. Both were illiterate, but Bentley, an epileptic with an IQ of 66, was especially susceptible to the malign influence of the other. His parents recognised the fact and forbade Derek from consorting with Craig, but to no avail.

TOP RIGHT: All four officers involved in the incident received awards from the Queen. (Left to right) Detective Sergeant Fairfax (George Cross), PC James MacDonald (George Medal), PC Norman Harrison (George Medal) and PC Robert Jaggs (British Empire Medal).

ABOVE: Frederick 'Fairy' Fairfax pictured with wife Muriel the day after the shooting.

OPPOSITE RIGHT: The now promoted Detective Sergeant Fairfax shows his son Allen the George Cross, presented to him at Buckingham Palace.

RIGHT: Detective Sergeant Fairfax and his wife arrive at the Old Bailey at the start of the trial. Bentley and Craig were charged with murdering PC Sidney Miles and with the attempted murder of DS Fairfax.

RIGHT MIDDLE: (Left to right) PC Macdonald, DC Fairfax and PC Jacks pictured during the court case.

Derek Bentley: 'Let him have it, Chris!'

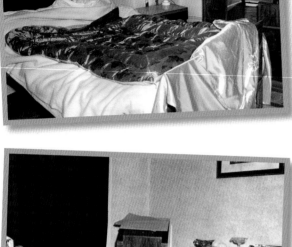

Equally culpable

The trial opened at the Central Criminal Court on 9 December, 1952, Craig and Bentley jointly charged with PC Miles's death. Both entered pleas of Not Guilty. Prosecuting counsel Mr Christmas Humphreys made it clear from the outset that while Craig's finger was on the trigger of the murder weapon, Bentley had incited his partner-in-crime and was equally culpable. It made no difference, he argued, that Bentley was already in police hands when the shooting took place. In law Bentley was party to the murder, though common sense was all that was needed to reach that conclusion.

It emerged that Craig had been fined for possession of a weapon a year earlier, and that he harboured ambitions of becoming a gunsmith. The younger defendant certainly had a chip on his shoulder, having been ridiculed during his time working in the storeroom of an engineering firm for his inability to read. The cultivation of the 'hard man' image was a way of acquiring status and covering up for his inadequacy.

But the rooftop bravado deserted Craig in the witness box, where he claimed he had shot PC Miles by accident. His passion, he said, was collecting weapons, disassembling them and putting them back together. He said he was not a good shot, and that he had fired aimlessly in a bid to scare the police officers away. Craig maintained he had no recollection of saying that he was filled with hate and was out to kill someone that night. He even had an answer for the rooftop dive, saying it was out of remorse for having injured an officer. Mr John Parris, acting for Craig, asked the jury to accept that he had not intended to kill Miles, citing the fact that he had been within a few feet of PC Fairfax, yet that officer had received only a flesh wound to the shoulder. He was not seeking an acquittal, but a verdict of manslaughter was appropriate in this case.

TOP LEFT, MIDDLE LEFT, LEFT AND ABOVE (INSET): During the trial several photographs of Bentley's home, including his collection of china, were released. Shots of the back room and the garden shed showed the equipment he used for repairing television and wireless sets.

ABOVE: The Home Secretary's flat in Great Peter Street. Crowds often gathered outside after the trial had finished in an effort to influence his response.

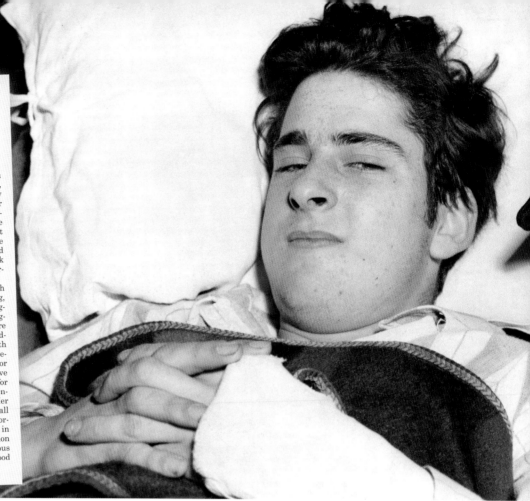

DECEMBER 12, 1952

Craig: 'One of the most dangerous criminals'

Christopher Craig, the 16-year-old gun-boy, and Derek William Bentley, 19, his fellow street-corner thug, were found guilty at the Old Bailey yesterday of the murder of P.C. Sidney Miles. Craig, too young for the death sentence, was ordered to be detained until the Queen's pleasure be known. Bentley was sentenced to death. In his case, the all-male jury, who were 77 minutes reaching their verdict, made a recommendation for mercy. When the verdict had been given the Clerk of Arraigns asked Craig and Bentley whether they had anything to say. Both looked down at the dock rail before them - and said nothing.

Lord Goddard, the Lord Chief Justice, had the black cap placed on his head. He said to Bentley: "You are 19 years of age. It is, therefore, my duty to pass on you the only sentence which the law can pass for the crime of wilful murder." Bentley raised his head only once as the sentence was read. He glanced at the judge when Lord Goddard came to the closing words, "May the Lord have mercy on your soul." The black cap was removed. Bentley was hurried below by two warders.

Craig stood in the dock with three warders."Christopher Craig, you are not 19, but in my judgment, and evidently in the judgment of the jury, you are the more guilty of the two," said Lord Goddard. "Your heart was filled with hate and you murdered a policeman without thought of his wife or family or himself. Never once have you expressed a word of sorrow for what you have done. I can only sentence you to be detained until Her Majesty's pleasure is known. I shall tell the Secretary of State when forwarding the recommendation in Bentley's case that in my opinion you are one of the most dangerous young criminals that has ever stood in that dock."

Deliberate act

Bentley maintained that he didn't know Craig had a gun, and denied saying 'Let him have it, Chris.' Summing up on his behalf, Mr F H Cassels said that the jury had to be sure that there was a prior agreement with Craig to use violence to resist arrest, and that Bentley had incited him to discharge his weapon. It was pointed out that Bentley showed no aggression towards the police officers, or any inclination to make a run for it. Surely he could have escaped the clutches of the injured PC Fairfax and rejoined Craig, had he wished to. Was it tenable that this same desperado who allegedly incited the shooting of PC Miles also meekly accepted his own capture?

In his summing up, presiding judge Lord Goddard all but ruled out the possibility of accidental death and a manslaughter verdict, directing the jury in the matter of the special protection accorded to the police: '…if a police officer has arrested, or is endeavouring to arrest, and that includes coming on the scene for the purpose of arrest, a person, and the arrest if effected would be lawful, and that person for the purpose of escape or of preventing or hindering the arrest does a wilful, that is to say an intentional act which causes the death of an officer, he is guilty of murder whether or not he intended to kill or cause grievous bodily harm.'

The Lord Chief Justice emphasised that while the outcome may have been accidental – the death of PC Miles – the perpetrators were still guilty of murder if the weapon had been deliberately discharged. The only leeway offered to the jury was if they found that the firing of the gun was itself accidental. But since Craig had emptied the revolver and reloaded, Lord Goddard opined that it was hard to see this as anything other than a deliberate act.

ABOVE AND BELOW: During the court case which opened on 9 December 1952, Craig was transported between Brixton Prison hospital and the Old Bailey by stretcher. During the fall from the roof he had broken an arm and fractured his spine.

Giving evidence at the trial, his father told the court that Craig had left school at 15 unable to read or write due to word blindness and had often been ridiculed because of this. He also had an obsession with firearms.

Death sentence passed

Turning to the case against Bentley, the judge stressed that if he was aware that Craig was carrying a gun, and there was an understanding that violence might be used to resist arrest, he was equally guilty of murder. It was no defence to say that he didn't believe his accomplice would use the weapon, or go to the lengths he did. The judge declared that it hardly seemed credible that Craig, a braggart with a passion for firearms, would not have shown Bentley the weapon he was carrying. But the crucial piece of evidence against Bentley was the utterance 'Let him have it, Chris', attested to by Fairfax, Macdonald and Harrison. Could it be that three brave public servants, who had demonstrated such admirable devotion to duty that night, had all been mistaken, or made sworn statements they knew to be untrue? And if Bentley did utter those words, it showed that he knew Craig had a gun and was urging him to use it.

Some seventy-five minutes later, a Guilty verdict was returned on both, with a recommendation for mercy in the case of Bentley. Craig, the guiltier party according to the judge, was over the age of criminal responsibility but not old enough to receive a capital sentence. He was given an indeterminate jail sentence. The jury's wishes regarding Bentley were overlooked as a death sentence was passed.

ABOVE: A detective carries a basket of exhibits into court. Jumbled together were PC Miles's cap and Craig's trilby alongside a knife, a mask and some ammunition.

ABOVE RIGHT: Bentley tries to hide his face as he is driven away from court.

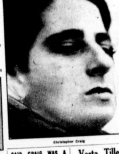

The Evening News

CRAIG AND BENTLEY BOTH FOUND GUILTY OF MURDER

Bentley to Die: Craig Detained During the Queen's Pleasure

HEART FULL OF HATE, JUDGE TELLS CRAIG

KEPT A DATE—THEN WENT OUT TO KILL

The Boy from the Quiet Street

By JAMES ANDERSON

"EVENING NEWS" REPORTER

SIXTEEN - YEAR - OLD CHRISTOPHER CRAIG, AND DEREK BENTLEY, AGED 19, WERE BOTH FOUND GUILTY AT THE OLD BAILEY TO-DAY OF THE MURDER OF P.C. SIDNEY MILES.

The jury added a recommendation for mercy in the case of Bentley.

GIFFARD TOLD GIRL HE KILLED PARENTS—POLICE

Story of Meeting in Chelsea

Mother Alive When Thrown Over Cliff, Court Told

CRAIG TRIAL SENTENCES

QUEEN MARY GOES FOR A DRIVE

POLICE ARE PRAISED FOR GALLANTRY

More Turkeys —But the Price Is Going Up

'FULL OF HATE' No Word of Sorrow

DID BENTLEY KNOW? 'Can You Suppose...'

SAID CRAIG WAS A MAGNETIC PERSONALITY

Gunman of 16 Is Jailed

Vesta Tilley Leaves £84,000

A WELCOME FOR TITO, SAYS STRABOLGI

CORRESPONDENCE 'Significant'

BARING'S TRIP HOME ATTACKED

LATE EXTRA

WEATHER FORECAST

Maxwell Fyfe stands by decision after appeal by 200 MPs'

Derek William Bentley will be hanged at Wandsworth Jail at nine o'clock this morning for his part with 16-year-old Christopher Craig in the murder of P.C. Sidney Miles. Shortly before 11 o'clock last night the Home Secretary finally refused to recommend a reprieve. It was the third time in a few days that Sir David Maxwell Fyfe had said "No reprieve."

He gave his decision in a letter to Mr. Aneurin Bevan, who led a party of six Socialist M.Ps to interview him at the Home Office earlier last night and present him with a last-minute appeal signed by 200 M.Ps. Sir David's letter stated that he had given "very anxious consideration" to the case the M.Ps put up.

He fully appreciated the further points of emphasis they had presented and had considered them with an open mind. But he had decided there was no sufficient reason for him to change his mind. The balance, he felt, was still the other way. Consequently his decision must stand.

Five hours earlier he had sent a similar "No" by special Home Office messenger to the Bentleys' home at Norbury.

The fight for a life

For seven hours yesterday the Bentley case dominated the House of Commons.

Here is a brief time schedule of events:

4.30 p.m. After an hour's discussion Speaker W.S. Morrison ruled that in matters touching the prerogative a death sentence cannot be debated until it has been carried out.

5.30: Mr Silverman drew up an appeal begging the Home Secretary "even now" to recommend a reprieve.

6.30: About 100 Socialist M.Ps had signed this appeal. The Bentleys arrived at Westminster. Mrs. Craig and her daughter were also there.

8.30: Another 100 signatures had been added and the Socialist deputation were grouped around Sir David's desk on the softly carpeted floor of the draughty great room.

9.15: The deputation left - and at **10.45** they heard the decision.

Father holds back news from his wife

In the great Central Lobby of the House of Commons, stage of many stirring appeals, there has probably never been a more moving sight than that of last night when hundreds of people came in to urge their M.Ps to fight for Bentley. The atmosphere was hopeful then. Every moment it was expected that a reprieve would be announced.

But just before the House rose, the Home Secretary's private secretary, Mr. Whittock, arrived with a letter, handed it to Mr. Harry McGhee, one of the M.Ps who had formed the delegation. It was the Home Secretary's decision.

Tried everything

Mr. Bentley, who was sitting at a table drafting another telegram to the Queen, was called over by Mr. Tom Driberg, M.P., and given the news. Mr. Bentley moved away as though stunned. Then, speaking as casually as he could, he shepherded his wife and daughter out - he said he thought they had better go home as the House had risen.

After they had gone home, still talking hopefully of a reprieve, Mr. Bentley said: "All we can do now is pray. We have tried everything and it has failed." He was crying.

A friend telephoned to the Queen the telegram they had been drafting: "There is still time to save my son. Please help me" - Mrs. Lilian Rose Bentley. Earlier a telegram had gone to the Duke of Edinburgh from Mr. Niven Craig, father of Christopher Craig.

Derek Bentley saw his family for the last time from 3 p.m. to 3.30 p.m. yesterday. His mother brought him three last gifts: a photograph of his three dogs, Bob, Judy, and Flossie; a rosary; and a letter from a girl friend.

OPPOSITE BELOW RIGHT: Newspaper headlines after the verdict of guilty had been passed reflect the fact that both men were accused of murder – but because of the difference in their ages Bentley would hang, despite a recommendation for mercy from the jury. Craig was given an indeterminate sentence.

TOP RIGHT: Detectives pack up the evidence used during the trial. There was an immediate outcry after the verdict as many members of the public voiced their disagreement with the judge's decision.

RIGHT: In a wave of emotion, Bentley's father William protests at the verdict.

Clamour for reprieve

There was a clamour for Bentley to be reprieved. Hundreds of MPs were incensed at the prospect of a man said to have the mental age of an 11-year-old being hanged for a crime that was committed when he was already in custody. Their hands were tied by the Speaker, who ruled that the case could not be debated in the House until the sentence was carried out. Even Lord Goddard, who would be severely criticised for his partial handling of the trial, believed that Bentley would be reprieved. But Home Secretary Sir David Maxwell Fyfe ignored all petitions, and the convicted man went to the gallows at Wandsworth Prison on 28 January 1953.

Bentley's execution provoked considerable outrage. For almost forty years critics focused on the ambiguity of the words ascribed to Bentley on which the case against him turned. Might he not have been urging Craig to surrender the weapon instead of fire it? Remarkably, the defence made nothing of the possible dual meaning at the trial; only later did that linguistic uncertainty add further weight to claims that a miscarriage of justice had occurred.

Then a darker picture emerged, calling into question whether the words had been spoken at all. Bentley had denied ever saying 'Let him have it, Chris', and his rebuttal of the official version of events was supported by Craig. That had been construed as felons sticking together, but in 1989, their story was backed up by PC Claude Pain, who was also on the roof at the critical moment but not called as a witness. Fairfax, Harrison and Macdonald may not have been guilty of deliberate fabrication. They had to make ordered sense out of confusion and panic, piecing together their reports while traumatised by the death of a colleague. Having convinced themselves that the fateful words had been spoken, the officers perforce had to repudiate any counter-claim. The three men denied that Pain had been in the vicinity, and the latter, troubled by the events but nearing retirement and fearing the consequences of impugning the reputations of his colleagues, remained silent.

TOP: The Home Secretary refused to overturn the ruling and at 11pm, the night before Bentley was due to hang, crowds gathered outside the Home Office demonstrating against his decision. Inside six MPs including Aneurin Bevan were pleading with the Home Secretary to change his mind.

ABOVE: Telegrams sent to Bentley's parents from Winston Churchill and the Home Secretary, Sir David Maxwell Fyfe following appeals to overturn the judge's decision.

RIGHT: The notice of execution outside Wandsworth Prison announcing that Derek Bentley would hang at 9.00 am the following morning.

OPPOSITE BOTTOM: William Bentley and his daughter, Iris, arrive at the Home Office bearing packages that contained 6,800 signatures begging for a reprieve.

OPPOSITE ABOVE: The following morning crowds gathered in silence outside Wandsworth prison at 9.00am, just as Bentley was sent to the gallows.

Mr Bentley carries on fight

Mr. William Bentley, father of 19-year-old Derek Bentley who was executed yesterday, said last night: "I am going to fight on to get the law changed. "A lot of people are with me. Nearly 30,000 people signed for a reprieve for Derek. Like me, they cannot understand why a boy who was in custody when the murder was done should die, and the man who fired the shot should live." Sixteen-year-old Christopher Craig, found guilty with Bentley of the murder of P.C. Miles at Croydon, was sentenced to be detained during the Queen's pleasure.

Mr. Bentley said his wife and daughter will probably go to St. Leonards-on-Sea to the home of a sympathiser who has offered them a holiday. On Sunday afternoon he will drive to Marble Arch to join a demonstration which has been organised by Miss Anne Doran, a 25-year-old actress, and Mr. Darell Sykes, a 22-year-old salesman. After the execution yesterday Miss Doran went home to get a few hours sleep before going to the Gateway Theatre for the first night of a play. She takes the part of a murderess.

About 500 people were outside Wandsworth Jail when the notice of Bentley's execution was posted. Mr. Bentley drove through the crowd and collected some of his son's personal effects including his new overcoat. He went home and told his wife he had not yet been able to get the rest of Derek's clothes.

Hospital visit

At the inquest two hours later Dr. David Haler, a pathologist, said his examination had shown that Derek Bentley's brain was normal. When Mr. Bentley heard this he went to Guy's Hospital, where his son had once been treated, and got a medical report. "I handed this to a solicitor," said Mr. Bentley. "It shows my son's brain was not normal."

Derek Bentley: 'Let him have it, Chris!'

Bentley and Craig: Comment

Derek Bentley, aged 19, who was hanged yesterday for murder, was made to suffer the ultimate indignities by so-called "friends."

Most people will regard the scuffling and hysteria of the small crowd of notoriety-hunters outside the prison gates as highly distasteful. The condemned youth might have been spared a brawl over his body. He might have been allowed to pass from the world in decent silence. Instead, coins were thrown, glass smashed, and there were shouts of "Murder" and "Save him" - as though he were a national hero.

He was not. The hero in this case was Police Constable Miles, who was shot dead while protecting his fellow citizens. Having said this, we recognise and respect the large body of opinion which held that Bentley, who had not fired the fatal shot, and who had been recommended to mercy, should not have been executed.

Verdict

We commend the sincerity of the 200 M.Ps who signed a last-minute appeal for a reprieve, and of the six who, as a deputation, sought to persuade the Home Secretary to change his decision.

But we think they were wrong. They said that a new factor, "public reaction," had appeared and that the great majority of Bentley's fellow-countrymen thought that to hang him would be contrary to fair play and natural justice. The appellants, however, had no means of assessing the size of the majority (if any) which favoured a reprieve. Nor can we agree that "fair play" or "natural justice" should supersede the law. If this were admitted the courts would be robbed of their function - which is to reach a verdict in accordance with the evidence.

> The hero in this case was Police Constable Miles, who was shot dead while protecting his fellow citizens.

TOP LEFT: A prison official emerged from the gates at 9.10 am to post up another notice. Protestors immediately began to shout and throw missiles as police officers struggled to control the crowds.

TOP RIGHT: William and his wife Lillian on the day of their son's execution

RIGHT: Officers lead away one of the protestors. By the time of Bentley's execution the crowd outside the prison had swelled to more than 500 people.

ABOVE: That morning's newspapers had confirmed the Home Secretary's final refusal to change his mind despite an appeal signed by two hundred MPs.

CERTIFICATE OF SURGEON

DECLARATION OF SHERIFF
AND OTHERS

> It was established that Bentley knew his companion, Craig, to be armed. It was also stated that during the struggle with the police on the warehouse roof he shouted to Craig: 'Let him have it, Chris!' Those five words proved his guilt.

ABOVE: During the commotion the glass over the notices was smashed. Behind the broken shards the announcement of the execution and the doctor's confirmation of his death can be seen.

ABOVE RIGHT: Bentley's father and sister Iris stand grim-faced. They immediately began a campaign to clear his name.

BELOW: Bentley's father and sister pictured seven years later. Iris worked tirelessly to have the verdict overturned. She had some success in 1993 when Home Secretary Michael Howard gave a limited pardon, agreeing that the execution should not have taken place. The case was finally taken to the Court of Appeal and in July 1998 the conviction was finally quashed. Lord Goddard, the judge that made the original decision, also received severe criticism for his handling of the case.

JANUARY 29, 1953

Justice

In politics "public reaction", can be a valuable guide. But it can all too easily pervert the course of justice. Derek Bentley had justice.

He was properly tried and sentenced. He appealed, but his appeal was dismissed. What the M.Ps endeavoured to do, in effect, was to re-open the case; but it is not for the House of Commons to re-try criminal causes.

The law in the matter under discussion is clear. It says that if two or more persons set out on a foray which is likely to end in murder, and murder results, all are equally culpable. It was established that Bentley knew his companion, Craig, to be armed. It was also stated that during the struggle with the police on the warehouse roof he shouted to Craig: "Let him have it, Chris!" Those five words proved his guilt.

Courage

This is generally admitted. But many people thought that since Craig - who killed the policeman - was too young to be hanged, Bentley - who did not - should also have escaped the gallows. But if this argument were admitted there would be nothing to stop any older man giving a lethal weapon to a boy in some burglarious enterprise, knowing that if murder were done neither of them would hang. In any case, Bentley's guilt was not made less by the fact that Craig was younger.

In all this sorry business tribute must be paid to Sir David Maxwell Fyfe, the Home Secretary, who has carried out a difficult and distressing task with courage and dignity. We should all remember that he has stood fast not merely in a blind adherence to the letter of the law but so that the interests of the community shall be served.

Derek Bentley: 'Let him have it, Chris!'

Conviction quashed

Iris Bentley, Derek's sister, campaigned tirelessly to clear the stain on the family name. A partial victory was achieved in 1993, when Home Secretary Michael Howard accepted that a limited pardon was appropriate, on the grounds that a capital sentence should not have been passed. He refused to budge on the issue of the verdict, however, which he deemed correct. That wasn't enough for the Bentley family, who took the case to the Court of Appeal, where the conviction was quashed in July 1998. Lord Goddard came in for severe criticism over his handling of the trial. He was self-avowedly on the 'hang 'em and flog 'em' wing of the judicial spectrum, and his direction of the jury was interpreted as a determined effort to ensure that someone paid the full price for the death of PC Miles. Craig might have been able to avoid the noose; Bentley wouldn't.

The ruling came too late for Iris Bentley, who lost her battle against cancer a year earlier. Christopher Craig, who spent ten years behind bars for his part in the events of 2 November 1952, emerged from the shadows to place on record his own deep remorse and pass comment on the decision that exonerated his teenage friend. 'Today, after 46 years, the conviction of Derek Bentley has been quashed and his name cleared. While I am grateful and relieved about this, I am saddened that it has taken those 46 years for the authorities in this country to admit the truth.'

A limited pardon wasn't enough for the Bentley family, who took the case to the Court of Appeal, where the conviction was quashed in July 1998.

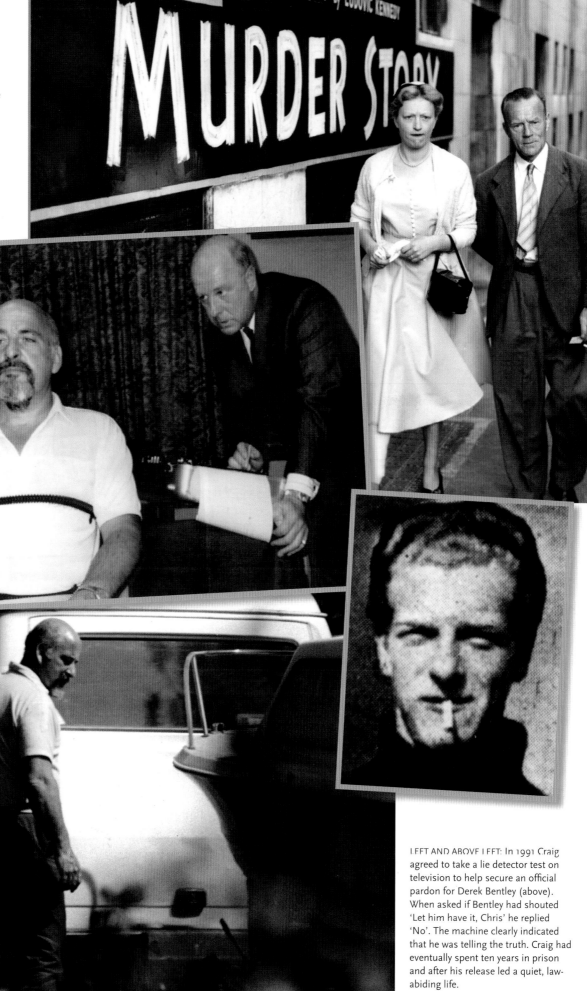

RIGHT: William and Iris arriving at the Cambridge Theatre in London for the opening night of 'Murder Story' written by Ludovic Kennedy. The plot of the play bore a very close resemblance to the crimes committed by Bentley and Craig.

OPPOSITE: William, Lillian and Iris Bentley made the journey to Wandsworth prison 20 years after Derek's execution to place wreathes in his memory.

LEFT AND ABOVE LEFT: In 1991 Craig agreed to take a lie detector test on television to help secure an official pardon for Derek Bentley (above). When asked if Bentley had shouted 'Let him have it, Chris' he replied 'No'. The machine clearly indicated that he was telling the truth. Craig had eventually spent ten years in prison and after his release led a quiet, law-abiding life.

Drummond Murders

'Politics play an important part in this brutal murder. Whoever the murderer may be, I believe he has trailed Sir Jack Drummond since his arrival from Villefranches at the end of last month. Robbery is not the motive of the crime and I think the murderer believes his victim played an important part in the British political intelligence contrary to his own ideals.'

M. Espariat, Mayor of Lurs

Distinguished biochemist

Sir Jack Cecil Drummond, born January 12, 1891, was a well-known British biochemist married to Anne and with one daughter, Elizabeth, born on March 23, 1942. He had a distinguished career during the Second World War, using his expertise in nutrition to ensure that rationing led to added protein and vitamins in the diet of the poor and a reduced intake of meat, fats, sugar and eggs among the better off. After the war it became clear that this had resulted in a general improvement in the nation's health. Drummond was knighted in 1944 and subsequently became head of research at Boots.

> On August 4, 1952 they set up camp by the side of the N96 in Provence, next to a footpath leading to the nearby river Durance.

In summer 1952, the Drummond family set off on a touring holiday in France, travelling to the Côte d'Azur to stay with friends. On August 4, 1952 they set up camp by the side of the N96 in Provence, next to a footpath leading to the nearby river Durance. A few metres away was a farmhouse, home to the Dominici family, 75-year-old Gaston and his wife Marie, along with their son, his wife and their baby. Early the following morning the Dominici son discovered the bodies of the Drummond family and raised the alarm.

Great Alps Search for Drummond Killers

Police dogs were tonight searching the gorges and desolate Alpine slopes near Lurs, in Southern France, for the murderers of Sir Jack Drummond, 61, Britain's wartime food expert, his wife, and ten-year-old daughter, Elizabeth. Hundreds of police, under the direction of the Marseilles Murder Squad, have been told that they will be on 24-hours-a-day duty until the killers are found. It was stated here that two senior Scotland Yard detectives will fly to Marseilles to take part in the inquiries.

One of the dogs, 'Wash,' attached to the gendarmerie at Digne, was shown the body of Elizabeth and immediately set off along the main Marseilles-Grenoble railway line in the direction of Thoard, a few miles north. Gendarmes tonight found the murder weapon - a 'Rock-ola' repeater, normally used by the U.S. Army. The gun had been thrown into one of the few pools of water in the dried-up bed of the River Durance. Examination of the weapon showed that it had jammed after nine rounds had been fired.

'For that reason,' a police officer state, 'the killer was compelled to club the child to death instead of shooting her.'

The initials 'R.M.C.' were stamped on the butt, which was also decorated with two crossed guns, the emblem of several French Colonial regiments. Police are faced with considerable difficulty in tracing the source of the weapon as many guns of the same type were dropped by parachute to Resistance fighters during the war.

Unbelievable savagery

The murders were discovered at 6 a.m. by a farmer, M. Pierre Dominici, who told detectives: 'I was returning to my farm, La Grand'Terre, after repairing the banks of a dyke. I saw a young girl lying by the roadside. She was wearing white pyjamas and seemed to be asleep. Then I saw that her head was covered with blood.' She had been struck with unbelievable savagery, M. Dominici said, apparently with a gun butt.

'I began to run for help,' he continued, 'when I came across a woman wearing a red dress who had been shot in the chest. A few yards away there was a car with a G.B. plate, a Hillman, numbered NNK 686. On the other side of the road was a man. He had fallen on his face and had also been shot.'

Lonely spot

M. Dominici halted a passing motor cyclist, who reported to the police at Forcalquier eight miles away. Afterwards he remembered having heard five or six shots from the direction of the road during the night, M. Dominici added. Other inhabitants of the lonely hill region, bordering Napoleon's route over the Alps, told police they saw two men in shorts in the area late yesterday evening. A long-distance lorry-driver reported that at about 11 p.m., he saw a motor cycle and sidecar nearby.

> Police are faced with considerable difficulty in tracing the source of the weapon as many guns of the same type were dropped by parachute to Resistance fighters during the war.

OPPOSITE : Gaston Dominici addresses the court at Digne in southern France during his trial for the murder of Sir Jack Drummond and his family. Dominici's son had found the bodies of the Drummond family on August 5, 1952 and contacted the police.

TOP RIGHT: Gaston Dominici laughed as a witness was giving evidence during his trial. Originally, he had confessed to the murders but later withdrew his confession claiming that he was trying to protect the rest of his family.

RIGHT: Dominici's wife Marie (right), and daughter-in-law Yvette, leave the courthouse in Digne.

LEFT: Dominici's eldest son Clovis insisted that his father was guilty. However, he argued that his father should be pitied as he had lived well all his life and fell victim to a moment of madness.

BELOW (INSET): Gaston Dominici hides his face in his handkerchief and weeps as Maitre Louis Sabatier sums up for the prosecution. He was found guilty and sentenced to death by guillotine. This was later reduced to life imprisonment when queries over the conduct of the investigation were raised.

The family were seen eating supper beside their car after erecting a tent and laying out a light, modern camping mattress. It is believed that they turned in about 11 pm.

AUGUST 6, 1952

Bullet wounds

The Drummonds arrived at the site last night about 8.30, travelling from Digne. They stopped at one of the only sheltered spots for miles around - a bend in the road perched on the edge of a ravine 70ft. above the River Durance. The family were seen eating supper beside their car after erecting a tent and laying out a light, modern camping mattress. It is believed that they turned in about 11 p.m. Police are working on the theory that they were attacked approximately 2 1/2 hours later and that Lady Drummond was shot first. Sir Jack and his daughter were evidently killed while attempting to flee. There were signs of a struggle, and, from skin under Elizabeth's fingernails, it is possible that she severely scratched her aggressor. Sir Jack was shot three times in the back and was also wounded in one hand, apparently while trying to defend

himself. Lady Drummond had five bullet wounds in the right side.

Dr. Henri Dragon said: 'Elizabeth had run in her bare feet and there were footmarks in the earth behind her. At present it seems likely that the killing was unpremeditated and followed a struggle when the victims awoke as someone was robbing their car. There were still a few pieces of luggage in the vehicle but no clothes.

Two strangers

One unexplained factor is the presence last night of two other strangers in the area who were apparently not French. They approached M. Dominici's farm some time after he had seen the Drummonds and shouted out a request in a language that he did not recognize. It was two hours before the victims were identified because their passports as well as their clothing had been stolen. Their names were finally found through a school notebook in which Elizabeth had been doing her holiday homework, and through a postcard that she had begun to write, saying, 'I am as happy as ever.'

Detectives stated earlier that they were anxious to interview two couples who were seen near Lurs last night. Those whom they were making 'every effort' to trace, they said, were two motor cyclists, believed to be foreigners. The other couple were in a fast, black car of a French make and with a front-wheel drive.

Food Packs Saved Lives

Sir Jack Drummond, Britain's No. 1 food expert, planned our wartime diet, saved the people of Malta from starving during the siege of the island, and invented an emergency food for the famine-stricken people of Europe. He was scientific adviser to the Ministry of Food from 1939 till 1946, and Lord Woolton, wartime Minister of Food, said of him: 'I was more fortunate than any man deserved to be in finding him.' One of his best-known wartime recipes was 'Blitz Broth,' a soup made available in air-raid shelters. His greatest invention, a pre-digested food in liquid form, saved innumerable lives in Europe. Concentrated foods suggested or perfected by Sir Jack Drummond had been dropped to the French Maquis at the spot where he was murdered.

Gaston Dominici convicted

Police suspicion soon fell on the Dominici family, and under questioning Gaston Dominici confessed – although he had always been regarded as a pillar of the local community and had no apparent motive. He later withdrew his confession, saying he was just trying to protect the rest of his family. In 1952 a known German criminal claimed he had carried out the murders with three accomplices while travelling to Marseilles to carry out a robbery, but this was never investigated further. Many also believe that the motive for the murders dated back to the war, and that Sir Jack may have been a spy.

In November 1954 Gaston Dominici was convicted of the murders. He was sentenced to the guillotine, but this later became life imprisonment after major queries were raised about the investigation and the conduct of the trial and subsequent enquiries failed to come to a firm conclusion. Dominici was released in 1959, although he was never pardoned or retried. His grandson, Alain, has always protested that his grandfather was innocent.

RIGHT: Dominici pictured before his arrest talking with reporters near the spot where Drummond and his family were murdered.

BELOW: On the third anniversary of the Drummond killings detectives reconstruct the crime. Police believed after this renewed investigation that there may have been a second murderer.

In November 1954 Gaston Dominici was convicted of the murders. He was sentenced to the guillotine.

Teddington towpath murders:
'One of Scotland Yard's most notable triumphs in a century'

They were both expected home that evening, but neither of them appeared.

Bicycle ride

On Sunday May 31, 1953, two days before Queen Elizabeth II's coronation, two young girls, Barbara Songhurst and Christine Reed, set off on a bicycle ride from Hampton, a village on the Thames west of London. Barbara was 16, an assistant in a chemist shop who lived with her family in Princes Road, Teddington; her friend Christine was 18 and she also lived with her family, in Roy Crescent in nearby Hampton Hill. Between 11.00 and 11.30 am the two girls were seen cycling along the towpath next to the Thames, between Teddington and Twickenham. It was the last time they were seen alive; they were both expected home that evening, but neither of them appeared.

ABOVE: River police examine Teddington Lock with a water glass while Chief Detective Inspector Hannam holds a conference with other detectives on the bank. Behind them is the spot where Barbara Songhurst, 16, and Christine Reed, 18, were murdered.

LEFT: Hannam stands on the river bank and gives an order to a detective. Barbara's body had been found in the river the day after the murder.

OPPOSITE TOP: The scene of the crime: police search for the knife with which 16-year-old Barbara had been stabbed.

OPPOSITE BELOW: Mothers with young children in prams gather to watch the police search at the lock. Detectives found the girls' shoes along with bloodstains on the verge of the tow path which led them to the spot where they believed the murder took place.

OPPOSITE MIDDLE: Crowds of sightseers watch detectives search the woods near Teddington. After five days of searching both on land and in the river, the police decided to drain the Thames between Teddington and Richmond.

River Thames drained

The following day Barbara's body was found floating in the Thames near Water Lane in Richmond, some two miles downriver from where the girls had last been seen. Her skull was fractured and she had been beaten and raped, then stabbed several times. Her shoes were missing, but about a mile and a half from the point where the body was recovered – close to the towpath near Teddington Lock – detectives found two pairs of girls' shoes. Bloodstains on the verge of the towpath nearby led police to the place where they believed the girls had been attacked, after which Barbara's body had been thrown into the river, on the ebb tide some time between 10.00 and 11.00 pm on Sunday. There was no trace of the two bicycles – or of Christine, and Scotland Yard issued a description of her while police mowed grass near the towpath and police launches dragged the river. On June 2, Christine's bicycle was discovered in the river but there was still no sign of Christine herself or of the other bicycle. After five days of searching the police decided to drain the Thames between Teddington and Richmond, using the locks at these points, and on June 6, Christine's body was finally found; she proved to have similar injuries to Barbara.

Bloodstains on the verge of the towpath nearby led police to the place where they believed the girls had been attacked.

JUNE 4, 1953

Teddington lock

This was the scene on the tow-path near Teddington lock yesterday. All afternoon the police hunted for the knife with which Barbara Songhurst was stabbed. Last night it was announced that naval frogmen may be called in to help with the search.

Police investigating the Teddington Lock murder last night revealed that a blood stained stone found on the towpath has started a new line of inquiry.

They believe that Barbara Songhurst, the 16-year-old chemist's assistant was ambushed by a man or men who rushed out of the bushes as she was cycling home at about 11.10 p.m. on Sunday. Barbara was with her 18-year-old friend, Christina Reed, who is also believed to have been murdered but who has not been found.

Police believe that the front wheels of their bicycles were forced together, throwing both girls over the handlebars on to the hard gravel towpath.

The bloodstained stone coincides with a heavy bruise at the back of Barbara's head, received before death. A section of the river near Eel Pie Island was dragged by police late last night, after a report that an object which looked like a body had been seen floating near the island.

Teddington towpath murders

Alfred Whiteway arrested

Later that same month, on June 12, a man attempted to rape Patricia Birch in Windsor Great Park and then robbed her of several shillings. The police issued a photofit of the attacker, and two builders recognised Alfred Charles Whiteway and called the police. Whiteway was a 22-year-old labourer, who lived in Teddington with his parents. He was married, but his wife lived in nearby Kingston-upon-Thames – by all accounts, because the two of them could not afford their own accommodation. When Whiteway was arrested on June 28 he was carrying an axe, but somehow he managed to hide it under the seat in the police car on the way to the station. It was found later by a policeman cleaning the car, who at first didn't realize its significance and took it home to chop some wood. Although Whiteway eventually admitted the attack on Patricia, he was indignant at the charge of theft, claiming that he hadn't wanted any money but that the woman had thrust it at him. As they investigated the case, police soon began to link it with a similar attack on 14-year-old Kathleen Ringham, who on May 24 had survived the assault of a 'man with a chopper' on Oxshott Heath near London. Whiteway was charged with both attacks on July 1 and on July 15 he pleaded guilty at Richmond Court on two counts of assault.

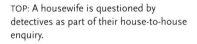

> When Whiteway was arrested he was carrying an axe, but somehow he managed to hide it.

TOP: A housewife is questioned by detectives as part of their house-to-house enquiry.

ABOVE: Two detectives check a ladies bicycle near Teddington lock in the hunt for the one Barbara Songhurst had been riding.

ABOVE LEFT: A notice fixed on the towpath warning that a three mile stretch of the Thames was to be drained. Five hundred boats moored between Teddington Lock and Richmond had to move into mid-stream to avoid capsizing.

LEFT: Police search the river bed of the Thames.

OPPOSITE TOP: Chief Inspector Hannam leaves with a parcel of 'interesting things' bought up by river police at Teddington.

OPPOSITE TOP (INSET) AND OPPOSITE BOTTOM: Police search for clues with a water glass, which allowed them to examine the river bed closely.

OPPOSITE MIDDLE LEFT: Police using a mine detector found a carpenter's file sharpened to a point and bloodstained.

OPPOSITE MIDDLE RIGHT: Detective Inspector Vivian (left) and Chief Inspector Hannam (right) wrap objects retrieved from the river bed in newspaper.

> *Whiteway had withdrawn his confession, claiming that it was a work of fiction, which the police had completely fabricated.*

Whiteway confession

However, it wasn't long before the police also began to consider him as a suspect for the rape and murder of Barbara and Christine – and at this point the policeman remembered the axe he had found in the police car and brought it into the station. Unfortunately all forensic evidence had been destroyed by several weeks of use, but when confronted with the axe and with evidence of blood that had been found in the seams and eyelets of his shoes, Whiteway broke down. He admitted to the police that he had killed the two girls and signed a statement to that effect, so on August 20 he was charged on two counts of murder and remanded for trial at the Old Bailey.

No reprieve

Whiteway was tried for murder in October 1953. He was defended by Peter Rawlinson, then a junior barrister but who later became Solicitor General and then Attorney General under three Conservative Prime Ministers. The prosecution claimed the defendant had knocked the girls out by throwing an axe or something similar at them, then raped and stabbed them. However, by now Whiteway had withdrawn his confession, claiming that it was a work of fiction, which the police had completely fabricated. Rawlinson cross-examined murder squad detective Herbert Hannam at length and pointed out many inconsistencies in the way the confession was worded, but the Press were indignant at any implication that the police were lying – and the jury agreed. On November 2, 1953, they took just over an hour to find Whiteway guilty and he was sentenced to death. Despite an appeal there was no reprieve, and he was hanged at Wandsworth Prison on December 22, 1953.

Ruth Ellis:
The last woman to be hanged in Britain

Ruth Ellis had a short and deeply troubled life. Abused by a succession of men, the insecure, unstable mother of two young children finally cracked over the Easter weekend of 1955, shooting dead her lover in a fit of jealous rage.

Betrayal

Ruth Neilson was born 9 October 1926 and brought up in Rhyl, North Wales. Her elder sister Muriel claimed that both she and Ruth were abused by their musician father, which, in the latter's case, would set the pattern for unhappy, dysfunctional relationships with men. Although she was an attractive woman – she would spend some time working as a photographic model – Ruth craved affection and attention, usually from the wrong type. She was needy and dependent, but the men in her life rarely offered dependability.

The Neilson family relocated to London during the war. Ruth had left school and was eking out a living in shops and factories when the next emotional blow struck. She fell for a French-Canadian soldier, Andre Clare, by whom she became pregnant. There was talk of marriage, but Clare omitted to inform her about his existing wife and family back in Canada. A son, Andrew, born in 1945, was the product of a union that ended in betrayal and abandonment.

Ruth drifted into Soho's sleazy club scene, which no doubt paid a lot better than the low-level clerical jobs she was used to. It may not have been part of the job description for her to sleep with the men who patronised the Court Club in Duke Street, though taking hostess work a stage further was an easy way to supplement her income.

> **Ellis emptied a revolver into Blakely. One bullet ricocheted off a wall and injured a passer-by, but the others found their target.**

LEFT: Ruth Ellis was the last woman to be hanged in Britain after she was found guilty of murdering racing driver, David Blakely. Ellis was reported in the media to have been 'utterly indifferent, disdainful in regard to her chances of survival.'

Stormy, obsessive relationship

In 1950 she married divorced dentist George Ellis, one of the club's regulars. He was seventeen years her senior and a chronic alcoholic. Ruth suffered many drink-fuelled assaults before she managed to escape, now with a second child, Georgina, to look after. She drifted back to what she knew: the club scene and hostess work. Former employer Morris Conley installed her as manager of the Little Club in Brompton Road, Knightsbridge, and it was here that she made the acquaintance of David Blakely. Superficially, Blakely was a good catch: ex-public schoolboy, good looking, well off, a playboy whose chief passion revolved around the glamorous world of motor racing. But scratch not very far beneath the surface and a less appealing picture was revealed. He was a philandering rogue capable of the most boorish behaviour when intoxicated – which was often – and not above resorting to using his fists on a woman.

Ellis and Blakely had a stormy, obsessive relationship, punctuated by violent rows and passionate reconciliations. Businessman Desmond Cussen seemed to offer salvation, and some hope of a better life. He was besotted with Ruth, but although she revelled in the adoring attention and had a brief sexual relationship with him, it was not a love match. Ruth was repeatedly drawn back to the bad penny, sharing a bed with Blakely even when she was living under Cussen's roof

Fired until the bullets ran out

By the spring of 1955, Blakely had had enough and wanted to sever all ties with Ellis. On 9 April, Good Friday, he sought sanctuary at the home of friends, the Findlaters, with whom he planned to spend the holiday weekend. Ellis became increasingly distraught and frustrated at her thwarted attempts to contact her lover. Convinced that he was having an affair with the Findlaters' nanny, she went round to the house and damaged his car, calming down only after the police were called. For Ellis it was merely a tactical withdrawal.

That Sunday the Findlaters hosted a party, and when Blakely and a friend, Clive Gunnell, slipped out for more supplies of beer and cigarettes, the spurned woman struck. As the two men came out of the Magdala public house in South Hill Park, Hampstead, Ellis emptied a revolver into Blakely. One bullet ricocheted off a wall and injured a passer-by, but the others found their target. Even when he was lying prostrate on the ground, with Gunnell crouching over to attend him, Ellis kept firing until the bullets ran out, then calmly asked for the police to be called. She was still holding the weapon when an off-duty officer arrested her. There was no doubt about the perpetrator, but had the crime been committed in cold blood? Ellis admitted her guilt on the night of her arrest, adding: 'I am confused.' Unfortunately for her, the ability of the defence to cite a disturbed state of mind during the commission of murder was far more constrained than it is today. Experts interviewed her and she was also given an ECG examination. They found no evidence of mental illness.

JUNE 22, 1955

Ruth Ellis jealousy appeal?

Mrs. Ruth Ellis turned to a nurse attendant in the dock at the Old Bailey yesterday and smiled as the jury announced their verdict: guilty of murder. That smile was the first sign of emotion the 28-year-old platinum blonde had given during her trial for shooting her lover, David Moffatt Blakely, 25-year-old racing motorist, in a Hampstead street on Easter Sunday. Mr. Justice Havers donned the black cap and spoke the death sentence. Before she walked calm and unassisted from the dock, Mrs. Ellis heard him say: "The jury have convicted you of murder. In my view it was the only verdict possible."

Permission was given for her father, Mr. Neilson, to see her in the cells before she was taken to Holloway Jail. Mr. Neilson and Mrs. Ellis's mother are caretakers of a block of Hampstead service flats.

Mrs. Ellis's legal advisers were last night considering the possibility of an appeal on a new point of law - that of provocation brought on by jealousy. It was the only defence offered by her lawyers, who asked for a verdict of manslaughter. The appeal, on the grounds that a woman thwarted in love is more irresponsible than a man, could be taken to the House of Lords. It is the first time that such a point of law has been offered in a murder trial.

> 'The jury have convicted you of murder. In my view it was the only possible verdict.'

ABOVE: Ruth Ellis with David Blakely, whom she shot outside a pub in Hampstead on Easter Sunday, 1955.

LEFT: The newspaper headline the day of Ruth Ellis' execution. Despite pleas from family and friends Ellis had refused to talk about the events leading up to the shooting. The day before the execution she changed her mind and claimed that another man had given her the gun, loaded it and driven her to the scene of the crime.

Not guilty plea

Ellis pleaded Not Guilty when she appeared at the Old Bailey, though by the time the jury retired, she had sealed her own fate. Defence counsel Melford Stevenson had wanted to focus on the provocation angle, telling the court that Ellis was 'driven to a frenzy which for the time being unseated her understanding'. He called a psychologist, who testified that women faced with infidelity tended to show impaired judgment to a greater extent than men in the same situation. She loved and hated Blakely at the same time; her mind was in a state of turmoil, a problem she resorted to the gun to solve. Stevenson hoped to persuade the jury that Ellis was of unsound mind when the crime was committed, and that manslaughter was, therefore, the appropriate charge.

The presiding judge, Sir Cecil Havers, was having none of that. He gave the jury no leeway in the matter by issuing the following ruling: '…where the question arises whether what would otherwise be murder may be reduced to manslaughter on the grounds of provocation, if there is no sufficient material, even upon a view of the evidence most favourable to the accused, that a reasonable person could be driven by transport of passion and loss of control to use violence and a continuance of violence, it is the duty of the judge, as a matter of law, to direct the jury that the evidence does not support a verdict of manslaughter. I have been constrained to rule in this case that there is not sufficient material… to reduce this killing from murder to manslaughter on the grounds of provocation.'

Havers said that if he had ruled in error, it would be rectified on appeal, but for now the jury was unable to return a manslaughter verdict.

'I intended to kill him'

Stevenson's hands were tied. He was undone by his own client who, in answer to a question from prosecutor Christmas Humphreys regarding intent, replied: 'It is obvious that when I shot him I intended to kill him'. Ellis had been caught with a smoking gun, admitted intent and, with manslaughter ruled out, Stevenson knew that the game was up. He declined to make further comment to the jury, for he decided he could make no worthwhile closing argument without contravening the judge's ruling. Humphreys chose not to make any closing remarks either to maintain equilibrium, though that was hardly too gracious an act since the outcome could only be in his favour.

The jury retired with the judge's solemn words ringing in their ears. 'I am bound to tell you this, that even if you accept every word of Mrs Ellis's evidence, there does not seem to be anything in it which establishes any sort of defence to the charge of murder.' It took just twenty minutes to return a Guilty verdict.

'It is obvious that when I shot him I intended to kill him.'

'A life for a life'

Ellis showed little inclination to appeal, calmly accepting the axiomatic wisdom of 'a life for a life'. It was left to others to take up the cudgels on her behalf and petition for a reprieve. In some ways that was strange, since it appeared to be a watertight with no obvious reason why she shouldn't follow the fifteen other women who had gone to the gallows since the turn of the century. The dissenting voices were up against it, for a pro-capital punishment Conservative Party had just been returned to office. The pleas for clemency fell upon the deaf ears of Home Secretary Gwilym Lloyd-George. Crowds gathered outside Holloway Prison, some chanting the names of Evans and Bentley before police restored order. They couldn't save Ruth Ellis, who was hanged on 13 July 1955. She was 28.

ABOVE: Ruth Ellis took on low level modelling work to make ends meet. Through this she became a nightclub hostess, which paid significantly more than the various waitress, factory and clerical jobs she had had since leaving school.

LEFT: David Blakely was a well-mannered former public school boy, but also a hard-drinking racing driver with expensive tastes.

OPPOSITE PAGE: Ruth Ellis was hanged on 13 July 1955 at Holloway prison. In 2003 Ellis's family members tried to have the conviction reduced to manslaughter on the grounds of severe provocation but their claims were rejected by the Court of Appeal.

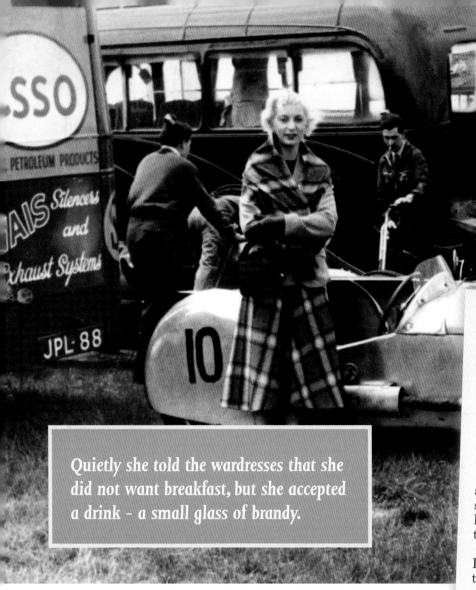

> Quietly she told the wardresses that she did not want breakfast, but she accepted a drink - a small glass of brandy.

JULY 14, 1955

'She died a brave woman'

In Holloway Prison last night the staff were saying that Ruth Ellis was the bravest woman ever to go to the gallows in Britain. For the 28-year-old mother who, eight hours before her execution, had broken down and pleaded for life, died calmly.

The emotion was all outside the prison walls. By 9 a.m. – the time of the execution – a crowd thousands strong surged behind a massive police cordon. By then Ruth Ellis had resigned herself to death. She was tranquil.

On her execution eve she had read a little from her Bible. Just before midnight she had said goodnight to the wardresses with her and composed herself for sleep – the deep sleep of exhaustion.

Refused breakfast

At 8.15 a.m. yesterday, while the crowd wept, prayed, and peered at the prison gates, she was roused by a gentle touch on the shoulder. Quietly she told the wardresses that she did not want breakfast, but she accepted a drink - a small glass of brandy.

At one minute to nine, while a street musician outside the walls played Bach's "Be Thou With Me When I Die," the prison governor, Dr. Charity Taylor, and the hangman entered her cell. With them were two men warders taken from duty at the prison gates, a wardress, the prison medical officer, and the chaplain. Of the women Ruth Ellis was the most composed.

In the silence outside the walls a radio somewhere intoned the chimes of Big Ben. A man threw the torn-up shreds of a newspaper in the air and shouted: "Another murder."

Abolition of capital punishment

The Ellis case was an important staging post on the road towards the abolition of capital punishment, though there were many struggles ahead for those wanted the ultimate sanction removed from the statute book. A year after Ellis's execution, the abolitionists went down by 143 votes in Parliament. Change was on the way, however, and in 1957 the concept of diminished responsibility officially became part of a defence counsel's armoury. Before then, provocation leading to retaliation 'in hot blood' was acceptable as a form of mitigation, but that didn't apply in the case of Ruth Ellis, hence the judge's ruling. The case was instrumental in widening the parameters in which the perpetrator's state of mind could be taken into account, though it came too late to help Ellis herself.

'Battered woman syndrome'

In 2003 members of the Ellis family tried to get the conviction reduced to manslaughter on grounds of severe provocation. Michael Mansfield QC argued that she had been subjected to numerous assaults, including one blow which caused her to miscarry ten days before the shooting. Ellis was already taking anti-depressants, and now had the loss of a child to contend with. Ellis, it was said, was suffering from 'battered woman syndrome' and should not have been found guilty of a capital offence. The Court of Appeal rejected those claims, stating that Ellis had been convicted in accordance with the law as it stood at the time.

There was a second contentious issue, glossed over during the original trial. Where had Ruth acquired the Smith & Wesson revolver she used on Blakely? On the eve of her execution, she told solicitor Victor Mishcon – who would later be ennobled and act as legal advisor to Princess Diana - that Desmond Cussen had

given her the weapon and taught her how to use it. Cussen even drove her to the Magdala pub, Ruth having told him that she intended to kill Blakely. Cussen had an obvious motive for wanting Blakely, his love rival, out of the way, and discussions took place over the possibility of charging Cussen as an accessory. In the end, those plans were dropped, for with Ellis dead, the case would have been impossible to try. Cussen's alleged involvement didn't help Ruth's cause, either, for it merely highlighted the calculating premeditation that justified a guilty verdict.

Ruth Ellis's body rested in the confines of Holloway Prison for sixteen years, her remains reinterred at St Mary's Church, Amersham when the prison was completely remodelled in 1971. There was no doubt that she was guilty of the crime for which she was tried; whether she received justice is a different matter.

Arthur Albert Jones

DECEMBER 12, 1960

Arc lights gleam through the cold December night... This was the scene last night as a detective searches for clues among the scrub and bracken of Yateley Common, where the body of a 12-year-old Girl Guide was found in a ditch by three boys.

Potential suspects

On Friday 28 October 1960 a young 12-year-old girl from Middlesex called Brenda Nash went missing while on her way home. She was last seen by her friend a mile from her home in Heston, Middlesex at 10pm.

Just weeks earlier an 11-year-old Girl guide, Barbara, had been assaulted in neighbouring Twickenham, also on a Friday night at 10pm, but she was able to give the police a good description of her attacker: plump, round-faced and with a scar on his right cheek; 5ft 8in tall with short dark hair and aged between 30 and 40. The man had posed as a policeman who wanted to question Barbara about her bike at the police station and took her away in his car. After the attack he brought her back almost to her doorstep. Crucially the description of a black Vauxhall narrowed the list of potential suspects. Consequently all owners of black Vauxhalls registered between 1951 and 1954, who lived in Middlesex and Surrey, were asked to account for their movements on the night Brenda disappeared.

28 NOVEMBER 1960

Teams of volunteer skin-divers plunged repeatedly into the cold and treacherous depths of the waterlogged gravel pits in West Middlesex yesterday in a new search for the body of 12-year-old Girl Guide Brenda Nash who disappeared a month ago. It was the biggest mass underwater search ever organised to help the police solve a crime in this country. For six hours 107 divers three of them girls, dived into the murky silt and slime of the extensive gravel pits behind the old Heston Airport and on either side of moor-lane, Staines. The divers, all volunteers, came from the sub-aqua clubs in Chelsea, Ilford, Hounslow, Uxbridge, Croydon and Bromley. Although their hunt did not yield a single clue, they are anxious to continue the underwater search next weekend.

When the divers assembled outside Norwood Green police station in Southall yesterday morning Detective-Superintendent Frederick Hixon, in charge of the search for Brenda, told them "You will find lots of strange things below the surface in these pits. Concentrate on looking for clothing." At times the divers were groping blindly through debris and dangerous silt 20ft below the surface.

TOP: Detectives search for clues among the scrubland of Yateley Common, where the body of 12-year-old Girl Guide Brenda Nash was found in a ditch.

ABOVE: Amateur frogmen from various clubs in South London are seen in the murky waters of the gravel pits at Heston, Middlesex, during the hunt for Brenda Nash. Stretched out along a safety line, one of the search teams checks the equipment before making a first dive.

LEFT: One of the volunteers taking part in the search is 28-year-old diver and mathematician Linden Blake.

DECEMBER 12, 1960

Brenda Nash, was found dead yesterday-44 days after she vanished. Her body was lying huddled at the bottom of a ditch in Yateley, Hampshire, 24 miles from her home in Middlesex. Brenda was still in her Girl Guide uniform. On her shoulders were the flashes of the 5th Heston troop. When the detectives saw them they were able to identify her instantly, and police announced "we are treating this as a case of murder." So ended the countrywide search for the 12-year-old, fairhaired girl who disappeared as she walked to her home in Bleriot Road from a guide meeting on October 28.

Cowboys

The body was found by three young brothers playing cowboys on the common by Yateley village, the sons of accountant Mr John Muir: Alistair, 12, Keith, nine, and Ian five. It was partly covered by dead grass and bracken, only 15ft from a footpath and 20 yards from the main Camberley-Reading road.

Mr Muir said at his home in Vicarage Road last night "Alistair came running home just after 12 o'clock to tell me there was a body on the common. I thought at first he meant the body of a dog or some animal. I went back with him. The other two boys were waiting. I sent them all home at once and telephoned the police."

Last night Scotland Yard experts worked in the soggy ditch under the direction of Detective Superintendent George Salter of the Yard forensic science laboratory. Home Office pathologist Keith Simpson arrived to conduct an on-the-spot examination.

> After the police had interviewed approximately 5,000 owners they had their man: Arthur Albert Jones.

TOP: The search headquarters with police, troops and volunteers set up in Cranford Park.

ABOVE: Detective Sgt Fred Malyon talks to girl guides in Springwell. Thirty detectives visited more than 60 Girl Guide meetings in and around Heston.

ABOVE RIGHT: Drawings made from the description given by Barbara led police to the attacker.

MIDDLE: The type of coat that Brenda was wearing when she disappeared. It was described as a beige coloured swagger coat, single breasted, with a large collar and fur trimmings.

Searching for an alibi

It wasn't until December 11, 44 days after she had vanished, that Brenda Nash's strangled body was found on Yateley Common, Hampshire. The following day a young hairdresser, who worked in London's West End, told police that one of her workmates had mentioned that her uncle had asked her to provide an alibi for the 28 October – the day Brenda Nash disappeared. The uncle turned out to be Arthur Jones. However, Jones was arrested and charged only with the September attack and sentenced to four years imprisonment.

It wasn't until Jones was serving his sentence for the assault, and confided to a prison officer that he had killed Brenda Nash, that the connection was made. Jones was brought back to the high court and tried for murder. Armed with a confession the jury took just seven minutes to find Arthur Jones guilty and this time he was sentenced to life imprisonment.

James Hanratty: The A6 Murders

James Hanratty was hanged for murder on 4 April 1962, one of the last men to be given a capital sentence before that sanction was removed from the statute book. The Hanratty case became a cause celebre as a phalanx of campaigners joined the family's fight to have the verdict overturned.

ABOVE: James Hanratty, the notorious A6 murderer. Hanratty was a professional car thief, convicted of the murder of Michael Gregsten at Deadman's Hill on August 22, 1961.

ABOVE RIGHT: The car that Hanratty hijacked after shooting Gregsten and Storie was found outside Redbridge Underground Station near Ilford.

Over the next forty years, home secretaries of both political hues were exhorted to re-examine the case that resulted in James Hanratty being sent to the gallows. It seemed that scientists had provided the definitive answer when they subjected key evidential artefacts to DNA analysis in 2002. However, the possibility that the samples were contaminated left many still steadfast in their belief that the twenty-one-day court proceedings - at the time the longest murder trial in British history – produced an unsafe conviction.

Tap on the window

The victims of the crime for which Hanratty was executed were 36-year-old physicist Michael Gregsten and 22-year-old laboratory technician Valerie Storie. They were colleagues at the Road Research Laboratory in Slough, and were also lovers. Gregsten was married with two young children, and although his wife knew of the affair, he and Storie had to use discretion to snatch their moments of intimacy.

On the night of 22 August, 1961 the couple were ostensibly planning the route for a staff car rally. After visiting a pub in Taplow, they drove to a lay-by in a cornfield near Maidenhead, where their amorous pursuits were interrupted by a tap on the window of Gregsten's Morris Minor. He wound down the window to find himself staring down the barrel of a handgun. The man pointing the weapon said it was a hold-up and that he was on the run from the law. Initially, he had a handkerchief covering the bottom half of his face, but that was removed when he climbed into the back seat and ordered Gregsten to drive. There followed a circuitous two-hour journey, which included a stop for petrol. With a gun pointing at his back, Gregsten couldn't alert anyone at the service station, though he did try to attract attention by flicking his reversing lights on and off. Some motorists would recall seeing the haphazard flashing, though none thought enough of it at the time to take any action.

Murder then rape

The journey ended some sixty miles away, on a stretch of the A6 near Luton called Deadman's Hill. The gunman ordered Gregsten to pull into a lay-by. He had said he was hungry as he hadn't eaten for some time, but now sleep appeared to be the priority. He said they would be tied up while he rested, and bound Storie's hands to the door handle, though so inexpertly that she claimed she was soon able to free herself. Gregsten then made a sudden movement which panicked the gunman into firing his revolver twice. Both bullets struck Gregsten in the head, almost certainly killing him instantaneously.

Storie was then raped, after which she begged the man to take the car and leave her with Gregsten. He appeared to consent to this and asked her to help in getting Gregsten's body out of the car. He also made her run through the car's controls, and took a small amount of money proffered by Storie. She had caught but a fleeting view of the attacker, when his face was illuminated in the headlights of a passing vehicle, but he wasn't taking any chances. He fired a number of shots, hitting Storie five times. Assuming that he had done for both eyewitnesses, the murderer and rapist drove off in the direction of Luton.

Murder weapon found

It had not been so difficult for Storie to feign death as she had spinal injuries that would leave her paralysed from the waist down. She was very much alive, though she had no idea whether she would survive the night. Storie later said that she thought of using stones to spell out 'blue eyes, brown hair' to help identify the attacker if she didn't make it, but couldn't find any within easy reach. In the event, she had to wait until 6.45 the next morning before a farm worker came to her rescue.

The Morris Minor was found later that day in Ilford, some 40 miles from where the shooting took place. The murder weapon was also soon in police hands. The Enfield .38 revolver that killed Michael Gregsten and maimed Valerie Storie was discovered under the seat of a London bus, along with sixty rounds of ammunition. An identikit picture of the wanted man was produced, based on Storie's fleeting view of the assailant. Apart from that, and the gunman's voice, there was precious little to go on. He had appeared from nowhere and disappeared into the night, having carried out a seemingly random attack.

> The Enfield .38 revolver that killed Michael Gregsten and maimed Valerie Storie was discovered under the seat of a London bus.

AUGUST 24, 1961

Wounded girl lives after A6 shooting

The hunt for the hitchhike killer of the A6 switched to Ilford, Essex, last night. The car that the killer hijacked late on Tuesday night after shooting dead the driver and seriously wounding a girl passenger was found outside Redbridge Underground Station, near Ilford. From Redbridge the Underground runs to Epping in one direction and through London in the other.

The hi-jacking was at Deadman's Hill, near Clophill, Bedfordshire - about 50 miles away. The killer shot down 34-year-old Michael Gregsten - a married man with two children - and 22-year-old Valerie Storie after forcing them to drive 40 miles at gunpoint from the Old Station Inn, Taplow, Buckinghamshire. A quarter of a mile past Clophill he told Gregsten to drive off the main highway into a side-road used as a lay-by. He ordered Gregsten out of the car and pumped five, .38 bullets into him.

Then he forced Miss Storie into the back seat and attempted to assault her. Terrified, she pleaded with him. The gunman ordered her back into the front seat and said: "Tell me how to drive this car. "When she had explained he fired the remaining bullet in his revolver into her chest and pushed her out of the car. He then calmly reloaded, fired another shot at Miss Storie, and drove off with a crash of gears. The couple were found early yesterday.

Last night Miss Storie was still too ill to give a full account of what happened. The wanted man is described as aged about 30, 5ft. 6in., medium build, with deep-set brown eyes, dark hair, and pale-faced; believed to be wearing a dark lounge suit. He speaks with a Cockney accent.

ABOVE: Thirty-six-year-old Michael Gregsten. He and his colleague Valerie Storie were having an affair.

LEFT: Mine detectors were used by the men of the Royal Engineers who were called in to search the scrubland on Deadman's Hill to find the murder weapon.

James Hanratty: The A6 Murders

'Be quiet, will you, I am finking'

A breakthrough came on 11 September, when two spent cartridges that had come from the murder weapon were found in a basement room at the Vienna Hotel, Maida Vale. The room's most recent occupant had been a Mr J Ryan, who gave a Kingsbury address. Police quickly learned that Jim Ryan was an alias used by James Hanratty. Another name in the frame was Peter Alphon, who had also stayed at the hotel under a false name. Hanratty and Alphon were both petty criminals well known to the police, though the latter was a better match for the identikit picture of the wanted man. Alphon gave himself up after being named in a press conference given by police on 22 September, but was ruled out when Storie failed to pick him out of an identity parade two days later. That left Hanratty as the lone suspect, despite the fact that Storie said the assailant was about her height – just over 5 ft 3 ins. Hanratty was 5ft 8 in.

The hunt was now on for James Hanratty, who had suspiciously gone to ground. Realising he was wanted in connection with the A6 murder, Hanratty called Superintendent Basil Acott on 6 October to protest his innocence. He was tracked down to Blackpool, where he was arrested five days later. Valerie Storie had by now been transferred to Stoke Mandeville hospital, where another identification parade was arranged. Once again, she faltered, failing to pick out Hanratty. A second line-up, in which the men paraded before her were told to speak, yielded a positive result. Storie remembered the assailant's poor elocution, notably when he commanded: 'Be quiet, will you, I am finking'. Those words had been uttered when the gunman shot Gregsten and Storie asked if they could get him to a doctor. Now, they were used to indict Hanratty on a murder charge, since he stood out in the 13-man line-up for being unable to pronounce 'th' correctly.

TOP: Gregsten with one of his sons.

BELOW: Police guard the car Hanratty hijacked after attacking Gregsten and Storie on the A6.

LEFT: The .38 revolver that was used to kill Gregsten and injure Storie was left on a London bus. Ballistic experts matched the bullets from the gun on the bus to the marks on the bullets that killed Gregsten.

OPPOSITE TOP RIGHT: Deadman's Hill, near Clop-hill, Bedfordshire , was the scene of the A6 murder. The victim, Michael Gregsten, was in a car with his colleague and lover, Valerie Storie. The two worked together at the Road Research Laboratory in Slough. They were allegedly planning a route for a staff car rally on the day of the murder.

OPPOSITE TOP LEFT: Two pictures of a killer were issued by Scotland Yard. They were built up using the Identikit system. Picture number 1 shows a man with slicked-down hair, thin eyebrows and lips, a sharply chiselled chin, slightly protruding ears and hooded eyes. It was drawn with the help of witnesses whose identities were not revealed. Picture 2 shows a man with dark wavy hair, heavier eye-brows, a thicker nose, fuller lips, and altogether bolder features. It was drawn with the help of Valerie Storie.

OPPOSITE BOTTOM RIGHT: Bernard Daley in the Stevonia café in Blackpool where he served Hanratty with coffee prior to his arrest.

The two minds of a killer

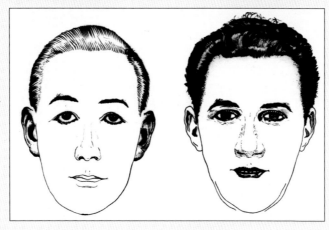

It is just seven days since the A6 gunman murdered Michael Gregsten and shot his friend Valerie Storie through the neck. Seven days in which Scotland Yard's top detectives have been asking themselves: "What kind of man are we hunting?" For this baffling crime does not fit into any known pattern. Was the murderer mad or sane? Was the motive rape, theft, or sadism? Is the man a loner, morbid introvert, likely to be found skulking at home? Or a Teddy Boy-type who loves dicing with danger, and may be haunting the dog tracks in fresh clothes?

Yesterday I went to Harley Street in search of answers to these questions - and found the top psychiatrists equally baffled. One expert on mental health said: "I would say the killer was mad in the legal and medical sense on the night of the murder. My guess is he suffers from paranoid schizophrenia.

Sane

"If so, he is likely to be a closed-in person. He may well be back at his work, apparently normal, but spending most of his leisure at home or in lodgings." Farther along the street I found a consultant in psychiatry at two London hospitals. He said: "I would guess the murderer is sane in the legal sense, but neurotic and unbalanced."

The killer was no ordinary homicidal sex maniac for he first held a gun at his victim's back for 5? hours. He was no ordinary homicidal thief for, offered Gregsten's well-filled wallet, he took only his driving licence, and used the car only to get away from the scene of his crime.

Let us assume for the moment that he is legally sane. Then he must be a stupid man, a braggart, a gambler cruel to the point of sadism. Who but a fool would have left his gun in a bus where it was sure to be found quickly? Who but a braggart would have parked the car near a station with two wheels on the pavement? Who but a gambler would have risked taking his victims to a petrol station?

Mad?

And only a man with a strong cruel streak would have waited 5? hours before killing and assaulting. But even this picture is faulty. A man of this type would surely have pocketed Gregsten's pound notes and given himself away before now by some fresh foolishness. So we are left with the more likely theory - that he is mad. But most madmen kill impulsively, yet he waited hours. Most sex maniacs strangle their victims yet he chose a gun.

The evidence is weighted on the side of the expert who labelled him as a paranoid schizophrenic. What are the chances of his murdering again? According to Harley Street, paranoid schizophrenics seldom kill twice.

But I wouldn't take a bet on that - and neither would Scotland Yard.

Anomalies

The trial opened at Bedford Assizes on 22 January 1962. Hanratty pleaded Not Guilty to the murder of Michael Gregsten, the only charge that was brought. Chief prosecuting counsel Graham Swanwick QC had other witnesses to support Storie's identification of the defendant. John Skillett was on his way to work the morning following the murder when a grey Morris Minor being driven erratically attracted his attention. It skidded and almost collided with him, and when he caught up with the car at a roundabout he wanted to give the driver a piece of his mind. Skillett said he got a clear look at the occupant, whom he identified as Hanratty. A pedestrian named James Trower witnessed the same incident and also identified Hanratty, though a passenger in Skillett's car picked out a different man in two different police line-ups. To cloud the picture further, Hanratty was experienced behind the wheel and therefore hardly likely to have been driving erratically, or, for that matter, to have needed instruction from Storie regarding the controls. Peter Alphon, the man the police eliminated from their enquiries, had not passed his test. This was just one of the anomalies that would lead to accusations that the police tailored the evidence to suit their case.

Another arose when Superintendent Acott took the stand. He testified that during a telephone call he received from Hanratty on 7 October 1961, the latter said he had been in Liverpool when the A6 murder was committed but couldn't name the people who could vouch for him as they were members of the criminal fraternity and didn't want the police brought to their door. Acott said he pressed for the names of the three men, but Hanratty refused to comply, saying he would take a chance on getting out of the bind without providing that information. Defence counsel Michael Sherrard seized upon this, saying that Hanratty had spoken only of 'some friends' who could corroborate his story; there had been no mention of the number of men who could furnish him with an alibi. Sherrard used this to mount a scathing attack on the police's record-keeping. He accused Acott of being selective with the evidence. The charge was that once the investigating team assured themselves that Hanratty was their man, they focused only on evidence which supported that view, ignoring any information that pointed in a different direction. Acott called that a 'disgraceful allegation'.

James Hanratty: The A6 Murders

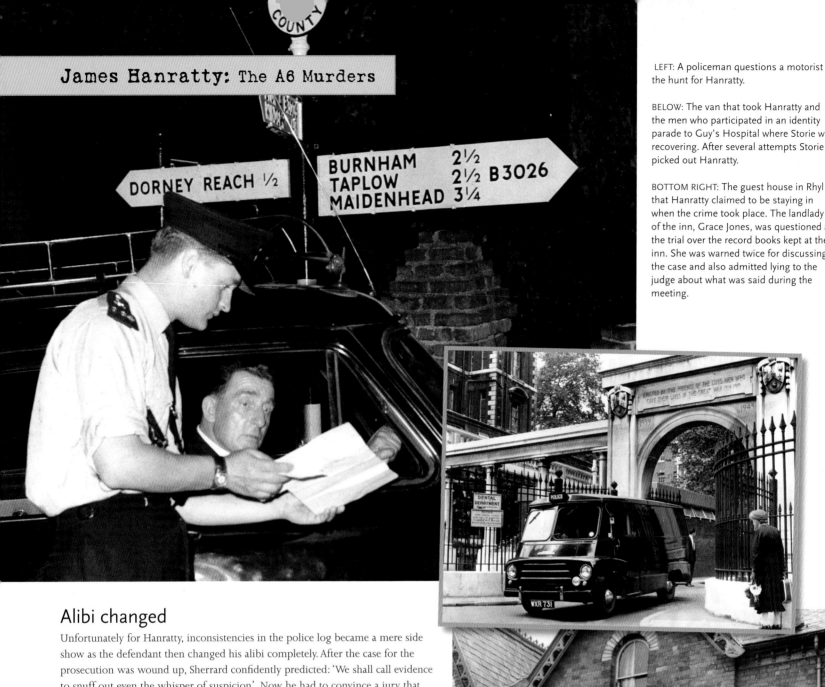

LEFT: A policeman questions a motorist in the hunt for Hanratty.

BELOW: The van that took Hanratty and the men who participated in an identity parade to Guy's Hospital where Storie was recovering. After several attempts Storie picked out Hanratty.

BOTTOM RIGHT: The guest house in Rhyl that Hanratty claimed to be staying in when the crime took place. The landlady of the inn, Grace Jones, was questioned at the trial over the record books kept at the inn. She was warned twice for discussing the case and also admitted lying to the judge about what was said during the meeting.

Alibi changed

Unfortunately for Hanratty, inconsistencies in the police log became a mere side show as the defendant then changed his alibi completely. After the case for the prosecution was wound up, Sherrard confidently predicted: 'We shall call evidence to snuff out even the whisper of suspicion'. Now he had to convince a jury that had just learned that the defendant's first alibi was total fabrication.

Hanratty went into the witness box to explain the dramatic volte-face regarding his whereabouts at the critical time. He testified that he was staying at a boarding house in Rhyl at the time of the murder, though he couldn't recall the exact location of the establishment or anyone there who might vouch for him. It was the flimsiness of that alibi that persuaded him to invent the story he recounted to the police. Hanratty said he spent the night of 21 August at the Vienna Hotel, travelling to Liverpool by train the following day. The purpose of the trip was to sell on some of the proceeds from burglaries he had recently committed. He recalled having a conversation with a woman in a sweet shop over directions, an incident to which a Mrs Olive Dinwoodie would give corroborating testimony. He claimed that he took a bus to Rhyl that evening, hoping to see a friend called Terry Evans. He returned to Liverpool on Thursday 24 August and was back in the capital early the following day.

> He testified that he was staying at a boarding house in Rhyl at the time of the murder, though he couldn't recall the exact location of the establishment or anyone there who might vouch for him.

'Perfect gentleman'

The hunt to locate the Rhyl guest house was on. Hanratty's recollection of a green bathroom in the attic led the police to Ingledene, an establishment in Kinmel Street. Landlady Grace Jones said that Hanratty had lodged with her during the week Aug 19-26. During cross-examination the prosecution elicited that Jones kept no records of guests who stayed just for a night or two, and thus could not be sure exactly when Hanratty resided at Ingledene. Swanwick said that Jones's testimony was not only unreliable, but suggested that she might be trying to drum up trade by using the trial as a ghoulish form of advertising.

Of Hanratty's changed story, Swanwick said that one of the hallmarks of a false alibi was when it was belatedly conceived. He accused Hanratty of substituting one set of lies for another. Swanwick also got Mrs Dinwoodie to concede that Hanratty merely looked like the man who had come into the Liverpool sweet shop. Hanratty countered by saying that the perpetrator of the A6 murder was "a savage", something that was not part of his make-up. 'I try to live a respectable life, apart from my housebreaking', he insisted. Defence counsel didn't try to downplay his client's misdemeanours, but made sure the jury was aware that none of his previous convictions were for sex crimes or crimes of violence. He wanted to stress that Hanratty was a thief, not a murderer or rapist. A former girlfriend was called as a character witness, and she testified that he always behaved like a perfect gentleman towards her. Michael Sherrard pressed home the point: even if Hanratty made up his first alibi, it didn't make him a murderer.

FEBRUARY 19, 1962

Sentenced to die

James Hanratty will be escorted from the condemned cell at Bedford Prison today to begin a second fight for his life. "Ginger Jim," 25-year-old convicted killer, will walk 75 paces past cells containing the jail's 178 other prisoners, to a distempered interview room. Across a scrubbed oak table he will confer with members of his legal team who are planning the appeal against his death sentence. Waiting for the report on the prison talks will be Michael Sherrard, 34, the defence counsel who almost collapsed in the stuffy, over-crowded Shire Hall court-room on Saturday night when the 11-man jury pronounced their verdict.

Hanratty - cocky, illiterate petty thief convicted of murdering Michael Gregsten, 36-year-old physicist last August, was whisked away from the court building minutes after stammering out from the dock: "I will appeal." Only a nervous licking of the lips revealed the tension he had undergone during the 21-day trial. Only once had the small-time crook who wanted to be big lost his nerve. In the cells below the court his temper flared. He slammed a door, nearly jamming the hand of a following warder. Then Hanratty was taken to the cell at Bedford Prison, where once Stanley Rouse, the blazing car murderer of the 30s had awaited execution. And there Ginger Jim, who had vowed to be a big criminal when the underworld labelled him "tea leaf" - a petty thief - broke down. He wept.

She just nodded

Forty miles away, at the same time, a nurse tip-toed through a soft-lit public ward at Stoke Mandeville Hospital, Buckinghamshire, and whispered the news of the verdict to 23-year-old Valerie Storie, who was raped and shot on Deadman's Hill. Valerie, now paralysed from the waist down, had fought off sleep that night to hear the result of Hanratty's trial; she just nodded. Then she slept. Soon she will be allowed out from the hospital to start work again at the offices where she met and became fond of Michael Gregsten. For her it will be the start of a new life.

Death sentence

The jury was out for almost ten hours before returning a Guilty verdict. Mr Justice Gorman passed a death sentence, which the Appeal Court found no reason to overturn or commute. Home Secretary Rab Butler took the same line, finding no grounds to grant a reprieve. James Hanratty was hanged at Bedford Prison on 4 April 1962. He was twenty-five years old.

The crusade to clear Hanratty's name began almost immediately. Over a dozen witnesses eventually came forward to place Hanratty in the north-west at the critical time. The Hanratty family argued that the police were less than assiduous in checking the second alibi, and even tried to sue Lord Butler for a breach of public duty in 1970. The suit was thrown out. Three years earlier, in May 1967, Peter Alphon had given a press conference in Paris in which he publicly confessed to the being the A6 murderer. The suggestion was that he had been paid by family members of the 'wronged' woman – Gregsten's wife – to give the couple a fright. It was a credible motive, something lacking in the case against Hanratty, and an unexplained £5,000 credit to Alphon's bank account seemed to add weight to the 'hired muscle' theory. Alphon subsequently retracted his statement, though that may have been born of fear that he might have faced criminal charges.

TOP LEFT: The Stevonia café in Blackpool where Hanratty was picked up by the police.

LEFT: The bill for the show at the Queen's Theatre that Hanratty supposedly went to see on the evening of his arrest. Two Blackpool detectives, making routine checks on teenage night haunts, found a man in a café who answered to the description of the A6 men that had been circulated by Scotland Yard.

MARCH 19, 1962

Father of Hanratty wants 250,000 to sign mercy petition

Mr. Hanratty, of Sycamore Grove, Kingsbury, London, NW, has left his window-cleaning business "until my son is reprieved". He is convinced of his innocence. Yesterday he said: "It is amazing the way people have responded. By the end of this week I expect to have at least 150,000 signatures. We have got people assisting all over Britain. "Not only that. Hundreds of people have written to us saying they are convinced of my son's innocence. Yet not one letter has said they think he was guilty."

Hanratty, due to hang on April 4, will be examined at Bedford Jail this week by medical and psychiatric experts, who are compiling a dossier which will be placed before Mr. R. A. Butler, the Home Secretary. Mr. Butler has already been sent a diagnosis from the St. Francis Hospital, Haywards Heath, Sussex, where Hanratty was admitted in 1952. At the hospital an exploratory brain operation was carried out. His brain appeared to be physically normal but, possibly on psychiatric grounds, Hanratty was diagnosed as mentally defective. This evidence, which was sent by the hospital to Brixton Jail two days after his arrest, has been in the possession of the police and his legal advisers.

LEFT: Hanratty is taken from Blackpool police station to Bedford police headquarters.

TOP LEFT: Hanratty was hanged on 4 April, 1962 at Bedford Prison. The crusade to clear his name began almost immediately

ABOVE AND OPPOSITE BOTTOM: Hanratty's perceived injustice attracted a huge following. John Lennon and Yoko Ono were among those helping Hanratty's father clear his son's name.

DNA samples

The Hanratty family finally got their wish in 1999, when the case was referred to the Court of Appeal. Hanratty's mother and brother provided DNA samples which were a match for material found on two exhibits: a handkerchief used to wrap the gun and an item of Valerie Storie's underwear. The odds against the DNA coming from anyone other than a member of the Hanratty family were estimated to be 2.5 million to one, and those findings were confirmed when Hanratty's body was exhumed and subjected to a DNA test in 2001.

Lord Chief Justice Lord Woolf said that the scientific analysis 'made what was a strong case even stronger' and ruled that the conviction was safe. Valerie Storie issued a statement saying that the tests proved what she had always maintained: that James Hanratty was the man who shot her and Michael Gregsten on the night of 22 August 1961.

It should have laid the matter to rest, but the Hanratty family were unmoved. They insisted that the evidence was contaminated. The very fact that forensics experts in the early sixties would have had no idea of the techniques that would be developed over the next forty years meant that they took little care when it came to handling exhibits. Geoffrey Bindman, the Hanratty family's legal representative, pointed out that exhibits were regularly transported in the same box, and were freely handled by any number of parties during storage and in court. It was a 'logical impossibility,' he said, that such potentially flawed evidence could be used to ascertain guilt. The DNA traces tying Hanratty to the murder were so microscopic, it was argued, they could easily have been the result of cross-contamination. The scientists, in turn, had their own rebuttal at the ready. If Hanratty's DNA had been transferred to the exhibits at a later date, the killer's DNA should have been on the material tested. No other DNA was found.

Element of doubt

While the scientific debate raged, it still left open the issue of how the police conducted their investigations. In other words, even if Hanratty were the perpetrator, there remained the question of procedural anomalies that left open to question whether he got a fair trial. Michael Mansfield QC, acting on behalf of the Hanratty family, said the police mishandled the case and the evidence that secured the conviction was 'fatally flawed'. Detective Superintendent Acott, who had since died, was singled out for particular criticism.

The balance of probability suggests that James Hanratty was indeed guilty of the crime for which he was hanged in 1962, though procedural irregularities and the possibility of the DNA test being compromised admit an element of doubt which his supporters continue to highlight.

APRIL 5, 1962

Jail stays quiet as Hanratty is executed

James Hanratty was hanged at Bedford Prison yesterday, for the A6 murder of physicist Michael Gregsten. There was no trouble inside the prison - no demonstration from the other prisoners. Nearly 200 people were outside the jail gates at 8 p.m., the time Hanratty was due to be executed. Three Oxford students had paraded for eight hours with banners reading: "End Legalised Murder," "No to Hanging," and "Hanging Is No Answer."

No notice was posted on the gates, but at 8.10 a.m. police started to disperse the crowd. Mr. Raymond Miles, 37, of Coombes Close, Bedford, placed a bunch of flowers at the prison entrance. A card with them said: "These flowers are for James Hanratty, who, like Evans and Bentley, has been murdered by our so-called civilised State." Shortly before Hanratty died he wrote to his mother, who is 45 on Friday.

TOP LEFT: An anonymous letter was sent to the editor of the *Yorkshire Evening News* in Leeds stating that Hanratty was innocent. The anonymous writer claimed responsibility for the A6 and the A9 murders.

TOP RIGHT AND TOP MIDDLE: Hanratty's father proceeded to protest his son's innocence even after his death. He is pictured staging a vigil outside the House of Commons and presenting a petition at 10 Downing Street as he pressed for a further enquiry.

Albert Henry DeSalvo: The Boston Strangler

Was it DeSalvo or not? The Strangler case that was never closed.

Albert Henry DeSalvo was born on September 3, 1931 in Chelsea, Massachusetts – a city just over the river from Boston – the son of Frank and Charlotte.

DeSalvo's father was a thoroughly unpleasant man who drank to excess and was often violent and abusive, and even before he reached his teens the youngster had been in trouble with the law many times. Although he was of average intelligence he did very poorly at school, but he later enlisted in the army, where he did well and was honourably discharged.

In October 1964, a man gained entrance to the home of a young woman in Boston by posing as a police officer. Once inside he tied her to a bed and sexually assaulted her, before apologizing and leaving. The police quickly recognized DeSalvo from the victim's description and he was arrested and charged with rape. As soon as his description was made public, many other women came forward claiming that DeSalvo had also attacked them and he was held in prison while charges were investigated. While there he confided to his cellmate, George Nassar, that he was really the infamous Boston Strangler.

TOP: Police capture DeSalvo in Lynn, Massachusetts, after he escaped from the mental hospital in which he was being detained. He admitted to strangling 13 women in the Boston area.

ABOVE: DeSalvo was the son of an abusive father who had been in trouble with the law countless times during his teens.

The profilers now decided that the killer was around thirty, of Mediterranean descent and a paranoid schizophrenic.

The first attack

The Boston Strangler had raped and murdered 13 women in and around Boston over the previous two years. The first attack was in June 1962 – a 55-year-old woman named Anna Slesers was found dead in her home in Boston; she had been sexually molested and strangled with the cord from her own bath robe. There were no signs of forced entry, so it was assumed she had known her attacker. A string of similar murders followed – there were another five throughout that year, all older women, all assaulted and most of them strangled in their own homes with items of their clothing. After the fourth murder, forensic profilers described the killer as being a fairly young man who hated his mother and had delusions of persecution.

However, in December 1962 the killer had abruptly changed track: the seventh victim, Sophie Clark, was only 19 and the eighth – found just under four weeks later, was 23. The profilers now decided that the killer was around thirty, of Mediterranean descent and a paranoid schizophrenic – a description that did fit DeSalvo. The next five victims included two older women and three much younger ones, and two of them were stabbed, not strangled, so by the beginning of 1964 the police had come to believe that the murders were probably the work of at least two killers. The last victim is generally accepted to be Mary Sullivan, a 19-year-old whose body was found early in January 1964, but several other women were strangled in Boston after her.

Murdered in prison

When interviewed after his confession DeSalvo knew details about the killings that had not been made public, but there were also a great many errors in his story. There was also no physical evidence tying him to any of the crimes. He was never charged or tried for any of the murders – he was imprisoned for life on charges of rape and robbery – and there is still considerable doubt that he was ever the Boston Strangler. In November 1973 he was murdered in the prison infirmary, and his killers have never been identified.

ABOVE LEFT: DeSalvo possessed information about the killings in Boston that had not been made public. However, there was no physical evidence tying him to the crimes and he was convicted and sentenced to life for rape and robbery but not for murder.

ABOVE: The cell in Bridgewater State Hospital that DeSalvo escaped from in February 1967.

TOP RIGHT: The quiet streets of Boston in early 1960s. Without any sign of forced entry into their dwellings, the women were assumed to have either known their assailant or have voluntarily allowed him into their homes.

The Great Train Robbery

'Let us clear out of the way any romantic notions of daredevilry. This is nothing less than a sordid crime of violence which was inspired by vast greed.' With that trenchant remark, delivered during the 1964 trial of the Great Train Robbers, Mr Justice Edmund Davies tried to dispel the myth that theirs had been a victimless caper and that they were deserving of the folk hero status they had been accorded by large swathes of the population.

Neither the judge's remarks nor the severe sentences he handed down had much effect on the public perception of the Great Train Robbery. It became a byword for Robin Hood-style criminality, and so captured the imagination that it was still making headlines forty years after the felony took place.

Shipment of used bank notes

The thieves' target was the Glasgow to London mail train. This service had been running for well over a century, and it was said that no successful robbery had been carried out in transit during that time. A gang of London-based criminals, most of them well known to the police, aimed to change that on the night of 7-8 August 1963.

The train left Glasgow at 6.50 pm, due at Euston just before 4 o'clock the following morning. There were no passengers aboard, just some seventy Post Office employees spread throughout the carriages engaged in sorting work during the nine-hour journey. The configuration of the carriages was critical. The diesel locomotive, manned by driver Jack Mills and fireman David Whitby, was pulling a baggage wagon and eleven mail coaches. It was the first of the mail coaches in which the gang was interested, for it contained the high-value registered mail consignment, including a large shipment of used banknotes. The recent bank holiday weekend made for even richer pickings than usual. It was common knowledge that the valuable packages were transported in that section of the train, and although it was governed by extra security measures, it gave the would-be thieves an important advantage when it came to planning the robbery.

FAR RIGHT: After being stopped, the diesel engine pulling two Post Office carriages was driven a mile down the track to Bridego Bridge where the robbers' haul was loaded onto trucks that had been waiting nearby.

RIGHT: The gang had tampered with a signal further up the line creating a false light, forcing the driver to come to a halt.

ABOVE: The stricken train was under tight police protection after being taken to Euston Station for further examination.

Diagram labels:
SEARS CROSSING. SIGNAL FAKED AT RED
TO LEIGHTON BUZZARD
TO TRING
TO LONDON
GANG'S LORRY PARKED HERE
ESCAPE ROAD
DRIVER FORCED TO BRING TRAIN HERE
RAILWAYMEN'S CAPS STOLEN FROM THIS HUT
TO CHEDDINGTON STATION
BRIDEGO BRIDGE

> Mills would be honoured for his courageous conduct and awarded 25 guineas, scant compensation for being left unable to work again.

Train halted

Just after 3.00 am the train reached Sears Crossing, near Cheddington, Buckinghamshire. Jack Mills spotted an amber light, warning him to proceed with caution, and he brought the train to a halt when he reached a red signal a little further on. What he did not realise was that the gang had rigged the lights, obscuring the green signal with a glove and using batteries to power the amber and red lamps that had prompted his reaction. Thieves had halted trains using these methods before, but the size and scale of this operation put it in a league of its own.

David Whitby left the engine compartment to use the trackside phone and try and establish the cause of the fault. Immediately he noticed that the wire had been cut, and was on his way back to inform Mills when he was overpowered by balaclava-wearing gang members. Mills himself resisted, battling with robbers on the footplate until he was clubbed with an iron bar, an assault that left him bleeding profusely from a head wound. Those who would romanticise a robbery carried out without the use of guns glossed over the vicious attack that left Jack Mills with permanent physical and psychological scars.

The engine and first two carriages were uncoupled and driven about a mile down the track to Bridego bridge. One of the gang members had been recruited for his train driving experience, but he failed to get to grips with this particular engine and so the injured Mills was pressed into service. The 58-year-old driver was able to furnish the police with little useful information, remarking on the slickness of the military-style operation. No orders were given; the gang members knew their jobs and carried them out efficiently. Mills would be honoured for his courageous conduct and awarded 25 guineas, scant compensation for being left unable to work again. He was living in straitened circumstances when leukaemia claimed his life in 1970.

SEPTEMBER 5, 1963

'If you shout I will kill you'

At 3.02 a.m. 57-year-old driver Mills slackened speed from 80 m.p.h. to obey the fake amber signal. Slowly he approached the red. The sorters in the two locked coaches were busy with hundreds of mailbags scooped from gantries alongside the line. They were unaware, even when the train stopped, that they were ambushed and that the two leading coaches had been uncoupled. At 3.05 a.m. Driver Mills halted his diesel engine. Fireman David Whitby, 26, takes up the story: 'I got down to go to the telephone at the signal. I found the wires had been cut. I went back to tell my driver.

As I did so I saw a man between the second and third coach.

It was then that one of the men carrying the flags came up to me. I said: "What's up, mate?" He walked across the line and said: "Come here." Suddenly he pushed me down the bank. Another man grabbed me, put his hand over my mouth and said: "If you shout I will kill you." I told him I would not shout. He took me back to the engine where I found they had coshed my mate. They put one handcuff on me and held the other end while they made my driver go forward to Sears Crossing. When we stopped the other handcuff was put on my mate. They made us get out of the engine and lie down by the side of the rail while they fought their way into the second coach. When they had finished unloading all the bags they put us with the G.P.O. men in the second coach. They told us to wait for half an hour and then left. The G.P.O. men had tried to stop them getting into their van but they broke in. We sat there until a guard came down the line from the ten uncoupled coaches.

ABOVE LEFT: A diagram clearly shows the stretch of line where the Glasgow-Euston mail train was held up.

ABOVE LEFT (INSET): A makeshift marker propped up beside a wheelbarrow showed gang members aboard the train the planned stopping point by the bridge.

ABOVE: Leatherslade Farm in Oakley, Buckinghamshire, had been chosen as the gang's hide-out after the robbery. Police swiftly located the property after John Maris, a local herdsman, had provided a tip-off after noticing strange activity around the building.

The Great Train Robbery

The gang formed a human chain to transfer the booty into a waiting lorry, and the travelling post office was quickly relieved of 120 packages, containing £2.6 million.

'Up special' attacked

At Bridego bridge the gang launched their attack on the registered mail carriage. Under normal circumstances this had to be opened by staff on the inside in response to a coded signal from the person without. That security mechanism counted for little against an onslaught of axes and sledgehammers. The four Post Office employees made a half-hearted attempt to barricade themselves in but it merely caused a short delay to the inevitable outcome. The gang formed a human chain to transfer the booty into a waiting lorry, and the travelling post office known as the 'Up Special' was quickly relieved of 120 packages, containing £2.6 million. Mills and Whitby were bundled into the security van with the four Post Office workers and told not to move for half an hour. The lorry disappeared into the night, the operation having gone like clockwork. Or so it seemed.

It had taken some time for the occupants of the uncoupled section of the train to realise why they had ground to a halt. When the penny dropped, a guard from those rearward carriages set off up the line towards Cheddington, for there was no means of communication available to him. He met up with staff from the forward carriages, and together they managed to stop a passing train and get a ride to Cheddington, when the alarm was finally raised. It was 4.15 am when the police were alerted to the audacious robbery, the biggest cash haul in the country's history.

AUGUST 14, 1963

The search of Leatherslade Farm at Oakley, Buckinghamshire - where since last Thursday the raiders had sorted and hidden their £2½ million loot - may take 3 days.

A telephone tip yesterday morning sent the Yard team, headed by Commander George Hatherill, racing to the farm - only hours after lorries and cars had been heard driving away early yesterday. And last night Mr. John Alfred Maris said he had seen lorries parked at the farm and had twice telephoned to Aylesbury police - first on Monday morning and again yesterday. Mr. Maris, a 33-year-old herdsman who lives less than a mile from Leatherslade, is the first claimant to part of the £260,000 reward. The garage was padlocked I had become suspicious about the house being sold because the property had been on the market for six months and suddenly it had changed hands overnight. I had never seen any visitors there or anybody who looked like a prospective buyer.

MIDDLE AND TOP LEFT: Over twenty members of Scotland Yard, including forensic scientists, prepare to search the farm. Several fingerprints were found and some of the gang's phone numbers were scribbled on the walls.

RIGHT MIDDLE: Only a few days after the robbery three men left a special court in Linslade, hiding their faces under blankets. William Boal and Roger Cordrey, the first two members of the gang to be arrested, were tracked down in Bournemouth after using some of the notes from the heist in a spending spree in the town. The third man was Alfred Pilgrim, who along with his wife Mary, was charged with receiving £860.

FAR RIGHT: An upright spade was found in front of the farm. It appeared the thieves had been digging a hole to burn the empty mail bags.

TOP RIGHT: Children play outside the post office in Oakley. This sleepy village was suddenly the centre of attention of the national media.

RIGHT: Robert Monteith, the local farmer who employed John Maris, voices his anger to the press. Roger Cooke, Member of Parliament for Twickenham, had accused locals of not doing enough to help catch the gang, bringing cries of protest from residents.

> The hideout, some twenty-five miles from the scene of the crime, was soon discovered after a local man reported suspicious movements.

AUGUST 9, 1963

Yard was given tape warning

How and why did the Great Train Robbery succeed? Mr. Reginald Bevins, Postmaster-General, cut short his holiday and flew to London last night to get the answers. Mr. Bevins put the haul of old banknotes and valuables at about £1 million - incredible enough. But Scotland Yard chiefs believe it reached the fantastic total of £3 million. Amazingly, the Yard had known for weeks that a mail train was to be robbed, probably "somewhere in Bucks." Yet this colossal sum travelled the length of England with no special security guard. On board the 12-coach Post Office mail train from Glasgow to Euston, apart from the driver and his mate, were some 70 unarmed sorters, working non-stop. All this and every other possible detail about the train, its load, the ambush spot and escape routes, were known to the man with the Midas touch who planned the raid.

Hideout discovered

Initially, there were few leads. The handcuffs that had been used to shackle Mills and Whitby were made by a Birmingham firm that kept a record of all its sales, but soon there were more fruitful lines of enquiry. The police assumed that the gang would have holed up somewhere not too far from the scene of the crime, for they would have been fearful of being out on the public highways once the news broke. It was a correct assumption, and the hideout, some twenty-five miles from the scene of the crime, was soon discovered after a local man reported suspicious movements. Not soon enough to apprehend any of the villains, but Leatherslade Farm, situated a few miles west of Aylesbury near the village of Brill, gave up enough clues to put the law on the scent of the villains. There were discarded mailbags, banknote wrappers and three abandoned vehicles. It was clear that the perpetrators had divided the spoils and made off in less conspicuous modes of transport. Attempts to obliterate finger and palmprints were woefully inadequate. The gang had even handed a gift to the forensics team with a print-laden Monopoly board, obviously used to while away the downtime during the planning stage. It was a colossal own-goal, considering that the men had a string of convictions and were well known to the capital's constabulary. And as if that weren't enough, the phone numbers of some of the men were found scrawled on a wall, including that of architect-in-chief Bruce Reynolds.

TOP LEFT: Boal and Cordrey were driven away from court as officers across the country continued to search for the rest of the gang members.

MIDDLE RIGHT: Rene Boal, charged with receiving £70 of the proceeds, and Mary Pilgrim, their heads protected with a police raincoat, were escorted into court.

RIGHT: Richard James, assistant buyer at a Chiswick garage, sold an Austin Healey sports car for £835 to a man and woman only 36 hours after the robbery. The sum was paid in cash using £5 notes. The lady gave a false name and address and the police rapidly circulated the car registration number throughout the country.

FAR RIGHT: A media frenzy surrounded the accused as they were escorted to and from the court under heavy police guard.

First arrests

On Thursday 15 August, just a week after robbery had taken place, the first arrests were made. Fingerprint evidence wasn't needed to nail Roger Cordrey and William Boal, who sealed their fate by going on a spending spree in Bournemouth. They splashed out wads of cash on a rented flat, three vehicles and a lock-up garage. The elderly widow with the garage to let became suspicious and contacted the police, who arrested Cordrey and Boal after a struggle. Some of the notes used to purchase the vehicles were identified as coming from the mail robbery, and a search of the flat, the garage and the cars revealed suitcases stuffed with money, £141,000 in total.

Fingerprint evidence wasn't needed to nail Roger Cordrey and William Boal, who sealed their fate by going on a spending spree in Bournemouth.

The reaction of the two men was typical of all the miscreants, and a further example of near-comical ineptitude. Under caution, Boal said: 'I am silly to get involved in this. I should have known better', which rather undermined his subsequent denial of any participation in the robbery. His amended story was that Cordrey owed him money and he tagged along on the Bournemouth trip in the hope of being repaid. Cordrey told him the cases contained glass, which he said he had no reason to disbelieve. As for Cordrey, he admitted that the money came from the robbery but denied taking part in the raid. He maintained that he was holding the money for someone he'd met at a race meeting.

THIS PAGE: Gang member James White had taken refuge with his wife in a caravan in Surrey. They had purchased it in cash three days after the robbery. However, realising the police were on their trail, they hid £35,000 behind the panelling in the caravan and in the tyres, then fled from the site. Police systematically took the caravan to pieces, finally locating the cash, while the search for the couple extended to the south coast.

AUGUST 23, 1974

Banknote bonfire

Charred scraps of paper and banknotes snatched by detectives from a bonfire in a London suburban garden were being examined early today by forensic scientists aiding the train robbery hunt. News of the find was telephoned to the home of Britain's top detective, Commander George Hatherill of Scotland Yard.

He ordered the clues gained from the back-garden South London bonfire - still smouldering when detectives found it - to be circulated to police throughout Britain. A Flying Squad team went to the house, a semi-detached home in a side street. They raked over the bonfire and tipped out pieces of charred notes and half-burned documents.

As this discovery was made police all over Britain were stepping up the hunt for two men the Yard wish to interview in connection with the £2,600,000 raid. Scotland Yard gave their names and issued photographs. One is a 6ft. 1in. cleft-chin Cockney, Bruce Richard Reynolds, 41. The other is James E. White, 43, with a Royal Artillery crest tattooed on his right forearm. Both live in London.

A third man named by the Yard, bookmaker Charles Frederick Wilson, 31, of Crescent Lane, Clapham, was charged at Aylesbury, Buckinghamshire, last night with being concerned in the train robbery. He will appear in court at Linslade this morning. Wilson was taken from his home to Cannon Row police station at lunchtime yesterday. His wife, Patricia, and three children stayed at home.

New hunt for 'Buster' Edwards and the Black Rose

Look around you this morning. You may see the couple pictured above. They are Ronald Edwards, 32, and his wife June Rose, 31, known as "Black Rose," whom Scotland Yard detectives investigating the Great Train Robbery would like to interview. The Yard believes the couple may be "not very far from London," with their daughter, Nicolette, two. Their hair may be dyed, but you could still recognise them. Edwards is one of five men police have said they would like to see since the raid at Cheddington, Buckinghamshire, on August 8. There is a substantial reward for information leading to the conviction of the train raiders. The mail robbery hearing will continue at Aylesbury today. Nine people are accused of conspiring to rob the Glasgow-London travelling Post Office and another six are accused of receiving part of the loot. Train trial opens today.

SEPTEMBER 5, 1963

Arrest no. 9

Another man was arrested last night and charged with taking part in the Great Train Robbery. He is Ronald Arthur Biggs, 34-year-old carpenter, of Alpine Road, Redhill Surrey. Police swooped on his small, detached house and turned out cupboards and drawers in the kitchen. Biggs was out, but his wife, Charmian, and sons Nicholas, three, and Christopher, five months, were at home. The detectives waited until he returned. He is the ninth person to be arrested by train raid police, and the fourth to be accused of taking part in the robbery. The other five are accused of receiving.

TOP LEFT: After the search of Leatherslade Farm was complete it was handed back to its owner Bernard Rixon. The robbers had paid a deposit on the property but never completed the purchase. Rixon planned to charge visitors an entry fee for guided tours.

FAR LEFT: The search for the gang was soon extended to Ireland when three men and a woman were seen in Dun Laoghaire freely spending money from a bag filled with £5 notes. After renting a flat for two months in advance, they spent six days there and then disappeared. Clem Furlong (pictured) had hired his Austin 7 to them for £20.

ABOVE LEFT: Mrs Betty Last, a resident of Bournemouth, had witnessed the arrest of Boal and Cordrey outside her house. The police found £100,000 in their cars.

ABOVE AND ABOVE (INSET): Two weeks after the raid police were following further leads and the search for the gang members was extended. Charles Wilson was arrested at his home in Clapham while descriptions of Bruce Reynolds and James White were widely circulated. Reynolds, a motor and antique dealer, had been living in a second-floor flat in Battersea.

FAR LEFT MIDDLE: The search also followed a lead to a house in Oxford where a landlady had rented out two rooms to two men the day after the raid. They had paid from a thick wad of £5 notes. Police believed that the house was used as another base from which to share out the proceeds.

139

One by one the robbers fell into police hands, invariably protesting their innocence despite the wealth of evidence stacked against them.

Nerve centre purchase

Back at Leatherslade Farm, the owner Bernard Rixon told how he had entered into negotiations to sell the property, a tale that would lead three more men into the dock. Brian Field, managing clerk for the London firm of solicitors acting for the proposed sale, had inspected the premises on behalf of the prospective purchaser, accompanied by another man, Leonard Field. The two men weren't related, other than being part of the team assembled to rob the mail train. After the viewing, a ten per cent deposit on the £5,550 purchase price was paid. The Rixons moved out on 29 July, but the balance was never paid, the transaction remaining uncompleted. Brian Field's boss, solicitor John Wheater, was also arrested and charged. The Rixons were soon making plans to turn Leatherslade Farm into a tourist attraction, charging visitors 2/6 for the privilege of seeing the Great Train Robbery's nerve centre.

Twelve apprehended

On 16 August a motorcyclist who pulled in by a wood near Dorking chanced upon four suitcases containing £100,000. In one of the cases there was a hotel receipt for an establishment in Hindelang, Germany, made out to Herr and Frau Field and dated February of that year. Brian Field's fingerprints were found on the case. Five days later, 31-year-old bookmaker Charles Wilson was in custody. His fingerprints had been among those found at the farm, yet he bullishly told police: 'I do not see how you can make it stick without the poppy (the loot) and you won't find that.' He was both right and wrong: the vast majority of the stolen money was never recovered, but that didn't help him to escape conviction.

One by one the robbers fell into police hands, invariably protesting their innocence despite the wealth of evidence stacked against them. By the time the trial opened at Aylesbury Assizes on 20 January 1964, twelve men had been apprehended and came to court facing a range of charges. The others in the dock were Ronald Biggs, James Hussey, Roy James, Thomas Wisbey, Douglas Gordon Goody and Robert Welch. All pleaded Not Guilty, except for Cordrey, who admitted to the charge of conspiring to stop the train – he was the signals expert - and receiving stolen money. His plea of Not Guilty to the robbery charge was accepted by the prosecution.

TOP RIGHT (INSET): The shop window of Bruce Reynold's antique business.

ABOVE RIGHT: Douglas Goody was arrested at the Grand Hotel in Leicester two weeks after the raid. He lived with his mother in Putney, where his fiancée Pat Cooper ran a hairdressing business for him.

TOP LEFT: Police had also managed to trace Reynolds and White to the Grafton Hotel in Bedford. Two men matching their description stayed for one night but had checked out before the police arrived.

ABOVE LEFT: John Daly's house in Sutton, Surrey. He and his wife had bought the house before the heist and filled the property with expensive furniture and gadgets. It appeared that no one had lived there since the robbery had taken place.

TOP RIGHT: James White was finally arrested at Littlestone-on-Sea in Kent, nearly three years later. Using the alias Bob Lane, he had lived in the flat with his wife Sheree and their baby, mixing freely with locals who were totally unaware that he was a wanted man.

LEFT: In December 1963 John Daly was brought in for questioning after being arrested at a flat in Eaton Square, Belgravia, where he and his wife Barbara had been staying with a 'Mrs Grant'. His wife was heavily pregnant with their second child at the time of his capture.

METROPOLITAN POLICE

On the 8th August, 1963, the Glasgow to Euston mail train was robbed of about two and a half million pounds.

Substantial rewards will be paid to persons giving such information as will lead to the apprehension and conviction of the persons responsible.

The assistance of the public is sought to trace the whereabouts of the after described persons:

RONALD EDWARDS alias RONALD CHRISTOPHER EDWARDS, also known as "BUSTER", aged 32, florist club owner, 5ft. 6in., stocky build, complexion fresh, hair dark brown, eyes brown, London accent, scar left of nose and right forearm.

JUNE ROSE EDWARDS, alias ROTHERY, aged 30, 5ft. 5in., hair black. May be accompanied by daughter NICOLETTE, aged about 3 years.

BARBARA MARIA DALY, alias ALLAN, aged 22, 5ft. 1in., hair brown. May be pregnant and accompanied by daughter LORRAINE PATRICIA, aged 1 year. JOHN THOMAS DALY, aged 31, born at New Ross, Eire, antique dealer, 5ft. 11in., complexion fresh, hair dark brown (wavy), eyes blue, scar right of forehead.

BRUCE RICHARD REYNOLDS, alias RAYMOND ETTRIDGE and GEORGE RACHEL, aged 31, born London, motor and antique dealer, 6ft. 1in., complexion fresh, hair light brown, eyes grey, may be wearing horn-rimmed or rimless spectacles, slight cleft in chin, scar left eyelid, cheek and right forearm.

FRANCIS REYNOLDS, aged about 24, 5ft. 2in., slim build, hair brown.

ROY JOHN JAMES, aged 27, born London, silversmith, 5ft. 6in., medium to slim build, complexion fresh, hair light brown, eyes hazel. Is a racing car driver.

JAMES EDWARD WHITE, alias JAMES BRYAN and JAMES EDWARD WHITEFOOT, uses many aliases, aged 43, born Paddington, London, cafe proprietor, 5ft. 10in., slim build, complexion sallow, hair and eyes brown, may wear moustache, Royal Artillery crest tattooed right forearm.

SHEREE WHITE, aged 30 to 35, 5ft. 6in., complexion light coffee-coloured, hair dark brown. May have 6 months old baby and be accompanied by white miniature poodle dog called "GIGI".

Persons having information are asked to telephone WHItehall 1212 or the nearest Police Station.

Final share-out

The Great Train Robbery gang was split up last night - to serve jail terms totalling 307 years. Immediately after Mr. Justice Edmund Davies passed the sentences, the 12 men in the dock were paired off. Each pair was carefully chosen to keep the most dangerous thugs apart. Then manacled and under heavy escort, they were taken to top security jails throughout Britain. They took with them the secret of where more than £2 million of the train-raid cash still is. The total stolen: £2,517,975. Recovered so far: Nearly £260,000 And they left behind their families, including 15 sons and daughters aged 15 months to 21 years.

Strain

Seven of them were jailed for 30 years - the longest sentences of the century apart from the 62 years imposed on Russian spy George Blake. Two faced 25 years, one 24, another 20, and one three years. One by one they were brought into the dock of the assize court at Aylesbury to face the judge. His voice betrayed the tremendous strain he was under as he took just 28 minutes to impose the 307 years jail. Mr. Justice Edmund Davies said in 1948 when he was Recorder of Swansea: "Stealing from railway vans is becoming a favourite national pastime. I intend to embark with others trying to crush it." The 30-year sentences reflect his hatred of violence and his determination to strip crime of any glamour.

'Stealing from railway vans is becoming a favourite national pastime. I intend to embark with others trying to crush it.'

TOP LEFT: The wanted poster put out by the Metropolitan Police in their attempt to apprehend the gang members.

FAR LEFT: Ronnie Biggs was soon brought in for questioning after his fingerprints were found in the farm.

LEFT: At the trial held in October, John Furnivall gave evidence against Cordery who had purchased a Rover car from him the day after the raid.

LEFT: Janet McIntyre, the receptionist from the Grand Hotel in Leicester, was called to confirm that Douglas Goody had stayed there on August 22. At this stage 18 people were accused of crimes relating to the robbery.

ABOVE: A year after the robbery several people were able to claim rewards that were offered for information about the crime. John Ahern and Esa Hargrave were given £10,000 to share after finding £100,000 in the woods near Dorking, Surrey.

'A diabolical crime'

The all-male jury returned guilty verdicts on all the defendants at the end of the 51-day trial. There was a brief hiatus before sentencing as a technical irregularity meant that Biggs had to be tried separately. After he, too, was convicted, Mr Justice Edmund Davies told the men their fate, creating a stir with the severity of the sentences he handed down. The fact that the accused maintained their innocence and showed no sign of remorse for their misdeeds played very badly the judge, who was in no mood to soft-pedal with the perpetrators of 'a diabolical crime'. Moreover, he pointed out that the lack of co-operation meant that the bulk of the stolen money had not been recovered. That meant that the thieves might be able to enjoy their ill-gotten gains after serving their time, something he was determined should not be in the near future. Biggs, Hussey, James, Wisbey, Goody, Welch and Wilson all received 30 years; Brian Field and Leonard Field 25 years each; William Boal 24 years; Roger Cordrey 20 years. On appeal, Boal and Cordrey's sentences were reduced to 14 years; Brian Field and Leonard Field's terms were cut to five years.

The judge said that John Wheater's case was the saddest. It was accepted that he had no foreknowledge of the crime when he did the conveyancing work on Leatherslade Farm, but he could have volunteered information regarding the purchase that would have helped the police enquiry. He was given three years, but with full remission served 22 months. During his time behind bars he was struck off the roll of solicitors.

> The all-male jury returned guilty verdicts on all the defendants at the end of the 51-day trial.

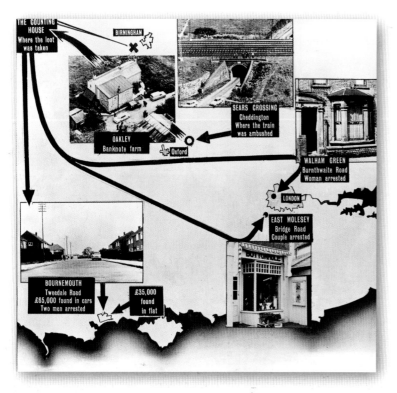

TOP MIDDLE AND TOP RIGHT: In July 1965 Ronnie Biggs (right) and Eric Flower (middle) both escaped from Wandsworth Prison. They had been jailed for 30 years and 12 years respectively.

LEFT: A diagram showing some of the key locations relating to the robbery and the hunt for the perpetrators.

MIDDLE RIGHT: John Daly under tight guard after his arrest in London.

ABOVE: In December 1963, £50,000 of the robbery proceeds were found after an anonymous tip-off. It was dumped in this telephone box in Southwark. There were two bags each weighing three-quarters of a hundredweight. The thieves had obviously decided that it was safer to abandon the money than spend it.

TOP LEFT: Tom Shepherd was another beneficiary of the train robbery rewards.

Fugitives

The trial took place with three gang members still at large: mastermind Bruce Reynolds, Ronald 'Buster' Edwards and Jimmy White. The number of wanted men increased to four on 12 August 1964, when Charles Wilson was sprung from Winson Green Prison in a daring raid. Wilson's liberators had acquired a set of duplicate keys to gain access to the inner doors, and they made good their escape over the 20-foot wall by means of a rope ladder. The fugitive went to ground in a small town 40 miles west of Montreal, where he took up residence with his wife and children. The long arm of the law reached him in January 1968 in the shape of Detective-superintendent Thomas Butler, the Flying Squad officer who led the original investigation. Butler had been tasked with bringing to book the Great Train Robbers still at liberty. His workload was eased when Jimmy White and Buster Edwards turned themselves in in 1966, but two names remained on his hit list. One of those was crossed off in November 1968, when Bruce Reynolds, the brains behind the operation, was tracked down to a villa overlooking Torquay harbour. Butler had been due to retire, having been granted special dispensation to be allowed to continue the hunt for Reynolds. That arrest should have closed the book, but by then another of the incarcerated crew had absconded.

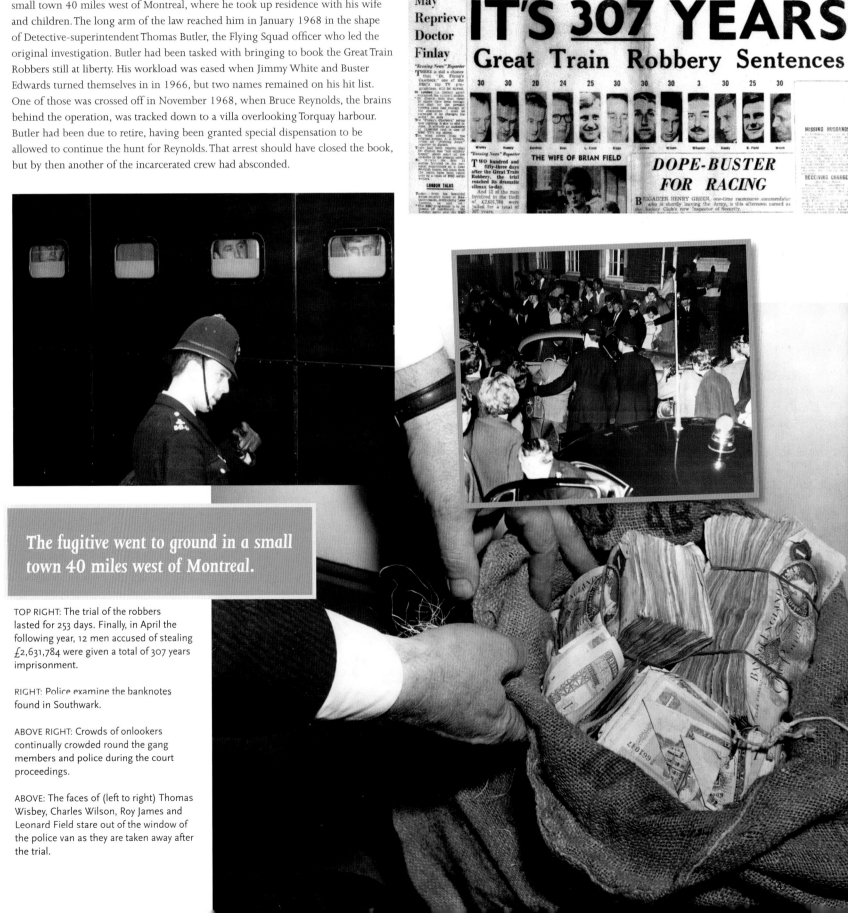

> ### The fugitive went to ground in a small town 40 miles west of Montreal.

TOP RIGHT: The trial of the robbers lasted for 253 days. Finally, in April the following year, 12 men accused of stealing £2,631,784 were given a total of 307 years imprisonment.

RIGHT: Police examine the banknotes found in Southwark.

ABOVE RIGHT: Crowds of onlookers continually crowded round the gang members and police during the court proceedings.

ABOVE: The faces of (left to right) Thomas Wisbey, Charles Wilson, Roy James and Leonard Field stare out of the window of the police van as they are taken away after the trial.

Buster Edwards turns up broke

SEPTEMBER 20, 1966

Ronald "Buster" Edwards, sought for three years after the Great Train Robbery, was "completely broke" when he gave himself up to police early yesterday. A senior police officer said this last night as Edwards, 35, slept in a cell at Aylesbury, Buckinghamshire. Edwards will appear in court at Linslade, ten miles away, today, on two charges concerning the robbery. He surrendered "by arrangement" to Scotland Yard Flying Squad men at a secret rendezvous in South London. The police officer said: "There had been no attempt on the part of Edwards to disguise himself. "But he had lost weight, looked much fitter and younger and his hair was a little grey. "We have been behind Edwards on a number of occasions, but he had always just gone when we arrived." It is known that Edwards attended a number of parties in South London after police began their hunt for him. Edwards's solicitor, Mr. Maurice Lesser, said last night: "I have seen Edwards and he authorised me to say that he voluntarily surrendered."

Edwards and his wife, June, 34, have a five-year old daughter, Nicolette. The surrender drama began at 1.15 a.m. yesterday, when Det. Chief-Supt. Thomas Butler, head of the Flying Squad, and Det.-Supt. Frank Williams, his second-in-command, were called by phone to Scotland Yard. They drove to an address in South London and met Edwards. An hour later the police car arrived back at Scotland Yard. At noon Edwards was driven from London with Superintendent Butler and a strong escort to Aylesbury police station. Edwards crouched in the back of the car. On the station notice board was a poster offering a substantial police reward for information about Edwards. It described him as a florist and club owner. Next to his photograph the poster showed one of his wife and a photograph of Bruce Reynolds, 31, a London motor and antique dealer. Reynolds is now the only man wanted for questioning about the robbery. He is believed to have been one of the masterminds behind the plot.

> 'We have been behind Edwards on a number of occasions, but he had always just gone when we arrived.'

TOP LEFT: Ronald 'Buster' Edwards, who lived in Southwark with his wife June and their two-year-old daughter Nicolette, was soon the subject of a police search. A gambler and boxer, he ran the 'Walk-In Club' in Lambeth Walk. Police suspected that the family were hiding on the Continent. Despite several leads, officers failed to find him but Edwards eventually gave himself up in September 1966 after the pressure of living for three years on the run.

TOP, ABOVE AND ABOVE LEFT: The following month he was taken to Linslade for a court hearing and was eventually imprisoned for 15 years for his part in the raid.

FAR LEFT: Edwards on his way to prison after sentencing.

RIGHT: Bruce Reynolds, who masterminded the robbery, was the last member of the gang to be tracked down. Following the guilty verdict in 1968, newspapers were quick to headline his 25-year sentence.

ABOVE: Reynolds had been renting a villa in Torquay with his wife Frances and their six-year-old son Nicholas. They had been planning to fly to Canada the following week. Parked outside the villa was the family's new Mini Cooper 'S'.

TOP RIGHT AND BOTTOM RIGHT: Reynolds, finally in police handcuffs after evading capture for five years

BELOW: James White had originally lived at Pett Bottom Farm in Elmstead, Essex. He had also given himself up to police.

ABOVE MIDDLE: After appearing in court in Leicester White was driven away to begin an 18-year sentence.

Evening News

Train robber says: Crime pays? You must be mad

IT'S 25 YEARS FOR REYNOLDS

The man with a cool brain

SIR MATT STEPS DOWN

'That's it, I suppose, I'm glad it's over'

The Great Train Robbery

Colourful life

Ronnie Biggs had been a minor player in the heist, yet he would become the most celebrated gang member for his dramatic escape and for successfully managing to evade recapture. Friends of Biggs came up with a simple but ingenious plan to get him out of Wandsworth Jail, and carried it out in broad daylight on 8 July 1965. A removals van was parked next to the prison's 20ft-high wall, and a rope ladder thrown over into the yard during the inmates' exercise period. Biggs shinned up the ladder and dropped through a hole cut in the vehicle's roof, followed by three uninvited inmates who seized their chance to escape. A waiting car whisked Biggs away to a colourful life on the run that would last for 36 years.

Biggs surfaced first in Australia, moving on to Rio de Janeiro in 1970 when he was threatened with exposure. He had had plastic surgery, but that didn't prevent the British press from tracking him down. Renowned Scotland Yard detective Jack Slipper was also on the case. He spent years trying to find the fugitive, and even when the quest was over he was thwarted by the lack of an extradition arrangement with Brazil. Biggs's position was made doubly secure when his girlfriend, nightclub dancer Raimunda de Castro, gave birth to son Michael. As the father of a Brazilian national Biggs was afforded even greater protection, able to enjoy the samba lifestyle unhindered. He suffered a scare in 1981 when a band of mercenary adventurers kidnapped him and took him to Barbados, hoping to claim a handsome reward. But once again the executive came to his aid, the island authorities ruling that he be allowed to return to Rio.

Free man

By 2001 Biggs's health was in decline and he returned of his own volition to the land of his birth. He spoke of his longing to stroll into a Margate pub and have a pint of bitter, but that was not an immediate prospect. With 28 years of his jail sentence still to run, Biggs would have been a centenarian were he to serve the entire stretch. That was never a serious possibility, and in the autumn of 2008, having completed one-third of his term, he was up before the parole board, hopeful that he would be released the following year. The 79-year-old Biggs had suffered a stroke, was being fed via a tube and had lost the power of speech. Those campaigning on his behalf said that he presented no threat to society, and taking into account the degree of overcrowding in British prisons it was reasonable to show compassion and grant Biggs his last wish: to be allowed to die a free man.

> By 2001 Biggs's health was in decline and he returned of his own volition to the land of his birth.

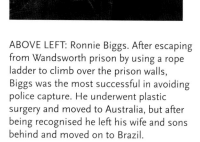

ABOVE LEFT: Ronnie Biggs. After escaping from Wandsworth prison by using a rope ladder to climb over the prison walls, Biggs was the most successful in avoiding police capture. He underwent plastic surgery and moved to Australia, but after being recognised he left his wife and sons behind and moved on to Brazil.

ABOVE: He was spotted again in Rio de Janeiro in 1974 but by then his girlfriend Raimunda de Castro (pictured) was pregnant with his son and the Brazilian authorities refused to extradite him.

TOP RIGHT: Biggs continued to live in Brazil for the next three decades with his son Michael. However, in 2001, at the age of 71, he decided to return to Britain and give himself up. He had 28 years of his sentence still to serve. He is still currently in prison despite having suffered a severe stroke but his family are hopeful that he will experience freedom before he dies.

LEFT: Seven of the gang attended a reunion in London to mark the publication of their paperback *The Train Robbers: Their Story*. Pictured from the left are: Buster Edwards, Tommy Wisbey, Jim White, Bruce Reynolds, Roger Cordrey, Charles Wilson and Jim Hussey.

FEBRUARY 2, 1974

Ronald Biggs arrested

The world hunt for escaped Great Train robber Ronald Biggs has ended after 3,128 days on the run. He has been detained in Rio de Janeiro, Brazil. Two Scotland Yard detectives are in Rio with him. Britain has not got an extradition treaty with Brazil, and detectives are trying to arrange for Biggs's voluntary return to serve his sentence - 30 years. Otherwise police can make a special extradition application to the Brazilian authorities.

The detectives, deputy head of the Flying Squad, Det. Chief Superintendent Jack Slipper and Det.-Sergeant Peter Jones, found Biggs in Room 909 at the £25-a-day Hotel Trocadero in Rio's Atlantic Avenue. They flew from London secretly on Wednesday after signing out in the Flying Squad duty book as being on annual leave.

Biggs was wearing only red bathing trunks when the detectives walked into his ninth-floor room. With him was a 22-year-old girl called Lucia, who burst into tears. Mr Slipper said to Biggs: 'Nice to see you again Ronnie. It's been a long time.' Despite plastic surgery to his face during his time on the run, Biggs, his grey hair slightly receding, was instantly recognisable to the detectives. Biggs told the detectives that he was planning to surrender. Apparently he was tired of looking over his shoulder for nearly nine years.

It is understood that Biggs, 41, is willing to return to London. Scotland Yard hope to have him back by the end of the weekend unless there are legal hitches.

FEBRUARY 6, 1974

Slipper of the Yard flies home without his man

Two tired and disconsolate policemen flew into Gatwick last night to tell Scotland Yard why Ronald Biggs missed the flight from Rio de Janeiro. 'Of course, we are disappointed,' said 49-year-old Det. Chief Supt. Jack Slipper. 'We went out to get Biggs and he was supposed to be coming back with us. But there it is. He's still in Rio and we're home without him.'

What foxed the Yard pair was that although Biggs at first expressed a wish to return to Britain, the Brazilian authorities had other ideas. 'I hope we may be going back for him in five or six weeks but I honestly have no idea. The position is now political and that's something I cannot talk about. I am feeling a bit fed-up. I just want to get back to some normal work.'

Biggs? 'Well, I respect him and he respects me, but we both know the score.'

ABOVE: Bruce Reynolds with his wife Angela and son. He now lives in charitable housing in Croydon and receives income support. Ironically, exactly 30 years after the robbery his own prized custom-made bike was stolen.

ABOVE MIDDLE: Reynolds and Edwards during the book launch party.

TOP INSET: After his release from jail Buster Edwards ran a flower stall outside Waterloo Station. He said that all he wanted to do was 'live an ordinary life'.

RIGHT: In December 1994 Edwards died after hanging himself, allegedly in remorse. Crowds lined the streets as 12 cars followed the hearse along the funeral route from his house in Camberwell to the crematorium in Streatham.

ABOVE: Thirty years after the robbery several people who were involved in the hunt for gang members met under Bridego Bridge. They included the local policeman, the station porter, a reporter and two men, who as children, had been car-spotters and had provided the police with several registration numbers.

Dallas: November 22, 1963
The violent death of a president who symbolised the hopes and dreams of a generation.

Texas was an important part of the re-election campaign, and to visit the state and not go to Dallas was unthinkable.

A sense of foreboding

There was a sense of foreboding in the Kennedy camp about the trip to Dallas. UN Ambassador Adlai Stevenson had visited the city the previous month and been given a hostile reception. Even Lyndon Johnson, one of the state's own sons, had fallen from favour, and there were no guarantees that his presence on the ticket for 1964 would reap electoral rewards. Texas was an important part of the re-election campaign, and to visit the state and not go to Dallas was unthinkable.

The whistle-stop tour was to take in five venues over two days. On the morning of 22 November, the Kennedys left Fort Worth for Dallas, the fourth leg of the trip. Things had gone well so far, the President and First Lady having been warmly received in San Antonio and Houston. There had been concerns that Jackie might be given a torrid time following a recent solo trip to Greece. She had received a lot of bad press over alleged revelry aboard Aristotle Onassis's yacht. According to reports, such behaviour ill became a woman who had so recently lost a child and whose husband was faced with such weighty affairs of state. These fears were quickly dispelled, however. Jackie carefully chose some conservative outfits for the Texas trip. This was a hedge against criticism that she was rather too fond of haute couture and life's luxuries, and lacked the common touch. Even so, she was the epitome of glamour and style and won the crowds over wherever she went. Halfway through the visit reports were already praising Jackie's sure-footed performance on the political stage and declaring her to be the jewel in the crown as far as her husband's re-election hopes were concerned.

Bullet-proof bubble removed

The couple left Fort Worth for Dallas in buoyant mood. Thirteen minutes later, Air Force One touched down at Love Field and the President and First Lady were soon working a highly receptive crowd. At 11.55 they took their places on the raised rear seat of the Lincoln convertible. Governor Connally and his wife Nellie sat on the jump seats opposite. It was a bright, clear day and the vehicle's bullet-proof bubble had been removed.

The motorcade made its way through the city, greeted enthusiastically by the crowds that lined the streets. The destination was the Trade Mart, where Jack was to make a speech. As the Lincoln turned into Dealey Plaza, three shots rang out. The first bullet struck Jack in the back. Before Secret Servicemen could reach the vehicle, the second bullet hit him in the back of the head. Governor Connally was also shot and seriously wounded. Jackie cradled her husband's head as the car sped to Parkland Hospital, just a few minutes' drive away. Kennedy's heart was still beating and the trauma team attempted a tracheotomy. But with virtually the entire right side of the brain now missing, it was a hopeless task. John F. Kennedy was declared dead at 1.00 p.m.

Appalling injuries

The security men who first attended the President knew there was no hope. The injuries were so appalling that some instinctively ran to Lyndon Johnson's car, which was some way behind the President's in the motorcade. Ninety-eight minutes after Kennedy was pronounced dead, Johnson took the 40-word oath of office and was sworn in as the 36th President of the United States. The brief ceremony took place aboard Air Force One, which was taking both him and Kennedy's body back to Washington. Jackie stood beside Johnson as he took the oath, her clothes still spattered with her husband's blood and tissue.

> **The first bullet struck Jack in the back. Before Secret Servicemen could reach the vehicle, the second bullet hit him in the back of the head.**

OPPOSITE: Jack Kennedy greeting women in Denver, Colorado, during the presidential election campaign in 1960.

TOP LEFT: Kennedy pictured amidst a storm of streamers and confetti as he drives though downtown Los Angeles on November 1, 1960 during the last few days of his presidential campaign. A week later he was elected the 35th president of the United States.

TOP RIGHT: President Kennedy and Costa Rican President Francisco Orlich wave to the crowd as they ride though the streets of San Jose.

ABOVE: President Kennedy at his desk in the White House.

As the convoy approached a huge underpass the President waved to the crowds. Mrs. Kennedy waved too and smiled. They had expected to face some unpopularity over political issues. Instead there were miles of cheers. And Mrs. Kennedy tuned to her husband and said: 'You can't say Dallas wasn't friendly to you'.

This was the moment the gunman, hiding in a nearby warehouse, chose. The first bullet, fired from high above, hit President Kennedy in the right temple and passed down to the neck. The second and third struck Governor Connally in the chest and wrist. President Kennedy slumped dying onto the back seat of his car. Mrs. Kennedy screamed 'Oh, no!' and fell to her knees to take his head in her arms.

Lee Harvey Oswald

Within a matter of hours the police had a suspect in custody. Lee Harvey Oswald, a 24-year-old former marine, had lived in the Soviet Union between 1959 and 1962. He worked as a clerk at the Texas School Book Depository on Elm Street, and police quickly concluded that this was the building from which the shots had been fired. A carbine and three empty shells were discovered on the 6th floor, and the weapon was traced back to Oswald. He was charged with murder, although rumours of a larger conspiracy began circulating almost immediately.

On 24 November, Oswald himself was shot and killed while being moved from the local police station to the state prison. In the two days he had spent in custody he had not confessed to firing the gun which killed Kennedy and wounded Connally. The man who shot him was Jack Ruby, a Dallas nightclub owner. Ruby was arrested and later convicted of Oswald's murder.

A carbine and three empty shells were discovered on the 6th floor, and the weapon was traced back to Oswald.

Oswald acted alone

President Johnson set up a commission under Chief Justice Earl Warren to investigate the events of 22 November. The report was delivered 10 months later, on 27 September 1964, and concluded that Oswald had acted alone. Ruby had perpetrated an individual act of revenge. In short, there was no wider conspiracy. These findings did nothing to end speculation. Between them Jack and Bobby had peered into some murky waters and made many enemies. They had taken on Jimmy Hoffa and the Teamsters Union; there had been dubious connections with the Mafia; Castro and the Kremlin also came under suspicion, while some thought it more than coincidental that the assassination followed so closely on the heels of Diem's murder in South Vietnam. Bobby was among the first to wonder if the CIA were implicated.

Rumours persisted for 15 years, when the House Select Committee on Assassinations finally shed new light on what happened in Dallas. Acoustics experts revealed that shots were fired from the grassy knoll on Dealey Plaza, as well as from the book depository. The identity of the perpetrators was - and remains - a mystery, but at least the theory of a disaffected individual was finally disproved.

Manhunt

An hour later, as a vast manhunt for the killer went on, came a dramatic gun battle in another part of Dallas. A cinema cashier, Mrs. Julie Postal, told police that a man 'who looked like he was running from something' was in the Texas Cinema in the Oak Cliff district. Patrolmen J. D. Tippit and M. N. Macdonald burst into the cinema. Oswald fled and in a street chase Tippit opened fire. The man fired back and the constable fell dead. Macdonald closed with the gunman, a strongly built man in a brown shirt, and received a 4in. gash in the face.

Then the man was overpowered. He said 'Well, it's all over now.' Police named him as Lee Oswald, chief suspect in the killing of the President. Later, they charged him with murdering Tippit. Then something of Oswald's strange life history began to emerge.

He is said to have gone to Russia in 1959 after being discharged from the U.S. Marine Corps. In Moscow he surrendered his passport to the American Embassy, saying he would never return to the U.S. and would seek Soviet citizenship. The Russians, according to U.S. Government sources, refused Oswald Soviet nationality but authorised him to live there.

Nothing more was heard of him until June 1962 when the U.S. Embassy announced he had returned to the U.S. with his 22-year-old Russian wife and their year-old daughter. He turned up later in New Orleans, where he became the chairman of a pro-Castro committee. He was fined for creating a disturbance while distributing 'Hands off Cuba' leaflets.

'Good suspect'

The chief of the Dallas police homicide division, Captain William Fritz, said tonight: 'He has not admitted anything yet, but he looks like a good suspect.'

Police said Oswald worked in a warehouse overlooking President Kennedy's route where the killer is thought to have hidden, and where a German Mauser rifle with a telescopic sight was found. Oswald's supervisor said he was in the warehouse at noon, local time, only half an hour before the assassination. Police who swarmed into the warehouse found the remains of fried chicken and paper on the floor of the fifth-floor room from which the shots were believed to have been fired - suggesting the assassin had spent some time there.

Acoustics experts revealed that shots were fired from the grassy knoll on Dealey Plaza, as well as from the book depository.

Assassination Scene
PRESIDENT JOHN FITZGERALD KENNEDY

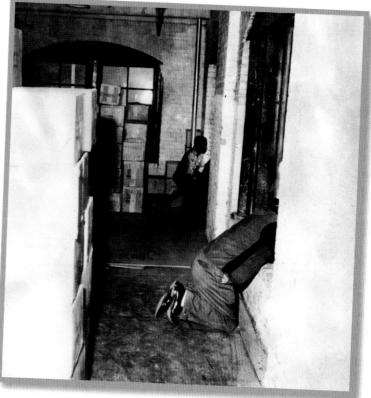

TOP: The assassination scene: Kennedy was shot from the sixth floor of the book depository as his motorcade drove past.

OPPOSITE TOP: President Kennedy and Jackie Kennedy pictured leaving Love Field shortly after their arrival in Dallas.

OPPOSITE TOP RIGHT: A man stands on the rear bumper of the President's car as Jackie Kennedy crouches over her husband after the shooting.

OPPOSITE BOTTOM RIGHT: Jackie Kennedy pictured getting into the ambulance carrying the body of her murdered husband at Andrews Air Force Base near Washington D.C.

ABOVE: Employees on the fifth floor of the book depository illustrate the positions they took when watching Kennedy's motorcade drive past. Oswald shot Kennedy from a window on the floor above.

ABOVE LEFT: Lee Oswald, a 24-year-old former marine, was captured and placed in custody within a matter of hours. He was discovered in a movie theatre and shot one of the arresting officers before being captured.

MARCH 7, 1964

New questions asked about Kennedy's assassination

By Mordecai Brienberg, Rhodes Scholar and lecturer

There is on file in Dallas an affidavit by the police officer who found a rifle on the sixth floor of the School Book Depository building [where Lee Oswald is said to have fired at President Kennedy]. That affidavit states that the weapon was a 7.65mm. Mauser. Henry Wade, Dallas District Attorney, on November 22 stated that this was the murder weapon and that Oswald's palm print was found on the weapon. The next day the F.B.I. released a report that Oswald purchased a rifle in March under the alias Hiddel. But this rifle was a 6.5mm. Italian carbine. After this report, Wade reversed his position; the rifle he had in his possession was an Italian carbine; it was no longer a Mauser.

The firing of a rifle leaves gunpowder traces on the hands and face, if it is fired from the shoulder. It would seem rather ridiculous for a person to have fired a rifle with telescopic sights from the hip. The results of paraffin tests (administered by Dallas police) were positive for Oswald's right and left hands. Paraffin tests on Oswald's face proved negative. Moreover, contrary to Wade's assertion on November 22 about palm-prints, the F.B.I. now states that "no palm-prints were found on the rifle."

Exit wound

The three doctors who attended the President immediately after the shooting told reporters at the hospital that one of the bullets entered the President's throat "just below the Adam's apple." There is a great difference between an entrance and an exit wound, and all three doctors claimed to have dealt daily with gun wounds. The bullet, the doctors further stated, ranged downward without exiting.

If the president had been shot as his car approached the T.S.B.D. building along Houston-street, Dallas, then the nature of the throat wound would be consistent with the allegation that the shots were fired from the sixth floor of that building. This was the first F.B.I. interpretation...

Photographs of the shooting indicate that the car was 75 to 100 yards past the building.

After the three physicians were questioned by the F.B.I. they issued a statement reversing their earlier view about the nature of the President's wound - on which they had been unanimous and definite. The throat wound, they now say, is an exit wound. These doctors state that they are unable to talk to reporters or to discuss the matter further.

Threshold of Greatness

John F. Kennedy took office determined to make his mark on history. Lyndon Johnson accepted the vice-presidency wondering whether yet another first executive would die in office and propel him into the top job. The events of Dallas, 22 November 1963, turned conjecture into reality for both men.

For a long time accounts of Kennedy's life and work became more akin to hagiography. His premature and violent death meant that his good qualities and achievements were magnified, his shortcomings and failures overlooked. The fact is that until November 1960 he knew more about how to win power than what to do with it. After taking office, he found that the learning curve was steep, and there were many reverses along the way. He grew in stature during his 1000-day tenure of the White House, and by the time of his death he was on the threshold of greatness.

But the balance-sheet approach fails to take account of the emotional impact Kennedy had, on both the American people and those beyond its shores. The world he envisioned and the ideals he espoused, touched people's lives in a way few statesmen have managed to do. He was more than an inspiring politician; he symbolized the hopes and dreams of a generation.

After the three physicians were questioned by the F.B.I. they issued a statement reversing their earlier view about the nature of the President's wound.

TOP LEFT: People of all ages and nationalities wrote their condolences in books placed inside American embassies all over the world.

TOP MIDDLE: Crowds read the sad news about Kennedy's death after it was posted at the American Embassy in London.

TOP RIGHT: Following Kennedy's assassination, Vice-President Lyndon Johnson was immediately sworn in as his replacement. Johnson had been two cars behind Kennedy in the fateful motorcade.

OPPOSITE TOP: Part of the C2766 Mannlicher-Carcano rifle found on the sixth floor of the depository building. Bullets from the shooting matched the rifle.

OPPOSITE BOTTOM: The lights in Piccadilly, London, were blacked out on the day of President Kennedy's funeral as a mark of respect.

Five bullets

The first police bulletin, overheard by a reporter waiting for the President's motorcade at a point farther along the route, was that "all firing appears to have come from the overpass" - in front of the car. The first radio accounts stated that a policeman rushed to the overpass and was seen chasing two persons on the overpass. Nothing further is ever mentioned about this report.

The front windshield of the President's car had a bullet hole in it. The Secret Service prevented reporters at the hospital from coming close enough to determine the direction of the bullet. The car was flown back to Washington and remained in the custody of the secret service. Eight days later the windshield was replaced. (It is not known whether the shattered windshield was destroyed.)

Finally four reporters of the Dallas Morning News, witnesses to the assassination, who were standing between the overpass and the T.S.B.D. building, all claim the shots were fired in front of the President's car. According to the official report three shots were fired. But there appears to have been five bullets.

Scapegoat?

Did Oswald fire five shots in five and a half seconds, when rifle experts are highly sceptical that an excellent marksman could have accurately fired three shots in that time? The shooting took place between 12.30 and 12.31 p.m. Oswald arrived at his apartment, according to his landlady, at 12.45. Another account states he arrived at 1 p.m. This report also mentions "choked downtown traffic." According to the official version, Oswald's taxi ride was about four miles. In uncongested traffic...the journey would take 12 minutes.

If Oswald arrived at 12.45 he would have had two minutes to (a) hide the weapon; (b) walk from the sixth to the second floor; (c) find coins and get a coke from the machine; (d) converse with a policeman; (e) leave the building and walk four blocks to a bus; (f) ride the bus several blocks; and (g) get off the bus and hail a taxi.

Granted that confusion existed, why, then, should the officials be continuously certain of one thing, Oswald's guilt? In the pressure for an arrest did the Dallas police consider Oswald an appropriate scapegoat because he was first on their list of "subversives"?

Dr. Brienberg's article appears in full in this week's Spectator.

Did Oswald fire five shots in five and a half seconds, when rifle experts are highly sceptical that an excellent marksman could have accurately fired three shots in that time?

Ian Brady & Myra Hindley: Moors Murders

To Ian Brady people were 'maggots', 'cabbages' and 'morons'; their extinction signified nothing. He amassed a library of books on murder, torture and sexual perversion.

In 1956 American writer Meyer Levin published Compulsion, a novel based on the extraordinary tale of two Chicago students convicted for murder in 1924. Nathan Leopold and Richard Loeb were outstanding scholars who chose to pit their superior wits against the police by committing the perfect crime. Intellect, they believed, could not be constrained by morality. They chose a victim at random, a 14-year-old boy, and sent a ransom demand to suggest that it was an abduction in the name of profit. In fact, the boy was already dead, which had been the sole object of the wicked enterprise.

Leopold and Loeb were not as quite as bright as they thought, for they made a catalogue of mistakes that led to their arrest. It was only the brilliant advocacy of the legendary Clarence Darrow that saved them from a capital sentence.

ABOVE LEFT: At age 11 Ian Brady passed the entrance examination for Shawlands Academy, a secondary school with a reputation for academic success, but he soon went off the rails. He was incarcerated several times for various petty crimes and was eventually declared criminally insane in 1985 and sent to Ashworth Psychiatric Hospital, where he remains to this day.

ABOVE MIDDLE: Myra Hindley met Brady in 1961 when she joined the secretarial staff at Milward's Merchandise Ltd. They soon became inseparable partners in a sado-masochistic relationship. Hindley spent 36 years behind bars, and remains the longest serving female prisoner in the annals of the British criminal justice system.

Obsession

Compulsion struck a chord with one particular reader, one who also espoused Nietzsche's 'superman' philosophy. He, too, became obsessed with committing the perfect crime, using dispensable individuals in pursuit of an intellectual exercise. To Ian Brady people were 'maggots', 'cabbages' and 'morons'; their extinction signified nothing. He amassed a library of books on murder, torture and sexual perversion. A favourite work was *The Life and Times of the Marquis de Sade*, and Brady endorsed beliefs such as: '…murder is a horror, but a horror often necessary, never criminal, and essential to tolerate in a republic'.

Brady might not have been quite an alpha student of the calibre of Leopold and Loeb, but he showed a lot of aptitude in his early years growing up in Glasgow. He was a loner with a chip on his shoulder, having to contend with rejection from both parents. He never knew his father, while his mother, Peggy Stewart, had to farm him out to another family as she was unable to cope. Even her visits dried up when she married Patrick Brady and relocated to Manchester. At eleven Brady passed the entrance examination for Shawlands Academy, a secondary school with a reputation for academic success, but he soon went off the rails.

> Brady was also fascinated by Nazism. Later, he would call his infamous girlfriend 'Hess', and she would even dye her hair blonde to conform to the 'Aryan' stereotype.

Sado-machistic relationship

Brady turned to petty crime, his misdemeanours earning him three court appearances and probation. The authorities thought the best hope of salvation lay in a reconciliation with his natural mother, and at sixteen Brady was ordered to move to Manchester. He took his stepfather's name and got a job as a porter, but failed to turn over a new leaf and his next brush with the law led to his first spell of incarceration. He used his time in prison to study bookkeeping, though he also immersed himself in a lot of unsavoury literature. As well as studying Nietzsche and de Sade, Brady was also fascinated by Nazism. Later, he would call his infamous girlfriend 'Hess', and she would even dye her hair blonde to conform to the 'Aryan' stereotype. Together they would carry out their own unspeakable agenda of imposing their warped superiority on those weaker than themselves.

Brady met Myra Hindley in 1961, when she joined the secretarial staff at Millward's Merchandise Ltd, the Gorton firm where he had worked as a stock clerk for the previous two years. Hindley, too, had a troubled upbringing. Her father had a drink problem and often beat her, a trait she developed when it came to settling differences of opinion with her peers. At the age of four, when her sister Maureen was born, Myra was sent to live with her paternal grandmother Ellen Maybury. She immersed herself in books and established deep friendships, perhaps trying to compensate for perceived rejection. Her capacity for obsessive, all-consuming relationships had a new focus when she started work at Millward's. She wrote in her diary of her attraction for the brooding Ian Brady, and before long they became inseparable partners in a sado-masochistic relationship. At last Brady had a confederate to help him act out his long-harboured dark fantasies.

First victims

The couple's first victim was 16-year-old Pauline Reade, a neighbour of Hindley's. On 12 July 1963 Pauline was on her way to a dance when she was lured by Hindley to go for a car ride. The advantage of having a woman fronting their depraved schemes quickly became apparent. Hindley drove Pauline out onto Saddleworth Moor, where Brady, who followed by motorbike, raped and killed her. After burying the body, they celebrated by drinking Drambuie.

Brady and Hindley plotted their crimes meticulously, their attention to detail extending to counting the buttons on their clothing before and after to ensure there was no evidence linking them to the scene. That degree of planning paid off in the case of Pauline Reade, and by the following year the local police had two more unsolved child disappearances on their files. 12-year-old John Kilbride disappeared from Ashton-under-Lyne market at around 5.30 pm on Saturday 23 November 1963. Seven months later, Keith Bennett, also aged twelve, disappeared while walking to his grandmother's house. Both boys were raped and strangled.

The evil acts themselves were not enough for Brady and Hindley; they wanted to document their deeds. Photographs of their next victim, and in particular a harrowing 16-minute tape recording of her ordeal, would help to secure a conviction and life sentences for the perpetrators.

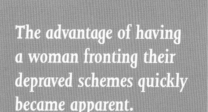

The advantage of having a woman fronting their depraved schemes quickly became apparent.

Sobbing and begging

10-year-old Lesley Ann Downey disappeared on Boxing Day afternoon 1964 when she and a group of friends visited a fairground a few minutes' walk from her Ancoats home. As with the previous three victims, a police search revealed no clues to her whereabouts, or what had befallen her. That day Hindley had driven her septuagenarian grandmother to visit her uncle, a regular practice. The usual arrangement was for Hindley to pick up Ellen Maybury at around 10 pm to take her home but on this occasion she called in to say that the roads, which had a light dusting of snow, were impassable. Eventually it would become clear that Hindley's grandmother could not be allowed to return to 16 Wardle Brook Avenue that evening because Lesley Ann was being held captive there. Pornographic photographs were taken, and the girl was recorded sobbing and begging to be released before she, too, was murdered and buried on the moor. Hindley picked up Ellen Maybury mid-morning the following day.

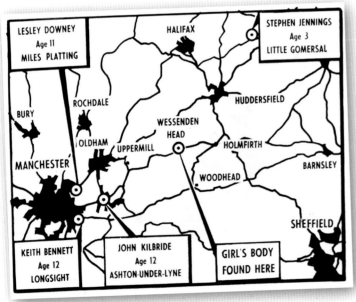

TOP RIGHT: Police hunt for bodies on the Derbyshire Moors in October 1965 after they had extended their search from Saddleworth Moor to the Snake Pass. Using sticks to prod the moorland peat, they attempted to find more of Brady and Hindley's victims.

MIDDLE RIGHT: Clothing was found on the moor two miles from Lesley Ann Downey's grave. Among the clothing were children's socks, a pleated red-and-black striped skirt, a woollen jumper and a nylon stocking.

ABOVE: Brady and Hindley were arrested after they claimed their fifth and final victim, 17-year-old Edward Evans. The murderous pair made the mistake of letting Hindley's brother-in-law into their dark secret. David Smith witnessed the murder of Evans and contacted the police.

Hunt for more victims on moor

More murder victims are expected to be found buried on the desolate Pennine moors where the body of a ten-year-old girl was discovered on Saturday. A police chief in one of Britain's biggest murder hunts, involving five police forces, said yesterday: "We are certain that more bodies will soon be found, possibly within the next few days. Everything points to this from the information we have so far gathered."

The girl found buried on a Yorkshire moor was identified last night as Lesley Ann Downey, missing since Boxing Day last year when she left her Manchester home to go to a fair. Her body was discovered in a shallow peat grave on Saddleworth Moor, near the main road from Ashton-under-Lyne, Lancashire, and Huddersfield.

Today more than 100 policemen carry on the digging which began on the moors six days ago. They had been told that several bodies were buried in the area.

Eight files

Yesterday police chiefs re-examined their files on eight people - three of them children - who have disappeared from the Manchester area over the past three years. Lesley was one of them.

Last week the murder squad detectives began to tear apart a house in Manchester. Floorboards were ripped up. Dust was collected from crevices and samples, with floorboards, were sent to the Home Office forensic science laboratory at Preston.

Detective Chief, Superintendent Arthur Benfield, head of Cheshire CID, who has taken charge of the combined investigation, last night held a conference at Hyde. A man is said to have boasted of carrying his victims to the moors by car and a man whose information first began the hunt has visited the area with detectives.

Last week's search was in vain. Then a woman was able to narrow the search area on Saturday night. Lesley's body was discovered in thickening mist by a young constable with only a few days' service.

> 'We are certain that more bodies will soon be found, possibly within the next few days.'

TOP RIGHT: Hindley and Brady with Hindley's sister Maureen. Maureen's husband, David Smith, was witness to the fifth and final murder. He and Maureen phoned the police and ended the 'Moors Murderers' killing spree.

MIDDLE RIGHT: The house on Wardle Brook Avenue.

LEFT AND ABOVE: A police squad digging in the garden of Ian Brady's home.

Butcher

The fifth murder proved to be Brady and Hindley's downfall. This time they widened the conspiracy net, drawing Hindley's brother-in-law into the murderous loop. David Smith married Hindley's younger sister Maureen in 1964, when he was just sixteen. He already had a criminal record, and Brady began to groom and school him in the matter of his favourite subjects and authors.

Over the summer months of 1965 Brady launched his machinations to involve Smith in a criminal act. First there was talk of a bank robbery, and Smith was even detailed to stake out one such outlet to observe the daily routine. Target practice sessions on the moors were arranged. Smith initially thought Brady's insistence that they had to be prepared to use firearms was mere bravado, as were his claims to have already committed 'three or four' murders. Brady answered the disbelief by saying he had photographic evidence of the crimes he had committed but wasn't prepared to reveal it yet.

On the evening of 6 October 1965 Hindley paid a call on her sister, and asked Smith to escort her home as the streetlights were not working. Hindley went into the house, telling Smith to wait for the landing light to be flashed on and off before approaching; she wanted to make sure that it was all right by Brady for him to enter. The signal was given and Smith was received by Brady, who invited him in, supposedly to collect some miniature wine bottles they were keeping for him. Brady went through to the living room and seconds later Smith heard screams coming from that direction. He rushed to investigate, in time to see Brady raining hatchet blows down upon the head of a youth.

Smith later said the act was carried out with as little emotion as a butcher carving a dead carcass.

Call to police

Brady used a length of lighting flex to strangle the last gurgling cries of the stricken teenager. When the body was rendered lifeless, he calmly lit a cigarette and exhorted Hindley to get a mop and cleaning materials. It was the 'messiest yet',
he said, a comment that would come under the microscope in court, for it contradicted Brady's assertion that references to other murders were a fiction constructed simply to impress Smith. Doctors identified fourteen separate blows to the head of the victim, 17-year-old Edward Evans, a vicious assault which left the room a blood-spattered mess. A terrified Smith helped Brady wrap the body in blankets and polythene sheeting and carry it upstairs into Hindley's bedroom.

It was after 3.00 am when Smith arrived home. He was violently sick, then he unburdened himself to Maureen. He was meant to return to 16 Wardle Brook Avenue later that day to help dispose of the body. Instead, at 6 am he called the police, taking a knife and screwdriver with him to the kiosk, so terrified was he that he might encounter Brady along the way.

> At 6 am he called the police, taking a knife and screwdriver with him to the kiosk, so terrified was he that he might encounter Brady along the way.

TOP: Brady pictured on the moors where he buried his victims. Hindley lured the children on to the moor, asking them to help her find a missing glove. Brady then attacked them, often raping them, and then buried their bodies in the peat.

BOTTOM: Canvas screens were placed around the spot where the second body was found on Saddleworth Moor.

DECEMBER 10, 1965

Brady killed without emotion, says Smith

Ian Brady showed no emotion during and after the murder of Edward Evans, 17-year-old David Smith told the Moorland murders case court at Hyde, Cheshire, yesterday. Brady rained axe blows on to the head and shoulders of his screaming victim without frenzy, Mr. Smith said in reply to Mr. W. L. Mars-Jones, QC. The blows were "almost positioned," he said. And later, while arrangements were being made for the disposal of Evans's body, the behaviour of Myra Hindley, Brady's woman friend, was normal. Neither she nor Brady showed any sign of agitation or worry, he claimed, and she reminisced about another body she said they had disposed of on the moors.

Mr. Smith, whose wife is Hindley's sister, stood for more than seven hours giving evidence yesterday

TOP LEFT: Mrs Crowther, wife of a farmer living near Saddleworth Moor, walks to the spot where she saw a man digging on the moor.

LEFT: Brady pictured arriving at the court where he was first charged with the Moors Murders. Brother-in-law, David Smith said he killed with little emotion, as a butcher would do when carving a dead carcass.

ABOVE: A youthful Brady relaxing at home. When a police team descended on 16 Wardle Brook Avenue they found Brady in the process of writing a letter to his employer saying he had hurt his ankle and was unfit for work. That, at least, was true, for Brady had been injured in the previous night's struggle.

Evidence uncovered

A police team descended on 16 Wardle Brook Avenue just after eight o'clock. They found Brady in the process of writing a letter to his employer saying he had hurt his ankle and was unfit for work. That, at least, was true, for Brady had been injured in the previous night's struggle. Hindley prevaricated over the whereabouts of the key to her locked bedroom, but when it became clear that the officers were not going to leave without searching the entire house, Brady capitulated. There had been 'a row' the previous night, he said, and the consequences of the altercation were to be found there.

Brady and Hindley both tried to implicate Smith. Brady described how he and Evans had had an argument, which came to blows just as Smith arrived. The latter had joined in the fracas, kicking Evans and beating him with a stick. Brady also said that references to other murders were exactly as Smith surmised: fanciful talk designed to impress him.

Attempts to convince police that this was a one-off incident, a fight that had gone too far and with Smith's hands equally bloodied, were soon shown up for what they were. A left-luggage ticket stub was found, which tied in with Smith's statement that he helped carry two suitcases to Hindley's Mini van on 5 October, the day before Edward Evans's murder. They were recovered from Manchester Central Station on October 15, and the books, photographs and tape recordings contained therein revealed the full horror of what they were dealing with. The contents included pictures of Lesley Ann Downey, which police were able to identify as having been taken in Hindley's bedroom. That prompted police to re-examine their open files on children who had disappeared in the recent past.

The pieces quickly fell into place. A 12-year-old girl who lived two doors from Brady and Hindley led police along the A635 to the spot on the moors where they had taken her for jaunts. She was lucky: her mistreatment extended only to being plied with alcohol.

APRIL 20, 1966

"Cleared the decks for murder"

Ian Brady and Myra Hindley "cleared the decks for murder" the night before killing 17-year-old Edward Evans at their home, the Attorney-General said yesterday. Sir Elwyn Jones, QC, was prosecuting in the "bodies on the moors" murder trial at Chester Assizes. In the dock accused of triple murder were Brady, 28, and Hindley, 23.

Photographs, tape recordings and books were removed from their house, said Sir Elwyn. These were deposited in two suitcases in the left luggage office at Manchester Central Station. The cases contained in-criminating material which put police on the trail that eventually led to the discovery of the graves of Lesley Ann Downey, ten, and John Kilbride, 12. By removing this evidence Brady and Hindley were preparing for the Evans murder, Sir Elwyn submitted. He said the three victims lived in or near Manchester. John vanished first and Lesley more than a year later. Evans died about nine and a half months after her disappearance. Extensive police inquiries for John and Lesley went on for months but their fate "remained sealed."

> *The pieces quickly fell into place. A 12-year-old girl who lived two doors from Brady and Hindley led police along the A635 to the spot on the moors where they had taken her for jaunts.*

TOP AND LEFT: Brady and Hindley leave Chester court in a police van after they had been sentenced to life imprisonment, having been found guilty of the charges brought against them.

Just over an hour after being sentenced the couple were driven from Chester Castle to Risley Remand Centre, near Warrington, Lancashire. Women hammered on the windows of the van carrying them as they drove through a crowd of 300 people outside the castle. Two dozen policemen tried to hold the crowd back.

Brady and Hindley were sentenced after the jury had been out for two hours and 22 minutes.

APRIL 20, 1966

Out of a detergent box comes an axe

From a carton labelled "Deepio, the complete multi-purpose detergent," the Attorney General took a plastic bag, and from the bag a small hand axe. All eyes were riveted on the familiar-looking firewood chopper as the chief lawyer of the land said with slow emphasis: "This is the weapon which the prosecution says Brady used to launch a murderous attack on Edward Evans."

Ian Brady and Myra Hindley, accused of the "Murders on the Moor," are charged with murdering a girl of ten, a boy of 12, a youth of 17. Today brought the latest act in a drama which opened on the dark Pennines and is now to be played out in this quiet country town.

Myra Hindley, 23, who had a new ash blonde rinse, played cat's cradle with her long fingers. When she made notes she replaced her ballpoint pen precisely on her pad, like the efficient shorthand typist she is. Occasionally, she tugged at the hem of her blue-grey suit, a fashionable three inches above her knees. Brady, on her right, hunched slackly in his chair, frowning and pressing the knuckle of his left forefinger to pursed lips. From time to time the two had whispered conversation, heads bowed.

TOP: Police resume digging on Saddleworth Moor, 20 years after Brady and Hindley's conviction. In 1986 Hindley and Brady cooperated in trying to find the graves of Pauline Reade and Keith Bennett.

ABOVE: Brady (right) is pictured on the moors with Detective Chief Inspector Peter Topping during the second visit to Shiny Brook.

SADDLEWORTH MOOR — Marsden — A62 — Meltham — Butterley Reservoir — B6107 — Diggle — Greenfield — A635 — Holmfirth — Dove Stone Reservoir — POLICE FIND NEW BODY IN THIS AREA — PA518 — 5 miles

SADDLEWORTH MOOR — Marsden — A62 — 5 miles — Meltham — Butterley Reservoir — B6107 — Shiny Brook — Diggle — ①③ — 4 — A635 — Holmfirth — ② — Greenfield — Dove Stone Reservoir

1 Body of Lesley Ann Downey found in 1965
2 Body of John Kilbride found in 1965
3 Body found Wednesday, July 1
4 Search for 4th body here

PA521

Life sentences

On 6 May 1966 at Chester Assizes, Ian Brady and Myra Hindley were convicted of murdering Edward Evans and Lesley Ann Downey. Brady alone was found guilty of the murder of John Kilbride, but Hindley was convicted of harbouring him in full knowledge that he had committed that murder. She was given seven years for the lesser charge, though that was academic. Brady and Hindley remained devoid of emotion throughout the proceedings, which closed a matter of months after the death sentence for capital crimes had been suspended. Presiding judge Mr Justice Fenton Atkinson sent them both down for life. Brady was 28, Hindley 23.

Ian Brady has never sought release. He was declared criminally insane in 1985 and sent to Ashworth Psychiatric Hospital, where he remains to this day. It is said that his attempts to end his life by going on hunger strike have been thwarted through force feeding.

Myra Hindley, by contrast, mounted a long campaign for freedom when she believed she had paid her debt to society. She claimed to have found God, took an Open University degree and turned her back on Brady, whom she said had indoctrinated and intimidated her. Lord Longford took up Hindley's cause and argued that she had been rehabilitated but successive home secretaries refused to sanction her release. The strength of feeling that her name and image provoked was shown to be undimmed in 1997 when artist Marcus Harvey exhibited a portrait made up of children's handprints at the Royal Academy. She died three years later, on 15 November 2002, aged sixty. Myra Hindley had spent thirty-six years behind bars, and remains the longest-serving female prisoner in the annals of the British criminal justice system.

TOP LEFT AND BELOW: The scene of the renewed hunt for the bodies of Reade and Bennett on Saddleworth Moor.

ABOVE AND LEFT: Diagrams illustrating the area to be searched in 1986. They also show where the other bodies were found more than 20 years before.

> Myra Hindley mounted a long campaign for freedom when she believed she had paid her debt to society. She claimed to have found God.

'In your case, Hindley, you have been found guilty of two equally horrible murders.'

MAY 7, 1966

Moors killers jailed for life

Ian Brady and Myra Hindley were both jailed for life yesterday. Brady, 28-year-old stock clerk, was convicted of murdering 17-year-old Edward Evans, ten-year old Lesley Ann Downey and 12-year-old John Kilbride. Hindley, a 23-year-old blonde short-hand typist, was found guilty of murdering Evans and Lesley Ann. The jury at Chester Assizes cleared her of killing John Kilbride, but convicted her of harbouring Brady knowing that he had killed the boy.

Just over an hour after being sentenced the couple were driven from Chester Castle to Risley Remand Centre, near Warrington, Lancashire. Women hammered on the windows of the van carrying them as they drove through a crowd of 300 people outside the castle.

Two dozen policemen tried to hold the crowd back.

The sentences on Brady and Hindley came after the jury had been out for two hours 22 minutes.

'Guilty, guilty, guilty'

It was 5.10 p.m. when Hindley was led into the glass-enclosed dock by two women prison officers. Seconds later, Brady took his place beside her. They stood as the jury filed into court.

The verdicts on the three charges against Brady were voiced firmly and clearly by the middle-aged foreman: "Guilty, guilty, guilty." Brady folded his arms across his chest and stared directly at the judge. When the judge asked Brady whether he had anything to say before sentence was passed, he said: "No, except the revolvers were bought in July 1964."[Earlier the jury had returned to court to ask about the date Hindley bought two revolvers. The judge consulted

counsel and told them that one was purchased in the summer of 1963 and the other in the autumn of the same year.]

Hindley was asked if she had anything to say. Almost inaudibly she replied: "No."

Then the judge told Brady: "Ian Brady, these were three calculated, cruel and cold-blooded murders. In your case, I pass the only sentence which the law now allows, and that is three concurrent sentences of life imprisonment." He added curtly: "Put him down."

As the sentence was delivered Hindley took a packet of mints from her pocket and slipped one into her mouth. Brady turned without looking at her and left the dock. Then the judge said: "In your case, Hindley, you have been found guilty of two equally horrible murders and an accessory after the fact of the murder of John Kilbride." On you I pass two concurrent sentences of life imprisonment and, in connection with the harbouring case, a concurrent sentence of seven years' imprisonment."

ABOVE LEFT: Detective Chief Inspector Peter Topping gives a press conference on Saddleworth Moor during the renewed search for the bodies of Brady and Hindley's victims.

ABOVE RIGHT: As the icy mist lifted in November 1986, eight dogs went to work in the continuing search for the bodies of Pauline Reade and Keith Bennett. Sergeant Neville Sharp worked with Jan, a keen-eyed collie.

NOVEMBER 19, 1986

Myra Hindley talks at last

Moors murderess Myra Hindley revealed last night why she is helping police search for two children missing since the Sixties. In a statement from prison, she said she had been moved by an anguished letter from the mother of one youngster. She had seen police and directed them to Pennine moorland in the search for Pauline Reade and Keith Bennett. Police will tomorrow begin hunting for their remains in the windswept area close to where Hindley and her lover Ian Brady buried John Kilbride, 12, and Lesley Anne Downey, ten, more than 20 years ago.

'Enormous distress'

In her statement dictated to solicitor Michael Fisher, 43-year-old Hindley said: 'I received a letter, the first ever, from the mother of one of the missing children, and this has caused me enormous distress. I have agreed to help the Manchester Police in any way possible, and have today identified from photographs and maps, places that I know were of particular interest to Ian Brady, some of which I visited with him.

In spite of a 22-year passage of time, I have searched my heart and memory and given whatever help I can give to the police. I'm glad at long last to have been able to have been given this opportunity and I will continue to do all that I can. I hope that one day people will be able to forgive the wrong I have done, and know the truth of what I have and have not done. But for now, I want the police to be able to conclude their inquiries so ending public speculation and the private anguish of those directly involved.'

The letter she referred to was sent by Winifred Johnson, the remarried mother of Keith Bennett. Mrs Johnson, 53, said last night: 'Never in my wildest dreams did I think Hindley would answer. I wrote asking her to search her conscience and think of me not knowing what had happened to my son. I don't know whether to believe her. I don't know why I should trust her. I'll have to wait and see. It's such a dreadful feeling that I might soon know the truth. I feel numb.'

'I received a letter, the first ever, from the mother of one of the missing children, and this has caused me enormous distress.'

TOP RIGHT AND FAR RIGHT: Detective Chief Superintendent Peter Topping with Mrs Winnie Johnson, the mother of Moors Murder victim, Keith Bennett.

ABOVE RIGHT: A Canberra aircraft flies over Saddleworth Moor taking photos in an attempt to help police in their search.

RIGHT AND OPPOSITE BELOW: Police work through bad weather as they try to locate the graves of Bennett and Reade in 1986. Massive security operations to protect Hindley and Brady were undertaken when the two assisted police on the moors in the search for the grave.

OPPOSITE TOP RIGHT: The house on Wardle Brook Avenue was demolished to deter morbid day trippers who frequently came to look at the home the killers shared.

Police find body on moors

Police hunting victims of the Moors murderers found a body yesterday. A skeleton, believed to be that of a girl, was unearthed by detectives searching Saddleworth Moor outside Manchester. It was in a shallow peat grave only yards from where 10-year-old Lesley Ann Downey, killed by Ian Brady and Myra Hindley 23 years ago, was found in 1965. Home Office pathologist Geoffrey Garrett was working through the night for clues to the body's identity.

Breakthrough

The scene, Hollin Brown Knoll, was lit by floodlights as police carried on the hunt. A senior detective commented: 'It has been a long, hard inquiry which has been dismissed as a waste of time. We have now made what we believe is a major breakthrough. We think we have found the body of a girl victim of the Moors murderers.'

The police made their grim find seven months after they launched the hunt for the bodies of 16-year-old Pauline Reade and 12-year-old Keith Bennett. The youngsters vanished during Brady and Hindley's reign of terror, and for 20 years detectives suspected the couple.

Then last December Hindley received a letter from Keith's mother, Mrs Winnie Johnson, and broke her silence to admit her involvement in the two disappearances and offer help to the police. She visited the Moors twice to point out possible burial sites.

Trial

The man leading the hunt, Detective Chief Superintendent Peter Topping, confirmed that a body had been removed from Saddleworth Moor in a phone call to Mrs Johnson. He told her: 'We have found a body - but it is not Keith.'

Mrs Johnson said: 'When Mr Topping told me they had found a body my heart stopped. When he told me it was definitely not Keith's he added immediately that the search for my son would continue. I know now that they will find him.'

Myra Hindley's solicitor, Mr Michael Fisher, said she would take the news 'very, very badly.' He went on: 'She is going to react, it is going to be very bad for her. It will be very upsetting and I know she will find it all extremely hard to take.' Mr Fisher said he was going to Cookham Wood prison in Kent, where Hindley is serving her sentence, 'as soon as I possibly can.'

Earlier this year Pauline Reade's father, 61-year-old Mr Amos Reade, said: 'Our family have lived through the sheer hell and torment of not knowing exactly what happened.' When Hindley made her statement about the two missing bodies, Pauline's mother, Mrs Joan Reade, said: 'For God's sake, tell the truth and give me a few peaceful years before it kills me. All I have left now is the hope that one day I will finally know the truth.'

'All I have left now is the hope that one day I will finally know the truth.'

MYRA HINDLEY NEAR TO DEATH

Priest gives last rites to gravely ill Moors murderer

By Hugh Muir

MOORS MURDERER Myra Hindley is near to death tonight and has received the last rites in hospital.

Hindley, 60, has suffered a suspected heart attack and a chest infection. The woman who lured trusting children into Ian Brady's clutches and helped him torture, abuse and kill them, is under police guard in a ward away from other patients at West Suffolk hospital in Bury St Edmunds, where she was taken after the heart scare at the beginning of the month.

A priest was called to her earlier today. Prison sources say her condition has deteriorated in the past 24 hours. She has

suffered increasing ill health since a suspected stroke two years ago. She and Brady, 64, were jailed for life in 1966 for the murders of 10-year-old Lesley Ann Downey in 1964 and Edward Evans, 17, in 1965. Brady was also convicted of murdering 12-year-old John Kilbride, with Hindley as an accessory. Twenty-one years later, they confessed to killing Pauline Reade, 16, and 12-year-old Keith Bennett.

Serving her 30th year behind bars at Highpoint Prison, Suffolk, Hindley collapsed amid continuing speculation about whether she should, under European law, be released from jail. Today her solicitor Andrew McCooey, who had been due to see her next week, said: 'Her health has not

Child killer Myra Hindley as she looked at the time of her trial for serial murder

Continued on Page 2

Evil life of Myra: Pages 8 & 9

Fire strike hits Tube and now RMT may walk out

By Dick Murray
Transport Editor

TUBE commuters faced a struggle home tonight again after dozens of train drivers refused to work because of the fire strike — although London Underground managers were able to run 40 per cent of services.

There was more bad news, however, for Tube users when the RMT union threatened to call a strike of its own, because management refused a promise not to discipline drivers who would not work during the fire walkout.

Tube strikers have claimed the system is unsafe without regular Fire Brigade cover. LU said its drivers had refused to work today, but Bobby Law, London regional organiser for the largest rail

Continued on Page 4

The Profumo Affair

John Profumo was a pillar of the Establishment, an Old Harrovian who entered Parliament aged 25 in 1940, following a distinguished period of military service. He married actress Valerie Hobson in 1954, and served the Macmillan government in a number of capacities before being appointed Secretary of State for War in 1960.

Rumours in parliament

The first hint that a glittering career might be under threat came in March 1963, when a group of Labour MPs led by George Wigg, under the protection of parliamentary privilege, demanded to know the truth regarding rumours of a relationship between a front bench spokesman and 'freelance model', Christine Keeler. At that point Profumo was not publicly named, the press not enjoying the immunity accorded to members of parliament, but in the Palace of Westminster and, no doubt, most of Fleet Street, the identity of the minister at the centre of the allegations was well known.

LEFT: John Profumo was Secretary of State for War in 1960. His position came under threat in March 1963 when his rumoured affair with Christine Keeler was viewed as a threat to national security.

TOP: Profumo wed actress Valerie Hobson in 1954. They are pictured leaving their wedding ceremony at St Columbus Church in December of that year.

ABOVE: Christine Keeler pushes through the crowd as she leaves the Marlyebone Court.

OPPOSITE LEFT: Keeler en route to visit Lord Denning. Denning conducted the inquiry into the security aspect of the Profumo affair. Keeler had asked for police protection claiming she was frightened.

OPPOSITE RIGHT: Valerie Hobson with Profumo at the Premier of the film 'A King in New York.' Hobson gave up acting shortly after marrying her second husband, Profumo.

Wigg and his Labour colleagues also inferred that Profumo might be able to shed light on a possible perversion of the course of justice. Keeler had failed to attend the Old Bailey trial of one John Edgecombe, in which she had been called as a witness. She was at the centre of a feud between Edgecombe and Aloysius 'Lucky' Gordon, both men having vied for her affection. Edgecombe had slashed Gordon with a knife and gone into hiding. On 14 December 1962 he turned up at a flat in Wimpole Mews, Marylebone, where Keeler was visiting her friend Mandy Rice-Davies. The fugitive wanted to enlist Keeler's help but never got over the threshold. Refused entry, Edgecombe put several bullets through the door and fled. It brought police and journalists running, but the Edgecombe case was a mere sideshow. What the Press and Parliament really wanted to know was the truth about rumours circulating regarding Keeler's relationship with the War Secretary.

Cliveden party

On 22 March 1963 Profumo came out fighting, warning that he would sue if the allegations were repeated outside the House. He said he had met Keeler at a party at Cliveden – Lord Astor's Buckinghamshire seat - in July 1961. Thereafter, he had been in Keeler's company on a number of occasions at a flat in Wimpole Mews owned by an acquaintance, osteopath Dr Stephen Ward. He stressed that there was nothing improper about their relationship. Barely two months later, on 5 June 1963, Profumo resigned both his Cabinet post and his seat in the Commons, admitting the 'grave misdemeanour' of having misled the House in his earlier remarks. Profumo had indeed met Christine Keeler at Cliveden in the summer of 1961, though the circumstances were somewhat less innocent than he first suggested.

Keeler and Rice-Davies meet Stephen Ward

Christine Keeler left home at sixteen, eventually finding work as a topless dancer at Murray's Club in Soho. There she befriended Mandy Rice-Davies, who also joined the establishment's payroll, and both girls fell into the orbit of club patron Stephen Ward.

In addition to his Wimpole Mews property, Ward also leased a cottage in the grounds of Lord Astor's estate. He and Keeler were at Cliveden the same weekend that Lord Astor was entertaining Profumo. Also present was Yevgeny Ivanov, naval attaché to the Russian Embassy. Profumo came across Keeler swimming in the nude, and he obtained her telephone number from Ward. The two embarked upon a brief affair, setting in motion a train of events that would leave a ministerial career in tatters and cost Stephen Ward his life.

MARCH 23, 1963
Profumo kills a rumour

"I understand that my name has been connected with the rumours about the disappearance of Miss Keeler. I would like to take the opportunity of making a personal statement about these matters.

"I last saw Miss Keeler in December 1961 and I have not seen her since. I have no idea where she is now. Any suggestion that I was in any way connected with or responsible for her absence from the trial at the Old Bailey is wholly and completely untrue. My wife and I first met Miss Keeler at a house party in July 1961. This was at Cliveden.

Among a number of people present were Dr. Stephen Ward, whom we already knew slightly, and Mr. Iva-nov, an attaché at the Russian Embassy. The only other occasion my wife and I met Mr. Ivanov was for a few moments at the official reception for Major Gagarin at the Soviet Embassy."

Closed

"My wife and I had a standing invitation to visit Dr. Ward, and between July and December 1961 I met Miss Keeler on about half a dozen occasions at Dr. Ward's flat when I called to see him and his friends. Miss Keeler and I were on friendly terms. There was no impropriety whatsoever in my acquaintanceship with Miss Keeler and I have made this statement because of what was said yesterday in the House by three hon. members and which remarks were protected by privilege. I shall not hesitate to issue writs for libel and slander if scandalous allegations are made or repeated outside this House."

Christine Keeler left home at sixteen, eventually finding work as a topless dancer at Murray's Club in Soho. There she befriended Mandy Rice-Davies.

> 'To my very deep regret I have to admit that this was not true and that I misled you and my colleagues, and the House. I ask you to understand that I did this to protect, as I thought, my wife and family, who were equally misled.'

Political dynamite

Keeler was co-habiting with Ward at the time she met Profumo, though they were not lovers. But Ward did move in elevated social circles, and he regarded it as no stain on his character if he took her to parties and she chose to consort with one or other of the guests. Nor was it an issue for him if those lovers chose to shower Keeler with gifts, as Profumo had done during their brief dalliance. The fact that Keeler was also sharing a bed with Ivanov turned the affair from a sex scandal into an incident that was political dynamite. It was less than a year since the Cuba missile crisis had brought East and West to the brink of nuclear conflagration, and the prospect of state secrets being bandied about during pillow talk alarmed the security services – unless, of course, it was to their advantage. MI5 knew of Keeler's liaison with Ivanov and encouraged it, hoping to profit from any information gleaned. But when the tables were turned and the Russian attaché tried to use Keeler as a conduit for finding out details of Britain's defence capability via Profumo, the alarm bells started ringing. It was as a result of MI5's intervention that Profumo abruptly ended the affair with Keeler, and the minister must have thought he had had a narrow escape. But events were spinning out of control. Once the press pack got a whiff of the scandal, the minister's fate was sealed.

Ward appears in the dock

Nor was Stephen Ward off the hook. The Government was keen to find out more about the man they regarded as the author of its misfortune. That investigation resulted in charges being brought against Ward, who was accused of living off the immoral earnings of Keeler, Rice-Davies and two other women, Vickie Barrett and Ronna Ricardo. Ward had a thriving professional practice and was also a successful artist, his works fetching hundreds of pounds. His gross income was said to be in the region of £5,500 per annum, the equivalent of some £70,000 today. But on 22 July 1963 Ward found himself in the dock at the Old Bailey, accused of running a vice ring, contravening the 1956 Sexual Offences Act.

Far from acknowledging Ward as a pimp, Christine Keeler gave evidence to the effect that he was out of pocket in his dealings with her. Yes, she occasionally gave him small amounts of cash when he was hard up, but those were a drop in the ocean compared with the sums he bestowed upon her; and the fact that she was living at his Wimpole Mews flat rent free merely added to the financial imbalance of their arrangement.

JUNE 6, 1963

Profumo quits

A letter, dated Tuesday and sent by 48-year-old Mr. Profumo to the Prime Minister, said:

'Dear Prime Minister: You will recollect that on March 22, following certain allegations made in Parliament, I made a personal statement. At that time a rumour had charged me with assisting in the disappearance of a witness and with being involved in some possible breach of security.'

'So serious were these charges that I allowed myself to think that my personal association with that witness, which had also been the subject of rumour, was by comparison of minor importance only. In my statement I said that there had been no impropriety in this association. To my very deep regret I have to admit that this was not true and that I misled you and my colleagues, and the House.

I ask you to understand that I did this to protect, as I thought, my wife and family, who were equally misled, as were my professional advisers. I have come to realise that, by this deception, I have been guilty of a grave misdemeanour, and despite the fact that there is no truth whatever in the other charges, I cannot remain a member of your administration, nor of the House of Commons.

I cannot tell you of my deep remorse for the embarrassment I have caused to you, to my colleagues in the Government, to my constituents, and to the party which I have served for the past 25 years. Yours sincerely - Jack Profumo.'

'He would, wouldn't he?'

Prosecuting counsel Mervyn Griffith-Jones faced a similar dead bat from Mandy Rice-Davies. She may have been just eighteen, three years younger than Keeler, but Rice-Davies gave an assured performance that proved resistant to any line of attack. In the earlier hearing at Marylebone Magistrates' Court, she provided the most quoted line of the entire affair. Responding to Lord Astor's denial that he had had sexual relations with her, she retorted: 'He would, wouldn't he?' At the Old Bailey trial she testified that in her brief time living at Ward's Wimpole Mews flat she paid £6 per week in rent and small sums on top of that, some £25 in total. But the court also heard that at other times Ward gave her money, and subsidised her use of the telephone. After doing the mathematics, it left a trifling amount that could have left either party in credit. It certainly didn't create a picture of a predatory 50-year-old Svengali figure exploiting an ingenuous teenager for every penny he could get.

JUNE 6, 1963

Youngest M.P

Yesterday's issue of *Paris-Match* also carried a correction to an earlier story about Mr. Profumo and Miss Keeler. A spokesman for the French magazine said Mr. Profumo had asked for the correction and it had been agreed that no court action would be taken if it were printed.

Mr. Profumo and his wife have a seven-year-old son. Miss Hobson has two children from a previous marriage. Mr. Profumo's first spell in the Commons was from 1940 to 1945, when he represented Kettering, Northamptonshire. For some time he was the youngest M.P. in the House. He became M.P. for Stratford-on-Avon in 1950. He has served as a Minister for nine years, as War Minister since 1960.

Mr. Profumo's resignation from his £5,000-a-year job as a Minister and his intention to resign as an M.P. will mean a by-election at Stratford. At the last general election Mr. Profumo had a 14,129 majority in a straight fight with Labour. Mr. Albert Bond, Tory agent at Stratford, said: "I have never met an M.P. who has been more assiduous to his duties than Mr. Profumo. This is a surprise."

Miss Keeler was at a Chelsea flat last night. Her business manager asked reporters how much they were prepared to pay for Miss Keeler's story.

OPPOSITE TOP: Profumo and his wife, Valerie. His affair with Keeler turned from a sex scandal into political dynamite when it became apparent that Keeler was also sharing a bed with Ivanov, the senior naval attaché at the Soviet Embassy.

RIGHT: Mandy Rice-Davies at London Airport after returning from Majorca. She told Scotland Yard about Keeler's friend Profumo while in an office at the airport.

TOP RIGHT: Mandy Rice-Davies and Christine Keeler arrive at court in 1963 for Stephen Ward's trial at the Old Bailey.

JUNE 11, 1963

Ward in court

Dr. Stephen Ward, 50-year-old society osteopath, was refused bail yesterday. Ward, accused of living on immoral earnings, heard Chief Inspector Samuel Herbert say: "My objection to bail is that there are likely to be a number of more serious charges. Throughout my inquiries this man has been in constant touch with witnesses and I fear if he is allowed bail he will interfere with prosecution witnesses."

Ward is charged with living "wholly or partly on the earnings of prostitution at 17, Wimpole Mews, London, W.1." on various dates between January 1, 1961 and June 8, 1963.

Chief Inspector Herbert said when he arrested Ward in North Watford, Hertfordshire, on Saturday and told him of the charge, he replied: "How dreadful. I shall deny it. Nobody will come forward to say it is true." Ward, who spent the weekend in the cells at Marylebone Lane police station in London, was remanded in custody for a week.

Ward is charged with living 'wholly or partly on the earnings of prostitution at 17, Wimpole Mews, London, W.1.'

Dirty tricks afoot

Had the case against Stephen Ward rested on those bald facts, an acquittal would have been all but assured. But there were dirty tricks afoot and defence counsel James Burge could see which way the wind was blowing. Rice-Davies said that she had had sexual intercourse with an Indian doctor on a number of occasions at Ward's flat, the man in question leaving between £15 and £25 after each visit. Ward denied this, stating that those liaisons had taken place elsewhere. Burge elicited from Rice-Davies that she had come under severe police pressure over separate misdemeanours, one relating to the theft of a television set, the other to serious motoring offences. The implication was clear: that as a quid pro quo for relocating the scene of the sexual encounters with the Indian doctor to Wimpole Mews, other possible charges against Rice-Davies would be dropped. Burge tried to get Rice-Davies to admit as much, but with no luck. For one thing it would have meant perjuring herself, and it also might have led to the other charges being revived and a spell back in Holloway Prison. She had already had a taste of conditions there and had no wish to repeat the experience. In short, Mandy fervently believed that Ward should have been acquitted, but that outcome came a distant second to self-preservation.

ABOVE: Profumo and his wife pictured on their return to London. Profumo fled the capital the day before his statement admitting to the House that he had lied about Christine Keeler.

TOP RIGHT: Christine Keeler's mother's house in Buckinghamshire.

RIGHT: Keeler and Rice-Davies driving from the court after the first day of the trial of Stephen Ward. Ward, a 50 year old osteopath, was accused of running a vice ring and living off the immoral earnings of the two women.

Solicitor says Miss Keeler spoke of Ivanov

Solicitor Mr. Michael Eddowes last night answered questions at a Press Conference about the letter that started a new Profumo sensation yesterday. Mr. Eddowes sent the letter to Mr. Macmillan. Christine Keeler, he claimed, had told him that Russian attaché Eugene Ivanov asked her to get military information from Mr. Profumo. He added that he passed this information to the Special Branch seven days after Mr. Profumo's statement of denial in the Commons on March 22.

Last night solicitors for Miss Keeler denied on her behalf that Ivanov had ever asked her to obtain military information from Mr. Profumo and denied that she had made any statement to that effect to anyone.

Mr. Eddowes, 60, claimed that the information allegedly requested by Ivanov concerned the date of delivery of nuclear warheads to West Germany. He also claimed in his letter that he had asked the Special Branch to interview five persons "with all of whom Miss Keeler had been intimately associated" so that the accuracy of his report could be checked.

Public duty

At his home in Knightsbridge Mr. Eddowes was questioned by reporters about the identity of the five. He said they were "frightfully unimportant" and were not M.Ps. Mr.

Eddowes said that the Special Branch had assured him that his report would be sent to the Prime Minister at once.

He added: "I wrote to Mr. Macmillan because something has obviously gone seriously wrong somewhere. My original information to the security services was plainly ignored. I was expecting to have a call this morning from at least some senior security officer as a result of my letter to the Prime Minister. Instead, all I had was a formal acknowledgment from the P.M's office. This convinced me that it was my public duty to publish my letter to him before the Commons debate on Monday.

It was on December 19 that the talk with Miss Keeler about military information took place," said Mr. Eddowes. "I had met her

briefly some time before," he said. "These were purely social meetings at Dr. Stephen Ward's flat. I was then getting treatment from Dr. Ward for a strained shoulder which I had damaged in a car crash."

Excited

He said that Miss Keeler phoned him and asked for advice. She said someone had tried to attack her and she was very worried.

"She asked me to go to see her and gave me an address in Marylebone. I went to see her. She was very upset and excited when I saw her. Some time before I had heard that she had had a relationship with both Profumo and Ivanov, and I thought that this would be a good opportunity to put questions about the possibility of espionage in this

direction. I asked her if Profumo and Ivanov were friends of hers. She said one would go out of one door as the other came in. I asked her if Ivanov had tried to get her to obtain information from Profumo. She said she had not got him any information, but Ivanov had asked her to get the date of the delivery of nuclear warheads to Germany."

Mr. Eddowes said he did nothing with the information at that time. He explained: "I was given to understand that the security police were watching both Profumo and Ivanov and had the matter in hand. This came from a source I had no reason to doubt." But when the Profumo denial was made in the House Mr. Eddowes realised, he said, that he must take action.

TOP: Mandy Rice-Davies in an Austin Seven Countryman at the 1960 motor show.

'I was given to understand that the security police were watching both Profumo and Ivanov and had the matter in hand.'

The Profumo Affair

Total fabrication

Prostitute Vickie Barrett described how she had been recruited by Ward, telling the court of her visits to Wimpole Mews to service a number of clients he had provided. It was said that whips and canes were her stock-in-trade, lurid revelations guaranteed to crank up the titillation and sleaze factor. 'If she is telling the truth,' said Ward, 'I am guilty.' But that was not the case, he insisted. In an impassioned outburst, the defendant rejected Barrett's testimony as total fabrication, but he knew that if enough mud was hurled, some was bound to stick. 'In the general atmosphere of villainy that has been built up around me anyone can make any suggestion about me. Anyone from the street can come forward to this court and I have to prove they are wrong.'

One witness who offered a chink of light was Ronna Ricardo. At the magistrates' court hearing she had been one of the jewels in the prosecution's crown, referring to numerous sexual liaisons she had had at Wimpole Mews, orchestrated by Ward. Now, she turned tail, saying that she had been pressurised into putting her name to the original statement. The police, she alleged, had threatened to take away her baby and have her sister put in a home if she did not implicate Ward in the procurement trade. Finally, here was some concrete evidence that a witness had been got at, that the authorities were determined to go to any lengths to secure a conviction. Ricardo's volte-face was a potential boon to the defence, though it did beg the question: was she lying at the magistrates' court, or was she lying now?

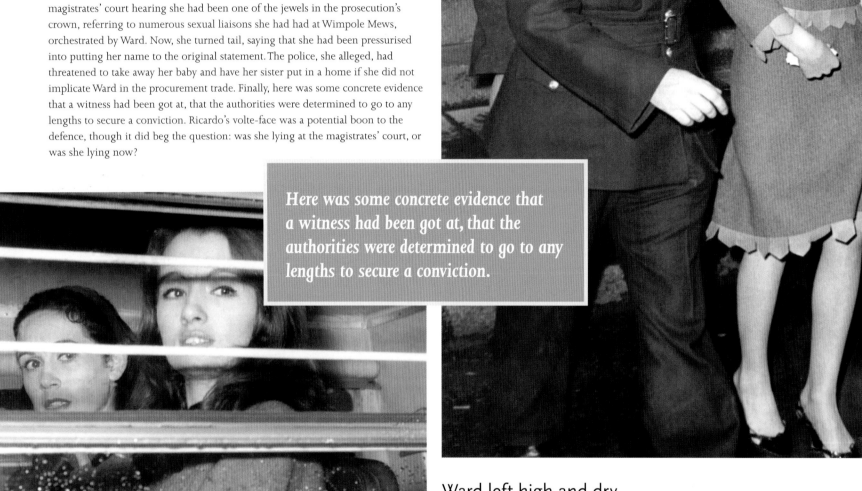

> Here was some concrete evidence that a witness had been got at, that the authorities were determined to go to any lengths to secure a conviction.

ABOVE AND RIGHT: Keeler was arrested on 6 September 1963 for conspiracy to obstruct the course of justice and perjury. She, and three others, concealed information that she was assaulted by someone else prior to the alleged attack by 'Lucky' Gordon.

Ward left high and dry

In his summing up Mr Justice Marshall said the picture that had emerged over the 10-day trial had not been a pretty one, but that it was important for the jury to refrain from adopting 'a Pecksniffian attitude'. The judge remarked upon the fact that Ward appeared to have been abandoned in his moment of greatest need. 'If Stephen Ward was telling the truth in the witness box, there are in this city many witnesses of high estate and low who could have come and testified support of his evidence.' In other words, the defendant seemed to have been left high and dry, a prescient comment as events transpired.

After four and a half hours' deliberation, the jury returned a Guilty verdict on two counts, those relating to living off the immoral earnings of Keeler and Rice-Davies. Ward was acquitted on the charge of procuring a girl under the age of twenty-one to have intercourse with a third person; and of living off the immoral earnings of Vickie Barrett.

Ward Convicted

Dr. Stephen Ward, his life still threatened by a drug overdose, was last night convicted of living on immoral earnings. After an absence of 4hr. 36min. the jury at the Old Bailey found him guilty of being kept partly by the prostitution of Christine Keeler and Mandy Rice-Davies.

The jury of 11 men and one woman cleared 50-year-old Ward of three other charges - living off the immoral earnings of Vickie Barrett and being involved in procuring two girls. The maximum sentence on each count on which Ward was found guilty is seven years. The sentences could be made consecutive, making 14 years' jail, or he could be fined.

Last night Ward was still "grievously ill" and deeply unconscious in St. Stephen's Hospital, Chelsea. He will be told the verdict as soon as he recovers.

Barbiturate overdose

Ward was not in court to hear the verdict. Fearing the worst after hearing the judge's summation, he had taken an overdose of barbiturates and lapsed into a coma. Mr Justice Marshal allowed the verdict to be given in Ward's absence, though he deferred passing sentence until such time as the defendant was well enough to attend. That time never came, for Stephen Ward died three days later. He never regained consciousness.

Vickie Barrett broke down when she heard the news, admitting that she had had intercourse only with Ward at his flat. Her testimony relating to a succession of other men she conducted business with at Wimpole Mews was all lies, a false account cooked up under duress. Of course, that particular fabrication hardly mattered inasmuch as Ward was exonerated on the specific charge relating to Barrett; but it did add further weight to the theory that evidence had been gained through coercion.

Ward's plea to Denning

The night Dr. Stephen Ward decided to take a fatal overdose of drugs he made a telephone call to an official of the Denning enquiry. Mr. T. A. Critchley, a Home Office Assistant Secretary helping Lord Denning in the inquiry into the security aspects of the Profumo affair, talked last night about his 20-minute conversation with Ward.

Mr. Critchley told me: "Dr. Ward mentioned the names of two of the girls with whom he had been associated and who had given evidence at his Old Bailey trial. He said he was particularly anxious that Lord Denning should examine their testimonies. It must have been about 9.30 last Tuesday evening when Dr. Ward phoned me at my home. He sounded calm and self-confident. I had the impression that he was phoning around some people to talk about things he might not have an opportunity to say later."

Lord Denning, who had already questioned Ward, almost certainly would have wanted to see him again.

Ward, 50-year-old osteopath, died in hospital on Saturday after more than 80 hours in a coma, without knowing that an Old Bailey jury had found him guilty of living on the immoral earnings of Christine Keeler and Marilyn Rice-Davies.

RIGHT: 'He is nearer to God than I am' — What Lord Longford said about John Profumo.

TOP RIGHT: Calling time: a letter sent to The Times in London, May, 1987, by some of Britain's most venerable figures asking for the Promumo Affair to be consigned to history.

A matter now for history?

From Lord Hailsham, CH, FRS, and others

Sir, The undersigned have noted the current publicity in relation to an episode now a quarter of a century old and feel it a good time to place on record their sense of admiration for the dignity and courage displayed by Mr and Mrs John Profumo and their family in that period.

This letter also records our feelings that it is now appropriate to consign the episode to history.

Yours faithfully,
HAILSHAM,
DROGHEDA,
CARRINGTON,
GOODMAN,
WEINSTOCK,
ROY JENKINS,
JAMES PRIOR,

9-11 Fulwood Place,
Gray's Inn, WC1.
May 20.

Profumo receives OBE

Christine Keeler's name became synonymous with the Permissive Society, the famous naked shot of her sitting astride a chair becoming one of the iconic images of the Swinging Sixties. Away from the glare of publicity John Profumo set about rebuilding his life and restoring his reputation. He turned to the voluntary sector, notably Toynbee Hall, a charitable institution in the East End with which he would be associated for the rest of his life. He took on menial tasks including washing up and cleaning toilets, and had to be persuaded to assume a senior role in the fund-raising arm of the charity. A landmark on the road to redemption came in 1975, when he was awarded a CBE for his charity work. Twenty years later, Margaret Thatcher invited Profumo to her 70th birthday party celebrations, hailing him as 'one of our national heroes'. He was placed next to the Queen, the rehabilitation complete.

John Profumo died on 10 March 2006, aged 91. For 43 years he maintained his silence on the scandal that rocked the Establishment, sold millions of newspapers and played no small part in the Conservative Party's defeat at the 1964 general election.

The Krays

'I'm not going to waste words on you. The sentence is that of life imprisonment. In my view, society has earned a rest from your activities and I recommend that you be detained for at least 30 years.'

With those words, uttered by Mr Justice Melford Stevenson at the Old Bailey on 5 March 1969, the curtain was brought down on the reign of the Kray twins, rulers of the East End underworld for over a decade. Remarkably, not everyone bade good riddance to gangland's most notorious figures. Stories of Ronnie and Reggie Kray's charitable giving were legion; they were ever willing to dip into their pockets in response to a hard-luck story, or fund a Christmas party for local pensioners. The streets, it was said, were far safer when the Krays ran the show. They also looked after the families of the 'aways', the euphemism given to their acolytes who were serving time. Both twins' funerals brought thousands out onto the streets of the capital; theirs was a tight-knit community that looked after its own. Yet the Krays' story was no romantic tale in which the only victims were hardened criminals who got what they deserved. Ronnie and Reggie built their empire on violence and intimidation and maintained it through fear, emulating the Mafia-style level of control that they had set out to achieve.

East Enders

The twins were born 24 October 1933 to Charles and Violet Kray, who already had a six-year-old son, named after his father. The boys' father was a peripheral figure during their upbringing, for he roamed the country as a travelling salesman. Not that Charles Snr would have made much of a role model, for he was a hard-drinking gambler who consorted with the local villains when he wasn't out on the road. He also showed his mettle when he was called up for military service, choosing to go on the run rather than fight for King and country.

At school Ronnie and Reggie were willing and co-operative, showing little indication that they would veer badly off the rails. They did show themselves to be handy with their fists, but initially that was in the controlled environment of the ring. The boys were keen and able boxers, inspired to put on the gloves by their maternal grandfather, who had fought under the name Jimmy 'Cannonball' Lee. They were treading a well-worn path, for many East Enders took up boxing as a way of channelling their aggression, and as a possible escape route from an impoverished existence in an unemployment blackspot.

The highlight of their boxing career came in 1951, when they fought on the same card in a junior championship staged at the Royal Albert Hall, but by then the twins had revealed that they weren't averse to a rather less noble art, with the gloves off. Two years earlier, they found themselves up on a GBH charge following an incident outside a dance hall. The twins were acquitted through lack of evidence, which would become a recurring theme over the next 20 years. It was no easy task to find someone willing to testify against the Krays, even in their teenage years.

'The Firm'

One of the early money-making scams they became involved in was sham auctions, where their muscle and boxing prowess came in handy. Stooges in the crowd ramped up prices before an unsuspecting purchaser secured his 'bargain'. When the penny dropped either they disappeared shamefacedly, not wanting to admit they had been taken for a ride, or, if they chose to confront the rogue operators, one of the Krays would be pressed into service. A favourite trick of Reggie's was to wait until the victim was remonstrating in full flow, then deliver a vicious uppercut. A blow to a slack jaw inflicted horrific injuries.

The boys' boxing careers came to an end when they were claimed for National Service in 1952. Army life didn't agree with them, and they spent much of the time incarcerated at Shepton Mallet military prison for absconding and a string of other misdemeanours before being dishonourably discharged in 1954. They took over the Regal billiard hall in Mile End, and after a few run-ins with the local hard cases, slowly established 'The Firm', the name given to the organisation that would rule the East End roost and to whom others paid their protection dues – if they knew what was good for them. Thuggery attracted thugs, and the twins brought some of them into their circle. Their timing was perfect, for the mid-fifties saw the retirement of Billy Hill and Jack 'Spot' Comer, two of the most notorious gangsters of the day. The Krays were ready and able to step into the vacuum created, though they had to see off several other contenders for the underworld crown.

> 'The Firm' was the name given to the organisation that would rule the East End roost and to whom others paid their protection dues.

APRIL 6, 1965

Boxers who became club owners

The Kray twins, ex-professional boxers, have run clubs in both the East End and the West End of London. As lightweights they won their first professional fights in July 1951. They were 17.

From the East End clubs they owned, The Double R, in Bow Road, and the Kentucky, in Mile End Road, the Krays organised concerts and parties in aid of the aged and crippled. They gave television sets to old people's homes; money to a Bethnal Green Darby and Joan club. Bethnal Green councillor Mr.

Bob Rosomond said: "When I was mayor I often met the Kray brothers at charity functions. On one occasion Ronnie Kray came to the town hall with Winifred Atwell, the pianist. He was showing her round the East End."

Two years ago the Krays took over Esmeralda's Barn, a rendezvous for debutantes and their escorts in Wilton-place, Knightsbridge. The twins - in frilly toreador dress shirts and black ties - moved into the "high life." They have been frequent callers backstage at West End theatres. At first nights, big boxing promotions and film premieres the Krays are always to be seen.

OPPOSITE: The three brothers Reggie, Charles and Ronnie in a handclasp of friendship.

TOP: Reggie Kray outside his house in Bethnal Green with his grandfather, Jimmy. He and Ronnie had just been acquitted of attempting to obtain protection money from Soho club owner Hew McGowan.

ABOVE: The twins flank mother Violet who was always a stalwart supporter of her boys. Ronnie and Reggie Kray were born on 24 October 1933 in Hoxton, East London, to Charles and Violet Kray. The couple already had a six-year-old son, also called Charlie, who was born on 9 July 1927.

The Krays

Loose cannon

Ronnie was the dominant partner in The Firm, styling himself as the 'Colonel' in their military-style operations. He was also unhinged, his psychosis diagnosed during a seven-year stretch he was given for violent assault in 1956. Ronnie had to be restrained with a straitjacket while serving at Winchester Prison, and was eventually certified insane and transferred to Long Grove Mental Hospital, Epsom. His grip on reality was tenuous and he suffered acute paranoia, at one time saying he was convinced that Reggie was a Soviet spy. Even so, Ronnie showed enough improvement to get himself released after serving half his sentence, or, at least, convinced the doctors that he was well enough to be given his freedom. In fact, he was dangerously psychotic, and even Reggie regarded him as a loose cannon whose wild unpredictability was having a damaging effect on their business interests.

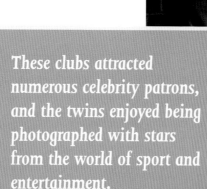

Untouchable

The Krays made a fortune from extortion and fraud, and operated illegal gambling dens. As well as taking regular protection payments, they also engaged in the practice of 'nipping', where members of the gang made random visits to premises they were 'securing' and helped themselves to some of the proceeds. One of their favourite scams was the 'long firm fraud'. Companies were set up, premises obtained and goods ordered from suppliers. Bills were paid promptly to begin with in order to increase their credit rating, at which point a huge order was placed and the operation closed down. The premises were often torched before the disappearing act.

> These clubs attracted numerous celebrity patrons, and the twins enjoyed being photographed with stars from the world of sport and entertainment.

On the surface, the Krays liked to present themselves as respectable businessmen, acquiring interests in several nightclubs, including Esmeralda's Barn in the upmarket West End, a stone's throw from Knightsbridge. These clubs attracted numerous celebrity patrons, and the twins enjoyed being photographed with stars from the world of sport and entertainment. One David Bailey photoshoot produced stark monochrome images that acquired iconic status, on a par with Twiggy and The Beatles in capturing the 60s zeitgeist. The Metropolitan Police Force knew that the empire was propped up by violence and intimidation, but proving it was another matter entirely. And events that occurred in the mid-sixties convinced the Krays even more that they were untouchable.

'Nipper' Read

Ronnie Kray was a known homosexual, and in 1964 the Mirror Group broke a sensational story linking a gangster with a Tory peer. The paper had photographic evidence of the liaison, but concerns over a possible lawsuit led the editor to run a tantalising headline: 'The Picture We Must Not Print'. The German magazine Stern had no such qualms and named Ronnie Kray and Lord Boothby as the protagonists in the story. The Mirror then backed down, issuing open apologies to both parties, and thereafter Fleet Street was pragmatically circumspect in its reporting of the capital's gangland ringleaders.

TOP, MIDDLE AND BOTTOM: When the twins attended Wood Close Primary School in Brick Lane there was no hint of their future criminal tendencies and they got on well with teachers and other pupils. The influence of their grandfather, Jimmy

'Cannonball' Lee, soon led both boys into amateur boxing, at that time a common pastime for working-class boys in the East End. However, by the time the boys turned professional they had already been in trouble with the law.

APRIL 6, 1965

Kray twins go free

Ronald Kray, 31, grinned at his twin brother Reginald outside their parents' home in London's East End yesterday and said: "Definitely it's the quiet life for us now." They had just left the dock at the Old Bailey's No. 1 Court. There they were cleared of charges of attempting to obtain protection money from a Soho club owner. The Krays, who had been in custody for three months after their arrest, were acquitted with a third man on the sixth day of a retrial after a jury in the first trial failed to agree.

The Krays, in blue Italian-cut suits, struggled through a crowd of their friends as they left the court. A bronze Jaguar took them to their lawyers' office and then to their parents' home in Vallance Road, Bethnal Green. There the two East Enders, who used to own the fashionable Esmeralda's Barn nightclub in Knightsbridge, were hugged and cheered by neighbours.

Their mother, Mrs. Violet Kray, ran out of the terrace house saying: "I'm almost crying, I'm so relieved." Reginald brought his typist girlfriend Frances Shea, 21, out of the house and hugged her. He said: "We're hoping to get married this week."

A representative of his firm of solicitors said: "Don't say anything." Then he turned to questioners and said: "Reginald has not made his mind up yet." Cars arrived and men hurried into the Kray house. A man from the solicitors' office opened the door from time to time. He said: "They're just having a quiet drink in the peace of their own home after the ordeal."

> Their mother, Mrs. Violet Kray, ran out of the terrace house saying: 'I'm almost crying, I'm so relieved'.

Krays' trial collapses

That same year, one club boss decided to call the Krays' bluff and go to the police instead of paying for the 'door services' offered. When Hew McCowan made a statement detailing how the Hideaway Club in Gerrard Street had been targeted by the Krays, it must have been music to the ears of Detective Superintendent Leonard 'Nipper' Read, the man tasked with breaking the stranglehold The Firm exerted on the capital. Unfortunately, it was not the hoped-for breakthrough. McCowan's manager, Sidney Vaughan, was to be a key witness, but he changed his story, telling Read he had had some kind of epiphany and that his original statement was false. Even worse, witnesses came forward to testify that McCowan had tried to suborn them into giving false evidence against the twins. There was a hung jury, and a retrial was ordered. That failed to go the distance, Mr Justice Lyell halting the proceedings and finding the defendants not guilty. It was partly in response to this case that the Labour government passed the 1967 Criminal Law Act, which allowed for 10-2 majority verdicts. Under the new system at least three jurors would have to be 'got at' to secure an acquittal, though that was of small comfort to DS Read when the case collapsed in 1965.

ABOVE RIGHT: The tenacious characteristics shown in the boxing ring were to be seen later on in their business activities with devastating effects. By the time Reggie and Ronnie finished their years of National Service in 1954 they were already immersed in a seedy world of criminal activity which would see them in court for the first of many appearances.

ABOVE LEFT AND TOP LEFT: Shortly after the case against the brothers collapsed at the Old Bailey in April 1965, Reggie married his girlfriend, Frances Shea. The wedding photographs were taken by the celebrated photographer David Bailey. As West End nightclub owners at this time the Krays mixed with many well-known peoplewhich gave them an air of respectability and in the 1960s they became celebrities in their own right, even appearing in interviews on television.

The Krays

'Most clubs are very respectable'

The twins celebrated by rubbing McCowan's nose in it, hosting a victory party at the Hideaway Club, which they had acquired and renamed El Morocco. The acquittal even brought them a platform on the BBC, where they gave a sanitised view of their business dealings. The occasional patron might overindulge and have to be dealt with, they said, but apart from that 'most clubs are very respectable'. Reggie took the opportunity to publicly announce his forthcoming nuptials, and in April 1965 married Frances Shea, whom he had known since she was a 16-year-old schoolgirl. It was a stormy relationship, Frances soon buckling under the stifling oppression of having every facet of her life ordered by her husband. After two months she left and returned to her family home, the marriage, apparently, never consummated. Reggie certainly shared his brother's homosexual predilections, and in local circles they were irreverently known as 'Gert and Daisy', though, naturally, not to their faces. In June 1967 Frances took an overdose of phenobarbitone, perhaps realising that there was only one sure way of walking out on the Krays.

> 'I have done my one, it is about time you did yours.'

First Victim

It was murder, not extortion that finally proved the Krays' undoing. Their first victim was George Cornell, a member of the South London Richardson gang, long-time enemies of the Krays. However, it wasn't a turf war that caused Ronnie Kray to go looking for Cornell on 9 March 1966. It was a matter of honour and respect, for Cornell had unwisely called Ronnie a 'fat poof'. It was also rumoured that he had shot a cousin of the Krays during a bar-room fracas, but the insult alone was enough for Ronnie to seek retribution. The showdown took place at the Blind Beggar public house in Aldgate. Ronnie and one of his lieutenants, John 'Ian' Barrie, confronted Cornell, who seemed unfazed, remarking, 'Well, look who's here.' They were to be his final words, for Kray unceremoniously put a bullet through his head. He had hardly chosen a remote location for the revenge killing – there were over two dozen people in the pub - yet the police struggled to find a single witness. East Enders were reticent enough to inform on one of their own, and fear of reprisals made it doubly difficult for the police to build a case against the Krays.

JANUARY 10, 1969

Rivals in violence

The Kray twins' rivalry in violence linked two terror murders committed 20 months apart, an Old Bailey jury was told yesterday. Mr Kenneth Jones, QC, prosecuting, said: 'During that intervening period arguments took place from time to time between Ronald and Reginald Kray... In the course of these arguments Ronald would say to his brother: "I have done my one, it is about time you did yours."'

Twenty months after the first murder, the second man was stabbed to death. Mr Jones said the reason for this murder was not hard to seek. 'Reginald Kray had decided to show that he was equal to his twin brother in violence and that he could kill too.'

> They were to be his final words, for Kray unceremoniously put a bullet through his head.

ABOVE, LEFT AND OPPOSITE RIGHT : Reggie married his childhood sweetheart Frances Shea at St James the Great with St Jude church in Bethnal Green on 19 April 1965. Veteran boxer Ted 'Kid' Lewis and former champions Terry Spinks and Terry Allen were among the guests. The marriage was short-lived, lasting only eight weeks, although it was never formally ended.

ABOVE: Frances died in June 1967 after taking an overdose of barbiturates. Reggie attended the hearing at St Pancras Coroner's Court with elder brother Charlie. The inquest ruled that that she had committed suicide.

OPPOSITE TOP LEFT: The Kray brothers arrive for a hearing at Bow Street Magistrate's court. On 8 May 1968 the Krays and 16 other members of their 'firm' were arrested when police raided their Braithwaite house in Old Street. Their arrest and incarceration before their trial helped to loosen the grip of fear they had on the community and many witnesses started to come forward.

Second murder

In December that year the twins committed their second murder. The victim was another villain, Frank Mitchell, a brute of a specimen known as the 'Mad Axe Man'. Mitchell was sprung from Dartmoor Prison, perhaps to help in a possible turf war with the Richardson mob, or maybe simply to keep a promise or render a favour. The escape plan went smoothly enough, and Mitchell was whisked away to a flat in London to lie low. But he became restless, and it seems the twins turned on the man they now regarded as a liability. On Christmas Eve 1966, Mitchell was told he was being taken to another safe house in the country, but as he piled into the waiting van he was shot at the Krays' behest by two of their henchmen. The body was never recovered and it remains, officially, an unsolved murder.

> Ronnie was becoming increasingly unstable. He had upped the ante dramatically with the cold-blooded execution of George Cornell, and wanted Reggie to show the same murderous intent.

Butchered

Ronnie was becoming increasingly unstable. He had upped the ante dramatically with the cold-blooded execution of George Cornell, and wanted Reggie to show the same murderous intent. Following Frances's death, the bond between the brothers was deeper than ever, and Reggie was more than willing to put himself on the same bloody footing. All that was needed was a suitable victim.

The initial target was Leslie Payne, the financial brains of the outfit who oversaw the long-firm cons and looked after The Firm's business interests. He was suspected of trying to cut a deal with the police and small-time crook Jack McVitie was recruited as hit man, paid a £100 retainer to do the job. McVitie was universally known as 'The Hat' for he was never seen without his trilby, which he wore to hide his receding hairline. His bald spot became the least of his problems when he not only failed to carry out his mission, but also let slip in an unguarded moment that he had ripped off the Kray twins and might kill them instead. With that he effectively signed his own death warrant. Ronnie and Reggie installed themselves at a Stoke Newington flat and told underlings to put the word out for McVitie to come and join the party. Jack walked right into the trap, and after a failed attempt to escape by jumping through a window, he faced the merciless wrath of the Kray twins. Told by Ronnie to take his death like a man, McVitie replied: 'I'll be a man but I don't want to die like one.' It made no difference, for Reggie butchered him with a carving knife, egged on by his brother. While they cleaned themselves up, some of their lieutenants got rid of the body, perhaps in deep water, perhaps in the foundations of some civil engineering project. It was never recovered.

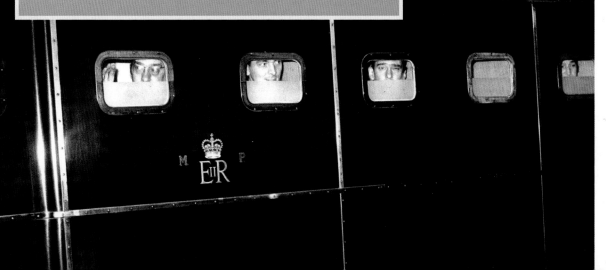

ABOVE LEFT: After the failure of the prosecution in May 1965, Inspector Leonard 'Nipper' Read tackled the problem of convicting the twins with renewed vigour. He frequently came up against the East End 'wall of silence', which discouraged anyone from providing information to the police.

LEFT: Members of the Kray gang return to the Old Bailey in an armoured van to receive their sentences.

058111 REG. KRAY

058109 C. KRAY

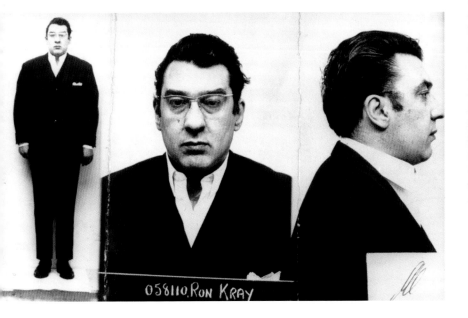

058110. RON KRAY

Terrified, bathed in sweat, like a caged animal, he tried to escape. He threw himself at the window and smashed it, but Reginald Kray and Ronald Kray pulled him back.

Tongues finally loosened

The wall of silence surrounding the Krays now began to crumble. All three murders had been gratuitous and irrational, leaving insiders fearing their turn might be next. Some thought the twins were now out of control, and were unnerved enough to want to see them toppled. That was the breakthrough Read had been waiting for. Until then no one dared speak out against the Krays while they were at large, and they would remain at large until someone spoke out against them. This Catch 22 cycle was broken in 1967, when two members of The Firm implicated the Krays after being arrested on other charges. Paul Elvey was carrying dynamite when he was taken into custody, and told police that the Krays intended to use it to blow up the house of one of their enemies. Elvey dragged Alan Cooper's name into it, and the latter, faced with a charge of conspiracy to murder, told police that he had been hired as a hit man by the Krays.

At 6 am on the morning of 8 May 1968 the police launched a co-ordinated sweep, hauling dozens of gang members into custody. Read himself arrested Ronnie and Reggie Kray. His hope that having all the villains out of commission might loosen a few tongues proved correct. Those with a grievance who now felt able to air it included Leslie Payne, who was aware of the threats against him and wanted out. He gave details of The Firm's fraudulent activities. Albert Donoghue, another trusty lieutenant, spilled the beans regarding the death of Frank Mitchell, while Ronnie Hart, a cousin to the Krays, gave chapter and verse on the events surrounding Jack McVitie's demise. John Dickson, who drove Ronnie and Ian Barrie to the Blind Beggar on the night George Cornell was gunned down, also jumped ship. With gang members turning tail, the Blind Beggar barmaid, who had insisted she'd seen nothing at the time and lived in fear for three years, now found the courage to come forward.

JANUARY 10, 1969

'The last brutal sequence of this whole foul incident was then enacted in the living room. McVitie was at last fully aware of what was to happen to him. This was no party. Terrified, bathed in sweat, like a caged animal, he tried to escape. He threw himself at the window and smashed it, but Reginald Kray and Ronald Kray pulled him back and started belabouring him with their fists. Then Ronald Kray, who had done his, held McVitie from behind, pinning his arms. Reginald Kray took up the knife, stabbed McVitie in the face, punched him over the heart and plunged the knife repeatedly into McVitie's body with his twin brother saying over and over again, "Kill him, Reg."

As he said the words 'Kill him, Reg!' Mr Jones' voice dropped to a hoarse whisper. He went on: 'McVitie fell to the floor gravely wounded, gasping for breath. The butchery was not complete. Reginald Kray stood astride him and plunged the knife into his neck twice, twisting it to make sure its deadly work was done.' Then, said Mr Jones, Ronald Albert Bender, one of the Krays' associates, felt McVitie's heart and pronounced him dead.

Mr Jones said that some weeks after the McVitie murder Ronald Kray told a man that if two women who knew that violence had been done said anything they would be 'done.' 'He enlarged just a little on this,' said Mr Jones. He said: "I've got a woman who could do this. I had her ready for Cornell's old woman."'

LEFT: Mug shots of the Krays. Once the gang members were in custody it was relatively easy to gain a conviction. The murder trial began on 8 January 1969 and lasted for 40 days.

Volatile

The Old Bailey trial began 8 January 1969 and ran for 40 days, the longest murder trial in British legal history. There was huge media interest, and black market tickets for the public gallery changed hands for £5 as everyone waited to see whether the prosecution, led by Kenneth Jones QC, could finally secure a conviction against the Krays. Albert Donaghue pleaded guilty to being an accessory to the murder of Jack McVitie, leaving the fate of ten men to be decided by the court. Mr Justice Melford Stevenson wanted to simplify the proceedings by numbering the defendants. Ronnie and Reggie were having none of that and the judge relented, though that would be their only victory during the proceedings.

The twins were volatile throughout. In one outburst Ronnie called the chief prosecuting counsel a 'fat slob' when he didn't like the line of questioning being pursued with one particular witness. To see an all-powerful underworld figure reduced to playground-style name-calling was an indication that the Krays were emasculated, their reign of terror over. On 5 March 1969 Reggie and Ronnie were both found guilty of the murder of Jack McVitie, and the latter was also convicted of murdering George Cornell. Of the other eight men in the dock only one walked free. Charlie Kray was found guilty on an accessory charge and given ten years.

ABOVE LEFT AND ABOVE RIGHT: Charlie Kray is driven away from Maidstone Jail in 1975 after serving seven years of his ten year sentence. After leaving prison he lived in Benidorm and tried to build a property development business. However, he was once again imprisoned in 1997 for 12 years after he was found guilty of masterminding a drugs deal. After suffering with chest pains he was taken from Parkhurst Prison on the Isle of Wight to hospital, where he died on 4 April 2000 aged 73.

BOTTOM RIGHT: Reggie arrives at the Old Church in Chingford for the funeral of his mother Violet, who died of cancer in August 1982. The notorious East End gangsters arrived separately – each handcuffed to a prison guard and flanked by police officers. Ronnie Kray was brought from Broadmoor Hospital for the criminally insane in Berkshire.

> *Ronald Joseph Hart stood in an Old Bailey witness box for 150 minutes yesterday and calmly told the Kray case jury that he saw Reginald Kray knife Jack 'The Hat' McVitie to death.*

Jack the Hat said 'I don't want to die'

Ronald Joseph Hart stood in an Old Bailey witness box for 150 minutes yesterday and calmly told the Kray case jury that he saw Reginald Kray knife Jack 'The Hat' McVitie to death. He claimed that he helped the Kray twins to drag McVitie from a window as he tried desperately to escape being killed. His evidence brought an outburst from Reginald Kray in the dock. He stood up, pointed to Hart in the witness box and shouted: 'If there was any stabbing done, it must have been done by you.'

Hart, 26, who was allowed to keep his address secret, said Ronald Kray posted him at the front window of a flat in Evering Road, Stoke Newington, London. It was his job to shout down when McVitie arrived. He followed McVitie and the escort of four men who had brought him into a basement room. He added: 'I saw Reggie Kray get McVitie up against the wall. McVitie had Reggie Kray's arm trapped under his arm. Reggie Kray was holding a gun in the hand that was trapped.

Then McVitie ran out into the passage. Ronnie Kray got hold of him, pushed him against the wall near the telephone and said: "Come on, Jack, be a man." McVitie said: "Yes, I'll be a man but I don't want to die like one." They went back into the room. McVitie was pushed into the settee. Reggie Kray tried to shoot him. Reggie pointed the gun at him and pulled the trigger. Nothing happened. McVitie made a run for the window. Reggie gave the gun to Ronnie Bender. Next thing I remember, Reggie and McVitie were up against the wall. Ronald Kray was trying to push the carving knife into McVitie's back. It was bending.

'McVitie ran across the room and smashed the window. Ronald Kray, Reggie Kray, Ronnie Bender and myself pulled him back. Then Reggie Kray got hold of the knife and stuck it in McVitie's face. Reggie punched him in the chest and started to stick the knife into his stomach about three or four times. Ronnie Kray was holding McVitie's arms from behind. McVitie was telling them to stop. Ronnie Kray was saying: "Kill him, Reg. Go on, Reg." Then McVitie fell on the floor. He was dying then ... Reggie Kray stood astride him and stuck the knife through his throat.'

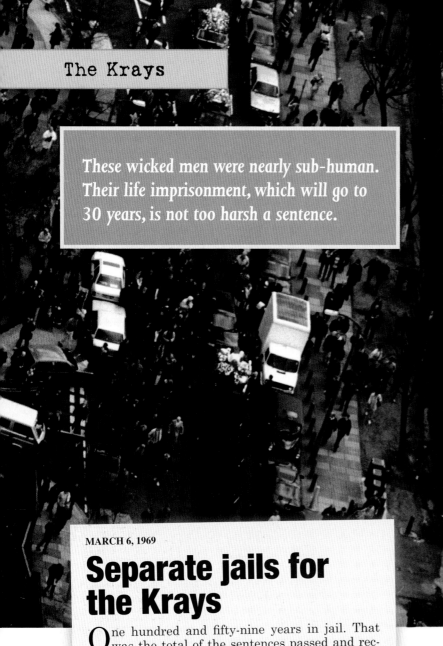

The Krays

> These wicked men were nearly sub-human. Their life imprisonment, which will go to 30 years, is not too harsh a sentence.

Separate jails for the Krays

One hundred and fifty-nine years in jail. That was the total of the sentences passed and recommended at the Old Bailey yesterday for the Kray twins and members of their 'murder firm.' The twins, Ronald and Reginald, now 35, will be old-age pensioners when they are released if the judge's proposals in his report on the case to the Home Secretary are carried out.

For Mr Justice Melford Stevenson sentenced them to life for murder and recommended that each twin should be kept in prison for 30 years. Four others found guilty of murder were jailed for life. The judge recommended two should serve 20 years and two 15 years. There would be no remission for good conduct for the twins.

Some of the Great Train Robbers who got 30-year sentences will serve a maximum of 20 with good conduct. The Kray sentences are among the longest given at the Old Bailey since the war.

ABOVE AND RIGHT: Ronnie Kray was given a traditional send off, with six black-plumed horses and a glass-sided hearse following his death in Wexham Park Hospital, Slough, on 17 March 1995. The infamous gangland killer died in hospital of a heart attack two days after collapsing at Broadmoor where he was serving a life sentence for murder. Ronnie's twin brother had been allowed out of Maidstone Prison for the day, handcuffed and accompanied by three prison guards. Thousands of mourners lined the funeral route waiting for the hearse and entourage of 20 black Daimlers to make its way from the funeral directors W. English and Son, past Vallance Road, where the twins were brought up, to St Matthew's Church, Bethnal Green.

Comment

HONEST citizens - and a few dishonest ones - will sleep more peacefully now that justice has overtaken the Kray gang. The enormity of their crimes, especially those of the killer twins, almost passes belief. We have heard of murder as a business, but this was murder as a sort of family competition. 'I've done mine,' says Ronald to Reginald, 'now it's your turn.' The court story of the ordeal of Jack McVitie, stabbed to death in cold blood, sends shivers down the spine.

These wicked men were nearly sub-human. Their life imprisonment, which will go to 30 years, is not too harsh a sentence. This outcome will inevitably lead to a renewal of the debate on capital punishment, especially when it is recalled that the taking of lives has earned the same penalty as that of the Great Train Robbers for the taking of property.

It is not often that so much unrelieved evil is disclosed in the British courts. But the disturbing thing is that the gangster has become much more common in this country than he used to be.

At one time the protection racket prospering on the proceeds of vice, blackmail, and armed menace was unknown here. It was something to read about under a Chicago date-line. But since the war it has grown to ugly proportions, and there is even talk of the Mafia muscling in. The gun, which was also rare in our underworld, is increasingly taking over. Punishment such as given to the Krays and to the leader of the Richardson 'torture gang' who got 25 years in 1967, should give pause to any who feel like emulating them.

But the only real deterrent is an alert and devoted police force, the debt to whom, as Mr Justice Melford Stevenson said, cannot be overstated or ever discharged.

30 years

The twins began their 30-year stretch in different prisons, Ronnie at Parkhurst, Reggie at Leicester. After representations from mother Violet, Reggie joined his brother at the Isle of Wight facility in spring 1971. Their first outing came 11 years later, to attend Violet's funeral. Charles Snr died shortly afterwards, in February 1983. By then they were separated again, Ronnie having been transferred to Broadmoor.

Reggie's third outing in 26 years came in March 1995, this time to attend the funeral of his twin brother, who had suffered a fatal heart attack. He was 61. Reggie spent five more years behind bars, and had just exceeded the minimum recommended term when he was released on compassionate grounds. He was suffering from terminal bladder cancer and enjoyed only a month of freedom before the disease claimed his life on 1 October 2000, three weeks short of his 67th birthday.

'Ronnie Kray has for years been portrayed as a criminal Robin Hood but at the end of the day he was a killer.'

MARCH 18, 1995

Ronnie Kray, killer with a fan club, dies in agony

Ronnie Kray, the East End gangster who attracted both hatred and respect, died of a heart attack yesterday. While friends and former enemies queued to praise a 'villain of honour', others dismissed him as nothing more than a cold-blooded murderer.

Kray, 61, a paranoid schizophrenic with a history of heart problems, died at the Wexham Park Hospital in Slough shortly after 9am. He had collapsed two days ago in Broadmoor, where he was serving a life sentence imposed in 1969 for the murder of George Cornell and Jack 'The Hat' McVitie.

Reggie's fury

Reggie Kray, who is also serving a life sentence for murder, is furious at finding out about his twin brother's death from an inmate who heard the news on a radio in Maidstone Prison. He said: 'I learned he was dead not from prison authorities, police or the hospital but from a fellow inmate. He knocked on my door and gave me the news and I collapsed in horror. I could not believe it.' Friends believe the death will add impetus to the campaign for his release on parole, possibly as early as this year.

The twins ran a brutal gang in London's East End during the late 1950s and 1960s which netted them a fortune and allowed them to live a life of luxury. They were local celebrities - liked by some, feared by many. Since their conviction, an industry has grown around them with books, T-shirts, television specials and a film starring pop star twins Gary and Martin Kemp of Spandau Ballet.

Reaction to the death was polarised. Actress Barbara Windsor said if the brothers had been judged by today's standards they would have been released a long time ago. 'They weren't menacing and did a lot for charity. They were charming with old people and women and they've been badly misrepresented for over 30 years. People could walk the streets in the East End in those days. It was a safer place.'

'Mad' Frankie Fraser, 70, a member of the notorious Richardson gang in the 1960s, said: 'He had very good principles. Women and children - he loved them. And he was very honourable.'

But reformed robber John McVicar said the twins were just hoodlums. 'I think it was significant that at their trial more people from their "firm" were prepared to give evidence against them than for.'

Laurie Johnson, deputy chairman of the Metropolitan Police Federation, said: 'Ronnie Kray has for years been portrayed as a criminal Robin Hood but at the end of the day he was a killer.'

TOP RIGHT: The Krays reached iconic status, revered and honoured by some and scorned and hated by others. Father Christopher Bedford, leading the funeral service, said: 'I feel that everybody has to be given a Christian burial and commended to God's mercy.'

MIDDLE LEFT: Charlie helps carry the coffin of brother Ronnie. Both Charlie and Reggie died in 2000 and joined Ronnie in the family burial site. He had originally purchased the plot back in 1967 as a resting place for his first wife, Frances Shea, and subsequently his mother, father, elder brother and then Ronnie had been buried there. Reggie had become ill while in Norfolk's Wayland Prison and was diagnosed with inoperable cancer of the bladder. Jack Straw, the British Home Secretary, approved his official release from prison on compassionate grounds in September 2000. He died peacefully in his sleep on 1 October, one month after his release.

TOP LEFT: Charlie and Reggie share a quiet moment at the graveside of brother Ronnie as he was buried with all the pomp and sentiment only the East End can muster.

Harry Roberts:
The Braybrook Street Massacre

Evening Standard

3 POLICEMEN SHOT DEAD NEAR SCRUBS

Q-car crew murdered

ENGLISH GIRLS IN ROW AT GAMES

They were planning to rob a rent collector, but a routine police check in Braybrook Street, a stone's throw from the walls of Wormwood Scrubs, led to a shoot-out that left them facing a triple murder charge.

AUGUST 13, 1966

Armed London Police Hunt Killers of Braybrook Street

Armed police joined the hunt last night for gunmen who killed three policemen in a London street. They were issued with .38 revolvers at Shepherd's Bush police station in West London. Other officers with teargas guns were held ready. A police officer said: "More guns will be issued if these men are cornered." Nearly 200 policemen from all parts of London were sent to Shepherd's Bush police station, headquarters of the hunt for the killers. Most were volunteers - men on leave or away on holiday hurried back to help the hunt.

ABOVE: The stark exterior of Wormwood Scrubs prison towers over Braybrook Street, Shepherd's Bush, where three policemen were mercilessly shot at point-blank range during a routine police check.

ABOVE (INSET): The evening newspapers related the grim events. A child witness had stated to the officers: 'They immediately started firing at the policemen'. Over a hundred police raced to the scene as they hunted for the Standard Vanguard car that had sped away from the area.

LEFT: Police cover the bodies of the dead officers. PC Geoffrey Fox, DS Christopher Head and DC David Wombwell were all in plain clothes and had been in an unmarked Triumph car.

TOP LEFT: Local resident Mrs Ida Collins was one of the first to give a witness statement to the police. Several people had been milling around the road as the events unfolded and fortunately a motorist had taken down the licence plate number.

RIGHT: The shrouded body of DS Head lies under the Triumph car.

ABOVE: The car is towed away. The windscreen, shattered by the shot that killed PC Fox, is clearly visible.

TOP RIGHT: Stunned local residents, including several children who had witnessed the shooting while playing in the street, watch as police examine the scene.

BELOW: Detectives meticulously search the area around one of the bodies, looking for any possible clues. The entire London police force was on alert and many off-duty officers joined in the hunt for the three men.

The name of Harry Roberts has reverberated around some football grounds over the past four decades, used in a tasteless chant targeted at the police. The man who inspired the unsavoury refrain was a petty criminal who had no qualms about committing cold-blooded murder if he were backed into a corner, and that is exactly the position in which he found himself on Friday 12 August 1966. Three policemen were shot dead in the incident, the worst death toll for serving officers attending a single incident since the Sidney Street siege of 1911.

Felonious pursuits

On that August afternoon Harry Roberts had car theft in mind. He and two confederates, John Duddy and John Witney, were cruising the streets of London's Shepherd's Bush area on the lookout for a vehicle that could be used in their felonious pursuits. They were planning to rob a rent collector, but a routine police check in Braybrook Street, a stone's throw from the walls of Wormwood Scrubs, led to a shoot-out that left them facing a triple murder charge.

The gang's blue Standard Vanguard estate was in a sorry condition, and it may well have been the sight of an exhaust tied up with string that first attracted the attention of three plain-clothes policemen on patrol in an unmarked Q car. The officers who thought they were dealing with a possible unroadworthy vehicle were DS Christopher Head, DC David Wombwell and PC Geoffrey Fox. It is quite possible that they then recognised one or more of the occupants, and the prospect of known criminals loitering in the environs of Wormwood Scrubs may have aroused their suspicions still further.

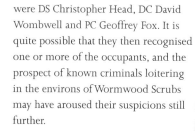

Harry Roberts: The Braybrook Street Massacre

Point-blank range

Head and Wombwell approached the car to question the driver, John Witney. Roberts was in the passenger seat, Duddy in the rear. The officers noticed that the car had no valid Road Fund Licence, and Witney explained that he couldn't tax the vehicle until it had passed its MOT test. On request he produced his driving licence and insurance certificate. That merely added to the list of misdemeanours, for the insurance had expired at noon that day, just over three hours earlier. As Witney pleaded for leniency, Roberts became nervous. If the police searched the car, they would find guns and live ammunition, putting the level of offence into a different bracket altogether. DS Head had gone to inspect the back of the Vanguard, and Roberts saw his chance. He produced a Luger and fired at PC Wombwell at point-blank range. The officer was struck in the left eye and killed instantly.

DS Head was shot in the back while trying to make it back to the patrol car and fell to the ground just in front of the vehicle. Duddy jumped out to join the fray, running to the nearside of the police car, where he fired at PC Fox through the glass. The .38 automatic was discharged twice more, and it was one of these bullets that inflicted a fatal head wound on the officer. The police car's engine was idling, and as Fox slumped forward, pressure was applied to the accelerator and the vehicle lurched forward and hit the stricken figure of DS Head. Roberts and Duddy ran back to the Vanguard, which sped away, leaving some wide-eyed onlookers believing they had witnessed part of a movie production.

> Roberts and Duddy ran back to the Vanguard, which sped away, leaving some wide-eyed onlookers believing they had witnessed part of a movie production.

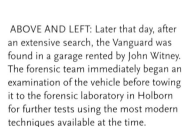

ABOVE AND LEFT: Later that day, after an extensive search, the Vanguard was found in a garage rented by John Witney. The forensic team immediately began an examination of the vehicle before towing it to the forensic laboratory in Holborn for further tests using the most modern techniques available at the time.

TOP: A local resident points to the garage in Vauxhall where the vehicle was found.

OPPOSITE BOTTOM: Frogmen working from a police launch on the River Thames. They were searching for the murder weapon which may have been thrown from Lambeth Bridge.

Drivers of all London's radio-controlled taxis were asked to look out for the gunmen's getaway car - a blue 1955 Standard Vanguard, believed to be a van converted into an estate car. Its number is PGT726. Scotland Yard started a street by street search of garages and yards for the car.

Death came to the three policemen on routine patrol in just four seconds - the time it took to fire a few rounds from one or more revolvers in quiet, sunny Braybrook Street, bordering Wormwood Scrubs Common. The three officers, all wearing plain clothes, stopped their Triumph 2000 Q car - Foxtrot One-One - to make a chance check on the Vanguard parked in Braybrook Street. Two men got out of the gunmen's car. One by one the three policemen, all unarmed, were shot down. They fell within yards of a group of frightened schoolchildren playing on the common, in the shadow of Wormwood Scrubs Jail.

Silent

The Yard, alerted by a 999 call, had radioed to the car believing it to be the nearest to the scene. For a few seconds Braybrook Street, a long crescent lined on one side by council houses was silent. Gunsmoke drifted in the air. The children had run clear. But soon dozens of policemen were on the spot. A senior Scotland Yard officer said: "It was the most callous crime I have known." So callous that PC Wombwell was believed to be holding his hands above his head to prove he was unarmed when he was gunned down.

A man's name scribbled on a pad beside the gear lever of the Q car may help the hunt. It was written by Sergeant Head shortly before the shooting. Police think he may have recognised a suspect in the parked Vanguard and had time to write down his name before he was shot.

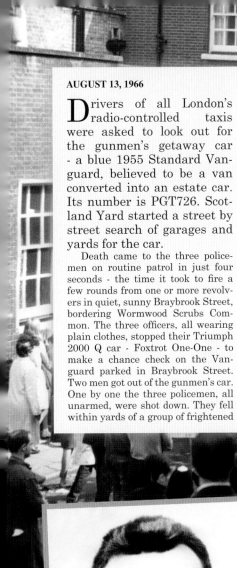

> For a few seconds Braybrook Street, a long crescent lined on one side by council houses was silent. Gunsmoke drifted in the air.

TOP: Witney was in police custody by the end of the day and the following Tuesday appeared at West London court where he was remanded in custody. He had revealed the names of Harry Roberts and John Duddy as his accomplices.

ABOVE LEFT: Police published the name and a detailed description of Harry Roberts, a known petty criminal, and received over 400 phone calls of sightings in the London area and many more from other parts of the country. Sir Joseph Simpson, Metropolitan Police Commissioner, consulted legal experts from the Director of Public Prosecution's office before deciding not to issue his photograph to the general public.

ABOVE AND ABOVE MIDDLE: Witney returned to court a week later where he was once again remanded in custody.

A passing motorist took down the registration number of the Vanguard, and before the day was out John Witney was in custody.

Outrage

The cold-blooded murder of three police officers in broad daylight shocked the nation. Donations flooded in, the only tangible way for many to express their outrage and support for the victims' families. Holiday camp magnate Sir Billy Butlin contributed £250,000 and the coffers soon swelled to over £1 million. Those funds were used to launch the Police Dependants' Trust, a body that continues to this day to support officers who have suffered debilitating injuries in the line of duty, and the bereaved families of policemen killed in service.

Witnesses

Metropolitan Police Commissioner Sir Joseph Simpson appealed to the criminal fraternity for help in tracking down the killers, convinced that even many underworld figures would have abhorred the shocking triple homicide. In the event, information from that quarter wasn't needed. There were a number of witnesses to the murders, including several children playing in the street. A passing motorist took down the registration number of the Vanguard, and before the day was out John Witney was in custody. He initially said that he had sold the vehicle that very morning, but when it was recovered from a garage that he rented in Lambeth, Witney realised that the game was up and confessed. At least, he confessed to being in the car with Roberts and Duddy, whom he named, but vehemently denied firing any shots. Duddy was arrested on 17 August, holed up in a tenement flat in his native city Glasgow. He, too, admitted to being present in the car but denied doing any of the shooting. On the flight back to London he changed his story and admitted to DI Jack Slipper that he had killed PC Fox. Harry Roberts proved to be a lot more elusive. He evaded capture for three months, despite one of the biggest manhunts in history. Roberts used his military training and survival skills to hide out in Epping Forest, an area he knew well from his childhood.

TOP LEFT, TOP MIDDLE AND BOTTOM LEFT: John Duddy was arrested in Glasgow five days after the shooting and was immediately flown back to London by DI Jack Slipper and DCI George Hensley, who guided him down the aircraft steps. He was forced to spend the flight with his head under a plastic raincoat in a separate compartment so his face was not seen by any of the crew or other passengers. After landing he was driven away for further questioning. During the flight he had admitted killing PC Fox.

LEFT: Children watch the police activity around the flat in the Calton area of Glasgow.

TOP RIGHT AND BELOW: Duddy was taken to West London court where he was also remanded in custody.

Parliamentary reaction

Roberts was still at large when the memorial service for the fallen officers was held at Westminster Abbey in early September. Outside there were banners calling for the re-introduction of capital punishment for the murder of police and prison officers, reversing parliament's decision of the previous year. Home Secretary Roy Jenkins said he understood the strength of feeling but explained that it would be wrong to institute a policy change on the strength of a single event, no matter how terrible and tragic that event might be. That autumn, Conservative MP Duncan Sandys sought to introduce a bill allowing the ultimate sanction to be available in certain circumstances. While there was much support for his view, the biggest cheer in the Commons debate followed the comment that most people would be able to sleep more easily if Timothy Evans were still alive. Leave to introduce the bill was voted down by a majority of 122.

The 'Braybrook Street Massacre' also brought forth calls for the police to armed. Sir Joseph Simpson's response to that kneejerk reaction was to say it would be a sad day in the country's history if officers routinely carried guns. However, the events of 12 August 1966 did lead to the formation of SO19, the police firearms unit, established in December that year.

ABOVE INSET: Donations poured in as the outraged public found a way to express their support for the victims' families. Police officers at Shepherds Bush station counted the donations which came to over £1,000. This scene was repeated throughout the country and many officers were handed money as they went about their daily tasks.

LEFT: At Scotland Yard, officers were opening letters of sympathy and donations.

TOP MIDDLE: Police search a house near King's Cross. The hunt was now on for Harry Roberts, the final member of the trio suspected of killing DS Head and DC Wombwell. An officer recognised Roberts in Gerrard Street, Soho, and followed him through a maze of streets near King's Cross. Police ringed the area as Roberts leapt on a bus and jumped off by the Sadler's Wells Theatre, Islington. Police swarmed through the theatre while performers were rehearsing.

TOP LEFT: As police continued to search the Islington area, residents from the Spa Green Estate watch as officers secure the roads.

TOP RIGHT: The hunt in Islington extended to a semi-derelict house. Sixty armed officers surrounded this property after a woman had seen a man jumping over a wall at the time of the search.

ABOVE: The West London Air terminal was also searched. Countless officers joined in to pursue their colleagues' killer.

Roberts finally in custody

The Old Bailey trial began on 14 November 1966. Roberts may not have been in the dock with Duddy and Witney but all three were on the charge sheet. Prosecuting counsel Elwyn Jones QC, the Attorney General, made it clear from the outset that the three men were jointly and severally responsible for the officers' deaths. That statement must have been a blow to Witney, for there was considerable evidence to support his story, namely, that he had taken no part in the shootings. He was to find that as far as the law was concerned, culpability was not restricted to the person who pulled the trigger.

Duddy and Witney pleaded Not Guilty. By 17 November, what would have been the fourth day of the trial, Harry Roberts was in custody, having been tracked down to a barn in Sawbridgeworth, Hertfordshire. It was decided that the three men should be tried together, and to give Roberts's counsel time to prepare a defence a retrial was ordered. That opened 5 December 1966. Witney and Duddy again entered Not Guilty pleas, while Roberts pleaded Guilty to the murder of Wombwell and Head, but Not Guilty in regard of the charge relating to PC Fox. He named Duddy as the man who fired the shot which killed that officer. Lillian Perry, who co-habited with Roberts, provided corroborating testimony. She said Roberts admitted to the murders when he returned home on the evening of 12 August. The following Monday, Perry said she accompanied him to buy camping equipment, after which the two parted, Roberts telling her: 'This is as far as we go together. I am on my own now.'

> *Elwyn Jones QC, the Attorney General, made it clear from the outset that the three men were jointly and severally responsible for the officers' deaths.*

ABOVE: Police alongside the road as the search for Roberts extended to Epping Forest in Essex.

TOP LEFT AND MIDDLE LEFT: Hundreds of officers meticulously search for any evidence in the undergrowth.

LEFT INSET: A pair of shorts and booking form signed 'Roberts' were eventually found in a barn at Standen Manor Farm in Hungerford, Berkshire. Cowman Jock Gordon had disturbed a man who then ran through a hedge and disappeared.

LEFT: An army helicopter joined the 250 officers in the search of the thick woods and farmland just south of Hungerford.

> Witney also said he was terrified of Roberts, who had threatened him with violence after the incident to ensure his silence and co-operation.

Salient facts

James Burge QC, acting for Roberts, called no evidence on his client's behalf. Duddy's counsel, James Comyn QC, took the same line, but made it clear that Harry Roberts was the chief instigator, something even Roberts's counsel conceded. Witney was the only one of the defendants to give evidence. He denied knowing that Roberts and Duddy were carrying guns, and insisted that his only experience of firearms had been during his Army training. Witney also said he was terrified of Roberts, who had threatened him with violence after the incident to ensure his silence and co-operation. Witney, a married man with two children, said he was in fear of his own life and that of his family. Duddy, perhaps to redress the balance, called Witney 'the brains of this outfit'.

During the six-day trial there was little dispute regarding the salient facts. The main point at issue was apportioning responsibility for the crimes. The prosecution argued for all three to be treated as one, while the defence sought to establish gradations of culpability. Solicitor General Sir Dingle Foot QC had taken over as chief prosecuting counsel, as the Attorney General was engaged on the inquiry into the Aberfan disaster. In his summing-up, he showed himself to be just as persistent as Elwyn Jones on the subject of joint responsibility. The jury, he said, had three matters to consider: Who carried out the shootings? Did the three share a common purpose in trying to avoid arrest? If Witney was not party to that common purpose, did he assist the other two in their escape, thereby becoming an accessory after the fact?

TOP LEFT: By now Roberts's picture had been released and this wanted poster offered a reward for information leading to his capture.

THIS PAGE: Harry Roberts was finally found and arrested on November 16, 1966, three months after the shooting and just after the start of the trial at the Old Bailey. Police had been searching Thorley Wood in Hertfordshire when Sergeant Peter Smith, armed with a revolver, searched a barn and noticed a bottle of methylated spirits and found Roberts hiding under a bale of straw. The fugitive gave himself up immediately and offered police no resistance. Half a mile away police also found his previous hideout – a tent thickly camouflaged with bushes and logs. Using techniques he had learnt in jungle survival training he had made storage areas for his kit and had emerged into the local area to buy provisions and newspapers. Roberts had abandoned the tent a few days before to use the barn instead.

I Murdered Two, Admits Roberts

Harry Roberts stood in the dock at the Old Bailey yesterday and admitted killing two of the three policemen shot dead near Wormwood Scrubs Prison in August. Roberts, a 30-year-old carpenter, pleaded guilty as the clerk read out the charges accusing him of murdering Detective Sergeant Christopher Head, 30, and Detective Constable David Wombwell, 26. But he gave a firm "not guilty" to the charge of murdering Police Constable Geoffrey Fox, the driver of the three-man "Q" car.

After a jury of 11 men and one woman had been sworn in Sir Dingle Foot told them: "The Crown say that this was a case of deliberate, cold-blooded murder. The Crown say that the men responsible for these murders, all equally responsible, were the three accused." In the dock with Roberts are John Duddy, 37, a carpenter, and John Witney, 36, also a carpenter. Duddy and Witney have pleaded not guilty and are being tried for the murders of all three policemen. Roberts - because he has pleaded guilty to murdering Sergeant Head and Constable Wombwell - is being tried only for the murder of P.C. Fox.

Sir Dingle said that on August 12 the three accused were in an old Standard Vanguard van belonging to Whitney. All three had loaded pistols and were planning to commit a criminal offence. They were spotted in Braybrook Street by a police Q car containing three police officers -Detective Sergeant Head, Detective Constable Wombwell and P.C. Fox.

> Sir Dingle Foot told them: 'The Crown say that this was a case of deliberate, cold-blooded murder.'

LEFT: The police van that carried Harry Roberts to Shepherd's Bush police station was greeted by a crowd of more than 1,000 who cheered the police and booed the occupant. Many had waited on the streets for over six hours.

ABOVE LEFT: Roberts, with his face covered, is led into Shepherd's Bush police station. He was immediately charged by detectives and received a two-minute visit from his mother Dorothy. He was due to appear in court the following morning. The trial of the three accused had already begun, despite Roberts's absence but it was then delayed until 5 December to allow his counsel to prepare his defence. All three were eventually found guilty, the jury deciding that Witney had equal guilt although he hadn't actually fired a gun.

ABOVE: Roberts, his faced covered, is taken to Brixton prison after a four-minute appearance at the Old Bailey.

TOP LEFT: The following year, while serving his sentence, Roberts made another journey to court handcuffed to two officers, to give evidence at the trial of Christos Costas. Costas was alleged to have sold Roberts the guns used to kill the officers at Braybrook Street. Under the raincoat he wore his prison uniform.

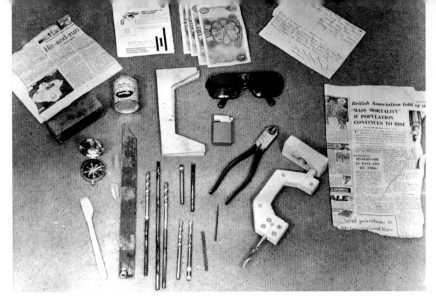

Witney just as guilty

The jury needed just thirty minutes to decide that Witney was just as guilty as the self-confessed murderers. After sentencing the three men to life imprisonment, with a recommendation that they serve a minimum of 30 years behind bars, Mr Justice Glyn-Jones added that the heinous nature of the crimes meant that in this case the life tariff might well be literal in its implementation.

John Duddy served fifteen years, which in his case was indeed a life sentence; he died in Parkhurst jail in February 1981, aged 52. John Witney spent 25 years behind bars, when it was decided he had paid his debt to society. He was released in 1991 and enjoyed eight years of freedom before his death, aged 69.

Harry Roberts is still in jail, now in his fifth decade of incarceration. His case has been reviewed by the Parole Board on a number of occasions since the recommended 30-year term expired in 1996. Roberts has done himself few favours with those empowered to grant his release, for his prison record includes escape attempts, contraband smuggling and abuse of home-leave privileges. Now a septuagenerian, Roberts is currently serving time at Littlehey, the low-security Category C prison in Cambridgeshire. With each passing year, the likelihood increases that the prime mover in the Braybrook Street Massacre will end his days behind bars.

> I think it likely that no Home Secretary in the future regarding the enormity of your crime will ever think fit to show mercy by releasing you.

DECEMBER 13, 1966

30 Years for Roberts and Gang

Harry Roberts and his two accomplices were jailed for a recommended minimum of 30 years at the Old Bailey yesterday for the murder of three London policemen. Mr. Justice Glyn Jones passed the statutory sentence of life imprisonment on the three men. Then he said: "Unless any Home Secretary in the future should be mindful of considering your release on licence, I have to make a recommendation you should not be released until 30 years have gone by."

Roberts, 30, John Duddy, 37, and John Witney, 36, stood impassive in the dock of No. 1 Court as the jury of 11 men and one woman found them all equally guilty of the three murders. The judge said: "You have been justly convicted of what is perhaps the most heinous crime that has been committed for a generation or more. I think it likely that no Home Secretary in the future regarding the enormity of your crime will ever think fit to show mercy by releasing you on licence. This is one of those cases in which a sentence of imprisonment for life may well be treated in the meaning of exactly what it says."

TOP LEFT: During his time in jail Roberts has made several escape attempts. In 1973, he used this escape kit to try to gain his freedom from Parkhurst prison. Roberts's last attempted escape from prison was in 1976 but since then he has tried to become model prisoner in the hope of gaining parole, but without success. Duddy died in prison and Witney was released in 1991, although he died eight years later.

TOP RIGHT: A police officer displays a card and donation sent after the shootings.

LEFT AND FAR LEFT: Twenty-five years after the shooting wreathes were laid at the memorial in Braybrook Street which marks the place where the three officers fell. Actors Roger Moore (right) and Michael Caine (left) attended the ceremony.

John Gotti

13 counts of murder, illegal gambling, extortion, tax evasion obstruction of justice...

Boy from the Bronx

John Joseph Gotti was born on October 27, 1940, the fifth of the eleven children of John J. Gotti, Sr. and his wife, Fannie. At first the Gotti family lived in a dirt-poor section of the South Bronx in New York, but by the time Gotti was ten they had moved up in the world to Brooklyn. At school he was the class bully – when he wasn't regularly playing truant – and by the time he was twelve he and two of his brothers were running errands for local mobsters. At fourteen he was badly injured when he and some other young boys tried to steal a cement mixer – it fell and crushed his toes, giving him a distinctive limp for the rest of his life.

At sixteen Gotti left school and joined the Fulton-Rockaway Boys, a teenage gang that concentrated on petty crime, rather than turf wars with other gangs. Gotti quickly rose to become leader, due to his hot temper and readiness to fight. He was arrested five times between 1957 and 1961, but the authorities could never make the charges stick. In 1962 he married Victoria DiGorgio, with whom he had had a child the previous year. The couple went on to have four more children, despite a tempestuous relationship due to Gotti's life of crime, his drinking, gambling and eye for other women.

New York Mafia

In 1966, Gotti became involved with a major New York Mafia Family controlled by Carlo Gambino, joining one of their crews that specialized in hijacking trucks from the nearby international airport. He was arrested and imprisoned once, but served only part of his three-year sentence.

Soon after his release in 1972 he rejoined his old crew and soon became close to Aniello Dellacroce, right-hand man of Carlo Gambino, which improved his status in the Mafia hierarchy. He was asked to kill mobster James McBratney, who had kidnapped one of the Family's associates, so he and two other men shot McBratney in front of several witnesses. Gotti was arrested for murder, but his lawyer managed to get the charge reduced to manslaughter and he served less than two years. When he came out, in 1977, he was promoted from associate to full Family member and took over as acting capo of his former crew. Under his rule it moved away from hijacking to the more profitable and less dangerous areas of gambling and loan sharking, but also began dealing in heroin – although there was a strict Family ruling against any involvement with drugs.

Power Struggle

Gotti continued to rise through the Mafia ranks, but in 1980 the accidental death of his 12-year-old son, Frank, caused his gambling habit to spiral out of control. Paul Castellano, who had become Don of the Family after the death of Carlo Gambino, began to question Gotti's fitness as capo – while in return Gotti questioned Castellano's leadership skills. The power struggle ended with Gotti arranging for Castellano's murder, leaving the way clear for him to assume control of the Family.

As Don of a leading Mafia Family, Gotti managed to create a public image of himself as a legendary rogue and his meticulous appearance and snappy suits led to him becoming known as the Dapper Don. He acquired his other nickname, the Teflon Don, after beating two prosecutions: in one, a witness who had complained of being assaulted by Gotti 'changed his mind' after the brakes of his truck were tampered with; in another, he was acquitted of racketeering after bribing one of the jury members. However, the FBI were closing in: they had secretly been taping Gotti and other leading Gambini Family members for many months, and Gotti's own second-in-command, Salvatore Gravano, had agreed to testify against him. On April 2, 1992 Gotti was convicted on 13 counts of murder, and on several other counts including illegal gambling, extortion, tax evasion and obstruction of justice. He was sentenced to 100 years in prison and sent to the maximum-security penitentiary in Marion, Illinois, but on June 10, 2002 he died of cancer.

OPPOSITE TOP LEFT: John Gotti is led out of FBI offices in lower Manhattan. The Mob boss was arrested at a social club in Little Italy along with other alleged Gambino family members in 1990.

OPPOSITE TOP RIGHT: Gotti listens to testimony during his trial. His own second-in-command, Salvatore Gravano, agreed to testify against him.

TOP RIGHT: Gotti arrives at New York State Supreme Court on the day of his sentencing.

ABOVE LEFT: 'Dapper Don' was convicted on 13 counts of murder, illegal gambling, extortion, tax evasion and obstruction of justice.

OPPOSITE BOTTOM LEFT: Supporters of Gotti try to overturn a Federal Marshal's car in front of the Brooklyn courthouse after hearing that Gotti had been sentenced to life without parole. Nearly 1,000 pro-Gotti demonstrators battled with police who were wearing riot gear.

RIGHT: The home of John Gotti in Queens, New York.

JUNE 25, 1992

Guilty of murder

Life imprisonment without parole for Mafia Godfather John Gotti, 51, will be a cell measuring 8ft by 7ft in a strict security jail. The most likely prison will be the bleak Marion jail in Illinois - one of the toughest in the country. It will seem a million miles from New York's Little Italy and the pasta cafes where Gotti once drank red wine and plotted against his enemies.

Gotti, head of the Gambino family, the most powerful crime syndicate in America, was found guilty of murder, racketeering, conspiracy, illegal gambling, obstruction of justice and tax fraud. He took his sentence yesterday in a New York court with dignity but the other players in the drama could have been on a movie set.

There was a near-riot by 1,000 supporters waving American flags, praise for Gotti's character from the owner of his favourite restaurant and music played on the court steps – the theme from the film The Godfather.

When the drama was over, Gotti was heading for jail while the street outside the Brooklyn federal court was littered with debris, broken glass, ripped-up banners and damaged cars.

Just the shadow of a smile crossed Gotti's face when the sentence was read out. His only reaction was later to whisper: "We've only begun to fight."

Gotti once named the Teflon Don because no charges ever stuck to him, is pinning all his hopes on an appeal. But, as far as the FBI is concerned, the cell key has already been thrown away.

Baader-Meinhof:
Germany's most notorious urban guerrillas

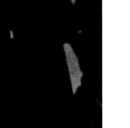

It was the 1967 killing of a young activist by police during a demonstration in Berlin that convinced Andreas Baader that the post-war authorities were little better than that which they had replaced.

Ulrike's links with Andreas Baader, terrorist son of a German historian, came to light after a daring raid on the Berlin Prison library.

MAY 10, 1976

The little innocent who grew up into a woman of terror

When they come to write the history of the women of the Twentieth Century, the name of Ulrike Meinhof will be given much more than a passing reference. For she made her own history . . . terrorising the very society within which she was brought up and educated. In a century when women gained more of their rights than ever before, they also took their share of something else. That something was violence.

Public Enemy Number One

Ulrike's links with Andreas Baader, terrorist son of a German historian, came to light after a daring raid on the Berlin Prison library. Baader was serving three years for setting fire to a department store in Frankfurt in 1968. Ulrike and two others wielding machine-guns burst into the reading room wounding a librarian, and snatched Andreas to freedom. On that day, May 14, 1970, the Baader-Meinhof gang was born.

In the following two years, every bomb attack and bank raid in West Germany was put down to the group. Ulrike was named Public Enemy Number One. She was captured in June, 1972, after 150,000 armed police had hunted her across Germany. When she and another member of her gang were captured in a flat in Hanover, they were guarding an arsenal of machine guns, hand grenades, pistols and ammunition. Last May, Ulrike with Baader and two others went on trial amid massive security costing £2 million. The court was a purpose-built fortress annexe to Stuttgart's Stammhein Prison.

Hostages

The four were charged with involvement in four murders, 54 attempted murders and a series of bombings, bank raids and arson attacks between August 1970 and May 1972. The charges also included bomb attacks on U.S. army bases in Heidelberg and Frankfurt in which four American soldiers were killed, and a bomb attack on a federal supreme court judge.

Ulrike and her co-defendants never denied responsibility for the guerilla violence, but their lawyers said the crimes were politically motivated. Yesterday - only hours after Ulrike was found dead in her cell at Stammhein at breakfast time - police and security units throughout Germany went on special alert.

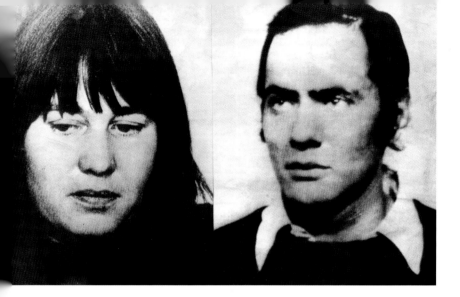

The Red Army Faction

The Baader-Meinhof Group was a name given by the German media to a left-wing gang of violent urban terrorists operating in West Germany over nearly thirty years, from the end of the 1960s. The group never used the term themselves – they called themselves the Red Army Faction (RAF). Founded by Andreas Baader and Ulrike Meinhof, along with several others, the group had an agenda of armed resistance and hoped to inspire a mass uprising against a capitalist government that included several ex-Nazis. In the early years they committed many crimes, including burning down department stores, robbing banks to obtain funds and bombing US military bases and German police stations. The main leaders, Baader, Meinhof, Gudrun Ensslin, Holger Meins and Jan-Carl Raspe were arrested in June 1972 and held in solitary confinement in Stammheim Prison near Stuttgart. They began a series of hunger strikes to protest at their treatment, which led to Meins dying of starvation in November 1974. Meinhof apparently committed suicide in her cell in May 1976, but the remaining three were found guilty of several murders and of running a terrorist organisation and were sentenced to life imprisonment in April 1977.

> 'These people belonged to a criminal organisation which advocated the use of force in what it called an anti-imperialist battle.'

Germany's autumn of terror

Meanwhile several people sympathetic to the original aims of the group took over and began a new wave of terror, starting with the attempted kidnap of the head of Dresdner Bank outside his home in July 1977, which became murder when he was shot and killed. They then kidnapped the president of the German Employers' Association, Hanns Martin Schleyer, and demanded the release of Baader, Ensslin and Raspe and eight other prisoners in exchange for his safe return. In October 1977, while the authorities were still delaying in hope of finding the kidnappers, a Lufthansa flight to Frankfurt was hijacked by a group of Arabs, who also wanted the German terrorists released, as well as two Palestinians imprisoned in Turkey. In addition they demanded $15 million in cash. Instead of complying the authorities took possession of the plane again after a brief assault in which all the Arabs were killed. The following day Baader, Ensslin and Raspe were found dead in their cells, also apparently having committed suicide. Schleyer was promptly shot by his kidnappers, and this period of internal turmoil became known as the German Autumn. The Baader-Meinhof Group continued to attack selected targets throughout the 1980s and 1990s, but was officially disbanded on April 20, 1998; during their period of operation they had killed more than 34 people, including several innocent bystanders.

> 'The revolution says: I was, I am, I will be again.' – The final statement of The Red Army Faction in 1998.

APRIL 29, 1977

Terror gang 'lived for death'

The era of terror caused by the Baader-Meinhof terror gang ended yesterday as the three surviving members were jailed for life. After a dry, two-hour summary of the evidence during their two-year trial, Chief Justice Eberhardt Foth announced the sentences and said: 'The trial is over.' As he spoke, there was not one whimper of interruption from the 200 people in the public galleries at Stuttgart Supreme Court, besieged by an army of security men.

Off to jail were taken Andreas Baader, Jan-Karl Raspe and Gudrun Ensslin - convicted of murdering four U.S. soldiers and a German policeman, 34 attempted murders, four plans to murder, and various charges of robbery, theft and causing explosions. They had refused to attend court to hear the judgment.

Judge Foth said: 'These people belonged to a criminal organisation which advocated the use of force in what it called an anti-imperialist battle. It did not stop short of murder. It is clear the accused went beyond the bounds of legality. The so-called political motive has had no influence on our decisions. The aim by the accused of political justification for their murders cannot be entertained. They wanted to murder. They violated the laws of a democratic country.'

OPPOSITE ABOVE: Ulrike Meinhof: an ideological leader of a terrorist group. Originally an intellectual drive to change society, the Red Army Faction quickly resorted to using violent means.

OPPOSITE BELOW: The casket bearing Meinhof: she apparently killed herself, at the age of 41, in her prison cell in 1976.

TOP RIGHT: Meinhof being led out of her apartment following her arrest in June 1972. Meinhof, Baader and their accomplices were charged with six bombings, the murder of a policeman, three attempted murders, six armed bank raids and the creation of an illegal armed underground movement.

TOP LEFT: Ulrike Meinhof and Andreas Baader. Several members of the underground movement continued the group's terrorist activities well after the deaths of both founders.

John Wayne Gacy: The killer clown

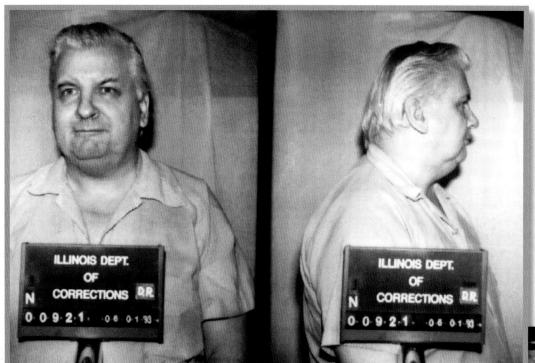

John Wayne Gacy, the 'killer clown', so-called for his part-time work as a children's entertainer, was convicted of the rape and murder of 33 males, following a six year reign of terror; he achieved notoriety as one of the most prolific serial killers in US history.

Health problems

John Wayne Gacy was born on St Patrick's Day – March 17 – 1942, in Chicago, the second of the three children of John Wayne Gacy Snr and his wife Marion. Gacy Snr was an alcoholic, who often physically attacked his wife and both physically and verbally abused his children, but Gacy Jnr worked hard to try and gain his father's approval. He was reasonably popular at school and in his Boy Scout troop and much of his childhood was unremarkable except for a couple of serious health problems. When he was eleven he was playing near some swings when one hit him hard on the head, causing a blood clot in his brain that led to regular blackouts until the clot was discovered and treated when he was sixteen. At seventeen he developed a heart problem that led to him being hospitalized several times throughout his life, although the exact cause of the problem was never diagnosed.

Community work

Initially Gacy dropped out of high school without graduating, but then he enrolled at business school where he discovered a true talent for salesmanship. He excelled in his first position as a management trainee at the Nunn-Bush Shoe Company and was transferred to manage a men's clothing outlet in Springfield, Illinois. While in Springfield, he became involved in several community organizations and devoted most of his free time to them. Many who knew him at this time considered him to be an upstanding young man, very ambitious and eager to make a name for himself. In 1964 he met and married Marlynn Myers, whose father owned the franchise on a string of Kentucky Fried Chicken outlets in Iowa. Gacy went to work for his father-in-law and the young couple moved to Iowa, where he again became involved with community work and the local Jaycees, a non-profit-making organization devoted to helping young people develop personal and leadership skills through service to others.

Rumours rife

Everything seemed to be going well for Gacy, but soon rumours began to spread about his sexual preference – he often had young boys with him and there were stories that he had made passes at several young men working in his restaurant. Most people discounted the rumours – until in 1968 Gacy was arrested and charged with the brutal rape of a teenage boy, and of then hiring another boy to beat up his victim to discourage him from pressing charges. He was convicted and given the maximum sentence of ten years, but after behaving as a model prisoner he was released on parole after only ten months. Meanwhile his wife had divorced him, so he returned to his hometown, Chicago, to begin a new life.

> Gacy was released on 24-hour surveillance, but soon evidence linked him firmly to one of the missing boys.

Young boys

Back in Chicago, Gacy seemed to turn his life around again: he got a job as a cook, his mother helped him to buy his own house and in 1972 he met and married Carole Hoff, a young divorcee with two daughters. The couple became friendly with the neighbours, and threw gigantic theme parties attended by hundreds of people – although sometimes guests commented that the house had a rather strange smell. In 1974, Gacy started his own contracting business carrying out decorating and maintenance work and hired several young men to work for him. Carole quickly noticed that her husband seemed more interested in these young boys than in her, and his moods had also become unpredictable – one minute good tempered and the next in a rage and throwing furniture around. She began divorce proceedings, which became final in March 1976.

The smell of death

Since his return to Chicago Gacy had continued to devote much of his spare time to community service, including dressing up as Pogo the clown to entertain children in hospital and at parties. He was generally considered to be a generous, hard-working and friendly man, but by 1978 he was also actively cruising for young men and rumours began to spread that he had made passes at some of his employees. Over the last few years several teenage boys had vanished without trace in the area, but in 1978 the mother of one young boy told police that he had been to see Gacy about a job and had not returned. Gacy was interviewed and said he knew nothing about the boy – but after carrying out a routine background check the police discovered his criminal record. They obtained a search warrant, thinking they would find the missing boy in Gacy's house, but although they found considerable evidence that something was going on, initially it was not clear what. Gacy was released on 24-hour surveillance, but soon evidence linked him firmly to one of the missing boys so a second search of the house was carried out. This time Cook County Medical Examiner Dr Robert Stein was called in and once inside the building he instantly recognized a strong smell of death and decay. The authorities soon uncovered 27 bodies buried in the crawlspace and under the garage – all male and ranging in age from nine to mid-20s – and later more bodies were found when the house was demolished, or were washed up in the nearby river.

Lethal injection

In 1980 Gacy was convicted of the torture, rape and murder of 33 boys and young men between 1972 and 1978, and sentenced to death. Although he managed to stay his execution by promising the authorities more information about his victims, on May 10, 1994, he was executed by lethal injection.

STORAGE SHED   GARAGE

WHERE FIRST VICTIMS WERE FOUND: UNDER GARAGE AND HOUSE

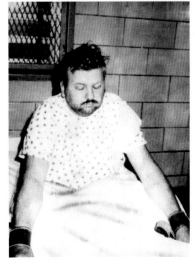

OPPOSITE TOP: In 1994 Gacy left his windowless cell after 14 years on death row. He was executed by lethal injection.

OPPOSITE MIDDLE: Gacy's wedding to his second wife, Carole Hoff, in June 1972. She divorced him in 1976 after it became clear he was more interested in young boys than her.

OPPOSITE BOTTOM: Cook County Medical Examiner, Dr Robert Stein, stands in a room at county morgue in Chicago. It contained the remains of the men who were found buried in the crawl space at Gacy's home.

TOP RIGHT: The house of death: Gacy buried the bodies under his home, many of them one on top of the other. Twenty-nine bodies were found on his property.

ABOVE: Gacy had been strapped to his bed in the hospital prison to stop him from harming himself or anyone else. He complained of a list of ailments in order to avoid being transferred to a cell block.

ABOVE: The building where Gacy's mother used to live. Grid patterns were drawn on the lawn of the apartment building where Chicago police searched for the bodies of more possible victims.

Charles Manson:
The Sharon Tate Murders

'Two men and three girls went to the residence. One man had a gun. The girls had knives. They parked their car so they would be able to get away quickly. 'They were dressed in black clothing and a man with wire cutters went up a pole outside and cut phone and electrical wires'.

> He grew up illiterate and anti-social and soon became involved in a series of petty criminal acts.

ABOVE: Charles Manson pictured during an interview which took place in jail after he was denied parole. His mother was an alcoholic who was in and out of prison when Manson was growing up.

TOP RIGHT: Actress Sharon Tate was nominated for a Golden Globe for her performance in *Valley of the Dolls*. In 1968 she married film director Roman Polanski.

Charles Milles Manson was born in Cincinnati, Ohio, on November 12, 1934, to an unmarried waitress called Kathleen Maddox. She later briefly married William Manson, who gave the child his last name. Kathleen was a heavy drinker who was in and out of prison, and Manson was brought up in a series of run-down hotels and institutions. He grew up illiterate and anti-social and soon became involved in a series of petty criminal acts, culminating in arrest for stealing cars. By March 1967 he had spent nearly half his life in prison.

After becoming involved with a librarian in San Francisco, Manson moved into her apartment. He soon established himself as a guru with a group of loyal followers, mostly young women, and in the summer of 1967 he and several of them set off to roam around in an old Volkswagen van. In the spring of 1968, two of Manson's girls became involved with Brian Wilson of the Beach Boys, and soon Manson and his entourage – now known as The Family – moved into the Wilson mansion. Here they met several people in the entertainment industry, including record producer Terry Melcher who was renting a house on Cielo Drive.

In March 1968 the Family members were cleared out of Wilson's house and established a new headquarters at Spahn's Movie Ranch in the Santa Susana Mountains. Manson became fixated on recording an album that would instigate widespread chaos and the rise of The Family to rule. He went looking for Melcher at Cielo Drive, which was now rented to Sharon Tate and her husband, film producer Roman Polanski.

'They were almost slaves, especially the women,' said one State trooper. 'They took orders without question.'

ABOVE: The cult leader is taken to court for a preliminary hearing on charges of possessing stolen property.

RIGHT: A police officer blocks the driveway whilst other policemen search in front of the house where a middle-aged couple were stabbed to death. The murders of Leno and Rosemary La Bianca bore striking similarities to that of the murders of Sharon Tate and her friends the day before.

BELOW: Man of a thousand faces: Manson's many different looks between 1969 and 1971.

In Satan's lair, where hate is the creed

They call themselves Satan's Slaves, or The Family. Now they are scattered, flushed by police from their hide-out. Ten are in custody, while detectives investigate a string of grisly and unsolved killings. When Sharon Tate was murdered The Family were living at the Spahn Movie Ranch, an old film company lot near Los Angeles. There, amid ramshackle ranch houses and barns, the group lived a communal life, with the women cooking and sharing their beds with the long-haired, bearded men who forayed out to steal. Then, according to police, they moved into Death Valley - an oven-hot and inhospitable desert area favoured by Californian hippies.

'They just bugged out for the desert,' said a man who saw their sudden evacuation after the murders. 'They even dug up their marijuana plants to take with them.'

They joined other groups to form a large commune, protected in military fashion by telescopes, walkie talkie radios, field telephones at a ring of lookout posts and an armoury of knives and shotguns. From their hideout they pillaged their way through California, robbing, stealing cars - and, according to the Los Angeles police, committing ritual murder. But police were on the gang's trail. Not at the time because of the murders, but because they were suspected of an epidemic of car thefts.

Hypnotic leader

The Family tried to cover up their tracks by setting up dummy camps, but State troopers tracked them back to Death Valley. The troopers found many of the women walking around naked. There were eight children in the group, including two babies suffering badly from malnutrition. Everyone had to swear allegiance to the hypnotic leader of The Family, singer Charles Manson, now in jail.

'They were almost slaves, especially the women,' said one State trooper. 'They took orders without question.'

The ranch where the commune lived is run by 80-year-old George Spahn. He said: 'Charlie and his friends came to spend the night during a rainstorm and never seemed to leave. Charlie came in and gave me 5,000 dollars several months before he took off. But he came in from time to time and got some of it back. He took a 2,000-dollar chunk so that he could help a religious cult called "The Fountain of the World".'

This centre stands a few miles away. Its head is a woman who calls herself Cardinal Nikoma.

Twenty-six of the hippies were arrested and ten of them held on a variety of charges, including car thefts. But the three named in connection with the Tate murders - Charles Watson, Patricia Krenwinkel and Linda Kasabian - were not among them.

DECEMBER 12, 1969

The man they call Satan

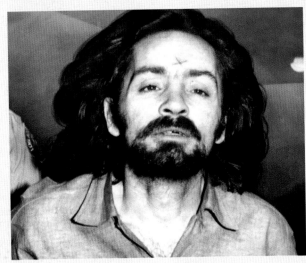

Charles Manson, leader of the hippie Satan's Slaves cult, which police say is involved in the Sharon Tate murders, ordered his followers to kill blindly out of revenge, a court was told by one of the girls who worships him. Susan Atkins, 21, said in Santa Monica that Manson ordered the murders 'as a symbol of protest.' Shelley Nadell, 31, who shared a cell in jail with her, said Miss Atkins told her the hippies 'released their souls' by taking part in murder rituals.

'The more they stabbed, the better they felt,' she said.

Miss Nadell's lawyer, Mr Wesley Russell, told reporters: 'Some of the murder victims are buried in the desert and their bodies probably will never be found. She was told of one boy who was decapitated.'

Miss Atkins appeared in court today, to plead not guilty to the murder of musician Gary Hinman, tortured and stabbed to death in Los Angeles last July - a fortnight before the Tate murders. She will be a key witness to the Sharon Tate grand jury inquiry in Los Angeles on Friday, when she gives her story of how she took part in the raid on Miss Tate's house when Miss Tate and her four friends were murdered last August. Three other hippies are held as suspects in the Tate murders and in the murders of a wealthy grocer and his wife the next day, but no-one has been charged. Miss Atkins's lawyer, Mr Richard Caballero, said that Charles Manson bore a grudge against Hinman and Terry Melcher, a previous occupant of Miss Tate's house.

Let me have my baby

When Manson decided on the murders he knew Melcher had left the house, but nevertheless ordered his 'slaves' to go there and 'murder everyone they found.' Miss Atkins's other lawyer, Mr Paul Caruso, said that during a five-hour interview she gave him this account of the murders at the Tate home, when Miss Tate, stylist Jay Sebring, coffee heiress Abigail Folger, playboy Voitek Frykowski and 18-year-old Steven Parent, a friend of the caretaker, were killed.

'Two men and three girls went to the residence. One man had a gun. The girls had knives. They parked their car so they would be able to get away quickly. They were dressed in black clothing and a man with wire cutters went up a pole outside and cut phone and electrical wires.

'They saw Parent starting to leave. He got into his car and was shot. 'Then a man went through an open window inside and opened the front door. The others went inside. 'Frykowsky was lying on the couch. Sharon Tate and Sebring were talking in her bedroom. The Folger girl was in another bedroom reading a book.

'Tate and Sebring were told to stay in the bedroom. Then they were brought out. Miss Tate became very apprehensive. She wanted to make sure her baby was not harmed. That was virtually all she pleaded about: "Let me have my baby." But she was killed.'

Manson is said to have given his followers a list of 11 and possibly 30 other people of hated affluent status for a similar fate. Their names are not divulged. He appeared in court in Independence, California, today to face charges of arson and robbery.

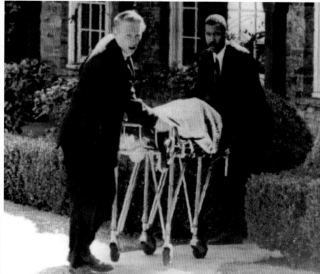

> 'Some of the murder victims are buried in the desert and their bodies probably will never be found.'

TOP LEFT: Manson pictured during his trial for the murder of Sharon Tate.

TOP RIGHT: An aerial view of Tate's home: 1. The spot near the swimming pool where Miss Folger was found. 2. Frykowski covered by sheets on the lawn. 3. Room where Tate and Sebring died. 4. Parent dead in car. 5. Where Garreston was arrested.

MIDDLE RIGHT: The body of Sharon Tate is taken from her home in Bel-Air. She was eight and a half months pregnant when she was brutally murdered.

RIGHT: A smile crosses Manson's face as he walks past girl employees in the Los Angeles Hall of Justice during in his murder trial.

'Satan' guilty

Charles Manson and two of his hippie slave girls were found guilty last night of murdering actress Sharon Tate and four friends. The Los Angeles court was silent for the first time in seven months as the jury shuffled in to give their verdicts. The seven men and five women jurors also convicted them and a third Manson-cult girl of murdering wealthy supermarket chief Leno La Bianca and his wife.

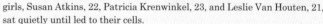

As the verdicts were announced Manson shouted: 'We're still not allowed to put on a defence. You won't outlive that, old man.' The three girls, Susan Atkins, 22, Patricia Krenwinkel, 23, and Leslie Van Houten, 21, sat quietly until led to their cells.

Appeals could delay the final verdict for years and, if the sentence is death, it will almost certainly never be carried out. Manson, 36, could join Sirhan Sirhan, Robert Kennedy's killer, on death row in San Quentin prison. A Supreme Court test case has stopped all death sentences throughout America since 1967. The cult leader is unlikely, however, to be released before he is at least 50.

Dirty work

For police, the verdicts closed the book on a case which opened in August 1969, when Miss Tate and three friends were found stabbed at the actress's home. Manson left the dirty work of his cult to his zombie-like girl followers. While they followed his orders, he stayed behind at Spahn Ranch, the rundown Wild West ranch where the cult strummed guitars and took drugs.

Manson smiled and winked at the jury. But as he was led away he told Judge Older: 'You'll never live to see that day' - meaning the day of his execution. Even after the verdicts, Manson's wild-eyed mesmeric powers seemed almost untarnished.

A group of girls, some of the 35 to 50 who had lived with him and obeyed his every command, squatted on the pavement outside the courtroom.

One of them said: 'We will wait, however long it takes, for our father to come back to us.'

Manson sentence 'just' says Sharon's father

And so it ended, the trial that jolted millions of American parents into examining the scary new values of their children's generation. Twelve Los Angeles jurors unanimously decreed the gas chamber for Charles Manson and his three girl 'Zombie' killers who slaughtered actress Sharon Tate and six other people. The final confrontation between the man who thought he was Christ and the jurors who suspected he might be Satan was as extraordinary as the whole bizarre, sordid trial. Manson, 36, and the girls made so much noise that Judge Charles Older turned them out - and the girls were not present to hear their own death sentences. Appeals, or abolition of the death penalty, could keep them out of the apple-green gas chamber in San Quentin prison. But Sharon Tate's father, the man who fought longest and hardest and spent much of his own money on the case, was satisfied. 'There is still justice,' said Lieut-Colonel Paul Tate, a retired Army intelligence officer.

TOP LEFT: Manson pictured on his way to be sentenced on March 29, 1971. He wasn't present in the court room when he was sentenced to the gas chamber, the judge having sent him into an adjacent room for disrupting the court.

ABOVE: Manson on his way to court. He threatened that murder and bloodshed would follow if he was sentenced to death.

LEFT: Sharon Tate pictured in 1966.

Ted Bundy

No one knows exactly where and when Bundy began killing. Many experts believe he may have started killing as far back as his early teens. After more than a decade of vigorous denials, Bundy eventually confessed to 30 murders.

Ted Bundy

Theodore Robert Bundy, commonly known as Ted Bundy, was born on November 25, 1946 in Burlington, Vermont, USA. His mother, Louise Cowell, was not married and his birth certificate listed Lloyd Marshall as the father, although there were suspicions that paternity actually lay with Louise's abusive father, Samuel. As a result of the confusion and social stigma surrounding his birth, Bundy grew up believing that his grandparents were his parents and that Louise was his sister. When Bundy was just four, he and Louise moved to Tacoma, Washington, to live with relatives. Here the child's surname was changed to Nelson, for reasons that are not clear, but not long after this Louise met and married Johnny Bundy. Louise's new husband legally adopted the child, so giving him his final surname of Bundy. However, all Johnny's attempts to develop a father-son relationship with Bundy were rebuffed — and the child still believed that Louise was his sister, not his mother.

Traumatic discovery

Although rather withdrawn, Bundy was a good student at school and was active in the local Methodist church and the Boy Scouts. However, he was already developing a fascination with death and sexual violence, looking through books and magazines for descriptions and images of violent and pornographic acts. In 1965 he graduated from high school and went to the University of Puget Sound (UPS), but after only two semesters he transferred to the University of Washington in Seattle. Here he began a serious relationship with another student that lasted until 1968; she broke off with Bundy after she graduated, tired of his lack of drive. Devastated emotionally, Bundy decided to visit his birthplace — where he made the traumatic discovery that his sister Louise was really his mother.

He was already developing a fascination with death and sexual violence.

ABOVE: Ted Bundy had an unusual upbringing – he was led to believe his mother was his sister and was raised by his grandparents, who he thought were his parents.

ABOVE LEFT (INSET): A wanted poster distributed by the FBI after Bundy was placed on the '10 most wanted' list. Bundy was arrested in Florida on a stolen car charge and then identified as the fugitive wanted in 36 rape or murder cases.

LEFT: Bundy after his original arrest. During his detainment he managed to escape several times. Following one escape he started a new series of attacks in Florida.

Law school

From this point on, Bundy became focused and driven. He began dating a secretary and re-enrolled at UW, majoring in psychology. He became involved in politics, supporting then working for the Republican Party, and in 1973 he was accepted in law school at UPS. Things appeared to be going well, but in the summer of 1973 Bundy met up again with his old student girlfriend and they began a relationship – although he carried on seeing the secretary too. Despite this he proposed to his old love and was accepted – then abruptly dropped her, just as she had dropped him years before.

Murder spree

Soon after this, Bundy's murderous spree began – although on Death Row he told a reporter that his first murder was in 1972 and his first attempt to kidnap a woman was in 1969. However, his first victim is generally accepted to be an 18-year-old student at UW, who was beaten and sexually assaulted in her room early in January 1974. She survived, but suffered permanent brain damage. The first murder was another student, Linda Healy, who disappeared in Seattle at the end of January and was never

He was arrested within a few days, tried, convicted and sentenced to death for murders in several states.

seen again. Soon female students were vanishing on a regular basis from university campuses in several states, as well as other women from a variety of public places. Bundy's modus operandi was often the adoption of a fake injury with a cast to his arm or leg; he would ask for help in carrying something to his car – a Volkswagen Beetle – and would then abduct and murder his helper. He was handsome and charming on the surface, so most victims offered help without question.

Bundy's confession

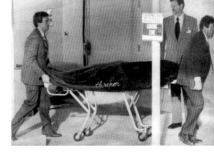

On August 16, 1975, Bundy was arrested in Utah – not for murder but for failure to stop for a police officer. However, he was soon connected to a string of missing girls, and on March 1, 1976 he was sentenced to 15 years. He was then extradited to Colorado to face further charges, and at the courthouse he promptly escaped. Recaptured after six days, he escaped again six months later and started a new series of attacks in Florida. This time he was arrested within a few days, tried, convicted and sentenced to death for murders in several states. Over the next decade of appeals Bundy insisted he was innocent, but with execution finally unavoidable he confessed to 30 murders. The true total remains unknown, although most people agree it was around 35. On January 24, 1989, Bundy was executed in the electric chair at Florida State Prison. Before he died, he told the press that violent pornography had helped to shape and mould his behaviour.

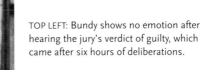

TOP LEFT: Bundy shows no emotion after hearing the jury's verdict of guilty, which came after six hours of deliberations.

ABOVE LEFT: Bundy holds a copy of the Miami Herald in court as he describes to judge Edward Cowart that a controversial photograph of himself that appeared in the paper made him out to be a villain and an idiot.

LEFT: Judge Cowart reads the verdict: the jury found Bundy guilty and he was sentenced to the electric chair.

ABOVE: The body of Ted Bundy is taken to the Alachua County Medical Examiner's office following his execution on January 24, 1989. When his appeals failed and execution seemed imminent, Bundy admitted to 30 murders.

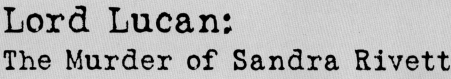

'He's murdered the nanny!' the woman cried, before collapsing and being rushed to St George's Hospital. Thus began a high-society mystery that has rumbled on unresolved for over 30 years.

ABOVE RIGHT: Lucan pictured in Portofino, in 1968 with Mrs Zoe Howard, wife of Greville Howard.

ABOVE LEFT: Lady Lucan pictured outside her Belgrave home. On the night of 7 November she staggered into the nearby Plumbers' Arms pub crying for help as blood poured from her head.

OPPOSITE TOP LEFT: Lord Lucan in a West End club, January, 1973.

OPPOSITE BOTTOM RIGHT: A policeman stands outside Lady Lucan's home in Lower Belgravia Street. When the police arrived at number 46 they found the body of 29-year-old nanny, Sandra Rivett.

Custody battle

On the night of 7 November 1974, the bloodied figure of a woman staggered into the Plumbers' Arms, a public house situated a few yards from her Belgravia home. It soon became clear that the cry for help was not just on her account. There had been another, less fortunate, victim.

The injured woman was Lady Lucan, nee Veronica Duncan. She had gained her title by dint of her marriage 11 years earlier to Richard John Bingham, 7th Earl of Lucan. Lord Lucan was an Old Etonian and former Coldstream Guardsman, following in the footsteps of his father, the 6th Earl, who served as the Chief Labour Whip in the House of Lords until his death in 1964.

Lord and Lady Lucan had three children, Frances (b. 1964), George (b. 1967) and Camilla (b. 1970). By 1972 the marriage had foundered and the children became the subject of a fierce custody battle. In March 1973 Lord Lucan obtained a court order giving him custody of the three children, but that decision was later overturned, a ruling that infuriated the earl. By the autumn of 1974, the couple had been living apart for almost two years and divorce proceedings were pending. It was a black time for Lord Lucan. He was an inveterate gambler who could win or lose thousands during an evening at the gaming tables. Friends called him 'Lucky' Lucan, but his good fortune seemed to have deserted him. He had incurred heavy financial losses, and the upkeep of two London houses following the marital breakdown represented a substantial additional burden. Many believe that on the night of 7 November 1974 Lord Lucan planned to relieve himself of at least one of the encumbrances weighing him down. In the months leading up to his disappearance Lucan reportedly told several friends that he wished to be rid of his wife.

Lucan named

Police arrived at 46 Lower Belgravia Street to find copious bloodstains on the stairs leading to the basement, at the foot of which was a sack containing the body of 29-year-old Sandra Rivett, the children's nanny. She had been clubbed to death with a blunt instrument. A piece of lead pipe covered in surgical tape was recovered from the scene, later confirmed as both the murder weapon and the implement with which Lady Lucan was attacked.

Police forced their way into Lord Lucan's flat in Elizabeth Street, but he was nowhere to be found. Not until the inquest seven months later would Lady Lucan publicly name her husband as the man who attacked her, though that revelation hardly came as a shock. For within days of the incident, Detective Chief Superintendent Roy Ranson, the man heading the inquiry, said that the police weren't looking for anyone else in connection with the crime, and on Tuesday 12 November warrants for Lord Lucan's arrest were issued on charges of murder and attempted murder.

> Twenty minutes passed and the nanny failed to return, so Lady Lucan went to investigate.

At the inquest, which took place in June 1975, Lady Lucan said she was watching television upstairs with Lady Frances when Sandra Rivett went to the basement kitchen to make tea just before 9 pm. Thursday was normally Sandra's night off - a fact of which Lord Lucan was aware - but that week she had taken Wednesday evening off instead. Twenty minutes passed and the nanny failed to return, so Lady Lucan went to investigate. She reached the ground floor and called out to Sandra's name, and it was then that she was attacked by her husband, whom she positively identified. He eventually broke off the assault, and, according to the countess, admitted accidentally killing the nanny. When he went to fetch a cloth to tend her injuries, Lady Lucan seized the chance to escape to the Plumbers' Arms and raise the alarm.

Screams

Police believe the attacker used lead piping. Moments later, Lady Lucan ran 100 yards to the Plumbers Arms to raise the alarm. She fell through the saloon bar door and screamed to head barman Derrick Whitehouse, 44: 'I've just come from a murder. Help me. 'Mr Whitehouse said yesterday: 'She was in a dreadful state. Hysterical and covered in deep cuts. We laid her on a bench and called the police 'She kept shouting "He's killed the nanny," and "My children, my children". There were about ten customers in the bar and one of them tried to quieten her.

'Within minutes of the 999 call, police smashed open the white front door of Lady Lucan's home and found Mrs Rivett's battered body wrapped in a canvas tent bag in the basement. Roadblocks were set up and teams of police began house-to-house inquiries. Other senior police went to the back of the block and knocked at the door of Lord Lucan's mews cottage in Eaton Row. When there was no reply they kicked open the yellow front door - but found that Lord Lucan had not been living there for some time.

Lord and Lady Lucan were married in the summer of 1963. Lady Lucan, then Miss Veronica Duncan, the debutante daughter of an Army major, was one of London's Society's most noted beauties.

Difficult

Lord Lucan - family motto 'Christ is my hope' - is the great-great grandson of the third earl, who led the Charge of the Light Brigade at Balaclava in the Crimean War. The Eton-educated former Coldstream Guards officer was regarded as the catch of the year. But the marriage proved a difficult one. The three children have been made wards of court. His love of baccarat and backgammon brought him into contact with leading film executives and he was screen-tested for the James Bond role won by Sean Connery.

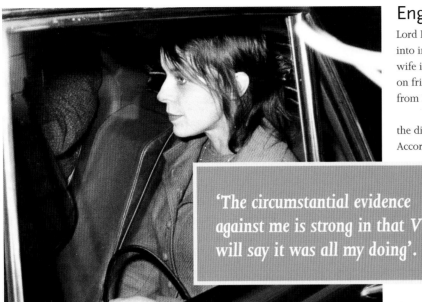

'The circumstantial evidence against me is strong in that V will say it was all my doing'.

Engaged in a violent struggle

Lord Lucan's version of events, pieced together from correspondence he entered into in the aftermath of the incident, differed markedly from that related by his wife in the coroner's court. At 11.30 pm on the night of the murder he called in on friends, the Maxwell-Scotts, who lived in Uckfield, Sussex, some 40 miles from Belgravia.

Ian Maxwell-Scott was not at home, and it was his wife Susan who received the dishevelled Lord Lucan; it was to be the last confirmed sighting of the peer. According to Mrs Maxwell-Scott, Lucan had been passing the family home when he looked through the basement window and saw a man engaged in a violent struggle with his wife. He had a key to the house and went to her aid, but slipped on a patch of blood and couldn't prevent the assailant from escaping. Lady Lucan became hysterical, accusing her husband of hiring an assassin, and fled the house while he was trying to calm her down and treat her wounds. Lucan made a telephone call to his mother relaying much the same story. He is said to have described it as a catastrophic evening of 'incredible coincidence'.

Lucan's story

Although in Lord Lucan's version of events he had no reason to reproach himself, he feared that things looked bad for him, as he indicated in a letter written to his brother-in-law William Shand-Kydd. 'The circumstantial evidence against me is strong in that V will say it was all my doing. I also will lie doggo for a bit....V has demonstrated her hatred for me in the past and would do anything to see me accused.' The letter also expressed concerns for his children. He said he did not want to put them through the agony of seeing their father in the dock, suggesting that he had no intention of facing criminal proceedings. Some interpreted this as an indication that he planned to disappear, others that he intended to take his own life. The letter was not only a clear rebuttal of Lady Lucan's version of events but an attempt to discredit the word of an embittered spouse.

CAUTION
BARGE WORKING
AHEAD
UNDERWATER
OBSTRUCTION

Holiday home

Detectives were also checking every major casino from Monte Carlo to Cannes, for the earl has played in most casinos in the south and police believe his gambling instincts are so strong he could pay a visit. Lord Lucan speaks French poorly but he has an extensive knowledge of the Riviera. Some of his friends are still at their homes there, but others have returned to England. Lord Lucan could easily be staying at a vacated holiday home.

In the United States, the FBI were interviewing relatives and several business associates of Lord Lucan. The move followed the discovery of a diary which he also used as an address book. Details were immediately sent to the French police HQ in Paris and to Washington via the Interpol network.

A major point in yesterday's decision to make public the arrest warrants was that Scotland Yard wanted all of Lord Lucan's friends to know that they risk facing criminal charges for either harbouring him or aiding him while on the run. Police accept that he has dedicated friends who would take the chance. Mrs Susan Maxwell Scott, the last person to see Lord Lucan, said she was 'amazed and aghast' that arrest warrants had been issued. Mrs Maxwell Scott, who was visited by Lord Lucan at her home at Uckfield, Sussex, just two hours after Mrs Rivett was found dead, said: 'He has to be innocent.'

POLICE

Car abandoned

Susan Maxwell-Scott said that Lord Lucan left at around 1.15 am on the morning of Friday 8 August. Two days later, the borrowed Ford Corsair in which he travelled to Sussex was found abandoned in Newhaven. It was stained with both type A and type B blood, matching the groups of Lady Lucan and Sandra Rivett respectively. A length of lead piping found in the boot matched the murder weapon found at the crime scene. The car's location fuelled speculation that Lord Lucan might have tried to flee the country by ferry, despite the fact that his passport was in police hands. Those who favoured the suicide theory suggested that he may not have intended to complete the crossing; perhaps he planned a watery grave.

> The feelings of hopelessness expressed in the letter gave further support to the idea that he intended to take the gentleman's way out and end it all.

Forensic evidence

The Corsair's owner was a friend of the peer's, Michael Stoop. Lucan had borrowed the vehicle as his own car, a Mercedes, had battery trouble. Stoop was also the recipient of a letter, which was read out in the coroner's court. In it Lucan referred to the missive sent to William Shand-Kydd detailing the events of 7 November, adding: '…but judging by my last effort in court no one, let alone a 67-year-old judge, would believe – and I no longer care, except that my children should be protected.' He obviously felt that a court case would go against him, as the custody battle had. The forensic evidence was certainly not in his favour. Most of the blood found in the basement was type B, Rivett's group, while the ground-floor deposits were mainly type A, Lady Lucan's group. That was consistent with the countess's story, not his. The feelings of hopelessness expressed in the letter gave further support to the idea that he intended to take the gentleman's way out and end it all.

OPPOSITE MIDDLE AND BOTTOM: Frogmen probed a hole near the swing bridge in Newhaven Harbour where bodies have been found in the past. After an hour the frogmen abandoned their hunt for Lord Lucan.

TOP LEFT: Police dog handles search for Lord Lucan on the downs above Newhaven Harbour.

ABOVE: Lord Lucan pictured during a holiday in Spain. His version of events, that was delivered through various correspondence, differed greatly from Lady Lucan's.

ABOVE LEFT: Evidence being carried out after the hearing into Sandra Rivett's murder. The Coronor's court committed Lord Lucan for trial at the Old Bailey but the police had yet to apprehend him.

OPPOSITE TOP: Lord and Lady Lucan had three children together and had been living apart from almost two years prior to the nanny's murder. During the inquest the QC acting for Lord Lucan's mother did his best to talk up Lady Lucan's alleged hatred of her husband, but the forensic evidence supported Lady Lucan's account.

LEFT: Lady Lucan publicly named her husband as the man who attacked her during the inquest, seven months after the incident.

JUNE 17, 1975

The night my nanny died

> I went downstairs again to Mummy's room at about 8.40. I asked Mummy where Sandra was and she said, 'Downstairs making tea.'

A sensational description by Lord Lucan's 10-year-old daughter of the night her nanny was murdered and her mother brutally attacked was read to a coroner's court yesterday. Lady Frances Bingham told of hearing a scream, then seeing her father with her mother, Lady Lucan, who was 'bleeding over her face and crying.'

Making tea

The statement said: On the Thursday evening we, that is, Mummy, George (her brother Lord Bingham, aged seven), Camilla (her sister, aged four), Sandra and I all had tea together. After tea I played one of my games in the nursery. At 7.20 I watched Top of the Pops on TV in the nursery. Mummy, Camilla, George and Sandra were downstairs watching The Six Million Dollar Man. I joined them at 8.05 and we all watched TV in Mummy's room. When the programme finished at 8.30 I went back to the nursery and played with my game. Sandra took Camilla and George upstairs and put them to bed. I had had my bath and I was wearing my pyjamas. I only stayed in the nursery about five minutes then I went downstairs again to Mummy's room at about 8.40. I asked Mummy where Sandra was and she said, 'Downstairs making tea.' After a while Mummy said that she wondered why Sandra was so long. I said I would go downstairs and see what was keeping Sandra. Mummy said No, she was going, and I said I would go with her. She said No, it was OK, she would go, and I stayed watching TV.

No light

Mummy left the room and left the door open. There was no light in the hall because the bulb doesn't work. Just after Mummy left the room I heard a scream. It sounded as though it came from a long way away. I thought that maybe the cat had scratched Mummy and she had screamed. I wasn't frightened by the scream and I stayed watching TV. At about 9.05 I ran to the door and called "Mummy." But there was no answer, so I left it. At 9.05 the news was on TV and Mummy and Daddy both walked into the room. Mummy was bleeding over her face and was crying. Mummy told me to go upstairs. Daddy didn't say anything to me and I said nothing to either of them. I only caught a glimpse of her. I don't know how much blood was on her face. As far as I can remember Daddy was wearing a pair of dark trousers and overcoat. I did not hear any conversation between Mummy and Daddy. I was on the bed when they came in the door.

Days off

I didn't see any blood on Daddy's clothes. I wondered what had happened but I didn't ask. I went upstairs and got into bed and read my book. I didn't hear anything from downstairs. After a little while - I don't know how long - I heard Daddy calling for Mummy. He was calling "Veronica, where are you?" I got up and looked down and saw Daddy coming out of the nursery. He went into the bathroom, came straight out and went downstairs.

During the last weekend I spent with Daddy, Camilla told Daddy that Sandra had boyfriends and went out with them. Daddy asked when she went out with them and Camilla said she went out with them on her days off. Then Daddy asked me when her days off were and I said Thursdays.

RIGHT: Many of Lord Lucan's belongings were auctioned off at Christie's auctioneers in order to pay off his massive gambling debts. Following his disappearance, it became apparent that Lord Lucan had accrued around £65,000 worth of debts.

Committed for trial

The court proceedings lasted four days and produced a sensational outcome. Lord Lucan was named as Sandra Rivett's murderer. It was highly unusual to name a perpetrator at a coroner's court, and indeed, legislation was passed in 1977 to outlaw such a practice. But following the jury's verdict, coroner Dr Gavin Thurston duly committed Lord Lucan for trial at the Old Bailey. First, of course, the police had to apprehend him.

JUNE 20, 1975

After half an hour, the verdict: Lucan killed her

Lord Lucan was the killer of his children's nanny, an inquest jury decided yesterday. The six men and three women took just 31 minutes to reach the verdict that 29-year-old Mrs Sandra Rivett was battered to death by the earl, who vanished soon afterwards.

The earl's mother, Kaitilin, Dowager Countess Lucan, who gave evidence that suggested her son was innocent, sat with her face downcast, breathing deeply. Coroner Dr Gavin Thurston, who summed up the three days of evidence in 70 minutes before the jury retired, formally announced that 'Richard John Bingham, Earl of Lucan, did on the 7th November 1974, in the City of Westminster, murder Sandra Eleanor Rivett.'

No one to commit

He said it was very rare for a jury to name someone in their verdict and added: 'It is my duty to commit that person for trial to the Central Criminal Court.' But in this case there was no one to commit for trial, and the verdict would remain 'on the file'.

> The six men and three women took just 31 minutes to reach the verdict that 29-year-old Mrs Sandra Rivett was battered to death by the earl.

Declared dead

Since 1974, there have been numerous 'sightings' of Lord Lucan in all corners of the globe, but all the trails turned out to be false. In 1999 the 7th Earl of Lucan was declared legally dead by the High Court, though that wasn't enough to persuade the House of Lords to allow his son to take his seat in the Upper Chamber.

The peer's disappearance left the book open, an invitation to speculators and theorists. Was Lord Lucan a murderer, as the coroner's court found? Did he hire a bungling hitman, who mistook Sandra Rivett for Lady Lucan? Was Lord Lucan the hero of the hour, saving his wife from a vicious attack by an unknown assailant? Did he commit suicide, fearing that he wouldn't be believed? Or is he alive and well, still in hiding?

TOP LEFT: Lord Lucan's coronet and peer's robes were auctioned in order to pay the missing earl's creditors.

TOP RIGHT: Lady Lucan with picture of a man held in Australia, who police believed to be Lucan. Since his disappearance on 8 November 1974 there have been many claimed sightings but none these have been verified.

ABOVE: Lady Lucan photographed at home in 1976. Her husband was declared dead by the High Court in 1999. The House of Lords failed to accept there is enough evidence to prove Lord Lucan is dead and has denied his son's request to take his seat in the Upper Chamber.

Patty Hearst:
Heiress on the FBI's 'Ten Most Wanted' list

Kidnap victim

The security videotape had caught the whole event on camera and police were surprised to see that one of the women was Patty Hearst, an heiress missing for over two months. And she didn't appear to have been under duress; she was waving a gun around and looked very much a part of the action.

The granddaughter of legendary newspaper publisher William Randolph Hearst – on whom Orson Welles' Citizen Kane was partly based – Patricia Campbell Hearst was born on February 20, 1954 in San Francisco, California. Her family lived in Hillsborough, an affluent San Francisco suburb, where Patty attended the Crystal Springs School for Girls. Later she went to the Santa Catalina School for Girls in Monterey, but as she reached her teens she began to rebel, fighting with the nuns, taking drugs and experimenting with sex. At her previous school she had met Steven Weed, who was one of the maths teachers, and the two of them first became lovers, then planned to marry. Patty soon moved in with her fiancé and when he was awarded a teaching fellowship at the University of California the two of them moved to Berkeley, where Patty enrolled for her sophomore year.

Symbionese Liberation Army

Despite the general student unrest at that time Patty was not involved with any political activist groups, but on February 4, 1974, two men and a woman broke into her apartment and kidnapped her at gunpoint. At first news of the kidnapping was kept quiet, but soon it became the focus of media coverage around the world. Her kidnappers called themselves the Symbionese Liberation Army (SLA) and appeared to be led by Donald DeFreeze, under the assumed name of Field Marshall Cinque Mtume. DeFreeze demanded total obedience and worship from his followers and planned to encourage the poor and underprivileged to rise up in revolution by attacking the rich and influential. At first the SLA tried to exchange Patty for members of their group in prison, but when this was refused by the authorities they demanded that the Hearst family distribute $70 worth of food to every poor person in California – which would have cost about $400 million. Patty's father donated several millions in food to the needy around San Francisco, but much of it was diverted by other radical groups or sold on at a profit – and the SLA still refused to free Patty, on the grounds that the food had not been good quality. The SLA had also wanted their propaganda published, which Hearst had done, but when they wanted more food distributed he refused unless Patty was returned safely. All communication stopped abruptly, and Patty's family feared the worst.

> *At first news of the kidnapping was kept quiet, but soon it became the focus of media coverage around the world.*

At 9.40 am on April 15, 1974, four women and a man walked into a branch of the Hibernia Bank in San Francisco carrying guns. Less than five minutes later they left, having robbed the bank of over $10,000 and wounded two bystanders.

Under duress

Meanwhile, DeFreeze had realised that Patty's social standing could be used to further his cause, so he began to work on her using psychological techniques. She was kept in isolation much of the time, blindfolded in a cupboard, and not allowed any privacy when using the bathroom. She was often abused verbally and sexually by members of the gang, told that she had been abandoned by her family, and fed lies about how the SLA was oppressed by the establishment. The SLA began to release tapes of Patty's voice to the media in which she talked of the SLA's aims and condemned the capitalist crimes of her family, with each tape exhibiting a shift in her attitude towards the SLA. The Hearst family believed the tapes were made under duress, but a photograph of Patty appeared dressed as a revolutionary with a rifle in her arms, standing next to the SLA's symbol, a seven-headed cobra. Another tape confirmed that she had joined the SLA and had taken a new name – 'Tania', after the girlfriend of Che Guevara. Soon after this she took part in the Hibernia Bank raid.

Seven-headed cobra

When the Attorney General saw the footage from the bank, he ruled that Patty had been a willing participant and issued a warrant for her arrest as a material witness. However, a month later she took part in another raid on a shop in Los Angeles, at which point her name was placed on the FBI's 'Ten Most Wanted' list. The following day DeFreeze was killed in a police shoot-out, along with five other members of the SLA. Patty vanished with two of the remaining members, but the FBI was on her trail and she was arrested on September 18, 1975. In the days following her arrest Patty maintained her allegiance to the SLA, making the Black Power salute and giving 'urban guerrilla' as her occupation. However, by the time of her trial for bank robbery and illegal use of firearms in February 1976, a transformation had been wrought. Gone were the revolutionary clothes – Patty now looked like the young heiress she had been before the kidnapping. Her defence was that she had been brainwashed – and that she had later not returned to her parents because she was in fear of her life. The judge and jury did not believe her story, which featured several inconsistencies, and she was found guilty on both counts and sentenced to seven years in prison. After serving nearly two years she was released by President Jimmy Carter, and President Bill Clinton granted her a full pardon on January 20, 2001. She married former bodyguard Bernard Shaw and now lives in New York and Connecticut.

> The Hearst family believed the tapes were made under duress, but a photograph appeared of Patty dressed as a revolutionary with a rifle in her arms.

OPPOSTE TOP LEFT: Granddaughter of newspaper publisher William Randolph Hearst, Patty Hearst was kidnapped by the Symbionese Liberation Army in 1974.

OPPOSITE BELOW LEFT: Posters at the University of California, where Hearst was a student. Tania was the name Hearst adopted when she joined the Symbionese Liberation Army.

OPPOSITE BOTTOM RIGHT: The wanted poster that was put out during the search for Hearst. It also pictures two other members of the terrorist group, William and Emily Harris.

ABOVE MIDDLE RIGHT: The house in San Francisco where Hearst was captured by an FBI agent.

TOP LEFT AND ABOVE: Hearst was pictured in the hold up of the Hibernia Bank in San Francisco. Her family released a letter from a New York expert that claimed that the pictures of her during the raid showed she was an unwilling participant.

RIGHT: Hearst was found guilty of the bank robbery and illegal use of fire arms and sentenced to seven years in prison, despite her defence that she was brainwashed. President Jimmy Carter released her after two years and President Clinton granted her a full pardon in 2001.

Mayfair bank robbery:
Britain's biggest bank robbery

NOVEMBER 13, 1976

The man believed to have masterminded Britain's biggest bank robbery sunned himself in Morocco yesterday after an extradition bungle which astonished Scotland Yard. Frank Maple, a 37-year-old Londoner, was enjoying his freedom while other people were convicted at The Old Bailey for their parts in the raid on the Bank of America vaults in Mayfair.

The robbers got away with gold, jewels and cash worth £8 million at a conservative estimate, but possibly as much as £20 million. Many of the jewels are priceless. Maple is one of four men both the Yard and wide world gangs hunting the men would like to find, and the Yardmen thought they had him once. The Flying Squad discovered that he was living in Spain at an £18,000 villa he bought in Marbella on the Costa del Sol, a few weeks after the robbery in April last year.

Detective Chief Inspector Michael O'Leary, went to Madrid and Spanish police agreed to his request that they should detain Maple as 'an undesirable alien' while formal extradition papers were prepared.

25 April 1975

Six armed men using a duplicate key broke into a Mayfair bank last night and walked out two hours later with cash and jewellery worth well over £8,000,000. The gang opened the vault 'like a child's piggy bank,' said police.

ABOVE, LEFT AND OPPOSITE MIDDLE: The Bank of America in Mayfair where six armed men stole £8 million. They had obtained the safe codes from Stuart Buckley who worked in the bank.

BOTTOM LEFT: Ms Farida almost collapsed when she learned that her entire collection of jewels had been stolen in the raid. They were worth more than £200,000.

BOTTOM MIDDLE: John Pugliese, another customer of the bank, pictured during his wait to find out whether his coins, valued at more than six figures, had been stolen.

LEFT: Anxious customers wait outside the bank to find out if the contents of their safety deposit boxes had been stolen.

OPPOSITE TOP: The bank's fire exit – the entrance used by the thieves. They were let in by their 'inside man', Stuart Buckley.

OPPOSITE BOTTOM: Silvio's Café in Cannon Street, London. The gang held regular operational meetings here over coffee and sandwiches.

Anyone standing still for more than a moment is liable to be swept off the pavement by the final wave in the tide of home-rushing secretaries, solicitors' clerks and office workers. But on Thursday, April 24, 1975, eight men were doing their best to avoid the jostling crowds and at the same time merge into the surroundings.

In fact all were watching for a signal from a white Ford van parked outside the Bank of America, an institution they regarded as a goose about to be robbed of a golden egg.

All clear

For behind its unromantic exterior an estimated £15 million was stacked in scores of black steel deposit boxes reaching almost from floor to ceiling in the basement vault. The signal that was to begin the biggest bank raid yet came when 26-year-old Stuart Buckley flashed an all-clear on the headlights of the white van.

The bank staff had gone home. It was time to move in. One by one the eight watchers walked through the glass-fronted doors leading into the complex of offices and flats in which the bank is housed. Once inside, all pulled stocking masks over their heads and some drew guns. Then silently and in Indian file they headed for the vault.

They had come well prepared. The leader of the file opened a locked door with a skeleton key and led the gang straight to their objective. Up one flight of stairs they went to the first floor, down another to the main banking hall, and then down a third flight to the basement. Just one pace sideways to the left of a partitioned alcove, where a clerk sat in normal banking hours, and they were facing the 8ft by 4ft steel door to the vault.

The fact that they knew exactly how to get to the vault was not surprising. Some of the gang had raided the bank six months before. That time the raid had to be abandoned when the drill bit of their Black and Decker melted on the vault door. This time there was no need to drill. They had the combination of the lock neatly written on a piece of white paper.

Successful criminals need luck, and Buckley had been blessed with a giant-sized share. Soon after he finished a prison sentence for receiving, the electrical contracting business he ran from his home in Canford Road, Battersea, was employed by the bank. Buckley became the gang's man on the inside. That was luck. What happened next, was a gift from the gods. On the bank's instructions, he went to work checking electrical circuits, a job which meant working above the ceiling of a passage that led to the vault. During the job Buckley struck gold. His screwdriver slipped and put a hole through the ceiling plaster. He peered through... and realised he was the unseen witness as two bank workers turned the dials to open the vault.

Locksmith

Buckley reported back to the gang's controllers at one of their operational meetings, held regularly over coffee and sandwiches in Silvio's Café in Cannon Street. A few days later Buckley once more crawled out over the ceiling. This time he took a miniature telescope with him and came away with the full combination. There was more to do. Two locks needed attention. Buckley smuggled into the bank 52-year-old Leonard Wilde, known in the underworld as John the Boche, the Quiet Man. Wilde, and several others in the gang, were given tours of the bank by Buckley, who told anyone who appeared interested that they were his workmates. Wilde was no electrician. He was, however an excellent locksmith. And at 5.45 on that evening in April, it all paid off. The combination lock clicked back, the vault door swung easily open and the eight masked raiders moved inside.

The real work was about to begin. An electric drill was plugged in and its noise echoed around the vault as it bit through the metal catches of safe deposit boxes.

He peered through ... and realised he was the unseen witness as two bank workers turned the dials to open the vault.

Mastermind escapes

"Whatever has happened to it, it will not be used for your benefit," Judge King-Hamilton said as he passed the longest sentences on those who masterminded Britain's biggest bank raid robbery.

The main evidence in the trial came from Stuart Buckley who turned police informant.

Leonard Wilde was sent to jail for 23 years and Peter Colson, 32, for 21 years. Others in the gang were sentenced to periods ranging from 18 years for robbery to three years for receiving stolen goods.

However, Frank Maple, who masterminded the crime, escaped justice. He left Britain shortly after the robbery and is believed to be in the African state of Morocco, which has no extradition treaty with the UK. Buckley received seven years for his part in the raid.

Donald Neilson: The Black Panther

On the morning of 14 January 1975, Dorothy Whittle made the shocking discovery that her 17-year-old daughter Lesley had been abducted during the night from their comfortable home in Highley, Shropshire. Three messages imprinted on Dymo-tape were found in the lounge, leaving no doubt over the explanation for Lesley's disappearance.

Ransom demands

One of the messages set out a ransom demand of £50,000, which was to be taken to a telephone box at Swan shopping centre, Kidderminster, that evening. The bag-carrier would receive a phone call with further instructions. The tape message carried a dark warning: 'From the time you answer you are on a time limit. If police or tricks death.'

The kidnapper had chosen his target carefully. Lesley's father had built up a thriving coach company, and on his death in 1970 had left £82,000 in trust for his teenage daughter. This information had featured in the press, and obviously one criminally-minded media watcher had seen it as an opportunity for a big payday.

Lesley's 31-year-old brother Ronald kept the phone box appointment, though he had not complied fully with the kidnapper's request, for he was in two-way radio communication with the police. A news blackout was vital to the success of the operation but the story leaked out and the assignation was aborted. The Whittle family faced an anxious wait for the kidnapper to make further contact.

The following day, a shooting took place at a transport depot in Dudley, an incident that seemed to have no connection with Lesley's abduction. Gerald Smith, a security guard at the Freightliner depot, noticed a man loitering suspiciously near the perimeter fence. He intended to report the incident but was stopped in his tracks by a hail of gunfire. Smith was hit six times, yet still managed to raise the alarm and give a description of his attacker. Ballistics experts examined the spent cartridges and were able to establish that the same weapon had been used in attacks on sub-post offices by Britain's most wanted criminal, the Black Panther.

Sub post-office raids

There had been a spate of sub-post office robberies over recent years, the perpetrator often making off with paltry sums. One such raid in 1972 had resulted in the postmaster being shot. He was a lucky survivor, but over the previous twelve months three more have-a-go heroes had been fatally wounded. Donald Skepper was shot dead when his Harrogate premises were hit in February 1974; Derek Astin suffered the same fate during a robbery in Accrington the following September; and two months later, Sidney Grayland died from gunshot wounds after he struggled with the interloper at the sub-post office run by his wife in Langley, West Midlands. The Post Office had put up a £25,000 reward for information that led to the killer being brought to book, but thus far he had eluded the long arm of the law. The 'Black Panther' tag wasn't just a reference to his hooded appearance; it also encapsulated the stealthy, feline quality he seemed to possess for melting away after committing a crime.

Police make links

Meanwhile, there had been significant developments in the abduction case. On 16 January, the Whittle family received a call containing a recorded message; it was Lesley's voice with instructions from the kidnapper regarding payment of the ransom. Ronald Whittle followed a Dymo-tape trail that led to Bathpool Park, near Kidsgrove. He was to look out for a flashing torch, the signal from the kidnapper. While Whittle was still struggling to find the park in the darkness of the small hours, a courting couple pulled up at the appointed place. The lovers were spooked by the flashlight and drove off, and the kidnapper also retreated, thinking it was a police trap.

A few days later, police discovered a link between the Black Panther's latest attack and the Whittle inquiry. They ran a check on a Morris 1300 saloon that had been left near the Freightliner depot and found that it had been stolen. Inside the vehicle was the gun that had shot Gerald Smith, a cassette tape of Lesley's voice and a pair of her slippers. There were also some numbered envelopes containing Dymo-tape messages that obviously formed a ransom trail. The investigating officers now knew that the man wanted for the post office homicides, the shooting of Gerald Smith and the abduction of Lesley Whittle were one and the same: the Black Panther.

> *The lovers were spooked by the flashlight and drove off, and the kidnapper also retreated, thinking it was a police trap.*

OPPOSITE LEFT: Britain's most wanted man, Donald Neilson, commonly known as 'The Black Panther'. Born Donald Nappey on 1 August 1936, Neilson was jailed for life in July 1976 for the murder of 17-year-old Shropshire heiress Lesley Whittle and three sub-postmasters in post office robberies.

OPPOSITE RIGHT: Chilling reminders of the secret life of Neilson: one of his sinister, trademark hoods and his sawn-off shotgun were found among an assortment of equipment when police searched his Bradford home following his arrest in the Nottinghamshire village of Rainworth in December 1975.

TOP RIGHT: A 'For Sale' notice marks the home of Nielson in Grangefield Avenue in Bradford, Yorkshire, where the jobbing builder lived with his wife, Irene, and 14-year-old daughter Kathryn. He had married Irene in 1955 and it was she who persuaded him not to pursue a career in the armed forces, but to settle down in Bradford.

ABOVE: Neilson had enjoyed the discipline and routine of National Service when he was a teenager. Although he did not join the army on a permanent basis, he continued to indulge his interest in the outdoor life and often took his wife and daughter on camping trips and outings involving survival activities and manoeuvres.

LEFT: The locked attic in Neilson's house where police found a stash of guns and a recording of Lesley Whittle's message giving instructions for the ransom payment.

Underground tunnels

It wasn't until 6 March that police made a thorough search of Bathpool Park. By then some schoolboys playing in the area had already made two important discoveries. They found the kidnapper's torch and a Dymo-tape message that read: 'Drop suitcase in hole'. After an intensive overground search of the park, police turned their attention to what lay beneath their feet. Where was the 'hole' referred to in the message? They learned that there was a network of underground tunnels, built to carry storm water from the surrounding hills. At the bottom of one 60-foot shaft leading down to one of the culverts, they found a platform which had obviously been used as a camp, for there was a sleeping bag, food and drink. They also found Lesley Whittle's lifeless naked body, with a wire ligature round her neck. The post mortem revealed that she had died of vagal inhibition, not asphyxiation. The vagus is a cranial nerve that regulates heartbeat and breathing; Lesley had died from shock before the noose had done its work. The time of death was estimated to be within days of the abduction.

> **McKenzie braked hard and White grabbed the shotgun, which discharged, injuring his hand.**

Diligent policework

The police drew a blank trying to trace where the goods recovered from the Morris 1300 and the underground camp might have been bought. Photofit images and the taped voice of the Black Panther drew a huge response when they were screened on television, but produced no significant lead. Months passed and it seemed that the trail had gone cold, the Black Panther once again showing his talent for going to ground. The breakthrough, when it came, was the result of diligent police work on the part of two young constables on Panda patrol in the Nottinghamshire village of Mansfield Woodhouse. PC Stuart McKenzie and PC Anthony White decided to question a man carrying a holdall who was loitering suspiciously in the vicinity of the local post office. He produced a sawn-off shotgun and forced the officers into the patrol car. McKenzie took the wheel while the gunman occupied the passenger seat, pointing his weapon at the constable's ribs. White was in the back of the vehicle.

As they passed through the village of Rainworth, the officers made their play. McKenzie braked hard and White grabbed the shotgun, which discharged, injuring his hand. Two men queuing in a nearby fish and chip shop rushed to the officers' assistance and the gunman was soon overpowered. McKenzie and White didn't know it yet but they had arrested the Black Panther.

FEBRUARY 15, 1975

Do you know him?

The police have nicknamed him the Black Panther - unconsciously, perhaps, giving him a touch of glamour his exploits hardly deserve. He is Britain's most wanted man - suspected of the kidnapping of 17-year-old heiress Lesley Whittle and the murders since 1971 of three sub-postmasters and another 20 or so raids on post offices around the country. The police cannot definitely put a name to him.

Astonishing dossier

But they have built up an astonishing dossier of the personality, background and appearance of the man they cannot name. Oddly, perhaps, in a man who is a merciless killer, he has shown compassion for women. And that fact alone leads the police to believe that Lesley Whittle may still be alive. One instance was during an armed robbery when he loosened the bonds on a woman after she complained that they were too tight. In another case he covered a woman with a blanket when she told him she was cold.

Other clues have formed a general profile of the kidnapper. The cloth cap and anorak or coat he wears may be part of a disguise. But police are convinced that he is a Black Country man. Witnesses have described him as about 35 to 40 years old, with black, wavy hair, not too long and from new trousers found in the abandoned stolen car police know he is between 5ft. 4in. and 5ft. 6in. tall and wears clothes with 29in. legs and a 32in. waist. He may have been in the Services. He has been seen carrying a large blue RAF webbing pack and walks in a brisk, military fashion.

LEFT: A police search of the Black Panther's lair in the attic of his Bradford home yielded a haul of army accessories including knives, guns and ammunition. Some wire which matched that used to tether Lesley in the underground drainage shaft was also discovered.

ABOVE AND RIGHT: It was a chance breakthrough that led to the arrest of Nielson and the subsequent search of his family home. He had been spotted acting suspiciously outside a post office in Mansfield by two patrolling policemen. As they questioned him, he pulled out a gun and forced them to drive him away. Following a violent struggle he was brought under control and detained, although at this stage the police still were unaware exactly who they had just captured.

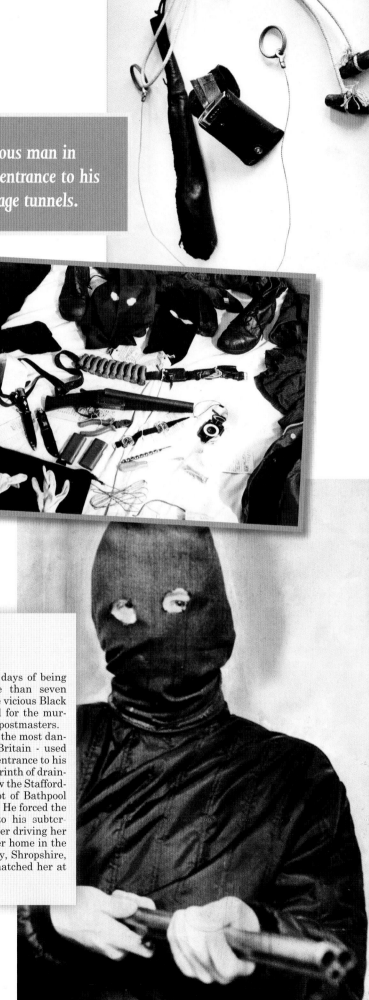

Hideout

Every hour of the murder hunt now strengthens police theories that the Panther is an itinerant construction worker who helped to tunnel the drainage scheme where he made his hideout. Nine years ago British Rail drove a tunnel and line through the park and fresh drains were built with the scheme. These carry surface water from the park and the overflow from its lake. They were added to a maze of existing drains - some 8ft. high - which served nearby sewer works and a canal. There are several entrances to the complex and in one part an underground canal. The whole area beneath the park is criss-crossed by tunnels, some of which police did not suspect existed but which the killer used freely.

> The Panther - the most dangerous man in Britain - used the shaft as the entrance to his hideout in a labyrinth of drainage tunnels.

Rage

It seems that he forced Lesley into the shaft, dressed only in her nightclothes. Then he tied her up and returned to the surface to await the arrival of her 31-year-old brother, Mr Ronald Whittle, with the £50,000 ransom. But when things went wrong the Panther returned in a rage to kill the girl, who had been left standing on the ledge with her hands bound. The ransom money was to be thrown down the shaft where Lesley's body was found. Her killer would have collected it and run off into the maze of tunnels, leaving Mr Whittle to discover his sister.

Tough

Mr Jack Trow, of Long Row, Kidsgrove, who worked on the drainage scheme nine years ago as a ganger, said: 'There were some tough types on the job. I thought about it and a couple might have fitted the bill from the impression I have of the Panther. There was one gang of tunnel men from Scotland who were very tough, and there were also quite a few from the Black Country.'

Police are examining a number of things found in the shaft. They include changes of clothing, Lesley's candlewick dressing gown, and a sleeping bag. They are also examining the underside of a manhole cover leading to the hideout on which the word 'death' had been scrawled. The cover was beneath one which marked the entrance to the shaft where Lesley's body was found. The scrawl is believed by detectives to be the Panther's sick postscript to his hideous crime.

TOP RIGHT: More items discovered in the police search included a wire saw from an RAF survival kit, a leather cosh, a cigarette lighter with a razor blade and a toggle cord.

MIDDLE RIGHT: Neilson was wearing some of the pictured clothing, including an anorak and cap, when he was arrested. It was only when his car and home were searched that police realised the person they had arrested was the Black Panther, the man responsible for the murder of the Shropshire student and three postmasters.

RIGHT: A police reconstruction of how the Black Panther appeared to his victims. Neilson's first casualty, Lancashire postmaster, Leslie Richardson, had given the police an accurate description after he was shot in the first of the violent robberies in February 1972.

MARCH 10, 1975

Lesley died of fright

Fear killed Lesley Whittle after her kidnapper tethered her by a wire cable to a ladder in the blackness of a 60ft. deep drainage shaft. The 17-year-old heiress died of fright when she plunged 45 feet down the shaft from a ledge near the top. She was found hanging from the wire which had been fixed round her neck. Lesley is believed to have been pushed off the ledge by her killer. A five-hour post mortem disclosed yesterday that Lesley died of vagal inhibition - a massive shock to the heart brought on by fear. Police now believe that she died within days of being kidnapped more than seven weeks ago by the vicious Black Panther, wanted for the murder of three sub-postmasters.

The Panther - the most dangerous man in Britain - used the shaft as the entrance to his hideout in a labyrinth of drainage tunnels below the Staffordshire beauty spot of Bathpool Park, Kidsgrove. He forced the terrified girl into his subterranean world after driving her 70 miles from her home in the village of Highley, Shropshire, where he had snatched her at gunpoint.

Donald Neilson: The Black Panther

Arsenal of weapons

The man identified himself as Donald Neilson, a 39-year-old self-employed builder who lived in Grangefield Avenue, Bradford, with his wife and daughter. The holdall he was carrying when challenged contained two of his trademark hoods, and a search of his house revealed all the Panther paraphernalia, including an arsenal of weapons, a press for making false number plates and wire of the type that had been used to tether Lesley Whittle by the neck. These were kept in a locked attic, away from the prying eyes of his family, who were unaware of the double life Neilson was leading.

Details of the Black Panther's history emerged. Donald Neilson was born 1 August 1936, growing up in Morley, near Leeds. His family name was actually Nappey, which made him the butt of schoolboy jokes during his impressionable years. His home life was hardly any happier, and he suffered a major blow at the age of 11 when he lost his mother to cancer. By the time he reached adulthood – and rid himself of the surname that had blighted his formative years – Neilson was a loner with a chip on his shoulder. He married mill worker Irene Tate in 1955, the union producing one daughter, Kathryn. Neilson did his National Service in the King's Own Yorkshire Light Infantry, and although he had an undistinguished record as a soldier, he developed an obsession with the trappings of the military lifestyle. His forte was survival techniques, and he would even take his wife and child out on manoeuvres. Neilson tried his hand at several lines of work, none of which brought him much success or satisfaction. When he chalked up yet another failure in the building trade, he turned to armed robbery, planning his crimes with military precision. A feature of his preparations was choosing hides where he could go to ground until the heat was off, surviving on meagre rations. As far as his family and neighbours were concerned he was busy working away from home.

> *His forte was survival techniques, and he would even take his wife and child out on manoeuvres.*

Years of planning

The post office raids had not been very lucrative, and reading about heiress Lesley Whittle had given him the idea for a big score. He had spent over two years planning the operation. The original ransom trail was to have led to the Freightliner depot; the altercation that led to the shooting of Gerald Smith caused him to abandon that plan and choose Bathpool Park as the drop-off point instead.

> *Only a man familiar with the system could have picked such a superb hiding place.*

Tethered

The spot included two shafts, one down which Lesley's 31-year-old brother Mr Ronald Whittle was instructed to throw £50,000 ransom and 150 yards away the 62ft. deep one where the girl was held prisoner, tethered to a platform by a wire rope round her neck.

MARCH 17, 1975

How kidnapper planned to outwit the police

This is the underground hideout of the Black Panther, part of a damp and stinking maze of tunnels where he kept heiress Lesley Whittle a terrified prisoner and finally killed her. It was an ideal hiding place. Few had any idea of the existence of the labyrinth more than 60ft. below the ground ... and more important for the man who knew he would be hunted by hundreds of police, it had four escape routes.

But before he could use them the Panther had to ensure that the 5ft. high drainage tunnels beneath Bathpool Park at Kidsgrove, Staffordshire, would not be flooded. The way he did this - and the careful selection of his hideaway - has convinced police that he has an intimate knowledge of the drainage system, and probably helped to construct it.

Some time before 17-year-old Lesley was kidnapped from her home in the village of Highley, Shropshire, in January, the Panther turned off the valves which allowed overflow water from a reservoir half a mile away to escape into the drainage tunnels. At this time of year the hideout is normally up to 5ft. deep in floodwater. With the valves off the killer reduced the depth to a mere two inches. Only a man familiar with the system could have known how to do it. Only a man familiar with the system could have picked such a superb hiding place among the maze of underground piping. It was no random choice.

LEFT: A signed receipt from Neilson's struggling business. By the time Neilson kidnapped the teenage heiress in 1975, he was already a multiple murderer, having previously supplemented his limited earnings as a builder by robbing post offices at gunpoint.

ABOVE: Police issued a re-constructed image of the kidnapper – 'Britain's Public Enemy Number 1' during the hunt for the abductor of the teenage schoolgirl. Nielsen had carefully chosen his victim who had been left a five-figure sum by her deceased father in his will.

TOP RIGHT: Nielson's van photographed at his home in Thornbury, Bradford. The non-fatal shooting of postmaster Leslie Richardson was followed by more violent robberies and three other postmasters were shot dead in similar incidents.

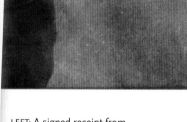

The quiet odd-job man from Grangefield Avenue

The arrest of odd-job man Donald K. Neilson, the family man with a daughter he adored, has shocked his neighbours in a city suburb. Today Neilson, 35, will be accused in connection with the murder of 17-year-old Lesley Whittle, whose body was found in a drainage shaft last March at Kidsgrove. He ran his builder's and joiner's business from three garages behind his house in Grangefield Avenue, Thornbury, two miles from Bradford city centre.

Yesterday detectives were still in the stone-built terraced house on the main Leeds-Bradford road, 72 hours after he was detained at Mansfield, Nottinghamshire. His wife, Sheila, and daughter Catherine, 14, have been taken away by police who have been involved in Britain's biggest-ever manhunt.

'Castro'

Neilson was known as 'Castro' to the man who knew him better than anyone. Mr Keith Walker, 38, who lived next door to him for ten years until a few months ago, said: 'I gave him the name because of the clothing he always wore - a jacket, jeans and boots. I don't think he was ever in the Army, although he looked every inch a part-time paratrooper and drove about in a Champ, a military Land-Rover.

He was an odd-job man who occasionally helped me on jobs when I had a building business. He was a fantastic worker, tireless and utterly fearless. I've seen him walk up and down a roof and swing down a rope lowered round the chimney. He kept himself very fit with swimming and hiking. His only amusements were swimming and going to the pictures regularly. He liked good westerns. He was also fond of music, mainly film themes. His favourite record was A Fistful of Dollars. He idolised his daughter and took her everywhere with him. He took her swimming and to a disco dance once a week.

I felt a chill down my spine when I heard he was the man detained in connection with Lesley Whittle's death.' Mr Walker said Neilson told him he had bought a house in Pudsey when he put his home up for sale a few months ago. He added: 'I'm probably the only person who became friendly with him and got close to him but I still only went in his house twice in ten years and have no idea about his background before I knew him. From his accent I'd place him coming from somewhere in the Midlands on the Shropshire side. His wife spoke with a Yorkshire accent although I sometimes wondered if they were actually married because to me they acted more like brother and sister.'

MIDDLE RIGHT: The van alleged to have been used by the Black Panther when he kidnapped Lesley Whittle. Nielson had earned this sobriquet from the media because of his practice of wearing a dark-coloured balaclava during the post-office robberies.

BOTTOM RIGHT: The Mercedes believed to have been used by Donald Nielson. The police flagged down the car, which had been reported stolen in Sutton Coldfield three hours earlier, on the M1 near St Albans, Hertfordshire. The fugitive once again eluded capture when he jumped out of the moving car and ran off.

He looked every inch a part-time paratrooper and drove about in a Champ, a military Land-Rover.

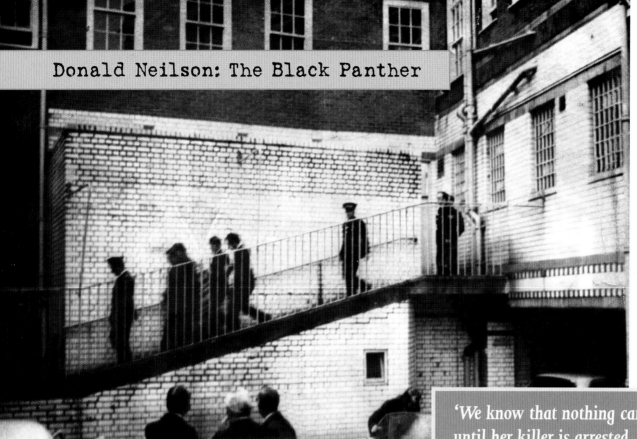

BOTTOM: A crowd of 300 jeered and shouted as 39-year-old Donald Nielson was driven to court. Extra police with their dogs had been brought in to control the hostile mob.

OPPOSITE LEFT: Covered by a plaid blanket Neilson cowers in the back of one of the convoy of five police cars which drove him to court. He was to be charged with four murders, as well as the serious offences of attempted murder, GBH, robbery, kidnapping and possession of firearms.

LEFT: Neilson being taken down a flight of steps on his way to court. He was led handcuffed into the dock of the packed courtroom by Detective Inspector Wally Boreham and Detective Chief Inspector Len Barnes.

> **'We know that nothing can bring Lesley back, but until her killer is arrested, charged and convicted there must always be a feeling of gloom.'**

DECEMBER 15, 1975

Callous

He made concrete blocks and for a time rented a garage to make wooden sheds. But nothing seemed to work out right for him and even his taxi business folded up after only nine months. He often went off camping in his hiking gear and would take his wife and daughter with him. He called me Kiddo but for a time we fell out because of the way he treated one of his dogs, a mongrel bitch, which was killed because he let it roam the streets. I found it dead in the road, put it on his doorstep and told him it would remind him of being callous when he claimed he loved dogs.

My wife saw him on Thursday night when they caught the same bus to Leeds.' Another neighbour said: 'His wife and daughter also kept themselves apart. I never knew the child to have playmates when she was younger. Mrs Neilson had a job as a cleaner at a city centre store.'

Neilson had a quick military-style walk. He once owned two Alsatians which he had referred to as 'Army dogs.' About six years ago he changed his name by deed poll from Nappy. 'I think he felt it was embarrassing, particularly for his daughter,' said a neighbour. He ran an old van and Land-Rover. But six weeks ago he bought a new Toyota van from the garage across the road.

Scientists and detectives have been working behind the blue venetian blinds at Neilson's house for nearly two days and have taken away clothing, papers, cameras, torches, and a mattress. Detectives at Kidsgrove will hold a top-level conference today. One thing that will be discussed is when an identification parade is to be held. It will be attended by security guard Gerald Smith, shot six times by a man at the freightliner depot in Dudley, Worcestershire.

Cloud lifts for a village

Ron Whittle smiled for the first time in 11 months yesterday, and spoke of the cloud that has lifted from the village of Highley in Shropshire. At the same time the Vicar, the Rev John Brittain, who declared that the Devil himself had trod the village, told parishioners that their prayers had been answered.

Mr Whittle, a coach proprietor, is 32, but grey streaks in his black hair betray the agony the family has been through since his sister Lesley was kidnapped on the wild, windy night of January 14. Yesterday a brief phone call from Detective Chief Superintendent Bob Booth, head of the West Mercia CID, told him that 'the hunt for the kidnapper and the murderer was at an end'. Mr Whittle said: 'The news was the best Christmas present that anyone could wish for. We know that nothing can bring Lesley back, but until her killer is arrested, charged and convicted there must always be a feeling of gloom.' Finally, Mr Whittle - recalling that he had been under suspicion among some members of the public because of his likeness to an artist's impression of the ruthless kidnapper-killer - said: 'I hope the news will put paid to any rumours.'

FAR RIGHT: The frenzied crowd hammer their fists on the outside of the van which ferried the Black Panther to his trial at Oxford Crown Court which started on June 14, 1976.

BOTTOM: A blanket covering her head, Mrs Irene Nielson leaves Stone police station with her solicitor. She was taken to the station 24 hours after her husband was jailed for life for murdering three sub-postmasters and heiress Lesley Whittle and seven offences in connection with the thefts from post offices.

Neilson is currently in his fourth decade behind bars, one of Britain's longest-serving prisoners.

Neilson pleads not guilty

Neilson was tried at Oxford Crown Court, as it was decided that feelings were running so high in the Black Panther's target territory that he could not be guaranteed a fair trial. He accepted the kidnapping charge but pleaded not guilty on the four counts of murder. There were also charges of attempted murder in relation to Gerald Smith and Anthony White. Smith died four months before the case went to court, but Neilson escaped a fifth murder charge because of an ancient statute which stated that a victim had to succumb to injuries within a year and a day for it to be deemed murder. The law has since been amended.

Neilson maintained that the gun had been fired accidentally in the struggles that took place in the post offices, and that Lesley had lost her footing on the platform when he returned from the abortive meeting with Ronald Whittle. The prosecution maintained that he felt angry and cheated when he returned to the culvert empty handed and pushed her off the ledge in a fit of rage. The jury agreed. Donald Neilson was sentenced to life imprisonment by Mr Justice Marr-Jones, who recommended that in this case the tariff should be interpreted literally. Successive home secretaries have endorsed that decision, and Neilson is currently in his fourth decade behind bars, one of Britain's longest-serving prisoners.

Peter Sutcliffe: 'The Yorkshire Ripper'

In the early hours of 5 July 1975, 34-year-old Anna Rogulskyj was brutally attacked with a hammer and knife in Keighley, fortunate indeed to survive what was a frenzied onslaught. Three months later, Wilma McCann wasn't so lucky. The 28-year-old mother of four worked the red-light district of Chapeltown, a Leeds suburb. She suffered major trauma to the head and multiple stab wounds, her body dumped on a playing field just 100 yards from her home. It was 30 October 1975; the Yorkshire Ripper's killing spree was under way.

The wave of attacks led to the biggest manhunt in British history, but it would be five years before the killer was brought to justice. In that time, 13 women were butchered, and there were seven more attempted murders. At least, that was the official tally; the actual figures were undoubtedly higher. The mutilation of the victims' bodies inevitably brought forth comparisons with the infamous Whitechapel murders of 1888. The hunt for the Yorkshire Ripper was on.

The man they were looking for was Peter William Sutcliffe. And they found him long before he had claimed his thirteenth victim. Sutcliffe was interviewed on nine separate occasions during the course of the inquiry, but slipped through the net each time. He enjoyed some huge slices of good fortune, and was also helped by an administrative load that swamped the investigating team. Over the five-year period, 250,000 people were interviewed, 30,000 statements taken, 5 million car registrations checked. With computer technology in its infancy, the police database consisted of an unwieldy card index system and shoeboxes filled with documents. It didn't take much for an individual name to be buried in the paper chase, and Peter Sutcliffe profited from the bureaucratic quagmire.

A target for bullies

Sutcliffe was born in Bingley on 2 June 1946, the eldest of John and Kathleen Sutcliffe's six children. An introverted and sensitive child, he preferred reading and clinging to his beloved mother's skirts to indulging in roughhouse games. At school he was something of a loner, neither joining in with the usual boys' pursuits nor chasing the girls. He was a target for the bullies, which led to bouts of truancy. It was hardly surprising that he left school at 15 with fewer qualifications than his studiousness merited.

Incidents in Sutcliffe's late teens showed that he wasn't just a shy misfit or late developer, but someone with the potential for darker deeds. He struggled to adjust to the world of work, his desultory jobs including a stint as a gravedigger. His workmates recalled his ghoulish penchant for taking trophies from the corpses; and there was also talk of necrophilia. Sutcliffe had his first brushes with the law during this period. There was a string of motoring offences, and he was convicted of attempted theft from a parked vehicle. A foreshadowing of what was to come occurred in 1969, when he was questioned by a policeman after his car was spotted in a red-light area of Bradford. He had a hammer in his possession but it was construed only as an implement that might have been used in the furtherance of robbery. He escaped with a £25 fine.

> In 1969 Sutcliffe was questioned by a policeman after his car was spotted in a red-light area of Bradford. He had a hammer in his possession.

Police record

Peter Sutcliffe's mugshot, showing a man with dark curly hair, moustache and beard, was now in the system. The word 'hammer' also appeared on the same file under the 'method' heading, though connected with theft, not assault. Over the next six years, there were a number of unsolved attacks on women in the Yorkshire region, several of the victims describing a man whose face was already in the police records. Unfortunately, no one made a connection between the assaults, or spotted that the descriptions matched that of the man convicted of being in possession of an offensive weapon in 1969. It meant that by the mid-1970s Peter Sutcliffe had only a minor record of petty criminality.

> It didn't take much for an individual name to be buried in the paper chase, and Peter Sutcliffe profited from the bureaucratic quagmire.

OPPOSITE TOP: Peter Sutcliffe at Dewsbury Court where he was accused murdering 13 women.

OPPOSITE BOTTOM RIGHT: Peter Sutcliffe left school at the age of 15 and took on a series menial jobs. During one spell as a grave digger, he claimed God had spoken to him.

TOP RIGHT: The house at 90 Kirkgate Shipley, Yorkshire, where Peter Sutcliffe was born.

ABOVE: The Sutcliffe family moved to this house in Manor Road, Cottingley, Yorkshire, when Sutcliffe was four. He was introverted and sensitive as a child. At school he was a loner and a target for bullies, which led to his bouts of truancy.

LEFT: The sex shop in Bradford where Sutcliffe had an accommodation address. As a young man he frequented prostitutes and it was with them that he began his killing spree.

THE CROWN BAR

On one occasion, in August 1975, Sutcliffe disappeared for 20 minutes during a night out in Halifax.

CLARK Transport

Police visit

In the early seventies, Sutcliffe conducted a long, slow courtship with Sonia Szurma, the daughter of Czech immigrants. It almost foundered when Sonia began seeing someone else, and Sutcliffe sought solace in the arms of one of Bradford's prostitutes. He paid ten pounds but couldn't go through with the deal, only to find that her pimp did not deal in refunds. A few weeks later he showed his capacity for violence by clubbing a prostitute over the head with a brick, mistaking her for the woman he believed had cheated him. The victim noted down his licence number and it resulted in a police visit. As the woman decided not to press charges, Sutcliffe escaped with a caution. He would claim his hostility towards prostitutes dated from this period.

Peter and Sonia patched things up and finally tied the knot in 1974. Sonia had trained as a teacher but she was not the most stable companion, having suffered a mental breakdown during which she imagined seeing stigmata on her hands. The couple's prospects appeared much rosier when Sutcliffe gained his HGV licence and they moved into their dream house, a smart property in Garden Lane, in the Heaton district of Bradford. To the outside world Sutcliffe was a hard worker and devoted husband. In fact, he was leading a double life, cruising the local red-light zones, often in the company of long-time friend Trevor Birdsall. On one such occasion, in August 1975, Sutcliffe disappeared for 20 minutes during a night out in Halifax. The next day Birdsall learned of a vicious attack on 46-year-old cleaner Olive Smelt. Sutcliffe had already bragged of one assault and Birdsall harboured grave suspicions regarding this incident. He didn't act on them, but became increasingly troubled by Sutcliffe's fixation regarding prostitutes. Years later, in November 1980, Birdsall would finally take his concerns to the police, but by the time that information was processed Sutcliffe was in custody. And 13 women had been brutally murdered.

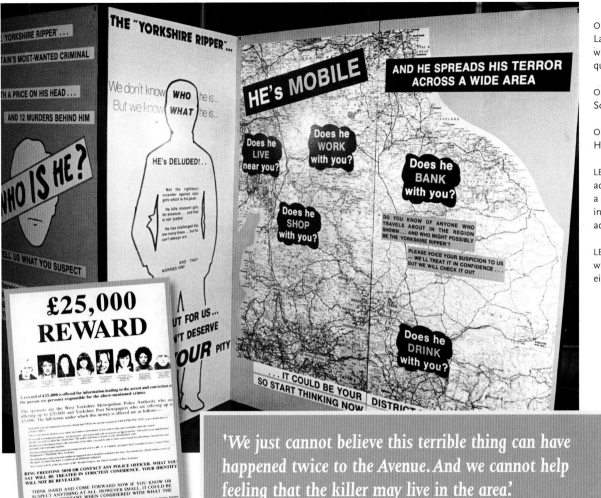

THE "YORKSHIRE RIPPER"...

We don't know **WHO** he is...
But we know **WHAT** he is...

HE's DELUDED!...

Not the righteous crusader against vice-girls which is his pose.

He kills innocent girls for pleasure... and that is not justice.

He has challenged the law many times... but he can't always win...

AND THAT WORRIES HIM!

'YORKSHIRE RIPPER'...
...TAIN'S MOST-WANTED CRIMINAL
...TH A PRICE ON HIS HEAD...
AND 12 MURDERS BEHIND HIM

WHO IS HE?

...ELL US WHAT YOU SUSPECT

£25,000 REWARD

HE's MOBILE

AND HE SPREADS HIS TERROR ACROSS A WIDE AREA

Does he LIVE near you?
Does he WORK with you?
Does he BANK with you?
Does he SHOP with you?

DO YOU KNOW OF ANYONE WHO TRAVELS ABOUT IN THE REGION SHOWN... AND WHO MIGHT POSSIBLY BE THE 'YORKSHIRE RIPPER'?

PLEASE VOICE YOUR SUSPICION TO US — WE'LL TREAT IT IN CONFIDENCE... BUT WE WILL CHECK IT OUT

Does he DRINK with you?

...IT COULD BE YOUR DISTRICT
SO START THINKING NOW

...UT FOR US...
...N'T DESERVE
...OUR PITY

'We just cannot believe this terrible thing can have happened twice to the Avenue. And we cannot help feeling that the killer may live in the area.'

HELP US CATCH THE RIPPER

● HAVE YOU SEEN THE HANDWRITING?
● HAVE YOU HEARD THE TAPE?

IF YOU HAVEN'T IT'S ON THE BACK PAGE

IF YOU HAVEN'T RING THE NEAREST OF THE FOLLOWING TELEPHONE NUMBERS
LEEDS (0532) 464111   MANCHESTER (061) 246 8060
BRADFORD (0274) 36511   NEWCASTLE (0632) 8075

OPPOSITE TOP: Sutcliffe's house in Garden Lane, Bradford. He and his Czech-born wife, Sonia, moved there when she qualified as a teacher in 1977.

OPPOSTE LEFT: The Crow Bar in Holytown, Scotland, where Sutcliffe drank.

OPPOSITE RIGHT: Sutcliffe obtained an HGV licence in June 1975.

LEFT AND BELOW: The world's first advertising campaign designed to catch a killer. The campaign cost £1 million and included billboard, newspaper and radio advertising.

LEFT INSET: A poster offering a reward, which was released in 1979. It shows eight of the Ripper's victims.

JUNE 27, 1977

Jayne, 16, may be Ripper's victim No. 5

A girl of 16 found battered to death yesterday may be the fifth victim of a woman-hating killer. The girl, Jayne McDonald, came from the same road, Scott Hall Avenue, Leeds, as the first victim 20 months ago. Children found Jayne's body in an adventure playground next to the Chapeltown Community Centre in the heart of Leeds's bedsitter land. Three prostitutes have been murdered in the same area over the past 20 months. A fourth victim in Bradford may also have been killed by the same man. All were battered, stabbed and butchered by a brutal killer police have dubbed the 'Ripper of Leeds.'

But police think that Jayne, a supermarket assistant, became a victim by accident. West Yorkshire's assistant Chief Constable, Mr George Oldfield, said: 'Obviously it is too early to speculate but the possibility of a link is very much in my mind.

Terrified

If she is another victim of the same killer then she was probably picked on at random.' Jayne and the first victim, 24-year-old prostitute Wilma McCann, lived only a few doors apart. Neighbour Mrs Violet Webster said: 'We just cannot believe this terrible thing can have happened twice to the avenue. And we cannot help feeling that the killer may live in the area. Women and people with young daughters are terrified by what has happened. Jayne was a very pretty and well brought up, respectable girl. We just pray that the killer is caught before it happens again.'

Murder cases linked

Although there were strong similarities regarding the attacks on Anna Rogulskyj and Olive Smelt in the summer of 1975, not least the head injuries consistent with hammer blows, many months passed before these were linked, either to each other or to the Ripper inquiry. As far as the police were concerned, Wilma McCann was the first victim. Following her death in October 1975, the police were wrestling with the possibility that there might be no link between the murderer and the victim. An anonymous sexual encounter that had taken a violent turn made their task much more difficult, though there were clues. Wilma had gone clubbing, and was seen trying to hitch a lift home in the early hours of the morning. There were reports of her drunkenly trying to wave down a vehicle to get a lift home, and one mentioned seeing her get into a brightly-coloured fastback car driven by a man with a drooping moustache. At the time Peter Sutcliffe owned a lime green Ford Capri.

Three months later, in January 1976, 42-year-old Emily Jackson was killed with the same modus operandi: two severe blows to the head and this time over 50 stab wounds. The cruciform shape of the latter injuries suggested that the most likely weapon was a Phillips screwdriver. The killer left the impression of a size-seven bootprint on the victim's thigh, and another in the ground nearby, but it was too common a type to be regarded as a major lead. It transpired that Jackson's husband, Sydney, had driven her to a pub in Chapeltown, leaving her to get on with 'business' while he had a drink. They had arranged to meet later to travel home together, an appointment Emily never kept. There were clear links between the McCann and Jackson cases, and police began issuing warnings for street workers to be on their guard. 'Ripper' headlines began appearing in the press, though it would be a while longer before the term 'Yorkshire Ripper' was coined.

Pressure on the police

In February 1977 the body of Irene Richardson was found in Roundhay Park, Leeds, by day a popular swathe of amenity land, by night a popular place for prostitutes to service their clients. Tyre tracks found close to the body were believed to be of the killer's car, potentially a significant breakthrough. A tread pattern was not quite a fingerprint, but the odds of finding a repeat pattern were over 100 million to one against. But first they had to trace the vehicle. The tyres could have come from any one of fifty models, and that left police with 50,000 vehicles to check in the West Yorkshire area. One of those was a Ford Corsair, the car Peter Sutcliffe was now driving. Of course, the suspect car could have had its tyres changed, or been sold or scrapped, but the police began the painstaking elimination process.

Two months after Irene Richardson was killed, the Ripper struck outside Leeds for the first time. The body of Patricia Atkinson was found lying on the bed of her Bradford flat. There was another bootprint, this time on the crumpled bedding, making it more difficult to analyse, but it could have come from a size seven Wellington similar to those found at the scene of Emily Jackson's murder.

The fifth victim was 16-year-old shoe shop worker Jayne MacDonald, whose body was found on a patch of waste ground next to a children's play park in Chapeltown. Distastefully, she was described in some parts of the media as the first 'innocent' victim. Jayne was walking home through a red-light district and it seems Sutcliffe mistook her for a streetwalker. The pressure on West Yorkshire Police to apprehend the killer was ratcheted up another notch, prompting Assistant Chief Constable George Oldfield to take over the running of the inquiry.

Oldfield's problem was the same as that which faced his predecessor, namely, the random nature of the attacks and the lack of connection between perpetrator and victim. And the hunting ground widened in October 1977 when the Ripper crossed the Pennines to claim his sixth victim.

Fear

The refusal of police to give details of the injuries suffered by the Ripper's victims served to increase the fear among women and led to grotesque speculation. After the rumours, forensic evidence was revealed which suggested the type of weapons the Ripper used - a hammer and a screwdriver. His attacks, according to one detective, came with a blow on the back of the head with the hammer.

In cities, towns and villages throughout the North of England mothers have lectured their daughters, boys have been sure to escort their girl friends to the doorsteps and women who had to work at night reduced their fear and their earnings by making their journeys in taxis.

Fear also grew into resentment. After the 13th killing, of Jacqueline Hill, in November, feminist groups stormed cinemas in Leeds and Bradford showing films which glamorised violence against women. On college campuses women began to arm themselves against attack with knives, hatpins, scissors and butane gas whistles. Queues of women, from pensioners to teenagers, formed in shops in the Ripper's territory to buy high-pitched pocket alarms.

All the time, the police hunt went on. It cost £4 million, involved 1,000 officers. Now an arrest has been made ... by two uniformed bobbies making routine checks on cars.

> *Tyre tracks found close to the body were believed to be of the killer's car, potentially a significant breakthrough.*

The net tightens

Twenty-year-old prostitute Jean Jordan worked the Moss Side area of Manchester and perhaps felt she was safe from the maniac on the loose in the neighbouring county. Or, like many streetwalkers who ignored police warnings, felt she had no choice but to carry on working and take the risk. Sutcliffe was disturbed as he tried to hide Jordan's body in some bushes and was forced to beat a hasty retreat. The body was found over a week later by a man trawling a patch of waste ground for bricks to use in a construction project. His name was Bruce Jones, who would go on to become a household name playing loutish, workshy Les Battersby in Coronation Street. The body he lighted upon was in such an horrific state that it could not have lain in the open undiscovered for such a long time. And it hadn't. Sutcliffe had returned to the scene of the crime and moved the body. Why? Because he was searching for the crisp new five-pound note he had paid up front for Jean's services. He feared it was traceable and wanted to retrieve it before the police did. The search proved fruitless, and the note was found in Jean's handbag some 50 yards from the body.

> The body was found over a week later by a man trawling a patch of waste ground for bricks to use in a construction project.

Investigations produced a short list of around 40 companies who might have used the note for payroll purposes. It included the engineering firm Sutcliffe worked for, T and WH Clark. That still meant around 7000 potential suspects but it represented a significant tightening of the net. Sutcliffe was interviewed twice in early November 1977. He said he had no five-pound notes left from his wages of the last week in September. Invited to account for his movements on 1 and 9 October, the days that the Ripper had killed Jean Jordan and returned to the body to search for the banknote, he said he was at home on both occasions, the second of them hosting a housewarming party. Sonia corroborated the story. The officers were satisfied and paid scant attention to the red Ford Corsair parked outside, a vehicle whose tyres would have been a match for those found at the scene of the Richardson murder.

With modern computer technology it would have been a simple task to cross-reference the 7,000 employees who might have received the five-pound note against the 50,000 car owners whose vehicle might have left its mark in Roundhay Park. Sutcliffe's name would have appeared in the results of such an exercise. As it was, the senior investigating officers were forced to concede that the £5 note would not lead them to the Ripper's door.

OPPOSITE TOP LEFT: Photofits of the Yorkshire Ripper (Left: made after Josephine Whitaker was murdered in April 1979. Below: made from a description by Tracey Browne. Right: issued after the attack on Marilyn Moore in December 1977).

OPPOSITE BOTTOM: As part of the £1 Million advertising campaign the police released a special newspaper with the front page headline 'Help Us Catch The Ripper'.

TOP LEFT AND ABOVE: The police incident room in Leeds. Immense pressure was put on the police to capture the Ripper.

RIGHT: Chief Constable Ronald Gregory and Detective Chief Superintendent Jim Hobson at the launch of the 'Flush Out the Ripper' campaign.

Peter Sutcliffe: 'The Yorkshire Ripper'

Sutcliffe's new hunting ground

Just before Christmas there was another breakthrough, an attack in which the victim survived to give a good description of her assailant – a man with dark curly hair, drooping moustache and beard. Dozens of similar descriptions were on file relating to attacks dating back over several years, but because they were not deemed part of the Ripper inquiry – in one case because a different size hammer had been used – the pattern was missed. Not until after Sutcliffe was in jail and the investigation was being reviewed were all these photofit images assembled as a collection. Taken as a group they screamed Peter Sutcliffe, and this oversight would be one of the key points in a damning inquiry into the handling of the case.

In January 1978 the Ripper chose a new hunting ground, Huddersfield. He killed 18-year-old Helen Rytka, who had gone onto the streets with her sister Rita. They got separated and Rita never saw Helen again. Her body was found in a lumber yard where prostitutes habitually took their clients. In May of that year Manchester-based prostitute Vera Millward met her end. Police found tyre tracks that matched those found at the scene of the Richardson murder. Vehicle experts from the Manchester force whittled the list of suspect cars down to just two - Ford Corsair and Ford Cortina Mark 1 - but the hierarchy in that constabulary had by then lost faith in that avenue as a route to finding the killer. Back in West Yorkshire the team persisted with the tyre line of inquiry, but were unaware of their colleagues' findings. By the time Sutcliffe was interviewed as part of the tyre track investigation, he had got rid of the Corsair, and the new owner had changed the tyres.

Police believed the Ripper went to ground after killing Vera Millward, though there were several non-fatal attacks on women in 1978 which were not laid at the Ripper's door. The victims gave the now-familiar description: dark curly hair, drooping moustache and goatee beard. One mentioned a Sunbeam Rapier, the model Sutcliffe had acquired after getting rid of the Corsair. These attacks were not deemed part of the Ripper inquiry.

> *The victims gave the now-familiar description: dark curly hair, drooping moustache and goatee beard.*

THE "YORKSHIRE RIPPER"... THE UNACCEPTABLE FACE OF VEN...
by a monster who sees himself as Judge,
Executioner to women suspected of easy

IGNORE THE RIPPER AND HE'LL GO AWAY... TO KILL AGAIN.

OCTOBER 4, 1979

Ripper alert as girl dies

The Yorkshire Ripper is feared to have killed his twelfth victim. The blood-covered body of a girl in her early twenties was found yesterday afternoon near a red light district of Bradford. The body of his latest victim, bearing mutilations similar to those which are the killer's trademarks, was found among a dilapidated row of terraced houses at Ash Grove, near the Manningham red light district.

Exhausted

The houses are in a back lane which runs almost to the entrance of Bradford University. The grim discovery was made in the garden of No. 13 by a patrolling policeman. Detectives believe that the girl, as yet unidentified, had lain there since the weekend. The house is unoccupied.

Last night the entire area was sealed off as 100 officers made house-to-house inquiries. A post-mortem was carried out by Home Office pathologist Professor David Gee, the man who has examined all the Ripper's victims. The body was found less than a mile from where two of the Ripper's victims were found.

The man leading the hunt for the Ripper, West Yorkshire's Assistant Chief Constable, Mr George Oldfield, is at present on the sick list after exhausting himself in the search for the psychopath. One of the first officers called to the scene of the new inquiry was Chief Superintendent Jack Ridgway, who is heading the investigation into two Ripper murders in Manchester.

The Ripper last struck five months ago. The majority of his victims had been prostitutes but then he killed 19-year-old building society secretary Josephine Whitaker as she returned home after visiting her grandparents in Halifax.

TOP RIGHT AND ABOVE: An ongoing advertising campaign had been launched because of the police's desperation to catch the killer tormenting Yorkshire.

OPPOSITE TOP LEFT: Letters sent from the Ripper to the police, including a poem entitled 'Clueless.'

OPPOSITE TOP RIGHT: A man with the Ripper tape which contained an arrogant but eerie message from the murderer. He said: 'I can't see myself being nicked just yet.'

OPPOSITE BOTTOM LEFT: Police at the front and back doors of number 2 Alfred Street in Darlington. The house was brought to the attention of the police when a women looking for her lost child went into the empty terrace house and found an exercise book that contained newspaper cuttings about the Ripper's victims.

Police on a wild goose chase

1978 provided a major turning point in the investigation, one that saw police veer off in the wrong direction. They were taken in by a number of letters and a cassette tape recording, purporting to be from the Ripper himself. The first letter, dated March 1978, affirmed the writer's desire to rid the streets of prostitutes, and taunted police over their inability to catch him. 'Warn whores to keep off streets cause I feel it coming on again', it ran, though there was remorse over the death of the 'young lassie' Jayne MacDonald, which had been a mistake. It was signed 'Jack the Ripper'. There was a Sunderland postmark, which the writer told them to ignore, but ACC Oldfield and his senior officers came round to the view that that was a double bluff. The focus of the inquiry turned to Sunderland and the search for 'Wearside Jack', as he was dubbed.

This turn of events was disastrous for the inquiry but a boon for Sutcliffe. Had the many assaults on file deemed unconnected with the Ripper investigation been taken into account, they would have suggested that the attacker was a local, not from the north east. The fact that the police believed 'Wearside Jack' was the man they were after had a particular effect on Trevor Birdsall, who put off reporting his suspicions regarding his friend Peter Sutcliffe.

Even as George Oldfield played the tape at a press conference, convinced that the voice and handwriting would lead to an early arrest, there were a few dissenting voices on the investigating team. 'Wearside Jack' had used a lot of phraseology from the original Ripper's correspondence to the police in 1888, and some felt there had to be a possibility that it was an elaborate hoax, taking media reports and feeding them back in the style of the 19th century serial murderer. The writer had said nothing that could not have been gleaned from the blanket reportage. On the contrary, he gave a clear indication that his only source of information was media accounts, but it took a neat piece of detective work to spot the inconsistency that suggested the road to Sunderland was a wild goose chase.

The search for 'Wearside Jack' was disastrous for the inquiry but a boon for Sutcliffe.

HELP US STOP THE RIPPER FROM KILLING AGAIN.

LOOK AT HIS HANDWRITING.

LISTEN TO HIS VOICE.
PHONE LEEDS (0532) 464111.

IF YOU RECOG...   REPORT IT TO YOUR LOCAL POLICE

JANUARY 5, 1981

Ripper - a man is held

Detectives were last night questioning a man in connection with the Yorkshire Ripper murders which have claimed 13 women victims in five years. He will appear in court today on what the police say will be 'a very serious charge.'

In a dramatic statement, West Yorkshire's Chief Constable Ronald Gregory, beaming and linking arms with his senior officers involved in the Ripper hunt, said: 'We are all absolutely delighted, totally delighted with the developments at this stage.'

The man was arrested in the red light district of Sheffield on Friday night as he sat with a woman in a car parked in a dimly-lit alley. Two uniformed policemen, 47-year-old sergeant Robert Ring and probationer PC Robert Hydes, 31, were on vice patrol making routine checks on vehicles in the area. They radioed the registration number of the Rover V8 car to the national police computer. Back came the reply: The number plates had been stolen.

No Wearside accent

It was down to simple mathematics. In January 1978, the same month that Helen Rytka was killed, the Yorkshire Ripper also picked up 21-year-old Yvonne Pearson from Bradford's red-light district. Her body lay undiscovered on a patch of waste ground for around eight weeks, and it was this time lag that was key. 'Wearside Jack's' first letter was written after Yvonne Pearson was killed but before the body was discovered. His body count should have included Pearson but it didn't, suggesting he was merely rehashing details already in the public domain. That was confirmed when a subsequent letter, written after Pearson's murder had been reported, now included her in the tally. Failure to spot the anomaly sooner gave Sutcliffe valuable breathing space.

The amount of time and resources devoted to the Northumbria connection made it difficult for the senior investigating team to backtrack; it would have necessitated admitting that many thousands of man hours had been wasted in an inquiry whose costs had already reached astronomical proportions. That blinkered view helped Sutcliffe in the next round of police interviews. His Sunbeam Rapier was logged for making multiple appearances in red-light areas that were under surveillance. Again he successfully fobbed them off, helped by Sonia, who corroborated his every word. Interviewing officers were told to adopt a softly-softly approach in questioning men about repeat visits to red-light districts; they weren't interested in exposing peccadilloes or rocking marital boats. Thus, when Sutcliffe claimed he had travelled through such areas during the course of his work, it was readily accepted. There were no checks to ascertain whether Sutcliffe could have been on legitimate business at the times he was spotted – checks that would have exposed his story as a lie – but thousands of follow-up interviews would have further burdened an inquiry that was already creaking under its own weight. The officers' suspicions weren't totally allayed, but Sutcliffe patently did not have a Wearside accent, which at the time trumped all incriminating evidence relating to tyre tread patterns, five-pound notes and even photofit descriptions.

> **Failure to spot the anomaly sooner gave Sutcliffe valuable breathing space.**

TOP RIGHT: A Billboard that was part of the advertising campaign to catch the Ripper.

TOP LEFT: Sutcliffe was apprehended when police picked him up for suspected kerb-crawling. When police realised the car he was in had fake number plates, he was taken in for questioning.

MIDDLE: A map showing Sutcliffe's trail of murder across Yorkshire and Lancashire.

OPPOSITE TOP RIGHT: The grave Sutcliffe was digging when he claimed he heard the voice of God. Sutcliffe undertook two stints of grave-digging in the 1960s.

OPPOSITE BOTTOM RIGHT: A crowd gathered at Dewsbury Court in 1981. Sutcliffe pleaded not guilty to 13 counts of murder but guilty to manslaughter and seven counts of attempted murder.

Hoax revealed

Officially, the Ripper resurfaced in Halifax on 4 April 1979, killing 19-year-old building society employee Josephine Whittaker, who was accosted while walking home from a visit to her grandparents. Size seven bootprints were found near the body, and there were also bite marks on the body, made by someone with an eighth-of-an-inch gap between the front teeth. Peter Sutcliffe had such a dental profile.

Barbara Leach, a 20-year-old student at Bradford University, was murdered on 2 September 1979, the 11th Ripper victim. Shortly afterwards, police took a telephone call from Wearside Jack admitting the hoax, and they finally switched their focus back to the hub of the killing ground. An elaborate re-enactment of banking business for the period prior to Jean Jordan's death was staged, in an effort to narrow the field of possible recipients of the five-pound note. That exercise produced a list of 250 people, employees of a dozen firms in the Shipley area. Among those was T and WH Clark. Sutcliffe was interviewed on three more occasions, with no conclusive outcome. He couldn't be ruled out, but there was nothing concrete to tie him to the murders.

Sutcliffe lay low until August 1980, when the body of 47-year-old civil servant Marguerite Walls was found dumped in the grounds of a mansion in Pudsey. She had been garrotted, a change of modus operandi that gave police cause to doubt whether it was the work of the Ripper. The murder of 19-year-old Jacqueline Hill in November saw a return to the normal method of bludgeoning with a hammer and ripping with a knife. The body of the Leeds University student was found close to her hall of residence.

> **Sutcliffe knew he was in trouble. He managed to get rid of a hammer and knife before he was taken in for questioning.**

Routine police work corners Sutcliffe

It was now that Trevor Birdsall finally took his suspicions concerning Peter Sutcliffe to the police. Before they could be acted upon, the whole case was blown wide open, not by incisive analysis on the part of top detectives but by routine policework from two diligent foot soldiers.

On 2 Jan 1981 Sergeant Robert Ring and PC Robert Hydes were out on patrol in Sheffield when they approached a parked car. They wanted to question the driver and the woman who had climbed into vehicle beside him. The man identified himself as John Williams, but couldn't name his passenger, confirming their suspicions that they had a kerb crawler on their hands. A call to the station revealed that they might have stumbled upon a more serious misdemeanour, for the car had false number plates.

Peter Sutcliffe knew he was in trouble. Under the pretext of wanting to relieve himself, he managed to get rid of a hammer and knife before he was taken in for questioning. There his identity was revealed, and it was found that he had been interviewed a number of times in connection with the Ripper inquiry. At first he admitted only to attaching false plates to his car, and was cool enough to ditch a second knife in the cistern of the station toilet.

The officers were now beginning to think they had caught a much bigger fish. The suspect was whisked away to Dewsbury for questioning by a member of the Ripper team, then Sergeant Ring recalled the roadside comfort break and dashed back to the scene of the arrest. There he recovered the discarded tools of the Ripper's brutal trade. If there was any doubt over who had put them there, it was dispelled after a visit to the Sutcliffes' home. In the kitchen there was a knife block with one of the set missing. The blade that was in police hands fitted the space perfectly.

Peter Sutcliffe: 'The Yorkshire Ripper'

The jury found Peter Sutcliffe to be sane and answerable for his crimes, convicting him on 13 counts of murder.

JANUARY 5, 1981

No Geordie accent

The officers moved in and the man was taken for questioning by detectives. Within hours, they decided to contact the special Ripper Squad Mr Gregory had set up at Leeds, 30 miles away. Detectives from the squad drove to Sheffield and took the man back to Leeds. Later he was moved to a new, top-security police station nearby at Dewsbury. Despite well-publicised police theories, the man has no Geordie accent - he is from Bradford. He is married and in his early thirties. His wife was interviewed by Ripper Squad detectives yesterday and was then taken to Dewsbury to see him.

The man, believed to be a lorry driver, lives in a detached, double-fronted house in the Bradford suburb of Heaton. Neighbours thought his wife was a part-time teacher and said she spoke several languages. One described them as 'an ordinary quiet couple. The woman was very fond of the garden.' The man was sometimes seen repairing cars outside.

Police spent the weekend examining the house and are believed to have taken away several objects in plastic bags. The Ripper's early victims were prostitutes and good-time girls who frequented pubs and clubs. But then, as those murdered came to include a shop assistant, a building society clerk and two university students, it became chillingly clear that no woman, in the Leeds-Bradford area of West Yorkshire especially, was safe from him.

Sutcliffe's confession

A confession soon followed, in which Sutcliffe detailed all his grisly deeds, describing himself as a 'beast'. His counsel sought to negotiate a manslaughter charge on the grounds of diminished responsibility, and Sutcliffe now spoke of hearing voices urging him to rid the world of prostitutes. The defence team was content with the plea bargain, but the judge, Mr Justice Boreham, was having none of it. He insisted that the case go to trial to determine whether Peter Sutcliffe was truly mad, or merely bad.

The pre-trial consensus gave way to the normal adversarial court proceedings. The prosecution, led by Attorney General Sir Michael Havers, argued that Sutcliffe simulated symptoms of mental disorder in order to avoid a murder conviction. In doing so he had fooled the psychiatrists who diagnosed that he was suffering from paranoid schizophrenia.

Defence counsel James Chadwin QC called Sutcliffe to give evidence, to allow the jury to hear what he had told doctors and decide for themselves on his state of mind. The court heard of a severe blow to the head, sustained in a teenage motorcycle accident; of the antipathy he bore towards prostitutes after an unsatisfactory run-in with a member of that profession in his youth; and of the divine call which prompted the killing spree. The prosecution established that Sutcliffe had lied to the police and his wife on a number of occasions and had shown himself to be accomplished in that art. Was it not reasonable, therefore, to suppose he had demonstrated that same underhand talent in his conversations with the medical professionals?

Transferred to Broadmoor

The jury found Peter Sutcliffe to be sane and answerable for his crimes, convicting him on 13 counts of murder by a 10-2 majority after seven hours' deliberation. It was 22 May 1981; almost six years had passed since the death of Wilma McCann, officially, the Yorkshire Ripper's first victim.

Sutcliffe was sentenced to life imprisonment with a recommendation that he serve a minimum of 30 years. In 1984 Home Secretary Leon Brittan finally bowed to expert medical opinion, accepting that Sutcliffe was suffering from paranoid schizophrenia and allowing him to be transferred from Parkhurst to Broadmoor. Whether Sutcliffe was a delusional psychotic in need of care or a clever manipulator of the system who should be serving time in an ordinary prison remains open to question. Less contentious is the view that he should be held in a secure facility and is unlikely ever to be released back into the community. In May 2008 Home Secretary Jacqui Smith said she could not envisage circumstances in which Sutcliffe - now calling himself Peter Coonan - could be released. It quashed the hopes of the prisoner, whose legal representatives maintained that the 30-year tariff was never formalised and as such constituted a breach of human rights.

Ripper: not guilty plea

Sir Michael told the jury: 'You have to consider whether this man sought to pull the wool over the doctors' eyes. You have to decide whether as a clever callous murderer he deliberately set out to create a cock-and-bull story to avoid conviction for murder.' For none of that detail was ever told to the police.

Before the jury was sworn in, Sutcliffe's 30-year-old wife Sonia, who had been sitting to the right of the dock with her mother Mrs. Maria Szurma, left the court escorted by a policewoman and did not return. She is thought to be a defence witness. Sutcliffe stared straight ahead and did not even give a fleeting glance towards his wife as she left the famous No. 1 court with her mother.

Luck

Last week, he pleaded not guilty to the murder of 13 women but guilty to manslaughter on the grounds of diminished responsibility. He admitted attempting to murder seven other women. But the Judge, Mr. Justice Boreham, expressed 'grave anxieties' about the pleas and decided a jury should be empanelled.

Only once did a flicker of expression cross Sutcliffe's bearded face. He smiled when a juror named Sutcliffe was called into the box. Then for 4½ hours Sir Michael recounted in harrowing and grisly detail the Ripper's catalogue of 'sadistic' killings and attacks on women.

Incredibly, last Christmas he even walked past one of his victims who had survived, Mrs Maureen Long. He recognised her instantly but she walked by. It was the kind of luck which had enabled him to escape arrest for five years. Sir Michael revealed yesterday that Sutcliffe was questioned nine times because his car was seen in red-light districts in the North. But each time he was let go.

Throughout his 'crusade' Sutcliffe, a Bradford lorry driver, believed he was being protected by God - and even claimed the fake letters and tapes sent to police were the work of God to mislead police.

2006 DNA test

The Byford Report into the conduct of the Ripper inquiry was extremely critical of West Yorkshire police. It highlighted procedural lapses, systemic failures and ill-judged decisions, all of which meant that Sutcliffe remained at large longer than he should have. One of the gravest miscalculations surrounded the 'Wearside Jack' hoax. That mystery was cleared up in March 2006, when the hoaxer's identity was finally revealed. A DNA sample from saliva deposited on one of the envelopes was matched to a Sunderland resident who had been convicted on a drunk and disorderly charge. 49-year-old John Humble was an alcoholic loner and social inadequate with a record of petty crime dating back to his teens. He was given an eight-year prison sentence for perverting course of justice, closing the book on one of the most infamous cases in criminal history.

> Sutcliffe was questioned nine times because his car was seen in red-light districts in the North. But each time he was let go.

LEFT AND OPPOSITE BELOW: Sutcliffe in January 1981 as he is taken to court to face the charges bought against him for the murders of 13 women.

OPPOSITE TOP: Sutcliffe leaves the Old Bailey in a police van after he received a life sentence. He was found guilty on all 13 counts of murder and seven attempted murders.

TOP: Sutcliffe pictured as he leaves court in Newport, Isle of Wight, where he appeared after being attacked at Parkhurst prison by fellow inmate James Costello.

Australia's trial of the century:
A young life cut short and a mother who fought for justice

On the night of August 17, 1980, Lindy Chamberlain reported that her daughter Azaria had been taken from her tent by a dingo. A massive search was organised, but all that was found were remains of some of the bloody clothes.

Azaria Chamberlain

Lindy Chamberlain was born Alice Lynne Murchinson on March 4, 1948 on the North Island of New Zealand, the daughter of a Seventh Day Adventist pastor. Her family later moved to Australia and in November 1969 she married Michael Leigh Chamberlain, also a Seventh Day Adventist pastor. Lindy trained as a dressmaker and made wedding dresses to order, as well as performing the normal duties of a clergyman's wife. She and her husband had two sons, Aidan and Reagan, but longed for a daughter and on June 11, 1980 Azaria Chantel Loren Chamberlain was born.

Dingo tracks

In August 1980 the Chamberlain family were on holiday, staying at a campsite near Ayers Rock (now Uluru) in Australia. On the evening of August 17, Lindy Chamberlain put baby Azaria down to sleep in their tent, then went back outside to join Michael and their sons. Later that night several people heard a baby cry, and when Lindy went to check on Azaria she saw a dingo just outside the tent – and the baby was gone. Dingo tracks were seen in and around the tent and there was blood on the mattress and leading away into the bush. The alarm was quickly raised and aboriginal and white trackers tried to find the child, but she had totally vanished. A week later a tourist found bloody clothes – including the jumpsuit Azaria had been wearing – near an area of dingo lairs, but not her matinee jacket. Others at the campsite and the police first on the scene, who had met Lindy and her husband and seen everything first hand, accepted that this was a natural tragedy – and the Head Ranger had earlier warned that dingoes were becoming too bold near the campsite and that something like this might happen.

Police criticised

The first Coroner's inquest in February 1981 confirmed that a dingo had killed Azaria, but meanwhile wild rumours were spreading; of odd behaviour, pagan sacrifice and murder. They seem to have begun partly because some people believed that a wild dog would never take a fully-clothed baby, partly because some thought Lindy seemed eerily composed under the circumstances, partly because of Azaria's unusual name, and partly because people did not understand her parents' religion. The Coroner strongly criticised the police handling of the initial investigation, feeling that some officers had collected evidence on the basis that a dingo was not involved rather than with an open mind.

After a further eight months' investigation the verdict of the first inquest was overturned, and a second inquest in February 1982 made no finding but bound the Chamberlains over for trial. The prosecution alleged that Linda had killed her daughter, based on bloodstains on the jumpsuit and the assumption that a dingo could not have removed the baby's clothes intact, as they were found. Defence evidence that a dingo could tear through strong fabric with its teeth and remove meat from a paper wrap without tearing it – and that a dingo had previously been seen removing a three-year old from a car at the same campsite – was ignored. In October 1982 Lindy was found guilty of murder and given a life sentence with hard labour, her husband was found guilty of helping to conceal the crime and received an eighteen month suspended sentence. For the next three and a half years, the Chamberlains fought to prove their innocence and public pressure to release Lindy grew.

> Evidence that a dingo had previously been seen removing a three-year old from a car at the same campsite was ignored.

Finally declared innocent

In February 1986 people searching for a fallen climber found Azaria's missing matinee jacket at Ayers Rock, and after pressure was brought to bear by a local reporter, Frank Alcorta, Lindy was finally released. The following June the Chamberlains were cleared of all guilt or responsibility in their baby's death and offered a pardon – but this still indicates guilt in Australia. It was not until 1988 that the Chamberlains were finally declared to be innocent, but even today the cause of Azaria's death remains open.

OPPOSITE TOP: Lindy Chamberlain pictured after being committed for trial in Alice Springs. The first coroner's inquest had confirmed that a dingo had killed her child. This was then overturned and she spent the next seven years living a nightmare, nearly three of them in prison.

OPPOSITE BELOW: Ayers Rock (Uluru), where Lindy's family were staying in a public campsite when baby Azaria went missing.

TOP LEFT: The prosecution alleged that Lindy Chamberlain had killed her daughter based on the bloodstains on the jumpsuit and the assumption that a dingo could not have removed the baby's clothes intact as they were found.

TOP MIDDLE: Lindy Chamberlain descends the stairs of a jet in Darwin with two police officers and an official from the sheriff's office of the federal court in Sydney.

TOP RIGHT: Lindy Chamberlain pictured after she was sentenced to life imprisonment with hard labour. She was released from Darwin jail after serving three years in 1986.

ABOVE LEFT: Ten years after Azaria's disappearance Chamberlain launched a book entitled "Lindy Chamberlain: Through My Eyes."

ABOVE RIGHT: In 1988 the Chamberlains were finally declared to be innocent.

Wayne Williams: The Atlanta murders

There was considerable racial tension in Atlanta, Georgia, in the late 1970s and early 1980s. The city had an African-American mayor but the balance of power was still with the white administration and although the area was booming economically many African-Americans were still very poor. Over a two year period, twenty-nine African-American children, adolescents and adults were killed.

Growing fears

A serious crime problem had given Atlanta a reputation as a dangerous place, particularly after a young white doctor attending a convention was shot and killed during a robbery by two African-Americans. Meanwhile the African-American population was targeted by the Ku Klux Klan, which was still very active in the area.

In July 1979 two 14-year-old African-Americans, Edward Hope Smith and Albert Evans, went missing and were both found dead; Edward had been shot and Albert suffocated, possibly by strangulation. In October 14-year-old Milton Harvey disappeared while on an errand for his mother – unlike the other two boys he came from an affluent home, but like them he was African-American. However, the alarm was finally raised when 9-year-old Yusef Bell vanished on the way to the shops; his body was found in an abandoned school and he had been strangled. A few days later Milton's body was found, but too badly decomposed to establish a cause of death. Until this point the four murders had not been connected, but now fears began to grow that they were racially motivated and that the Ku Klux Klan was involved. Camille Bell, Yusef's mother, was particularly vocal in her criticism of the authorities and was promised a full investigation.

Two murders in one month

In the following months there were no more significant murders, but in March 1980 the killings began again. Between then and November 1980 thirteen children were killed, ranging in age from seven to sixteen but all African-American – although this time two of them were girls. However, the authorities were still not treating the murders as the work of a serial killer, although after considerable public pressure they announced a task force would look at the cases together. The killings stopped in December, but in January 1981 there were two murders in the same month. The task force compiled a list of cases they thought were related, but this was always controversial. Many people insisted there were other killings that should have been included on the basis of geographical proximity, or because the victims knew each other, or because of similarities in method, while some of those on the list had no obvious connection. The last child victim added was Timothy Hill in March 1981 – the twenty-third child to be killed in just two years. After this the victims were all young adults – another six deaths between March and May 1981.

> Between March and November 1980 thirteen children were killed, ranging in age from seven to sixteen.

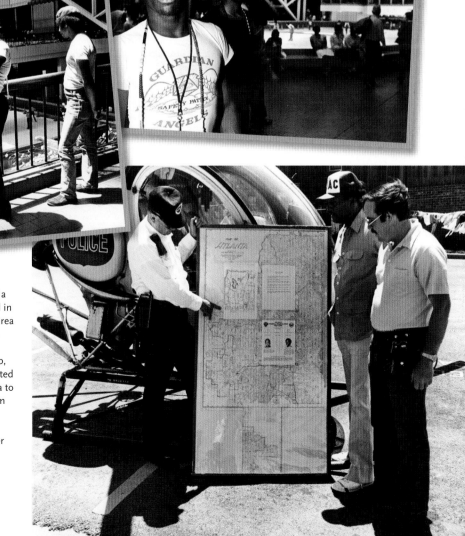

OPPOSITE ABOVE: Two people search for bodies in woodland in Atlanta. Every week searches took place to find the bodies of missing children.

OPPOSITE BELOW: Police remove the body of 21-year-old Larry Rogers from the abandoned apartment where it was discovered. He was the 23rd victim in Atlanta's string of youth slayings.

TOP RIGHT: A police man directs his colleagues toward the floating body of a naked black male. The body was found in the Chattahoochee River in the same area where five other bodies were dumped.

ABOVE: Members of the vigilante group, 'Guardian Angels'. The group was started in New York and came down to Atlanta to patrol the streets in a bid to make them safer.

RIGHT: Three men stand by a helicopter pointing at a map showing the search areas.

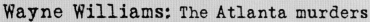

Wayne Williams: The Atlanta murders

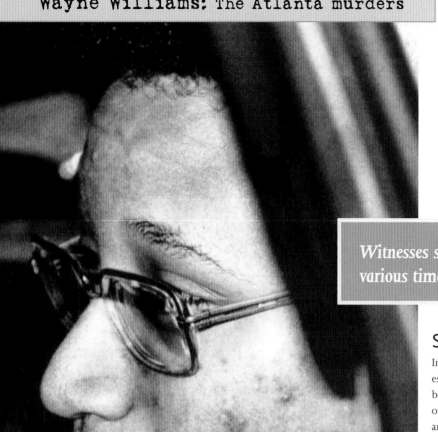

Witnesses said Williams had cuts and scratches on his arms at various times – and he had known some of the victims.

Stake-out

In May 1981, the police announced they were studying fibres from the bodies to establish a common factor. They believed this would prompt the murderer to dump bodies in a nearby river so they would be cleansed, and had accordingly staked out the bridge. On May 22, 1981, their patience was rewarded: they heard a splash and a car driving away, and stopped young African-American Wayne Williams to question him about what he had thrown off the bridge.

Wayne Bertram Williams was born on May 27, 1958 in the Dixie Hills area of Atlanta, the only child of Homer and Faye Williams, both schoolteachers. He still lived with his doting parents, from whose house he broadcast on his own amateur radio station and he had been know to make up unlikely stories about major record deals he was about to pull off. Williams had never been in serious trouble with the police – although he had been arrested briefly when he was eighteen for impersonating a police officer. When interviewed he insisted he was merely driving in search of the home of a young woman who he planned to audition and that he had thrown nothing into the river. However, when police checked the address and phone number of the woman, it proved not to exist.

Forensic studies

A few days later the naked body of 27-year-old Nathaniel Cater was discovered in the river. He had vanished several days earlier – and the medical examiner put the time of death at around the time Williams had allegedly thrown something off the bridge, although he could not determine a cause of death. Meanwhile forensic studies established that some fibres found on the victims matched fibres from the Williams' home, while dog hairs on some bodies were similar to those from their dog. Witnesses said Williams had cuts and scratches on his arms at various times – and he had known some of the victims. Finally he was arrested – but only for the murder of Cater and another man, Jimmy Payne.

OPPOSITE: Wayne Williams being taken to a hearing in Atlanta after he was charged with two of the homicides. Police believed Williams to be guilty of all of the youth murders over the two years but he was only tried for two.

TOP LEFT: Williams pictured carrying a legal pad as he is escorted to court to begin his second day at trial.

TOP RIGHT: Williams waves to photographers as he leaves the Atlanta jail to face arraignment on the murder charges brought against him.

TOP MIDDLE: Williams is taken to court where a 15-year-old testified that he had made homosexual advances to him. The unidentified youth also said he saw Lubie Jeter, another victim, get into a car with Williams.

ABOVE: Williams sits in the back of a police car on his way to court for the fifth week of his murder trial. In January 1982 he was found guilty of both murders and sentenced to two terms of life imprisonment.

Verdict doubts

The trial began on December 28, 1981. The defence was handicapped by lack of time and funds, so they were not able to counteract the authoritative evidence of the FBI forensic laboratories about the fibres, which was the main thrust of the prosecution. The jury was never told that the fibres in question were by no means rare, so it was likely the victims had come into contact with them elsewhere – and that no fibres or hairs from any victim had been found in the Williams home. Reports of Cater being seen alive – by several people who knew him – after Williams was supposed to have thrown him off the bridge were not discovered until it was too late.

In January 1982 Williams was found guilty of the murders of Cater and Payne and sentenced to two terms of life imprisonment. The police promptly announced that 22 other murders were now solved – even though Williams had never been tried for them. Many people have serious doubts about his guilt – including families of some of the victims – and for several years after he was imprisoned the unsolved murders of children and young adults continued in the Atlanta area.

2007 DNA tests

On January 29, 2007 lawyers for the state of Georgia agreed to allow DNA testing of dog hair that was used to convict Wayne Williams. The decision came in a response to a filing as part of Williams' efforts to appeal his conviction and life sentence. Williams' lawyer, Jack Martin, asked a Fulton County Superior Court judge to allow DNA tests on dog and human hair and blood that might help win Williams a new trial.

On June 26, 2007 the test results were released but failed to exonerate Williams.

> In January 1982 Williams was found guilty and sentenced to two terms of life imprisonment.

Jeffrey Dahmer

While looking for a weapon policemen found incriminating photographs – and the apartment soon gave up its other grim secrets.

Personality change

Jeffrey Dahmer was born on May 21, 1960, in Milwaukee County, Wisconsin, to Lionel and Joyce Dahmer. At first he appeared to be a typical toddler, but when he was six there was considerable upheaval in his life: he underwent surgery for a hernia, his younger brother was born and the family moved from Wisconsin to Bath, Ohio. It was around this time that Dahmer's personality began to change and he gradually became a withdrawn and insecure loner.

In Ohio Dahmer attended Revere High School, where he achieved average grades but also began to drink heavily. When he was 18 his parents divorced and afterwards the teenager lived with his father, who was often away. In June 1978 Dahmer met hitchhiker Steven Hicks, who he invited back home. The two of them drank and had sex, but when Hicks wanted to leave Dahmer killed him and cut up the body, burying the parts in garbage bags in the woods around his father's house.

After high school Dahmer enrolled at Ohio State University but after two semesters he dropped out. In 1979 he enlisted in the army for six years, but after two years he was discharged because of drunken behaviour and went back to Wisconsin to live with his grandmother. Several times during the next six years he was in trouble, being arrested for disorderly conduct in 1981, for exposing himself in 1982, for masturbating in public in 1986 and for sexually fondling a young boy in 1987.

'Over four years Dahmer murdered at least fifteen young men, enticing them home with promises of money or sex'.

LEFT: The beginning of jury selection in the trial at Milwaukee County Court in January 1992.

OPPOSITE TOP RIGHT: The sealed off apartment rented by Jeffrey Dahmer. It contained parts of 11 different bodies.

OPPOSITE MIDDLE RIGHT: Dahmer pleaded guilty to the charges bought against him but claimed insanity. The jury found him totally sane and guilty of all counts of murder. He was sentenced to 957 years in prison.

OPPOSITE BOTTOM LEFT: Dahmer after his arrest in 1991. Three years later, in 1994, he was murdered in prison by inmate Christopher Scarver.

TOP: Dahmer was accused of enticing young men to his home with the promise of sex or money before drugging and killing them.

LEFT: Dahmer enters the courtroom on 6 August 1991. He was charged with 12 counts of murder and the judge increased Dahmer's bail to five million dollars.

Incriminating photographs

In September 1987, Dahmer met Steven Toumi in a gay bar; after drinking heavily they booked into a hotel room. According to Dahmer, the following morning he woke to find Toumi dead. Dahmer bought a large suitcase to carry the body home, where he indulged in necrophilia before dismembering it and disposing of the parts in the rubbish. Over the next four years, Dahmer murdered at least fifteen young men, enticing them home with promises of money or sex, drugging and killing them, having sex with the corpse, then dismembering the body. He took photographs at various stages and often kept souvenirs – skulls or body parts. In July 1991 Dahmer's luck ran out. A young man was found in the street with a handcuff on one wrist, claiming Dahmer had threatened him with a knife. While looking for the weapon policemen found incriminating photographs – and the apartment soon gave up its other grim secrets.

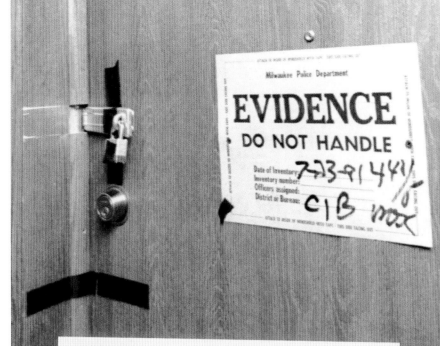

> Some of the details of the case were so horrific that jurors were offered professional counselling after the trial.

At his trial, Dahmer pleaded guilty by reason of insanity, but despite his gruesome rituals being recounted in detail the jury found him to be totally sane and guilty of fifteen murders. He was sentenced to fifteen consecutive life terms, a total of 957 years in prison, but on November 28, 1994, inmate Christopher Scarver killed both him and another prisoner.

MAY 17, 1992

Thank God, he will never be free again

Relatives of the victims of homosexual serial killer Jeffrey Dahmer yesterday wept with relief that he would never be freed. He is expected to be locked up for the rest of his life today after a jury found that he was sane when he murdered and dismembered 15 young men over a period of 13 years. Dahmer, 31, who pleaded guilty but insane, is unlikely to get parole. His lawyer had argued that his acts of necrophilia and cannibalism would only have been committed by a mentally sick man.

The jury of seven men and five women took five hours to decide that the former chocolate factory worker was accountable for his actions. When their verdict was announced after a three-week trial in Milwaukee, Wisconsin - which does not have the death penalty - his victims' relatives clutched each other and wept or cheered. 'I'm happy this man will never walk the streets again,' said Janie Hagen, sister of victim Richard Guerrero. Louis Rios, a relative of murdered Tony Hughes, sobbed: 'Thank God! I've been praying every night he would not be found insane.'

Linked to the devil

Dahmer's routine was to cruise gay bars and bath-houses luring young men to his flat where, after sex, he would slip sleeping pills into their drink, strangle or stab them, butcher the corpse and eat some body parts.

Dahmer told doctors he felt linked to the devil and had fuelled his depravity with pornography and repeated viewing of the occult film, Exorcist III. Some of the details of the case were so horrific that jurors were offered professional counselling after the trial.

In court, Dahmer rarely displayed the charm, humour, intelligence and remorse his lawyers attributed to him. But after the verdict, defence lawyer Gerald Boyle said he was 'very ashamed' and had offered to make himself available for research into serial killers.

At least six of his victims' families have filed multi-million-pound civil suits against the killer. While Dahmer currently has no assets, they want to make sure of first claim to any money he may eventually receive from films or books.

243

Brinks-Mat:
The biggest robbery ever staged in Britain

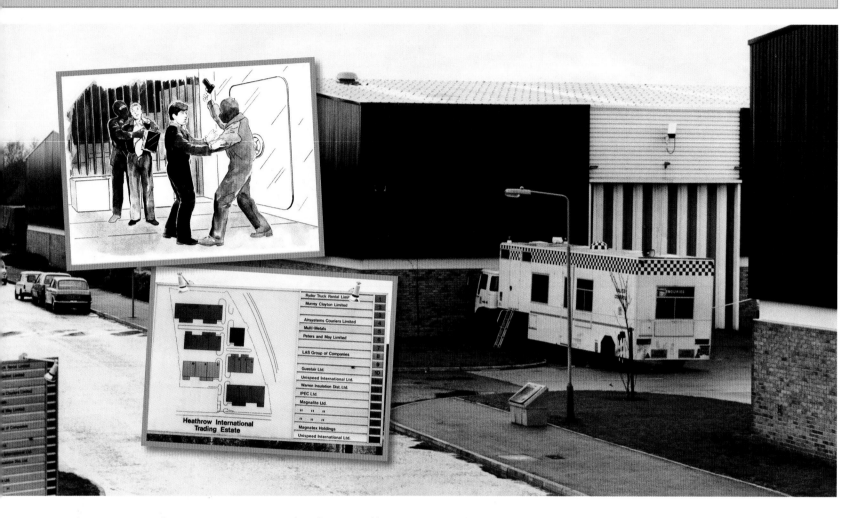

The gang who got away with £26 million in the weekend's Great Gold Robbery defeated some of the most advanced electronic gadgetry in the world with stark unsophisticated torture.

November 28, 1983

£26 million haul

In the 1980s, the warehouses of the Heathrow International Trading Estate were used as short-term holding bays for precious metals and gemstones on their way into and out of the country via the nearby airport. Over the years the multi-million-pound freight had become a magnet for criminals, so much so that the warehouse complex was dubbed 'Thief Row Airport'. In April 1983 thieves made off with £6 million from a Security Express depot, but that record haul was dwarfed seven months later when an armed gang raided the Brinks-Mat warehouse and got away with £26 million, the biggest robbery ever staged in Britain.

Six masked gunmen struck at around 6.40 am on Saturday 26 November 1983. The timing was crucial, for the valuables were guarded purely by electronic means until the day shift came on duty at 6.30 am. The thieves' plan required the co-operation of security staff, and they showed they were prepared to go to extreme lengths to ensure swift compliance.

6800 gold bars

The guards were handcuffed and blindfolded, their legs bound with tape. Two had their clothing cut away and petrol poured onto their bare skin, with the threat of being set alight if they didn't tell the gang what they wanted to know. The men targeted were the crew supervisor and the 'key man', who controlled all the doors and the alarm system. Each knew half of the combination to the vault, information that was soon surrendered. Only then did the gang realise that they had hit struck gold, quite literally. They had expected a three-million-pound cash haul; what they got instead was 6800 gold bars worth £22 million, a consignment bound for Hong Kong later that day. It was in the warehouse for one night only; the raiders had been fortuitous indeed. The bullion weighed three tons, and even with the aid of forklift trucks it took two hours to load the booty. They had to commandeer another vehicle, for their van was not up to the task, but were clean away by the time one of the security staff managed to free himself and raise the alarm.

> They had expected a three-million-pound cash haul; what they got instead was 6800 gold bars worth £22 million.

NOVEMBER 28, 1983

Electronic

When the electronic secrets had been surrendered, the gang went to work with military precision knowing that no alarms would be sounded. The gang, all armed with pistols and wearing balaclavas, had to race to pack their haul into a lorry and leave before a genuine collection van due later in the morning turned up.

Using the security firm's own fork lift trucks they began removing 76 blue-grey cardboard boxes from the strongroom. Each measured 10in. by 7in. by 4in. and weighed one hundredweight. In all they contained 6,800 gold bars, each numbered and impressed with a refiner's stamp.

The genuine security staff sighted only three of the robbers. But they say they heard voices and movements indicating there were six in all. The raid was over within an hour. The gang drove off - after closing the warehouse doors behind them and threatening the staff with death if anyone tried to raise the alarm. But by 8.30 a shocked guard managed to press an alarm button.

Inside information

This was 'no mean robbery team', said Commander Frank Cater, head of Scotland Yard's Flying Squad. It was undoubtedly a well-planned heist, but almost immediately police suspected that the gang had inside information. Employees were screened and one of the staff on duty when the heist took place was found to have connections with someone well known to Scotland Yard. The guard was Anthony Black, whose sister's partner was Brian Robinson, a notorious underworld figure known as 'The Colonel' for his organisational ability. Robinson was soon splashing large amounts of cash around, suggesting that the police were on the right lines.

Black cracked under questioning and confessed to his part in the heist. He supplied information regarding daily routine, photographs of the interior layout and a key to the warehouse door for duplication purposes. He also gave the signal that started the raid. Black turned Queen's Evidence when he was tried in February 1984, and was given a lenient six-year jail sentence in return for his co-operation.

Information supplied by Black led to three more arrests. Brian Robinson was tried at the Old Bailey in October 1984 along with Michael McAvoy and Anthony White. All denied the charges. Robinson and McAvoy were convicted and jailed for 25 years; White was acquitted due to lack of evidence.

OPPOSITE PAGE TOP: The anonymous warehouse where the gang struck.

OPPOSITE PAGE INSET BELOW: The estate plan which had no Brinks-Mat name next to Unit 7: Brinks-Mat understandably did not wish to advertise its presence on the industrial estate.

OPPOSITE PAGE INSET ABOVE: The gang tortured security guards until they gave up the security codes for the vaults inside. They poured petrol over one man and

threatened to set his clothes alight, they stabbed another in the hand and pistol-whipped a third.

OPPOSITE PAGE BOTTOM: The phone book that showed exactly where to locate Brinks-Mat. The gang had an insider, Anthony Black, whose sister's partner, Brian Robinson, was a notorious underworld figure.

ABOVE: Police on the hunt for the bullion worth £22 million raid the home

of jeweller John Palmer. Palmer was away on holiday when the police moved in on those suspected of handling the Brinks-Mat gold. He was one of 20 wanted men named later that year by Scotland Yard. When he eventually returned to England he faced trial for handling Brinks-Mat gold. Despite a hidden gold smelter at his home, the Old Bailey jury accepted his assertion that he did not know he was

smelting Brinks-Mat ingots, and acquitted him. His business partner Garth Chappell, who was at the heart of the operation to disguise and pass the bullion back on to the legitimate gold market, was jailed for 10 years. Palmer was later forced to pay a substantial sum to loss adjustors acting for Brinks-Mat.

> *A series of suspicious transactions at a Bristol bank led police to Hollywood Cottage, West Kingsdown, Kent.*

Following the money trail

By now police had tracked down five men wanted in connection with both the Brinks-Mat raid, and the Security Express robbery seven months earlier. They were living the high life on the Costa del Sol, but the police were thwarted by the absence of extradition arrangements between Britain and Spain, which had ceased in 1978.

The money trail proved a more fruitful line of inquiry. A series of suspicious transactions at a Bristol bank led police to Hollywood Cottage, West Kingsdown, Kent, the 26-acre estate of 38-year-old Kenneth Noye. Police suspected that the gold was being taken from here to a Bristol-based company and put the property under surveillance. They were right. Noye had been brought in for his knowledge of the precious metals market, and in particular his experience of smelting. It was his job to melt down the bullion and recast it into untraceable units that could be disposed of without attracting attention.

Police man killed

On 26 January 1985 DC John Fordham and DC Neil Murphy entered the grounds of Noye's property in advance of the execution of a search warrant. Noye was alerted by the barking of his Rottweilers and confronted the men with a knife. Murphy escaped and went to call assistance, but Fordham was attacked, suffering fatal stab wounds. Noye was cleared of murder, his counsel convincing the jury that he had acted in self-defence, a panic reprisal attack against an intruder. Fordham had been wearing a camouflage jacket and balaclava, and Noye insisted he hadn't identified himself as a police officer.

That verdict went in Noye's favour but he was still facing separate charges of laundering the stolen gold. He wasn't so fortunate in his next court appearance, fined £700,000 and given a 14-year jail term for handling the Brinks-Mat bullion. Two years after his release in 1994, Noye took another life. His victim was 21-year-old Stephen Cameron, stabbed in an apparent road rage incident, though it was later suggested that the altercation was over a drug deal. Noye's self-defence plea cut no ice this time; he was convicted of murder and given a life term.

DECEMBER 4, 1984

'Protect us' appeal by jury

Frightened jurors in the £26 million gold and diamond robbery case have appealed to police for protection. They are to be guarded day and night by armed officers even though the case has ended.

The jurors were among those who on Sunday found two men guilty of taking part in the robbery at Heathrow Airport a year ago. Yesterday the two, builder Michael McAvoy and motor trader Brian Robinson, were each jailed for 25 years at the Old Bailey.

Parties

Last night armed officers were on guard at the homes of worried jurors who had made their unprecedented plea for continued protection to Scotland Yard. The entire jury, including seven women, were under police guard throughout the four-week trial on the orders of the judge.

After the case, several told police they were afraid to go unprotected because of the insight the trial had given them into the operations of members of the bullion gang who had not been brought to justice. Scotland Yard agreed to extend the protection for worried jurors indefinitely. They will be guarded wherever they go. Armed officers will go shopping with housewives. They will attend Christmas parties with their charges, and be close to their homes during the night. The jurors' phones will continue to be monitored.

A quarter of a century on from the biggest heist in British history, many unanswered questions remain. It is believed that up to 15 people were involved in the Brinks-Mat robbery, which means that only a fraction of the perpetrators have been brought to book. Some may never be brought to justice, for several of those suspected of having played a part in the crime have met violent ends.

Perhaps even more intriguing is the whereabouts of the £26 million haul. Apart from the recovery of a dozen bars in the wake of Kenneth Noye's arrest, none of the bullion has been recovered. It is thought that anyone in possession of gold jewellery bought in Britain in the past 25 years is probably wearing part of the proceeds of the Brinks-Mat robbery.

> While it was the daring of the gang that allowed the raid to succeed, it was the expertise of the fences that allowed the loot to slip out of Britain so smoothly.

JULY 24, 1986

Luxury

Two separate gangs were employed; one to carry out the £26 million raid and take the gold to the three 'drop-off' points and one gang who were highly professional 'fences.'

Three members of the first gang are serving long sentences, while detectives would still like to question ex-East End publican Clifford Saxe, Ronnie Knight, the former husband of Carry On actress Barbara Windsor, and three others all living in luxury on the Spanish Costa del Sol beyond the reach of the Yard.

But while it was the daring of that gang that allowed the raid to succeed, it was the expertise of the fences that allowed the loot to slip out of Britain so smoothly. And the Old Bailey was told, it was to Kenneth Noye that the 'contract' fell for disposing of the three tons of gold.

He devised a brilliant plan. The gold was melted down at secret addresses. The size of the bars was changed and copper coins added to change their quality. Small parcels of the re-moulded gold were released on to the legitimate market by providing bogus documents to give it an 'honest background.' This part of the operation had an added lucrative twist - VAT was collected but never passed to Customs.

Ironically, it was this greed that put detectives on the trial of Noye. Police set up a watch on the bullion chain which began at Noye's £1 million home where the gold was collected in small parcels of 11 bars at a time.

Bankers

In one of the most extraordinary twists in the whole story, it was the bankers Johnson Matthey, who bought back most of the gold - it had been the bank which had originally owned the bullion stored at the Heathrow depot.

OPPOSITE PAGE AND TOP LEFT: : Police at Kenneth Noye's £1 million home. Noyes was tried for the murder of Detective Constable Fordham but convinced the jury that it was self-defence. Eleven Gold Bars were found hidden beside Noye's garage (opposite middle). Despite being found not guilty of murder he was convicted of laundering the stolen gold. He was fined £700,000 and sentenced to 14 years in jail.

TOP RIGHT: A police helicopter lands near West Kingsdown after filming the area surrounding Noye's home.

LEFT: Apart from the discovery of a dozen bars following Noye's arrest, none of the bullion has been recovered from the Brinks-Mat raid.

Dennis Nilsen

A routine plumbing call-out to a property in Muswell Hill in early February 1983 set in motion a train of events that would unmask one of Britain's most macabre mass murderers.

Cranley Gardens

A blockage in the waste system brought a drain-clearing operative to 23 Cranley Gardens in the north London suburb. He was taken aback when he lifted the manhole outside the property and saw the cause of the obstruction: lumps of flesh. He reported his macabre findings, but by the time the police came to investigate the following day, most of the organic material had disappeared. Most, but not all. There were enough traces to confirm that these were no animal remains; it was

OPPOSITE BOTTOM: Former policeman Dennis Andrew Nilsen is handcuffed to two officers after appearing in court accused of the murder of 20-year-old Stephen Sinclair of no fixed address. After a two-minute hearing he was remanded in custody by Highgate magistrates.

OPPOSITE ABOVE: In another of his many court appearances Nilson was charged with four more murders at an address in Melrose Avenue, Cricklewood, where he had lived prior to his move to 23 Cranley Gardens in the north London suburb of Muswell Hill.

LEFT: In 1961 Nilsen left school and enlisted in the British Army where he served for 11 years before leaving in 1972 to briefly join the police force. From the mid 1970s, Nilsen worked as a civil servant in a local Job Centre.

BELOW: Nilsen had moved to the attic flat at 23 Cranley Gardens in 1981. It proved far more difficult to dispose of his victims' remains in this confined setting and he had to improvise and find creative methods of disposal.

BOTTOM RIGHT: Nilson was born at 47 Academy Road in Fraserburgh, Scotland on 23 November 1945. He was the only child of his Scottish mother, Betty, and Norwegian father Olav Magnus Moksheim, who had adopted the surname Nilsen.

Grim discovery

The occupants of the ground-floor flat told DCI Peter Jay that there had been some strange comings and goings over the previous 24 hours involving the tenant who lived above them. His name was Dennis Nilsen, a 37-year-old civil servant who worked for the employment service. Jay challenged Nilsen when he arrived home, and the latter initially expressed surprise at the grim discovery. The pungent smell of decaying flesh in the top-floor flat told a different story, and the detective invited Nilsen to come clean and reveal the whereabouts of the rest of the body. Without hesitation Nilsen directed him to two plastic sacks inside the wardrobe. How many bodies were there, Jay enquired, one or two? Maybe 15 or 16 came the chillingly frank reply. Some of those had met their end in that house, most at his previous address, in Melrose Avenue, Cricklewood. The police thus found themselves in the strange situation of having cracked the case wide open almost before the inquiry had got under way. Even more bizarrely, they had solved a string of murders that weren't part of any current homicide investigation. Their task now was to piece together the evidence and try and put names to all the victims. Nilsen co-operated fully, giving chapter and verse on a killing spree stretching back over five years.

> How many bodies were there, Jay enquired, one or two? Maybe 15 or 16 came the chillingly frank reply.

Fascination with death

Dennis Andrew Nilsen was born 23 November 1945, growing up in Fraserburgh on the east coast of Scotland. His father, Olav, was a Norwegian immigrant who married local girl Betty Whyte in 1942. It wasn't a happy union, and Nilsen had long spells living with his maternal grandparents. They were strict Presbyterians who had little time for fun and frippery, yet Nilsen adored them. His first taste of death came in 1951, with the passing of his beloved grandfather. Nilsen viewed the body, more fascinated than shocked at being in the presence of a cadaver. It was a fascination that would remain with him into adulthood.

Nilsen was a something of a loner, his social development not helped by his confused feelings regarding his sexuality. He became further withdrawn when his mother remarried and had four more children by a man who had little time for his stepson. Soldiering provided an escape route. Nilsen became an army cadet in 1961 and went on to serve in the Catering Corps, rising to the rank of corporal by the time he returned to civilian life a decade later. His time in the military furnished him with the butchery skills that he would later use to render his victims into manageable pieces.

CRANLEY GARDENS N.10

FEBRUARY 11, 1983

Plumbing problems

The grisly investigation started when new tenants of a flat in the house at Cranley Gardens had plumbing problems and called in the Dyno-Rod firm. Plumber Mike Cattran came round - and discovered human remains in a drain. He called the police.

Forensic experts established that the remains were of three young men. Soon after their investigations began detectives took away a black and white mongrel dog. Then they went to the second house, in Melrose Avenue, Cricklewood, where a search was started last night under floodlights for, it is feared, 13 more victims.

The police had been told of several specific spots in the garden where they should dig and today will cover every inch of the ground and the house. They will be using sensors which respond to changes in earth temperature where remains are buried. The police face a huge problem of identification. There are unlikely to be fingerprints and it is thought that each victim's possessions and clothing were meticulously removed and disposed of.

Dark obsessions

There were brief spells as a probationary policeman with the Metropolitan force and as a security guard, after which Nilsen settled down to a life in the civil service as a Job Centre worker. His conscientiousness gained him promotion, and he also became an active trade unionist. Privately, however, his life was in turmoil. There were still dark obsessions with death, and when his first long-standing relationship broke down in 1977, Nilsen found a way to ensure that he would not face the desolation of rejection again. It was easy to pick up drifters and runaways in London, lost souls who would not be missed. To some he offered money, to others friendship, while there were those who were simply grateful for a roof over their head and a bed for the night. A private party usually followed, convivial at first with booze flowing freely. His victims were often undernourished and not in the rudest health, and when they were further incapacitated by their alcohol intake, Nilsen struck. Strangulation was the method he favoured, using his collection of neckties as ligatures. In his statement to the police Nilsen used his modus operandi to estimate how many lives he had claimed. 'I started with about 15 ties. I have only got one left.'

Ex-PC charged with murder

Scotland Yard detectives last night charged an ex-policeman with murder. He is 37-year-old Dennis Nilsen, now a Civil Servant. He will appear at Highgate court in North London this morning. Nilsen is charged with murdering Stephen Neil Sinclair, 20, of no fixed address, on or about February 1, 1983, at 23 Cranley Gardens, Muswell Hill, North London.

Resigned

Scottish-born Nilsen's home is a flat in Cranley Gardens. He is unmarried. He served as a probationary London police constable from December 1972 to December 1973 in 'Q' District, which is centred at Wembley. He joined the Metropolitan force immediately after leaving the Army, where he was in the Catering Corps.

After resigning voluntarily from the Metropolitan Police he worked as a security officer for a private firm and lately has been working with the Manpower Services Commission in the Kentish Town area of North London.

His father, Norwegian-born Olav Nilsen, served as a police sergeant in Bergen. He is now dead. Dennis Nilsen's mother, 62-year-old Elizabeth, is remarried to Mr Adam Scott, of Baird Road, Strichen, near Fraserburgh. She said: 'This has come as a great shock. I have not seen my son for about ten years. I have had phone calls and a letter now and again but very seldom. There are good connections between us, although he has not been here for ten years. I understood he was doing very well in his job.'

Stephen Sinclair grew up in the hamlet of St Martin's near the Scottish town of Perth. He was the foster child of retired traffic examiner Neil Sinclair and his wife Elizabeth, a needlework teacher. Mr Sinclair said yesterday: 'He left us several years ago and went to live in Perth. He stayed there for a while before moving south. We lost contact with him and he was never in touch again.'

Nilsen found a way to ensure that he would not face the desolation of rejection again. It was easy to pick up drifters and runaways in London.

TOP RIGHT: Nilsen served as a probationary London police constable in Wembley from December 1972 to December 1973. He had joined the Metropolitan force immediately after leaving the Army, where he served in the Catering Corps.

TOP LEFT: When he lived at 195 Melrose Avenue, Nilsen had access to a large garden which made it far easier to dispose of human remains.

FAR LEFT: When the police searched the house and gardens at Melrose Avenue, they were looking for the remains of 13 bodies. They used sensor equipment in order to try to establish where the corpses of the victims might be buried.

LEFT: A plastic make-shift tent erected in the back garden of the house at Melrose Avenue.

OPPOSITE PAGE: Army cadets were used to help with the grisly search at Melrose Gardens. The garden had provided Nilsen with a graveyard for burying parts of his numerous victims. He had also resorted to burning some body parts on bonfires, adding rubber tyres to mask the smell.

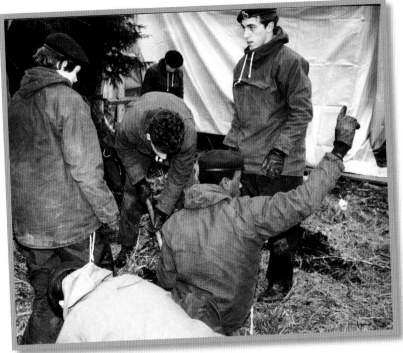

Fierce resistance

One victim, ex-Guardsman John Howlett, presented a tougher proposition.
He put up fierce resistance until Nilsen finished him off by drowning him in
the bath. Those who succumbed to the necktie treatment were also bathed,
and Nilsen would often share a bed with the corpse before disposing of the
body. In some cases the viscera were bagged up and left on waste ground, to be
devoured by scavenging animals. Another method was to boil down the remains
in a large cooking pot, while some body parts were burnt, tyres thrown onto
the bonfire to mask the smell of putrefaction. He also took to flushing some
of the soft tissue down the lavatory, the disposal technique that precipitated
his downfall.

Some men had lucky escapes. Douglas Stewart passed out in an alcoholic
haze, waking to find his legs lashed to the chair and Nilsen attacking him.
He managed to escape and reported the incident to the police, but found
that domestic tiffs between gay lovers were not a high priority for the local
constabulary. Paul Nobbs woke up feeling unwell after spending a drunken
night with Nilsen in November 1981. A hospital visit confirmed that someone
had tried to strangle him.

'Nothing can touch you now,' he recalled
uttering as he dispatched his final victim.

Dispensing life and death

Nilsen revelled in the power he exerted over his victims. During the Old Bailey
trial there would be references to his acting as a 'quasi-God', dispensing life or
death as the mood took him. 23-year-old Malcolm Barlow found himself on
the wrong end of that judgement call when chance put him in Dennis Nilsen's
path in September 1981. He collapsed outside 195 Melrose Avenue, and was
grateful when Nilsen came to his rescue and called an ambulance. Barlow
returned the next day to thank the Good Samaritan and was invited in for a
meal, which turned out to be his last. On 26 January 1983, Nilsen picked up
20-year-old Stephen Sinclair, a Scot who had had a troubled life, much of it
spent in institutions of one kind or another. Nilsen saw his death as an act of
mercy, putting an end to a lifetime of misery and suffering. 'Nothing can touch
you now,' he recalled uttering as he dispatched his final victim.

251

Dennis Nilsen

Nilsen's state of mind

Only half of the Nilsen's victims had been named by the time he went to trial on 24 October 1983. He thus faced six murder charges and two counts of attempted murder. A seventh victim, Graham Allen, had just been identified through dental records but that discovery came too late for inclusion on the indictment.

Most of the trial was spent trying to ascertain Nilsen's state of mind when he committed the crimes, and thus the level of responsibility he had to bear. He pleaded not guilty on grounds of diminished responsibility, defence counsel Ivan Lawrence QC arguing that manslaughter was the appropriate charge. Douglas Stewart and Paul Nobbs described their brushes with death, as did Carl Stotter, whose story came to light too late to appear on the charge sheet. Stotter recalled the night in May 1982 when he woke to find Nilsen at his throat. He passed out, and in a semi-conscious state became aware of being carried to the bathroom. Fortunately for Stotter, Nilsen had a change of heart on that occasion.

The defence produced two expert witnesses to pronounce on Nilsen's mental health. Dr Patrick Gallwey said Nilsen had paranoid and schizoid tendencies, which the defence hoped would satisfy the conditions for a plea of diminished responsibility as laid out in the 1957 Homicide Act. Dr James MacKeith testified that Nilsen had a personality disorder, which manifested itself as a craving for attention and desire for an enduring relationship. If the men he met during the one-night-stands showed apathy towards him, he took it as a rejection, a personal affront.

Nilsen covered the same ground in his statement to the police, which was read out in court. 'In the normal course of my life I feel I have normal powers of mental rationality and morality. When under pressure of work and extreme pain of social loneliness and utter misery I am drawn, compulsively, to means of temporary escape from reality.'

'Overwhelming desire to kill'

For the prosecution, Dr Paul Bowden agreed that Nilsen exhibited abnormal behaviour in his 'overwhelming desire to kill', but didn't concur with his fellow professionals that it was indicative of a severe personality disorder. In his opinion the defendant was cognisant of, and responsible for, the actions he had taken. Much of the evidence given by the expert witnesses was too abstruse for the lay person to follow. In his summation Mr Justice Croom-Johnson simplified matters, pointing out that mental abnormality was not a pre-requisite for evil intent. After 12 hours' deliberation the jury returned guilty verdicts with a 10-2 majority. Dennis Nilsen was given a life sentence, with a recommendation that he serve at least 25 years. He completed the minimum term in 2008, and although successive home secretaries had indicated that a whole-life tariff was applicable in this case, that ruling was being challenged in the European Court of Human Rights.

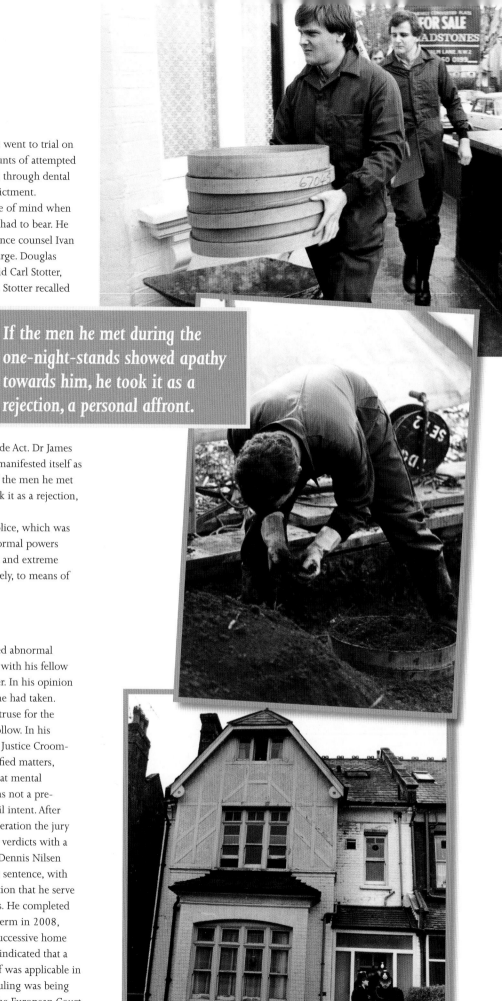

> If the men he met during the one-night-stands showed apathy towards him, he took it as a rejection, a personal affront.

'It amazes me I have no tear for my victims'

An astonishing insight into the mind of mass killer Dennis Nilsen was given to the Old Bailey yesterday. In a series of letters alleged to have been written from prison to the man who arrested him, he described his anguish, torment and the motivation which led him to kill.

At the start of the trial yesterday Mr Allan Green, prosecuting, said there was no dispute that Nilsen killed each of the men named in the murder charges. The only issue was whether he was guilty of murder or the lesser charge of manslaughter. Yesterday he sat with his hands clasped in the dock as Detective Chief Inspector Peter Jay read extracts from Nilsen's letters.

In the first, the author admits: 'There is no disputing I am a violent killer under certain circumstances. It amazes me I have no tears for these victims. I have no tears for myself, or those bereaved by my action. Am I a weak person, constantly under pressure, who just cannot cope with it, who escapes to revenge against society through the haze of a bottle of spirits? Or maybe it was because I was just born an evil man?'

Unbearable pressures

Another letter states: 'I am tragically a private person, not given to public tears. The enormity of the act has left me in permanent shock. The trouble was that, as my activities increased, so did the unbearable pressures which could only be escaped from by taking the best routes to oblivion via the bottle. I think I have sufficient principle and morality to know where the buck must come to rest. The evil was short-lived and cannot live for long inside. I have slain my own dragon as surely as the Press will slay me.'

Nilsen's letters expand on the part alcohol played in his life as a means of 'escaping from reality.' One letter says: 'This is achieved by taking increasing draughts of alcohol and plugging into stereo music which mentally removes me to a high plane of ecstasy, joy and tears. That is a totally emotional experience. I relive experiences from childhood to the present - taking out the bad bits.'

Headless

Two of the records which helped him into the state of 'true emotional experience' were Rick Wakeman's Criminal Record and the eight-minute long Oh, Superman, by Laurie Anderson. He said the latter helped him evoke an hypnotic trance. He once played it ten times in succession until the Bacardi ran out.

Nilsen also allegedly listed those that he remembered to have escaped alive from his flat. He recalled turning away a friend who had come to visit him from Exeter because: 'I would obviously not admit him when I had a headless, naked body lying on the floor of my front room.'

Cross-examined, Mr Jay said he had never come across a case when someone was 'so immediately willing to co-operate'. Nilsen had voluntarily given samples of blood, hair, and clothing, and even up until last week he had been offering to go over police photographs of missing people to see if he could identify them. Mr Jay agreed that Nilsen had always seemed matter-of-fact about the bodies.

The detective found it very difficult to associate him with the horrifying catalogue of events. The trial continues.

OPPOSITE TOP RIGHT, OPPOSITE MIDDLE RIGHT AND OPPOSITE BOTTOM LEFT: Sieves were used to sift through the debris in the back garden at Melrose Gardens.

LEFT: The white tent covers an area where the search had uncovered fragments of human skulls. Nilsen had willingly accompanied police to the house at 195 Melrose Avenue and pointed out where he had buried some of the bodies.

OPPOSITE BOTTOM RIGHT: Nilsen found it increasingly difficult to dispose of the corpses and neighbours had begun to complain about the smell. He had stored body parts under the floorboards and in various cupboards and chests.

ABOVE: Mrs Peggy MacPherson points to the blocked drain which precipitated the arrest of the mass murderer. Nilsen had used a variety of methods to dispose of the bodies, including chopping the entrails into small pieces and flushing them down the toilet.

OCTOBER 27, 1983

'It could have been thousands of bodies'

Dennis Nilsen told police he might have killed thousands of victims if he had not been caught, the Old Bailey heard yesterday. The former trainee policeman was said to have told officers: 'If I was arrested at the age of 65 then there may have been thousands of bodies behind me.'

Detective Superintendent Geoffrey Chambers, who conducted nine interviews with Nilsen, said the killer always believed he would be caught. He said that in his statement Nilsen said: 'I knew it would happen again. I was resigned to the fact that it would happen again and I would get caught eventually but I would do the best I could to dispose of the evidence.'

Shopping bags

Mr Chambers revealed details of how Nilsen got rid of the bodies of his young victims. He said that when Nilsen was living at Melrose Avenue, Cricklewood, he would cut the bodies up on the kitchen floor. The organs were buried in shopping bags in the garden while the remains were put under the floorboards with deodorant tablets. Nilsen sprayed the air twice daily with an air freshener and insecticide.

Before leaving the flat in 1981 he built a giant bonfire in the back garden, on which he burnt the stored bodies. Afterwards he crushed the ashes with a garden roller in case any pieces of bone were still visible and buried them in a corner of the garden.

Mr Chambers said that when Nilsen moved to Cranley Gardens, Muswell Hill, he used a different method of disposal. After strangling and drowning his victims Nilsen dissected the bodies with a kitchen knife and stored some of the flesh in the wardrobe of his bedroom.

The jury of eight men and four women were shown saucepans that Nilsen allegedly used to boil parts of the bodies before flushing them down the lavatory. Other pieces of flesh he would cut into strips - some the size of a fist - and also flushed away, said Mr Chambers.

Nilsen's last boast: There may be more

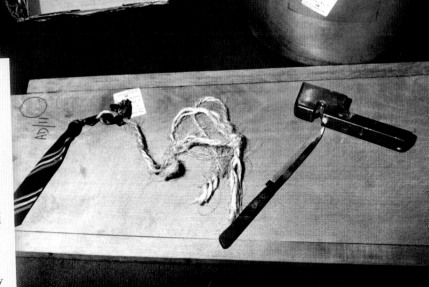

Britain's most macabre mass murderer, Dennis Nilsen, was given a life sentence of at least 25 years yesterday. And it was revealed that the man who admitted claiming 15 victims is to be re-interviewed by Scotland Yard after boasting: 'I may have killed a lot more.'

The statement was made by Nilsen as he sat in his cell below the famous No. 1 Court at the Old Bailey while waiting for the jury to return their verdicts on his crimes. He had recalled the 15 killings because the victims' bodies had been at his home, he said. But there could easily have been 'many more' because sometimes he had gone to other men's rooms for drinking sessions and it was possible that he had killed on those occasions. Detectives will now reopen the dossiers on unsolved murders of young men going back ten years.

Anxious to help

Last night his solicitor, Mr Ralph Haeems, said: 'He is anxious to help. He is willing for police to show him pictures of any young men in unsolved murder or suspicious death cases that might fit the pattern - and if he remembers being with them, he will say so.'

There was complete silence in the court yesterday when the jury of eight men and four women gave their verdicts after 12 hours 36 minutes of discussion. As the foreman announced that they had found him guilty by a majority of 10-2 on six charges of murder, Nilsen, 37, who was once a trainee policeman, bowed his head and stared at the wooden floor of the dock. He was also convicted by a majority of 10-2 on one charge of attempted murder. On the other, the jury's guilty verdict was unanimous.

Nilsen had described himself as 'the murderer of the century.' But in court he had maintained that his crimes were not murder, but manslaughter by reason of diminished responsibility.

Crowds

Nilsen, flanked in the dock by four burly prison officers, stood with his hands clasped tightly behind his back as Mr Justice Croom-Johnson told him: 'It may well be that even if the verdicts had been manslaughter, it would have been impossible for me to pass any other sentence than life imprisonment.'

With one final glance round the court, and still carrying the notes he had made throughout the ten-day trial, Nilsen - wearing the same cream shirt, blue tie, grey herringbone jacket and black trousers he wore each day - was led down to the cells.

Exhibits

A grisly array of the exhibits in the case went on display immediately after the end of the case. Photographers were shown the copper pot in which Nilsen boiled the heads of some of his victims. Police also displayed two knives that Nilsen had used to cut up the bodies. He had learned butchery techniques in the Army Catering Corps. With the knives was a sharpener and a wooden board on which Nilsen placed the remains before beginning the dissections. The display was in a disused Old Bailey court annexe opposite the Central

Criminal Court main building

For Chief Supt. Geoffrey Chambers and Det. Chief Insp. Peter Jay it was the final duty after weeks of painstaking work preparing the case against Nilsen - work which had led to their being congratulated by the judge.

OPPOSITE TOP RIGHT: Estate Agent Leon Roberts stands in the attic flat at 23 Cranley Gardens as it goes on sale in November 1983. The house had become known as the 'House of Horror'.

OPPOSITE TOP LEFT: The former home of the serial killer was open for viewing. After Nilsen's conviction in 1983, his former homes were sold cheaply to investors who renovated them and put them back on the market.

OPPOSITE BOTTOM LEFT: Dennis Nilsen leaves Highgate Magistrates' Court. He had been charged with six counts of murder and two charges of attempted murder.

RIGHT: The trial began at the Old Bailey on October 24, 1983. The charges were read and Nilsen pleaded 'Not Guilty' to each one. The jury were shown key exhibits found in the flat of the accused after his arrest. Among the prosecution witnesses were several of Nilsen's potential victims – those who had managed to escape from his clutches.

ABOVE RIGHT: Nilsen's solicitor, Ralph Haeems, decided to go for a defence of 'diminished responsibility', citing a personality disorder in Nilsen, thus asking for a charge of manslaughter.

RIGHT: Dennis Nilsen returns to court in June 1984 with a visible scar on his left cheek. The court heard how he had been attacked with a razor by a fellow prisoner.

Michael Ryan: The Hungerford Massacre

Daily Mail 20p

14 dead 16 wounded
BLOODBATH ON MARKET DAY

IN scenes straight from a horror video, a lone gunman rampaged through a little market town yesterday killing 14 people before, surrounded by police, he shot himself.

Sixteen more people were wounded during Michael Ryan's orgy of violence in and around his home town of Hungerford, Berkshire.

Gunned down: A young girl's body is put on a stretcher

August 20, 1987

In scenes straight from a horror video, a lone gunman rampaged through a little market town yesterday killing 14 people before, surrounded by police, he shot himself. Sixteen more people were wounded during Michael Ryan's orgy of violence in and around his home town of Hungerford, Berkshire. The dead included at least one policeman and four women including his own 60-year-old mother.

Ryan's first gun

Michael Robert Ryan was born on May 18, 1960 in Hungerford, Berkshire, the only child of Alfred Henry Ryan, a 55-year-old government building inspector known for being a perfectionist. His mother was Dorothy Ryan, a respected and popular member of the community who was twenty years younger than her husband. Ryan grew up in South View, Hungerford, a quiet, self-centred boy, who was short for his age and was often teased and bullied. He never retaliated, but instead began to avoid other children. Academically he was an underachiever and he later dropped out of college, finding low-paid work as a school caretaker. He continued to live with his parents, supported by his doting mother – who even bought him his first gun, an air rifle.

> **Even as the massacre was happening, Ryan offered no explanation as to why he had decided to go on the rampage.**

Licensed firearms

As soon as he was old enough Ryan began to collect a wide range of guns, which he proudly displayed in a locked cabinet in his bedroom. All his firearms were licensed – since he had no record of mental instability and no criminal record, there was no reason to refuse a licence application. He also bought army clothing and survival gear and subscribed to magazines on survival skills and guns, including *Soldiers of Fortune*.

When Ryan was 25 his father died of cancer. The loner became even more withdrawn and soon lost his job as a caretaker, instead spending his time working on cars or going off alone to the shooting range. Early in 1987 he joined the Tunnel Rifle and Pistol Club in Wiltshire; he spent a lot of time at the club, and the manager later reported that he was 'a very good shot', displaying consistent accuracy even over large distances. However, there was nothing to suggest that Ryan was anything other than a normal gun enthusiast, and the events of August 19, 1987 came totally out of the blue. Even as the massacre was happening, Ryan offered no explanation as to why he had decided to go on the rampage with his guns on that day.

OPPOSITE TOP: The scene of Ryan's rampage in Hungerford that claimed the lives of 16 people, himself included.

OPPOSITE BELOW RIGHT: Police officers pictured wearing protective clothing. They had been warned that Ryan was armed and dangerous.

TOP RIGHT AND LEFT: Ryan's house after he'd set it alight. The fire spread to three other adjoining houses.

ABOVE: Police cordon in Hungerford. Ryan had started his rampage outside his home town before returning to his house, where he shot his own mother and neighbours.

AUGUST 20, 1987

Catalogue of killings

Ryan, 27, a gun dealer and expert marksman, finally holed up in his old school, John O'Gaunt Comprehensive. Strapped to his wrist was a hand grenade. Police called in expert negotiators in the hope of taking him alive. But at 7pm a shot echoed through the empty school. Michael Ryan's reign of terror was over. And there was still no explanation for his incredible catalogue of killings.

Bodies still lay where he had shot them as they went about their daily routines on market day in Hungerford. An elderly man in his red-brick council home. A taxi driver still celebrating the birth of his first son shot to pieces over his steering wheel. A policeman's father blasted in his car. A policeman cut down with a calculated bullet in his back.

Ambulancemen and police had been unable to comb the area because of the threat of Ryan's bullets.

Two victims were fighting for life in intensive care at nearby Swindon. Trails of shattered windscreen glass, bloodstained pathways, scattered live ammunition and cars covered in blankets to conceal the ghastly outrage testified to the hours before. Police opened a casualty bureau to cope with enquiries about dead and injured. Nothing like it had ever been seen in Britain.

LEFT AND OPPOSITE TOP: Heavily armed firearm officers patrol Hungerford looking for Ryan. Later, police would received criticism that they were inadequately prepared to deal with the crisis.

ABOVE: Mr Deans pictured in his garage. Ryan made two attempts to shoot at Mr Deans' wife, who was lucky to have escaped with her life.

BELOW LEFT: An aerial view of the garage west of Hungerford. A motorcyclist who had witnessed Ryan shooting at Mrs Deans called 999.

BOTTOM: The scene in Hungerford High Street: police had informed locals to stay in their houses.

OPPOSITE BOTTOM: The Nursery Training College van that was damaged during the Hungerford shooting.

> At 7 pm a shot echoed through the empty school. Michael Ryan's reign of terror was over.

Indiscriminate killing

On the afternoon of 19 August 1987, Ryan began his massacre. His first victim, Susan Godfrey, a 35-year-old mother from Reading, was picnicking with her children when Ryan abducted her and shot her thirteen times in the back. Following the murder of Godfrey, Ryan drove along the A4 in the direction of Hungerford until he reached at a petrol station outside the town. Ryan shot at the cashier, missing twice, before fleeing and resuming his course towards the town.

Upon returning home, Ryan shot his dog, set his house on fire and began targeting his neighbours. After shooting five people on his street, he shot dead the first police officer to arrive on the scene, PC Roger Brereton, while he was still in his patrol car. He then began wandering through the town indiscriminately gunning down anyone he passed, and sometimes even breaking into homes and shooting the occupants. At some stage his mother had tried to stop his rampage, but he shot and killed her too. Within little more than an hour he had killed sixteen people and wounded a further sixteen. He then headed to his old school, the John o' Gaunt College, which was closed for the summer holidays. Police surrounded the building, and attempted to negotiate, but all attempts failed and Ryan turned the gun on himself.

As a massive police force moved in, the gunman disappeared. Two armoured vehicles were brought in from Scotland Yard.

AUGUST 20, 1987

Loner

Council worker Ryan, said by neighbours to be a former paratrooper, lived with his mother in South View, Hungerford. He was a loner with few girlfriends but a passion for guns; buying and selling antique weapons to finance his own collection. Yesterday morning he selected some of the deadliest weapons from his garden-shed arsenal. They included a Russian-made Kalashnikov automatic rifle. He wore combat gear and, Rambo-style, a headband. He was indiscriminate. An elderly neighbour, a young punk girl, a woman in a car. All joined his list of victims. Ryan advanced through the streets, firing right and left, reloading from a bag of cartridges on the chest of his sleeveless flak jacket. A soldier home on leave dived into a hedge as the menacing figure approached. Later he was to find body after body in the terrified town. As a massive police force moved in, the gunman disappeared. Two armoured vehicles were brought in from Scotland Yard.

Then Ryan was cornered in the Priory Road School. Caretaker John Miles took shelter in his house in the grounds with his two children and three maintenance men. Fortunately the school was empty because of holidays. With Ryan now surrounded by armed police the talking started by telephone. All the time they were aiming to bring him out alive. Chief constable Colin Smith said that, during the discussions, Ryan's demeanour seemed 'reasonable'. He gave no excuse for his actions.

The woman he loved most, his mother, was also dead from a single shot.

AUGUST 20, 1987

Final statistic

Then the shot ran out. At 8.07pm, officers with heat-seeking equipment reported that the gunman was in the corner of the school office and was not moving. Three minutes later they broke in. A rope was attached to the body's right leg in case it was booby-trapped. Then marksmen were told that the body had 'toppled over' and the siege was at an end. At 8.45 Mr Smith announced: 'The incident has been completed.'

Ryan himself was the 15th grim statistic of the Hungerford Massacre. South View, a terrace of four houses, was in ashes. The woman he loved most, his mother, was also dead from a single shot.

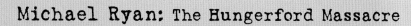

AUGUST 20, 1987

Rethink on gun laws

Mrs Thatcher, on holiday in Cornwall, was kept informed about the incident on a hotline from Downing Street. Almost a million guns are registered in Britain and yesterday's horrific events are certain to fuel demands for tighter controls. All Ryan's guns were legally registered. Growing public worry about violent crimes with firearms led the Government to insert new penalties in the Criminal Justice Bill which increased imprisonment from ten years to life on shooting offences.

And last night Home Office Minister Douglas Hogg promised a rethink on the gun laws. 'This is a ghastly incident and nothing I can say can really convey my feelings of sympathy to the families of the dead and injured,' he said. 'Obviously, the laws will be looked at as there are lessons to be learned from this incident.' Deputy Labour leader Roy Hattersley said: 'It is absolutely essential that a thorough and public inquiry examines the background to this tragedy - particularly the issue of gun licences and their availability.'

Today, Hungerford will try to come to terms with the appalling attack that shattered the community. Clergymen and police counselling officers will comfort the families of the dead and the maimed.

BOTTOM RIGHT: Empty cartridge cases fired by Ryan the day before the massacre. Ryan was a known gun enthusiast who obtained all his firearms legally.

BOTTOM LEFT: A spent cartridge from Ryan's Kalashnikov rifle. His rampage ended when he locked himself in his old school. Despite efforts to bring him out alive, he became the 15th person to die in the massacre.

TOP LEFT AND RIGHT: Ryan's guns pictured at a Hungerford press conference. The incident in Hungerford caused a complete rethink on gun laws and in 1988 the Firearms (Amendment) Act was passed. This banned the private ownership of semi-automatic rifles.

He was an only son, shunned by other children at his school and a 'bitter disappointment' to his father.

SEPTEMBER 25, 1987

Fantasies of a lone gunman

The fantasy world of Hungerford killer Michael Ryan was revealed yesterday. For the last year of his life he had surrounded himself in make believe. There were a number of non-existent girlfriends, marriage plans, wealthy friends, even a wife and child. He told stories that he held a pilot's licence, had flown helicopters and worked for a retired Army colonel who promised to buy him fast cars such as a Porsche or a Ferrari.

But, the inquest on Ryan and 15 of his 16 victims, heard, every detail was a figment of his imagination. In reality, 27-year-old Ryan was 'a rather sad and very, very lonely person', according to his aunt Mrs Constance Ryan. He had grown up an only son, shunned by other children at his school and a 'bitter disappointment' to his father. 'He was spoiled. The only time he asserted himself was when he carried a gun,' said Mrs Ryan, of Earlsfield, London SW. She told the inquest 'It seemed to me that he felt much more important and powerful when he carried a gun. He was not very big, unlike his father who was a tall and strong man. I think having a gun gave him that power.' Mrs Ryan described how her nephew told her he had pointed a gun at a man who got 'stroppy' while he was out shooting rabbits. 'He said that was the value of a gun,' she said.

MEMBERSHIP AND ATTENDANCE CARD

NAME RYAN MICHAEL
MEMBERSHIP Nos. R 62287
MEMBERSHIP CATEGORY PROVISIONAL

Grand plans

A friend of Ryan's mother, Mrs Eileen North, who knew Ryan all his life, described the fictitious 95-year-old colonel that Ryan had told his mother and acquaintants he worked for. Mrs North said in a statement: 'At one stage he was going to work for the colonel's tea plantation in India but that fell through because of a bad storm.' At times Ryan's mother Dorothy - who became one of his victims – was wrapped up in his fantasy world. Mrs North said the mother spoke of Ryan's engagements and of the grand plans that he had. Mrs Ryan told her Michael was to marry the colonel's nurse – but the wedding was postponed because the girl fell from a horse. Another time Mrs Ryan had told work friends that Michael had paid for her to take a trip to Venice on the Orient Express - but she had to cancel it because she could not get time off work.

Detective Superintendent John Childerley, who investigated the timetable of death, was asked by West Berkshire coroner Mr Charles Hoile about Ryan's mystery retired colonel. The Thames Valley police officer told the inquest: 'We have been unable to locate such an individual, and we believe all these stories were a figment of Ryan's imagination.'

SEPTEMBER 25, 1987

Sullen and moody

Charles Amor, who had briefly supervised Ryan on a Government community project for the unemployed, described the 5ft 6in gunman as 'sullen and moody.' Mr Amor said that on several occasions he had spoken to Ryan about guns. 'He said he always carried some gun in his waistband for protection,' said Mr Amor, of Thatcham, Berkshire. 'On another occasion he said he could supply anyone that wanted a gun with any type, of any calibre.'

A dealer in antique firearms, Alexander Gwilliam, who had sold Ryan a number of weapons, revealed more of the gunman's fantasies. In a statement Mr Gwilliam said: 'One story was that he was married to an Irish girl and had a furnished cottage and a child. But the marriage was not working out because his wife had failed to buy a birthday present for his mother. He also told me that he had found his wife in bed with an elderly uncle of his.' Mr Gwilliam added that Ryan told him his father had left him a lot of money. 'With the money he told me he and a partner were involved in a business renovating properties in London. They had at one stage ten or 12 men working for them but the partner had run away to Australia and left him bankrupt.'

TOP RIGHT: John Storms stands on the spot where he was shot by Michael Ryan. He was able to escape with his life thanks to the courage of Bob Barclay, who heard the shots and dragged Storms into his garden right in front of Ryan.

FAR RIGHT: Ambulance woman Linda Bright showing the bullet hole in the windscreen of her ambulance. Ryan attacked her and her colleague when they tried to tend one of his victims.

ABOVE: Funeral of P.C. Roger Brerton at St Mary's Church, Newbury, Berkshire. P.C. Jim Wood, who was in the car when Brerton was shot, Brerton's wife Liz, sons Sean and Paul , as well as Brerton's colleagues were present at the funeral.

The massacre led to the passing of the Firearms (Amendment) Act 1988, which banned the private ownership of semi-automatic rifles and restricted the use of shotguns with a magazine capable of holding more than two rounds.

O. J. Simpson: Murder Case

Orenthal James Simpson has more reason than most to be grateful for the double jeopardy failsafe that many legal systems adopt. The celebrated baseball star turned movie actor was acquitted of committing a savage double murder in 1994, but subsequently convicted on the same charge in a civil action. Only if new evidence came to light could O. J. Simpson find himself back in the dock in a criminal court, a highly unlikely scenario after so many years. But

the conflicting verdicts still leave open the tantalising question: did O.J. Simpson play a part in the murder of his ex-wife Nicole and her friend Ronald Goldman?

JUNE 18, 1994

O. J. Simpson is charged with double murder

American sports legend O.J. Simpson was last night charged with murdering his ex-wife and her boyfriend. He could face the gas chamber if found guilty. Simpson, a former American football hero turned Hollywood actor, is accused of killing Nicole Simpson, 35, and Ronald Goldman, 25. They were found dead outside Mrs Simpson's £400,000 townhouse in the exclusive Brentwood area of Los Angeles late on Sunday night.

Superstar status

Sporting prowess allowed OJ Simpson to swap his humble beginnings for superstar status and the opulent lifestyle that went with it. By the time he retired from top-level American football in 1979, Simpson had established himself as one of the game's all-time great running backs. Over the next decade, he carved a niche for himself as a sports pundit, and his good looks and affable personality opened up new doors. He already had a string of TV and film credits to his name, and retirement allowed him to take up more offers of acting work, notably a role in the 1988 hit movie The Naked Gun. He also had some lucrative endorsement deals, including fronting an advertising campaign for the car rental giant Hertz.

OPPOSITE LEFT: Orenthal James Simpson. His arrest and trial were among the most widely publicised in American history.

OPPOSITE RIGHT: In happier times the former football star carries the Olympic torch through the streets of Santa Monica, Los Angeles, during the opening ceremony of the 1984 Summer Olympics.

RIGHT: A few days after the double murder, Simpson was arrested and charged. At a preliminary hearing in Los Angeles in early July, Simpson looks over his shoulder to watch as his daughter, Arnelle, takes the witness stand.

BELOW: Simpson was represented by a team of attorneys including Gerald Uelman and Robert Shapiro, seen sitting next to the pensive defendant.

BOTTOM RIGHT: After failing to turn himself in, Simpson became the object of a low-speed car chase in a white Ford Bronco SUV. Simpson's friend, Al Cowlings, is seen walking away after the pursuit forced the fugitive to return to the driveway of his Brentwood home. The famous car chase through the streets of Los Angeles was broadcast live on national television.

Fairytale marriage

By then, Simpson had added a fairytale marriage to an already enviable lifestyle. In 1985 he married Nicole Brown, whom he had met when he was at the peak of his sporting career and she was a high school student waiting tables. It seemed to be a tale of romance and glamour, and there was further cause for celebration when Nicole bore OJ two children. But those close to the couple knew that appearance was out of kilter with reality. There was evidence of physical abuse, and that came to the attention of a wider public in 1989, when Nicole placed a 911 call in which she obviously feared for her safety. 'He's going to beat the s*** out of me,' she sobs at one point. Simpson was wont to dismiss such incidents as play-fighting, but even he couldn't gloss over the distressing scene played out on the tape. The marriage endured for three more years, when Nicole filed for divorce and was awarded a settlement of $433,000 plus $120,000 per annum in child support. Two years later, on the night of Sunday 12 June 1994, she was brutally hacked to death in the grounds of her Los Angeles home, and from the outset there was a considerable body of evidence pointing straight to her ex-husband.

> There was evidence of physical abuse, and that came to the attention of a wider public in 1989, when Nicole placed a 911 call.

JANUARY 25, 1995

O.J. 'spied on his former wife as she made love'

An obsessively jealous O.J. Simpson spied on his ex-wife as she made love to another man, it was claimed yesterday. The football superstar turned actor also stalked Nicole Simpson on dates, deliberately sitting opposite her in clubs and restaurants to intimidate her. Opening what has been billed as America's trial of the century, deputy district attorney Christopher Darden told the packed Los Angeles courtroom that Simpson killed Nicole for reasons 'as old as mankind'. 'He killed her for jealousy,' said Darden. 'He killed her because he couldn't have her, and if he couldn't have her, he didn't want anyone else to have her. By killing her, he committed the ultimate act of control.'

Simpson, 47, is charged with murdering Nicole, 35, and her friend Ronald Goldman, 25, on June 12 last year. Mr Darden said that when Nicole and Simpson split in 1992 she began dating a man called Keith. Simpson would turn up at restaurants and clubs and sit staring at them. Once, at 3am, he watched through a window as they made love. The next day, beside himself with anger, he told Nicole: 'I saw everything.' According to Darden, it was all 'part of cycle of domination' which began soon after Simpson and Nicole met.

Motive

When the LAPD arrived at the luxury Brentwood condo, they found a second body, that of 25-year-old Ronald Goldman. He was a friend of Nicole's – something more, some suggested – but that night he was said to be simply returning a pair of sunglasses Nicole had left behind at the restaurant where he worked. Police quickly deduced that the blade-wielding assailant had been a powerful individual – Nicole had been all but decapitated – and also that he had probably been known to her, for the wound pattern suggested proximity at the time of the attack. And if Goldman's role was indeed more than just a Good Samaritan, maybe jealousy was a possible motive? Unsurprisingly, the police's first port of call was to the nearby house of OJ Simpson, and it wasn't merely to break the news of his former wife's brutal murder.

> **As well as being hazy regarding his whereabouts on the night of 12 June, Simpson was also vague about a cut to his left hand.**

Shadowy figure

It was discovered that Simpson had flown to Chicago that very evening. He was questioned briefly, and it was arranged, somewhat generously given the nature of the crime, that he would turn himself in on Friday 17 June, the day after Nicole's funeral. His account of his movements on the fateful night convinced the investigating team even more that they had no need to look any further for the perpetrator of the double homicide. Simpson had booked a car and driver to take him to the airport for an 11.45pm flight to Chicago. The chauffeur, Allan Park, arrived at Simpson's house just before 10.30pm but got no response when he rang the doorbell. At around 10.50 Park saw a shadowy figure enter the property, and Simpson emerged shortly afterwards, claiming he had been at home the whole time but had fallen asleep.

Simpson had no alibi for the estimated time of the murders – sometime after 10pm – and his reaction to being told of Nicole's death was suspiciously atypical. He didn't ask where, when or how the crime had been committed, or if they had apprehended the killer. Was it because he already knew the answer to those questions?

As well as being hazy regarding his whereabouts on the night of 12 June, Simpson was also vague about a cut to his left hand. He eventually said he had caught it on a sharp edge on his Ford Bronco, but the prosecution would suggest a different explanation: that the wound had been inflicted in the struggle with the two murder victims.

LEFT: A black leather glove, which had the blood of both murder victims on it, had been found near the bodies.

TOP LEFT: O. J. Simpson shares a lighter moment with two of his attorneys, Robert Shapiro (left) and Johnny Cochran (right) during a hearing.

MIDDLE LEFT: Simpson looks relaxed as he listens to the testimony of Tom Lang during one of the many pre-trial hearings.

OPPOSITE BOTTOM RIGHT: Prisoner number BK4013970061794 entered a plea of not guilty and declared in court that he was, 'Absolutely, one hundred per cent, not guilty'.

OPPOSITE MIDDLE RIGHT AND OPPOSITE TOP RIGHT: In one of the most dramatic moments of the trial prosecutor Christopher Darden asked the defendant to put on the blood stained gloves he is alleged to have worn while stabbing the couple to death. Simpson struggled to pull on the left hand glove that had been found near the mutilated bodies, although he was able to pull on the right one with more ease. The defence claimed that the glove had been planted by police detective Mark Fuhrman in an attempt to frame the accused, whilst the prosecution argued that the glove had shrunk during the analysis carried out during blood-typing procedures.

Car chase

When the deadline for Simpson to turn himself in passed, the police went to his home to find that the bird had flown – maybe even expired. They found a note that included the words: 'Don't feel sorry for me, I've had a great life', though it also proclaimed his innocence, so it didn't add up as an indicator of guilt-ridden suicide. The prime suspect was now a fugitive, and the suicide angle was soon discounted as Simpson was spotted travelling on Interstate 405 in a vehicle driven by a friend. Traffic was heavy and it must have been one of the slowest car chases on record, yet the nation was held in thrall as the pursuit was broadcast live on television. It ended tamely enough as the vehicle was driven back to Simpson's Brentwood home and the wanted man was taken into custody. He had his passport and over $8,000 in his possession, plus a loaded gun and a false beard.

Physical evidence

At the indictment hearing Simpson entered a forthright plea: 'Absolutely, 100 percent not guilty.' When the trial opened on 24 January 1995, the prosecuting team, led by Marcia Clark, set about dismantling the defendant's bold assertion. Nicole's 911 distress call was played in court to set the groundwork: Simpson was presented as a violent, jealous ex-husband who couldn't bear to see his former partner with another man. Experts testified that shoe prints, clothing fibres, stray hairs and blood samples placed Simpson at the crime scene. A pair of blood-soaked socks was recovered from Simpson's home. The blood was Nicole's. One of the most crucial pieces of physical evidence was a pair of leather gloves, one of which was found near the bodies, the other at Simpson's house. Analysis of the bloodstains on the glove had involved freezing it, and prosecuting counsel was aware that they might have shrunk in the process. They had no intention of getting Simpson to try them on, fearing that it might rebound on them. But goaded by defence lawyer Johnny Cochran, they fell right into the 'Cinderella' trap. The glove was too small, and Cochran rammed home the point repeatedly to the jury: 'If it doesn't fit, you must acquit.'

> One of the most crucial pieces of physical evidence was a pair of leather gloves, one of which was found near the bodies.

OCTOBER 4, 1995

O.J. smirks at justice

At 10.07am, the bombshell. The woman clerk of the court began nervously gabbling out the verdict, momentarily stumbling on her words: 'In the matter of the People versus Orenthal James Simpson, case No. BA0797211, we the jury in the above entitled action find the defendant Orenthal James Simpson not guilty.'

A high, thin scream of horror and grief rent the dingy panelled courtroom. Kim Goldman, sister of the other victim Ron, tore pale, distraught fingers through her red hair, collapsing on to her stricken father's chest. Shortly afterwards, her father Fred stormed out of court, screaming at Simpson: 'Murderer! Murderer! Murderer!' Later he said: 'I deeply believe that this country lost today. Justice was not served.'

Simpson himself broke into a stunned, half-disbelieving smile at the verdict, then hugged Cochran. They'd done it! They'd pulled it off! There'd be no life imprisonment after all, no riots in the streets to avenge 'whitey's justice'.

Statement

It was to Jason, 24-year-old son from his first marriage, that the task fell of reading out a statement from the acquitted Simpson. His first priority, it said, would be to raise the two children he had with Nicole - Sydney, ten, and Justin, seven - in the way the couple 'had always planned'. But there was another duty. 'I will pursue my primary goal in life, the killer or killers who slaughtered Nicole and Mr Goldman,' ran the statement. 'They are out there somewhere. Whatever it takes to identify them and bring them in - I will provide somehow.'

The authorities took a different view. LA District Attorney Gil Garcetti said there would be no new hunt for the killers. 'We believe the evidence is there. The case is over.'

Seed of doubt

The cut on Simpson's left hand certainly looked like a knife wound, but there was no corresponding cut to the glove. The prosecution was thus alleging that OJ wasn't wearing the left-hand glove during the attack, but he did drop it at the scene before returning home. That raised the possibility that the evidence had been tampered with. The officer who found the matching glove at Simpson's house was Mark Fuhrman, one of the prosecution's star witnesses. He was presented as a model policeman but his reputation was badly tarnished after the defence had finished their cross-examination. Fuhrman was exposed as a racist who was not above planting evidence to secure a conviction. That undoubtedly struck home forcefully with the jury, of which nine members were black. Cochran branded Fuhrman 'America's worst nightmare, the personification of evil' as the defence strove to make race, not murder, the central theme. The State was forced to occupy the same ground in an attempt to refocus attention on what was actually on the charge sheet. Fuhrman, the prosecution was forced to concede, may have been 'the worst the LAPD has to offer', but his distasteful views did not mean that Simpson was innocent.

The insight into Fuhrman's character allowed the defence to offer a different interpretation of the facts: that both gloves had been at the murder scene, and Fuhrman removed one of them with the intention of implicating Simpson, first making sure that it was well smeared with Nicole's blood. If that were true, it followed that he must also have appropriated the socks from Simpson's house, taken them back to the crime scene to be similarly daubed, then placed them under OJ's bed to await discovery. Naturally, the prosecution protested that this was a groundless flight of fancy. For one thing, over a dozen officers were at the crime scene before Fuhrman put in an appearance, and all stated that there was only a single glove. If the picture the defence painted were true, then many more policemen must have been party to the conspiracy. Even so, once the idea of a vindictive, racist officer out to frame a black suspect was aired in court, an important seed of doubt had been sown.

The trail of blood and clues ignored by the jury

The jury took less than six hours to weigh up 45,000 pages of evidence and more than 1,000 exhibits. This is the hard prosecution evidence it ignored.

Gloves:

One was found near Goldman's body. Detective Mark Fuhrman claimed to have found its pair, smeared with blood, at Simpson's home. The prosecution argued that Simpson lost one glove during the killings and dropped the other while sneaking back.

Shoe prints:

Prints at the crime scene matched size 12 Bruno Magli sports shoes, a rare Italian-made model favoured by Simpson. FBI evidence matched the footprints to his shoes.

Socks:

DNA experts matched blood on black socks in Simpson's bedroom to his and Nicole's.

Timing:

The prosecution said Simpson had not been seen from about 9.40pm when he returned from a meal at McDonald's to 11pm when he finally answered a limousine driver's buzz at the gate. The driver said he saw a figure of Simpson's build cross the drive before O.J. appeared, claiming to have been asleep or in the shower. The prosecution said Simpson had driven to Nicole's between 10.10pm and 10.30pm, carried out the killings and raced home.

Hair and blood:

A knitted cap found at the scene carried hair like Simpson's. Some was also found on the victims' clothes. Their hair was found inside his Bronco, along with blood on the steering wheel, door and carpets. A trail of blood led from the bodies to the back of Nicole's home and from there to the Bronco in Simpson's drive.

Motive:

The prosecution produced evidence showing that Simpson was a jealous, controlling individual obsessed with his former wife whom he physically abused before and after their divorce.

> The officer who found the matching glove at Simpson's house was one of the prosecution's star witnesses.

Acquittal

The prosecution tried to recover lost ground by introducing evidence regarding Simpson's state of health. He was presented as being debilitated by arthritis, and thus lacking the strength and power that the assailant obviously possessed. Furthermore, he hadn't taken his customary anti-inflammatory drugs prior to the glove test, and it had left him with swollen joints. That explained why the glove didn't fit. Again they were wrong-footed by the defence team, who showed the court an exercise video Simpson had recently made showing him doing strenuous physical jerks.

DNA profiling was still in its infancy in the mid-1990s and the defence had little trouble producing their own witness to muddy the scientific waters. They were helped by the fact that some jurors confused DNA fingerprinting with blood-typing, and therefore downplayed evidence they believed could have implicated large swathes of the population.

> The jury took just three hours to deliberate over the nine-month-long trial. Simpson was acquitted, and in trying to temper any triumphal vindication vowed to track down his ex-wife's killer.

The jury took just three hours to deliberate over the nine-month-long trial. Simpson was acquitted, and in trying to temper any triumphal vindication vowed to track down his ex-wife's killer. That soon slipped off the agenda, not least because the victims' families launched a civil suit. The combination of a lower burden of proof and the new judge's tighter rein on the speculative racism angle cast a different hue on proceedings. Simpson hadn't testified in the criminal case but was called to the stand now, and he made an unconvincing witness. The jury found Simpson responsible for the 'wrongful deaths' of Nicole and Ronald Goldman, and with financial reparation the only available sanction, the court ordered Simpson to pay some $33 million in damages. The plaintiffs received only a fraction of that sum, helped by the law that ring-fenced Simpson's NFL pension fund, worth over $20,000 per month. However, the Brown and Goldman families were, presumably, more interested in the principle of culpability than squeezing the financial pips of the man they held responsible for the two deaths.

'Did he, didn't he?'

The great 'did he, didn't he?' debate rumbled on for a decade, and Simpson himself added further fuel to the fire when he cut a publishing deal for a book entitled *If I Did It*. It was not an admission, merely a fictionalised account of how he would have gone about committing the crime had he wanted to murder his ex-wife. There was an outcry, the public showing its disapproval for a tawdry money-making scheme on the back of a family tragedy. The book deal folded on the wave of antipathy.

Simpson hit the headlines again in 2008, when he was convicted on twelve charges relating to an armed robbery on a Las Vegas hotel the previous year. He and five other men raided the premises and made off with a number of items of memorabilia, which he claimed had been stolen from him. OJ Simpson was facing the prospect of years behind bars, possibly even life imprisonment, the sentence some thought he should have received thirteen years earlier.

OPPOSITE TOP LEFT: Sitting with his defence lawyers, Robert Shapiro and Johnny Cochran, a thoughtful looking O.J. Simpson listens to the evidence. Nicole Brown Simpson had filed for divorce two years before her death and during the trial evidence of domestic violence was presented to the court.

OPPOSITE BOTTOM LEFT: Defence attorney Johnny Cochran holds one of the defendant's hands to illustrate Simpson's debilitating arthritis which caused swelling and inflammation in the joints. The lawyer argued that this disability would limit his strength and prevent the football legend from causing any sort of bodily harm.

ABOVE: The widely publicised trial, often referred to as 'the trial of the century', concluded on October 3, 1995 when, after only three hours of deliberation, the jury returned a verdict of not guilty for the two murders. The verdict was seen live on TV by more than half of the U.S. population, making it one of the most watched events in American TV history.

RIGHT AND OPPOSITE BOTTOM RIGHT: After his acquittal O.J. Simpson travelled to England where he hoped to rehabilitate his image. His appearances included a visit to the prestigious Oxford Union, Oxford University's debating society. Britain's public relations guru, Max Clifford, was hired to coordinate coverage of Simpson's United Kingdom 'tour'.

The Wests: House of Horror

In August 1992 police turned up at the Gloucester home of Frederick and Rose West to investigate an allegation of child abuse. As a result of those enquiries, five children were removed from 25 Cromwell Street and taken into care, and West found himself facing a rape charge. He was saved by the fact that the abused daughter couldn't go through the further ordeal of having to relive the horrific events in court and give evidence against her father.

It seemed that West would not have to answer for his incestuous predilections, but a chance remark to a social worker changed all that, and the picture that emerged was much darker than the authorities imagined. It was noted that another daughter, Heather, was a conspicuous absentee from recent family photographs and home movies. The West children revealed the 'family joke', that their missing sister was buried under the patio at 25 Cromwell Street. It took police eighteen months to gather enough evidence to obtain a search warrant, and when they began digging, in February 1994, the 'House of Horrors' gave up its gruesome secrets.

TOP: The 'house of horror' — 25 Cromwell Street, Gloucester. Police attention was drawn to the house after allegations of child abuse. In 1994, after eighteen months of trying to obtain a search warrant, police began digging and the house of horrors revealed its secrets.

ABOVE: Missing poster for Catherine (Rena) Costello, Fred West's first wife. She and her daughter Charmaine were killed by Fred and Rosemary in 1971. Over 20 years later her relatives were still searching for her.

Perversion was the norm

Frederick West was born 29 September 1941 in the Herefordshire village of Much Marcle. His family had been agricultural labourers for generations, and Fred spent his childhood summers in the fields, helping with the harvest. He was driving a tractor by the age of nine, and the heavy farming workload took its toll on his education, for he was virtually illiterate when he left school at fourteen.

Physical and sexual abuse was rife in the West household. Fred's mother Daisy took his virginity, while the patriarch, Walter, regularly abused his daughters; perversion was the norm in their tied cottage. Fred took his cue from his easygoing father, who encouraged him to seize whatever opportunities came his way. Fred would interpret carpe diem as a green light for sating his lust, particularly after sustaining a serious head injury in a motorcycle accident at the age of sixteen. The family reported that Fred underwent a personality change, becoming an habitual liar and petty thief. His going off the rails reached a wider public two years later, when he was charged with impregnating his 13-year-old sister. The case was dropped when the girl refused to testify. Perhaps this early brush with the law, and the fact that he escaped censure, encouraged him to think he could take his sexual pleasure as he pleased with impunity.

MARCH 2, 1994

Specialist search teams

Heather West disappeared in 1987. Detectives are understood to have gone to her family house in Cromwell Street last week following tip-offs from a number of teenagers. Specialist search teams have been working in the 40ft by 15ft garden since Friday. A lane behind the houses has been closed to the public. Police used a small mechanical excavator to help remove the concrete paving stones forming a patio which covered a large part of the ill-kept garden. The excavator was also used to dig trenches in a grid, removing the top soil. To begin with, officers dug through the rain-sodden search with spades and used large sieves to search for clues. But their work halted temporarily with the discovery of the remains.

Home Office pathologist Bernard Knight, from Cardiff University, then began directing what Det Supt Bennett described as an 'archaeological-type' dig, painstakingly cataloguing and mapping the bones before removing them for forensic examination and identification.

The search of the garden is expected to last for several more days.

ABOVE AND LEFT: Police search the 'house of horror'. Among the nine bodies that were exhumed was that of Fred and Rosemary's daughter, Heather, who vanished when she was 16. It was a 'family joke' that if the other children did not behave, they would end up under the patio like Heather.

Diet of voyeurism

West was working as a lorry driver in 1962 when he picked up and befriended Scottish runaway Rena Costello. She was pregnant and trying to escape the clutches of the Asian pimp who was the baby's father. Fred and Rena married after a whirlwind romance and moved to Glasgow, where Charmaine was born the following March. Rena worked as a stripper and a prostitute, which merely excited a husband who had been raised on a diet of voyeurism. While Rena was selling sexual services, Fred got a job driving an ice-cream van, which afforded him numerous opportunities for extra-marital encounters. One such dalliance, with a girl called Ann McFall, became something more serious. Fred would call her the love of his life, yet she would be his first victim.

Rena gave birth to Fred's child, Anne Marie on 6 July 1964. The new arrival couldn't paper over the cracks of a volatile relationship, and a year later Fred returned to Much Marcle, taking both children with him. Ann McFall tracked him down there, becoming his childminder and mistress. She, too, became pregnant, but shortly before she was due to give birth, Ann was murdered and dismembered, her body buried in Fingerpost Field, a remote spot around fifteen miles from Gloucester. In a police interview some twenty-seven years later, West would cast the blame for Ann's death on Rena. The two women knew each other, and Rena did pay sporadic visits to Gloucester for short-term reconciliations, but this was not a crime committed by an enraged, jealous wife who had found herself supplanted in her husband's affections. Ann McFall undoubtedly perished at Fred's hands – hands that had become even more skilled in butchery through his current employment in an abattoir. Some believe Ann sealed her fate when she demanded that Fred marry her, others that she was killed when a violent sex game went too far. What is certain is that he now had blood on his hands, and once again he had got away with committing a crime.

Second Victim

West's second victim was probably Mary Bastholm, a 15-year-old waitress who disappeared in January 1968 while waiting at a bus stop. West patronised the café where Mary worked, and made off-the-record hints suggesting she numbered among his early victims. Her body has never been found. When West was finally brought to book, the police concentrated on building a case around the murders to which he had confessed. The case of Mary Bastholm thus remains unresolved, despite the strong indications pointing straight towards Fred West.

'Moved to London'

With Ann McFall dead and Rena back in Scotland, Fred needed practical help in looking after Charmaine and Anne Marie, who were being shunted in and out of care on a regular basis. He found it in the shape of 15-year-old Rose Letts, yet another casual pick-up while he was out on the road. She may have been twelve years his junior, but Rose was attracted to older men and the two hit it off immediately. She, too, had been brought up in a violent, abusive family; she, too, had been a slow learner at school; and she, too, had a strong sexual appetite. She moved into Fred's caravan home and was soon prostituting herself for him. Rose also fell pregnant, giving birth to Heather on 17 October 1970. A few weeks later, Fred was given a ten-month jail sentence for theft, leaving his 17-year-old lover to look after their new baby and the two older children. Rose handed out violent beatings, mirroring the parenting regime of her own tyrannical father. Charmaine, the more wilful of the two, came in for particularly severe treatment until sometime in June 1971, when she disappeared. According to her school record, she had 'moved to London', and Rose claimed that Rena took the child away. Charmaine never left Gloucester; her remains would be unearthed at the Midland Street flat where they were then living in May 1994. When the couple were arrested, there would be some difficulty in apportioning culpability. In that respect the events of 1971 were crucial, for the fact that Fred was incarcerated when Charmaine was killed was used as damning, incontrovertible evidence in the case against Rose.

MARCH 2, 1994

The garden of death

Police were last night trying to identify two more bodies found buried behind a Gloucester house. They were under the same patio as the remains of 16-year-old Heather West, discovered at the weekend. Her father, builder Fred West, 52, has been charged with her murder.

The two bodies found yesterday were both of adults or teenagers and had been buried some 5ft deep. The remains had been there so long it was impossible for experts to give an immediate estimate of their age or sex. Police are checking back through missing persons files. Unsolved cases in the area include that of 15-year-old Mary Bastholm, last seen leaving home to visit her boyfriend, and student Lucy Partington, 21.

As the painstaking examination of the garden of death went on yesterday, detectives were also said to have discovered a 'dungeon room' inside the semi-detached Victorian house. A neighbour, whose daughter used to play with the West family, said: 'She told me they had a cellar with a trap door covered by a carpet.'

Wife released on bail

Police are also poised to start digging up the grounds of West's former home in Bishops Cleeve, four miles from Cheltenham. Detectives are trying to trace all twice-married Mr West's children - neighbours have told them he had at least eight. His wife Rosemary, 40, was interviewed by police but released on bail on Sunday, pending further inquiries. She is understood to be staying with relatives.

> Charmaine, the more wilful of the two, came in for particularly severe treatment until sometime in June 1971, when she disappeared.

Commission of murder

The bond between Fred and Rose was now even stronger, for they were united by the commission of murder as well as by their deviant sexual proclivities. And when Rena came looking for her children later that summer, she couldn't be allowed to voice her suspicions. She was murdered – West said he smashed her head against a gate – and buried in the field adjacent to the one that housed the remains of Ann McFall.

Fred and Rose married in January 1972, and in September that year took up residence at 25 Cromwell Street. The family had just been swelled by the arrival of Mae, and again the Wests were in the market for a live-in nanny.

Caroline Owens was hired, but voted with her feet as soon as her employers tried to recruit her into a sex ring. Shortly afterwards, Fred and Rose happened upon Caroline while she was hitchhiking, and although she had been made to feel uncomfortable at the earlier lewd proposal, she also felt a pang of guilt for leaving them in the lurch. She accepted a ride, and was subjected to a 12-hour ordeal which included a sexual assault by both adults. Caroline was one of the lucky survivors, and although she made a statement to the police, she couldn't face court proceedings. The Wests escaped with a £100 fine.

> *Although one victim made a statement to the police, she couldn't face court proceedings. The Wests escaped with a £100 fine.*

OPPOSITE BELOW: Crowds gather outside the West's house on Cromwell Street, Gloucester. Among the victims found in the house was Shirley Robinson, who was eight months pregnant with Fred's child when he killed her in 1978.

TOP: Cement is poured into the foundations at the West's house on Cromwell Street. During their search police found a 50ft well below the property that West had covered over when he built an extension on the house.

ABOVE: The home where Fred West was born in Much Marcle, Herefordshire. West claimed that incest was accepted as part of the household and that his father introduced him to bestiality.

Victims silenced

25 Cromwell Street became a revolving door for all manner of waifs and strays, some answering advertisements placed by the Wests. With drink, drugs and sex on tap, the house was a magnet for young runaways, the very people Fred and Rose wanted to attract. Jordan's Brook, a nearby home for adolescent girls with troubled backgrounds also offered rich pickings for their evil intent. The youngsters they drew into their web were invariably looking for a sense of belonging and stability, and Cromwell Street offered just that, initially, at least.

After the narrow escape they had had with Caroline Owens, Fred and Rose were more determined than ever to silence their victims. Between 1973 and 1979 at least nine women met their end at Cromwell Street. Kneecaps and digits were routinely removed; decapitation was also common practice. One of the victims, Shirley Robinson, became pregnant by Fred and bragged that she might become the new Mrs West. She was eight months pregnant when she disappeared in May 1978.

APRIL 11, 1994

Grave is found in hunt for the first Mrs West

House of Horror detectives yesterday found what they believe are the remains of Frederick West's first wife buried in a field. They have spent two weeks searching the isolated Letterbox field for Catherine Costello, whose family have not seen or heard from her since 1969. The discovery, thought to be a small number of bones, was made at the field at Kempley on the Gloucestershire border with Herefordshire after West was taken there and pointed out a spot.

A pathologist will examine the remains today before digging begins again in the hope of making a formal identification. A Gloucester police spokesman said: 'We have got a positive line of inquiry of who we think the remains are, but it is too early to state at this stage.' Catherine's sister Georgina McCann trembled with shock at the door of her West Belfast home yesterday as she said: 'I was expecting this.'

The field at Kempley is a mile from West's childhood home at Much Marcle. Police have excavated more than 150 tons of earth while digging a 6ft wide, 4ft deep trench which by yesterday was more than 150ft long. Landowner Reg Watkins, 38, said: 'Fred West arrived here with a heavy police presence in the back of a riot van. He pointed out the spot to police and they marked it off.' Police used a £50,000 ground-penetrating radar device dubbed the Lawnmower to help in the search. Mr Watkins said: 'They passed a scanner over the place and a policeman told me they thought it had shown up one, maybe two bodies. They seemed to think they could be three feet down or so.'

Charged

Catherine married West in 1962 and they had two children - Anna, who still lives in Gloucester, and Charmaine, who disappeared in 1977. Police think her body may be hidden at 25 Midland Street, Gloucester, which they have yet to search. Builder West, 52, has been charged with the murders of nine women and girls whose bodies were found at his home at 25 Cromwell Street, Gloucester.

Years of abuse

The children also continued to suffer. Anne Marie testified that she was raped by her father at the age of eight, Rose holding her down while Fred penetrated her. She was later forced into prostitution, finally putting an end to the abuse when she left home in 1980, aged fifteen. Her gain was her half-sister Heather's loss. Heather was ten at the time, and the fact that Fred and Rose were her natural parents didn't spare her. She would endure seven years of abuse before she disappeared, probably after protesting too loudly. The violation created a special bond between the children. They knew what was happening was wrong, despite being told that incestuous relationships were normal, if not discussed openly. But they knew no lifestyle other than ill treatment, and also feared that if their parents were jailed for their actions, the family might be broken up.

The police were regular visitors to Cromwell Street in the 1970s, at the Wests' behest. Fred and Rose deflected attention from their own nefarious deeds by informing on their lodgers' drug taking, a ploy that helped them evade justice for twenty years. They were also extremely lucky. The parents of one of their victims, 19-year-old Linda Gough, turned up at the house in search of their missing daughter in 1973. Rose managed to fob them off with a tale that Linda had moved on, although she was wearing some of the dead girl's clothes at the time.

TOP LEFT: Fred West's police mug shot. His daughter Anne Marie testified that she was raped by her father at the age of eight whilst Rose held her down.

TOP RIGHT: Police use radar equipment in the hunt for bodies in Much Marcle. Rena Costello's and Anna McFall's bodies were found in fields near where West grew up.

ABOVE: The officer leading the enquiry into the Wests and DCI Moore in the yard of the 'house of horrors'.

OPPOSITE BELOW: The coach carrying the jury in the trial of Rosemary West arrives at 25 Cromwell Street.

Police uncover bodies

Rose's involvement was a key factor both in terms of recruiting victims and avoiding detection. Criminologists usually associate sexual sadism with males; women are seen as nurturers and carers, highly unlikely to participate in the violent abuse of any children, let alone their own. Caroline Owens said that she was wary about accepting a lift with Fred West until she saw there was an adult female in the passenger seat. It takes no great leap of the imagination to suppose how the less fortunate young women were also put at their ease by Rose's presence.

> They knew no lifestyle other than ill treatment, and also feared that if their parents were jailed for their actions, the family might be broken up.

By 1992, when police arrived at 25 Cromwell Street to investigate the rape allegation, Fred and Rose West had raised eleven children into what they termed 'our family of love'. Three of them had been fathered by Rose's clients, two were already dead. Once the police got the warrant that enabled them to search the house on 24 February 1994, events moved quickly. They soon found that the 'family joke' was all too real as Heather West's dismembered body was found. When a third femur was dug up, they realised they were dealing with more than a domestic murder case. On 4 March West made a statement admitting to 'a further (approx) nine killings, expressly, Charmaine, Rena, Linda Gough and others to be identified'. The remains of nine women were recovered from the 'House of Horrors' over a period of eleven days. Forensic scientists identified the victims by superimposing photographs onto the skulls. West took officers to the fields where Rena Costello and Ann McFall were buried, and while the excavation work was still ongoing there, Charmaine's body was found at 25 Midland Road.

JUNE 9, 1994

The dig of death

In the past eight weeks, officers have removed nearly 3,000 tons of earth. Using a JCB, a dumper truck, a conveyor belt system and a pump, they have carved out a pit big enough to house an Olympic swimming pool. The site, excavated by a team of 12 is almost 100ft long, more than 60ft wide and up to 8ft deep. Deeper holes have been sunk whenever a ground-penetrating radar indicates underground disturbances or voids. Examinations of the latest remains are expected to take weeks. Further searching will continue but police privately believe the final remains have now been discovered.

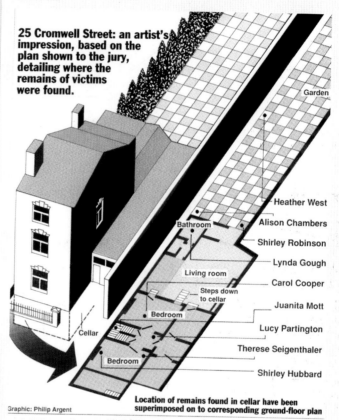

25 Cromwell Street: an artist's impression, based on the plan shown to the jury, detailing where the remains of victims were found.

Garden

Heather West
Alison Chambers
Shirley Robinson
Lynda Gough
Carol Cooper
Juanita Mott
Lucy Partington
Therese Seigenthaler
Shirley Hubbard

Bathroom
Living room
Steps down to cellar
Bedroom
Cellar
Bedroom

Location of remains found in cellar have been superimposed on to corresponding ground-floor plan

Graphic: Philip Argent

The hunt for the body of Anna - who came from Coatbridge in Lanarkshire, and worked briefly as a nanny for alleged mass killers Fred and Rosemary West in the early seventies - was launched in a corner of the field on April 13, when the infant corn crop was barely visible. By the time the search ended on Tuesday evening, the lush green plants were waving more than 2ft high in the sunshine. The dig had begun after the discovery, in adjacent Letterbox Field, of the body of Catherine West, Fred West's first wife.

> When a third femur was dug up, they realised they were dealing with more than a domestic case.

Complicity

Fred was much more forthcoming than Rose during police interviews, though there were many contradictory statements. For example, before Heather's body was found, he retracted his confession and said she was alive and well, working for a Middle East-based drugs syndicate. He spoke of being haunted by spirits, and offered a warped view of the crimes when he commented: 'Nobody went through hell. Enjoyment turned to disaster, that's what happened…most of it anyway'.

Rose was initially given bail and placed in a safe house, though police were convinced of her complicity from the outset. She was arrested on 23 April 1994, and from that moment, a wedge was driven between the confederates. Rose denied all knowledge of the crimes, laying all the blame at her husband's door. A week later, Fred again retracted his confessions, obliquely indicating that they had been issued as a cover up: 'From the very first day of this enquiry my main concern has been to protect other person or persons.' When the two came face to face at Gloucester Magistrates' Court on 13 December 1994, the first time they had seen each other in six months, Fred made a gesture of affection only to receive an icy rebuff. He now turned on Rose, telling police that earlier statements had been made to protect his wife.

NOVEMBER 23, 1995

Ten life sentences

Rose West last night began ten life sentences for the 'House of Horrors' killings. Mr Justice Mantell told her: 'If attention is paid to what I say you will never be released. 'West's face stayed as expressionless as it had been through all the evidence of the unimaginable cruelty she inflicted on her daughter Heather, stepdaughter Charmaine and eight other girls and women.

But her lawyers, who said they would appeal, admitted later that she had wept uncontrollably after the first three guilty verdicts were brought in on Tuesday. As the trial ended, a furious row broke over how the Wests were able to go on sexually abusing their own children and torturing and killing other victims for 25 years.

Strands of suspicion

There had been repeated warning signs about Rose West's sexual deviance and violence. Dozens of officials came into contact with the family but missed the clues that should have saved lives. The couple were fined for a violent sex attack on teenager Caroline Owens but no-one closely monitored them. The strands of suspicion were not pulled together even when the West children were treated at hospital on more than 30 occasions for unusual injuries. One was treated for a sexual disease and others suffered from squints and speech impediments - all conditions often associated with child abuse.

Education officials feared that Anna-Marie West was being abused at home but nothing was proved. There were no follow-up checks when her sister Charmaine, then eight, was recorded to have changed schools in 1971. In fact, she had been murdered. Social workers knew girls in their care were visiting 25, Cromwell Street but failed to discover they were being sexually abused there.

Yesterday the jury of four women and seven men ended their 13 hours of deliberations shortly before 1pm, bringing in unanimous verdicts of guilty on the seven charges outstanding overnight.

As the trial ended, a furious row broke out over how the Wests were able to go on sexually abusing their own children.

Life imprisonment

Fred West didn't live to answer in court to the twelve murder charges he faced. He took his own life at Winson Green Prison on 1 January 1995, using knotted bed linen as a noose. The trial of Rose West opened at Winchester Crown Court on 3 October that year. She had played no part in the deaths of Ann McFall or Rena Costello, which left her facing ten counts of murder. She pleaded innocent to all charges. Caroline Owens was a key witness, taking the stand twenty-three years after she had been the victim of the Wests' brutal assault. Her evidence, and that of other survivors, including Anne Marie West, was used to establish 'similar fact'. This held that if Rose was the chief aggressor in acts of sexual sadism against them, it was reasonable to suggest that the same situation pertained with the victims who had not survived.

Rose West opted to testify, against the advice of defence counsel. She stated that Fred dominated her, which rang very hollow when set against graphic accounts of her being the instigator of numerous acts of violence and abuse. She tried to present an image of soft-spoken respectability, but that was shot down when tapes of her screaming foul-mouthed vitriol at the police were played in court. After the six-week-long trial, the jury concurred with the prosecution statement, that the ten victims' 'last moments on earth were as objects of the sexual depravity of this woman and her husband'. On 22 November 1995 Rosemary West was convicted on all ten counts of murder and sentenced to life imprisonment.

'House of Horrors'

A year later, the bulldozers moved into Cromwell Street. The 'House of Horrors' was demolished and turned into a pedestrian walkway. The rubble was removed, crushed and incinerated to forestall the possibility of attracting souvenir hunters with a taste for the macabre. That den of iniquity was no more and had yielded all its secrets, but were there others? In the period leading up to Heather West's murder there are several years with no deaths attributed to Fred and Rose. Given their voracious appetite for sexual sadism, their rapacious capacity for torture, it seems unlikely that they allowed years to pass without indulging their depraved tendencies. Thus, the actual number of victims who fell prey to the Wests may never be known.

OPPOSITE BELOW: The jury arrives at 25 Cromwell Street. Rose West was tried at Winchester Crown Court and, unlike her husband, did not confess. She was found guilty on 10 counts of murder.

ABOVE: Crowds outside the 'house of horror'. Both Wests were convicted of murder and it was recommended they never be released.

OPPOSITE ABOVE: A police photograph of Rose West. A jury of four women and seven men found her guilty after 13 hours of deliberations.

JANUARY 2, 1995

House of Horrors man kills himself

Fred West hanged himself yesterday with two strips of his prison bed sheets. The man accused of the Gloucester 'House of Horrors' killings was found at 12.55pm in his cell at Winson Green jail, Birmingham. There was loud and sustained cheering among his 800 fellow-inmates as the news swept through the jail.

Final hours

The first detailed account of West's final hours was given exclusively to the Daily Mail. Prisoner WN 3617 spent New Year's Eve playing pool and watching television. New Year's Day began at 6.30am with breakfast of cereal followed by eggs, and he was then allowed into the exercise area. At noon he returned to his cell with his lunch of chicken soup and pork chops and was locked in. During the next hour, West put into action the plan to kill himself on landing D3 of the remand wing, according to prison sources.

At around 1pm, the door was due to be opened so he could wash his crockery and begin his period of 'association' with one other Category A prisoner - a game of pool had been suggested. Before this could happen, however, West jammed the door shut to make sure he would not be found. Next, according to one insider, he tore two strips of green sheet from his bedding and plaited them together for strength. This rope was knotted and threaded through a tiny air vent above the doorway as he stood on a chair. Kicking the chair away, West hanged himself, the weight of his body against the door acting as a barrier to the warders who forced their way in.

'Finally you have been brought to justice for your wicked, wicked crimes,' the High Court judge, Mr Justice Thayne Forbes, said. 'You abused the trust of these victims – you were, after all, their doctor.'

Unexpected death

On June 24, 1998, the former Mayoress of Hyde, Mrs Kathleen Grundy, was found dead at the age of 81. Her death was unexpected as she had not been ill – in fact she had been expected at an Age Concern club that day, where she helped to serve the meals. Soon after her death a firm of solicitors contacted her daughter, Angela Woodruff, about her mother's will, which they had received the day she died. Woodruff was immediately suspicious, as she was a solicitor specializing in probate so her own firm had always looked after her mother's affairs and they already held a will made in 1986. What was more the new will left everything to Dr Shipman, her mother's doctor – but failed to mention a second house that her mother had owned. Angela was sure the document was a forgery and gathered enough evidence to convince the police to exhume Mrs Grundy's body, which proved to contain traces of morphine. When interviewed Dr Shipman said Mrs Grundy had been suffering chest pains, that he had visited her on June 24 to take a blood sample, and produced medical records to back up the cause of death – but Angela Woodruf was insistent that her mother had been in good health.

ABOVE RIGHT: Hyde cemetery where most of Shipman's victims are buried.

LEFT: Frank Massey & Son Funeral Directors where Deborah Bambroffe first became concerned about Shipman's high patient death rate in November 1997.

OPPOSITE LEFT: Primrose Shipman on her way to sort out funeral arrangements for her husband. She spoke to Harold Shipman the night before he killed himself.

OPPOSITE TOP RIGHT: Shipman's former surgery in Hyde, Manchester, with a pharmacy next door.

OPPOSITE RIGHT: A map of Hyde, Cheshire, marking the addresses of the victims and possible victims of Harold Shipman.

Warning letter

Harold Fred Shipman was born in Nottingham on January 14, 1946. He did well at school, passing the 11-plus to enter the city's High Pavement Grammar school. In 1963, while he was studying for his A-levels, his mother Vera died from cancer at the age of only 43 and perhaps this led him to want to become a doctor. In 1965 he was offered a place at Leeds University to study medicine, and while still at university he met and married farmer's daughter Primrose Oxtoby. Shipman graduated in 1970 and first became a junior houseman at Pontefract General Infirmary in West Yorkshire, then went on to join a practice at Todmorden in the Pennines as a GP. Not long afterwards he began to have blackouts, which were at first attributed to epilepsy – until it was discovered that he had become addicted to painkillers and had been forging prescriptions to feed his habit. He resigned immediately and sought treatment, which led to him only being fined £600 and receiving a warning letter, rather than being struck off. After a course of psychiatric treatment Shipman was able to return to work as a clinical medical officer in Durham, but by 1977 he had become a GP again, joining the Donneybrook practice in Hyde, Greater Manchester. In 1992 he set up his own surgery in nearby Market Street – taking with him many of the Donneybrook patients.

It was discovered that he had become addicted to painkillers and had been forging prescriptions to feed his habit.

Body of ex-mayoress is exhumed after GP benefited from new will

DOCTOR QUIZZED OVER 20 DEATHS

DETECTIVES are investigating the deaths of 20 patients of a GP after he was left a fortune by an elderly widow.

By STEPHEN OLDFIELD and CHRIS BROOKE

JANUARY 5, 2001

Shipman joins list of world's worst serial killers

Estimates that Harold Shipman may have murdered 297 patients during his 24-year career as a doctor would make him one of the world's most prolific serial killers of modern times.

The worst known serial killer was Indian thug Behram, who strangled at least 931 victims with his yellow and white cloth strip, or ruhmal, in the Uttar Pradesh district of India between 1790 and 1840.

Transylvanian Elizabeth Bathory is thought to be the most prolific female murderer. She is believed to have killed about 650 girls between 1560 and 1615 in order to drink their blood and bathe in it - an act which she was convinced would preserve her youth.

Among the most prolific of British murderers was Mary Ann Cotton, who was hanged in Durham prison in 1873. She married three times and over some 20 years used arsenic to poison as many as 21 people - husbands, children, step-children, friends and relatives. Her motives were either insurance money, re-marriage or sheer spite. She was executed after being arrested following a spate of deaths at her home in County Durham in the 1870s.

Edinburgh body-snatchers Burke and Hare became serial killers after identifying the lucrative market for selling human bodies with no questions asked to the city's medical schools. The pair, labourers from Ulster, strangled people in Edinburgh's old town and sold the bodies. But the murder of their 16th victim led to their arrest, and Hare turned King's evidence, which sent Burke to his death on the gallows in January 1829. Hare is said to have died a pauper in London in 1859.

277

Murder investigation

Way back in 1985 the police had investigated the possible murder of one of Shipman's patients, but had taken no action against him. However, by the time of Mrs Grundy's death in 1998 several people had raised suspicions about the family doctor with the friendly bedside manner. A local undertaker had noted that they were carrying out quite a few funerals of elderly ladies who had lived alone and were patients of Shipman, while a joint practice across the road from Shipman's surgery had expressed concern to the coroner that the death rate at his practice was considerably higher than their own. Although the police were kept informed, a lack of evidence had meant that they could make no move – until Angela Woodruff came to them about her mother's will. They soon found the typewriter used to produce the will at Shipman's surgery and he was charged with forgery and then with the murder of Mrs Grundy.

Untimely deaths

As police began to investigate further, other people came forward with suspicions about the untimely death of elderly relatives. The police exhumed more bodies and soon Shipman was charged with a total of 15 murders as well as the forgery of Mrs Grundy's will, and committed for trial at Preston crown court. All 15 victims were elderly ladies, previously in good health, who had been attended by Shipman shortly before their death. It was alleged that he had injected each of them with morphine or diamorphine, then changed their medical records to back up the cause of death as given on the death certificate. Shipman denied all the charges, but on January 31, 2000, the jury pronounced him guilty after six days deliberation.

'Finally you have been brought to justice for your wicked, wicked crimes,' the High Court judge, Mr Justice Thayne Forbes, said. 'You abused the trust of these victims - you were, after all, their doctor. You used a calculating and cold-blooded perversion of your medical skills. You have shown no remorse. In your case life must mean life. You must spend the remainder of your days in prison.' The 54-year-old GP was given 15 life sentences to run concurrently for the murders, and four years for the forgery.

Shipman quizzed about further deaths

1 MAY 2001

Serial killer Harold Shipman was today on his way back to prison after being questioned at a police station for 30 hours in connection with nine suspicious deaths between 1974 and 1975.

Shipman, 55, was held at Halifax Police Station in West Yorkshire where he was taken yesterday morning.

At 3.15pm today a white police van with a police escort began the journey to take the mass murderer back to Frankland Prison near Durham. Shipman, of Hyde, Greater Manchester, was convicted in January 2000 of murdering 15 female patients after a lengthy trial at Preston Crown Court.

In January this year, detectives said that they were to investigate all 22 deaths certified by Shipman when he worked as a GP in Todmorden, West Yorkshire, for 18 months during the 1970s. Officers have since liaised with colleagues in Greater Manchester, prompted by a report into the serial killer which claimed that he could have murdered up to 300 patients.

Shipman worked in Todmorden between 1974 and 1976. He moved to Hyde in 1977 and stayed there until his arrest. The GP was convicted of murdering 15 women by giving them lethal doses of the drug diamorphine - the medical term for heroin. Most of the women were killed in their own homes, with no one else present.

> *A local undertaker had noted that they were carrying out quite a few funerals of elderly ladies who had lived alone and were patients of Shipman.*

ABOVE LEFT: Artist's impression of Harold Shipman during his trial.

ABOVE (INSET): Details of the will of Kathleen Grundy, which was forged by Harold Shipman.

LEFT: Primrose Shipman, the widow of Harold Shipman, leaves her house in Walshford, North Yorkshire, the day after her husband's death. She was on her way to see the prison ombudsman who was about to begin his inquiry into the death of Dr Shipman.

OPPOSITE TOP RIGHT: Hyde cemetery, where most of Shipman's victims are buried. The total death toll will never be known.

OPPOSITE BOTTOM RIGHT: An aerial photograph of Hyde showing Shipman's surgery in Market Street (No. 1, bottom left) and the location of the homes of some of those he is thought to have murdered.

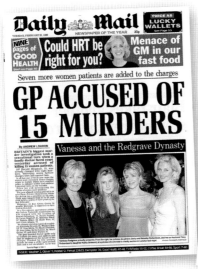

Shipman 'hooked on pain killer'

Serial killer Harold Shipman was so addicted to the pain killer pethidine that his wife Primrose had to accompany him on home visits, the inquiry investigating his death toll heard today.

Shipman, who took control of re-organising the drugs cabinet at the Abraham Ormerod Medical Centre in 1974 when he arrived in Todmorden, West Yorkshire, was so hooked on the drug that he suffered a series of blackouts when he was suffering withdrawal symptoms. But his partners at the practice, who had been called out to his home on a number of occasions after he had collapsed, believed he was suffering from epilepsy.

During a home visit to one patient in the town he hoarded prescriptions of diamorphine, promising to safely dispose of the drug. When matters came to a head in September 1975 Shipman, now serving life for the murders of 15 women patients, told his partners that he had become addicted to the pain killer because he did not believe in giving patients drugs he had not tried himself.

Christopher Melton QC told the hearing that Shipman had arrived in Todmorden in March 1974, an "enthusiastic, industrious" doctor who had impressed with his "even-temper". They had liked his "professional responsibility" and he seemed to be appreciated by his patients.

But during the course of the next 18 months Shipman began to lose his enthusiasm for the job, dropping in "productivity". Mr Melton said: "When he was confronted by the partners he explained to them that he first started taking the drug pethidine because he felt that he should not prescribe anything for his patients without having tried it himself." Later, in 1974 Shipman began to suffer blackouts.

"This came as a blow for the practice because it meant that Shipman could not do home visits alone." It was then, he said, that Primrose began to accompany her husband to the homes of patients who required visits.

Opening the hearing into the Todmorden investigations, where Shipman worked as a GP for 18 months, Mr Melton stressed it was likely that the overwhelming majority of the deaths investigated were the result of natural causes. Of the 31 investigated, Shipman had certified death on 22 occasions. Nine of the 31 were referred to the coroner. The doctor, who was convicted at Preston Crown Court in January last year, has remained in his prison cell in Frankland Jail, County Durham, during the inquiry. But after the end of the first phase of the hearings, when inquiry chairwoman Dame Janet Smith will produce an interim report determining how many victims he could have claimed, Shipman will be told of the findings and will be invited to respond.

'You abused the trust of these victims - you were, after all, their doctor. You used a calculating and cold-blooded perversion of your medical skills.'

Inquiry makes four reports

Afterwards an inquiry was set up to establish how Britain's most prolific convicted serial killer had escaped detection for so long, chaired by high court judge Dame Janet Smith. Its first report, published in 2002, concluded that he had killed at least 215 patients – and possibly as many as 260 – over a 23-year period. The list of victims included 171 women and 44 men, ranging in age from 41 to 93. In June 2002 the home secretary, David Blunkett, decreed that Shipman should serve the full life term with no parole. The second and third reports, published in 2003, criticised two police officers for their flawed investigation into Shipman just five months before he was caught, which had raised no concerns. The final report also called for an overhaul of the system of certifying deaths. On January 13, 2004, Shipman was found hanging in his cell in Wakefield prison, having apparently committed suicide.

> Dame Janet Smith said the culture within the medical profession led to an imbalance of being fair to doctors ahead of protecting patients.

SHIPMAN INQUIR

Chairman: Dame Janet Smith DBE

DECEMBER 9, 2004

Shipman probe: Doctors' watchdog fails patients

Doctors are too focused on "looking after their own" according to a "bruising" report into the case of serial killer Dr Harold Shipman published today. The watchdog in charge of regulating GPs, the General Medical Council, is heavily criticised for its procedures and its culture and has "fundamental" flaws, the report states.

The GMC sides too easily with its own profession and has failed to protect patients from rogue doctors. The 1,300 page report by Dame Janet Smith, a High Court judge in charge of the Shipman Inquiry, lists more than 100 recommendations for change.

Despite changes brought in by the GMC to get its own house in order, its culture has not changed enough to properly protect the public, Dame Janet said. "Having examined the evidence, I have been driven to the conclusion that the GMC has not, in the past, suc-ceeded in its primary purpose of protecting patients," she said.

"Instead it has, to a very significant degree, acted in the interests of doctors."

Dame Janet said the culture within the medical profession led to an imbalance of being fair to doctors ahead of protecting patients. And she said she did not "feel confident" the GMC will change in the "right direction".

She also criticised the GMC for not going far enough in its reforms since Shipman.

Mass killer Shipman, who worked at a one-man practice in Hyde, Greater Manchester, murdered at least 215 patients by lethal morphine injections. He was allowed to carry on practising by the GMC despite being convicted of drug offences in 1976 after becoming addicted to pethidine as a young doctor. Although he had a very high death rate among his patients, other doctors did not raise concerns to stop his 23-year killing spree. If the police, together with coroner John Pollard, had acted more quickly, the deaths of three Shipman patients would "probably" have been prevented, Dame Janet said.

25 AUGUST 2005

Prison criticised over Shipman suicide

The death of serial killer GP Harold Shipman at Wakefield Prison "could not have been predicted or prevented", a report by Prisons and Probation Ombudsman Stephen Shaw said toay.

But Mr Shaw made a series of criticisms of the prison authorities and said procedures for dealing with at-risk prisoners such as Shipman needed to be looked at again. He specifically criticised decisions made in relation to Shipman under the prison privileges scheme.

Shipman's privileges had been dropped from standard to basic because he refused to take part in offending behaviour courses in which inmates are encouraged to discuss their crimes and admit their guilt. The loss of privileges meant he could no longer afford to ring his wife and he was described as "very emotional" and "close to tears" by a prison doctor weeks before his death.

Mr Shaw dismissed allegations that Shipman had been taunted into killing himself in January last year by prison officers. But he added: "I am critical of the fact that staff at Wakefield do not appear to have been alerted to the man's long-term risk of suicide or what might finally trigger it."

Shipman killed himself while serving 15 life sentences for murder. He had only served four years. Some families of victims said they felt "cheated" and were angry at prison authorities that the mass murderer was able to take his own life.

The doctor, who killed at least 250 of his patients, made a ligature out of bed sheets and hanged himself from his cell window.

OPPOSITE LEFT: Danny Mellor, relative of Winifred Mellor, who was killed by Shipman, pictured outside Manchester Town Hall. To the left is solicitor Ann Alexander, who represented the relatives of the victims of Shipman.

OPPOSITE TOP RIGHT AND OPPOSITE MIDDLE RIGHT: Dame Janet Smith, who led Shipman enquiry, criticised the General Medical Council for not going far enough in its reforms following the Shipman case.

OPPOSITE BOTTOM RIGHT: Manchester coroner John Pollard pictured outside Manchester Town Hall where the second and third reports of the Harold Shipman Inquiry were delivered.

TOP RIGHT: Shipman pictured as he is brought out of Stalybridge police station. Shipman killed himself in Wakefield prison while serving 15 life sentences.

ABOVE MIDDLE: The word 'justice' was written on the shutters of Shipman's former surgery in Hyde.

RIGHT AND INSET: Market Street in Hyde, Manchester, where Shipman surgery was situated.

True Crime

Dr Hawley Harvey Crippen
Crippen (1862-1910) was the first criminal to be caught by using wireless communication. He was hanged at Pentonville Prison on November 23, 1910.

10

Archduke Franz Ferdinand
The Archduke's assassination in Sarajevo caused a declaration of war between Austria-Hungary and Serbia. As a result of the alliances each country had, World War One ensued.

18

Henri Desire Landru
Landru (1862-1922) was a French serial killer who bore a close similarity to the fictional character, Bluebeard. He was found guilty and beheaded by guillotine in Versailles on February 25, 1922.

20

Roscoe 'Fatty' Arbuckle
Comedian "Fatty" Arbuckle (1887-1933) was accused of the murder of Virginia Rappe in 1921. He was later acquitted of the crime.

24

Al Capone
Nicknamed 'Scarface', Capone (1899-1947) was seemingly untouchable for the murders he was guilty of. He was eventually arrested and imprisoned for tax evasion offences.

28

Bonnie and Clyde
Bonnie Parker (1910-1934) and Clyde Barrow (1909-1934) inflicted a wave of crime and mayhem across America during the Great Depression. The pair were killed in a shoot out in Bienville Parish, Louisiana.

34

The Lindbergh kidnapping
In 1932 the young child of aviation hero Charles Lindbergh was abducted from his bedroom. Despite the payment of a ransom, the baby was found dead weeks later. Bruno Hauptmann was tried and found guilty of the murder of Charles Lindbergh Jnr. He was executed on April 3, 1936.

38

John Dillinger
Dillinger (1903-1934) was America's most dangerous killer in the 1930s. His wave of crime came to an end after a shoot out outside the Biograph Theater, Chicago, in 1934.

48

John Christie
Christie (1899-1953) was a British serial killer who gave evidence in the trial of Timothy Evans, an innocent man who was tried and hanged for murders Christie had committed. Christie was finally apprehended and hanged at Pentonville Prison, July 15, 1953, on the same gallows as Evans. Evans was given a posthumous pardon.

52

Marcel Petiot
Petiot (1897-1946) was a French serial killer during the Second World War. Remains of 26 people were found in his home in Paris. He was beheaded by guillotine on May 25, 1946.

64

The Black Dahlia
Elizabeth Short (1924-1947), nicknamed 'The Black Dahlia', was the victim of a brutal murder. Her body was discovered completely cut in half. Her murder remains unresolved.

68

Geraghty and Jenkins
In 1947 Christopher James Geraghty, Charles Henry Jenkins and Peter Rolt held up a jewellery shop in Charlotte Street, London. They shot dead Alec de Antiquis, a father of six, when he tried to stop them. Peter Rolt was too young to receive a capital sentence. Geraghty and Jenkins were condemned to death and they were both hanged.

70

John George Haigh
Haigh (1909-1949) was a British serial killer active in the 1940s. Under the assumption that a body was needed in order to try him for his crimes, Haigh dissolved his victims' bodies in acid. He was hanged at Wandsworth Prison, August 10, 1949.

76

Lloyds Bank Raid
In 1949 Lloyds Bank in Bristol was held up and the bank manager George Black murdered. The culprit was never apprehended and the crime remains unsolved.

90

Double Jeopardy
Donald Hume was charged with the murder of Stanley Setty in 1949 but pleaded not guillty. He was found guilty of being an accessory after the fact and was sentenced to 8 years. When he was released he confessed to the murder. The laws on double jeopardy meant he could not be retried. Hume's continuation of his criminal ways landed him back in court and he was sentenced to hard labour for life.

92

Derek Bentley
Bentley (1933-1953) was tried and found guilty for his part in the murder of PC Sidney Miles. The killer, Bentley's friend Christopher Craig, was not old enough to receive a capital sentence. The judge sentenced Bentley to death, but Craig was only given a prison sentence and was released in 1963.

96

Drummond Murders

In 1954 Sir Jack Drummond and his family were murdered when they were holidaying in France. Gaston Dominici was found guilty of the murders and was sentenced to death by guillotine. This sentence was then commuted to life imprisonment. President Charles de Gaulle released him on humanitarian grounds.

110

Teddington towpath murders

In 1953 Barbara Songhurst and Christine Reed were murdered as they cycled along the towpath in Teddington. Alfred Charles Whiteway was found guilty of the murders and was hanged in 1953.

114

Ruth Ellis

Ruth Ellis (1926-1955) became the last woman in Britain to be hanged after she shot her lover, David Blakley, in a jealous rage. She was hanged at Holloway Prison on July 13, 1955.

118

Arthur Albert Jones

Jones was tried and convicted for the murder of schoolgirl Brenda Nash in 1960. He was sentenced to life imprisonment.

122

James Hanratty

Hanratty (1936-1962) was found guilty of committing the notorious A6 murder. His victim was Michael Gregsten. Valerie Storie, who was with Gregsten at the time of the attack, managed to escape with her life and identified Hanratty. He was hanged on April 4, 1962 at Bedford Prison.

124

Albert Henry DeSalvo

De Salvo (1931-1973), 'The Boston Strangler' confessed to murdering 13 women in the1960s. He was murdered in 1973 whilst serving his sentence of life imprisonment.

132

The Great Train Robbery

In 1963 a gang of robbers held up a postal train en route to London Euston and stole £2.6 million. Most of the gang were apprehended and sentenced to a total of 300 years. The mastermind of the heist was Bruce Reynolds who received 10 years for the crime. Gang member Ronnie Biggs escaped from jail whilst serving time and fled the country. In 2001, 35 years after his escape, he returned to Britain.

134

The assassination of JFK

John Kennedy (1917-1963), the 35th president of the United States, was assassinated in Dallas on November 22, 1963, by Lee Harvey Oswald.

148

Moors Murders

Brady (1938-) and Hindley (1942-2002) claimed 5 victims aged between 10 and 17, whom the pair buried on the Yorkshire moors in the 1960s. Hindley received two life sentences and died in 2002 after suffering a heart attack. Brady was given three life sentences, which he is still serving.

154

The Profumo Affair

John Profumo: 1915- 2006
The Profumo Affair was a political scandal in 1963. Profumo, the Secretary of State for War, reportedly had a brief relationship with Christine Keeler who was the mistress of a Russian spy. The scandal escalated and resulted in Profumo's resignation.

166

The Krays

Reggie Kray: 1933-2000
Ronnie Kray: 1933-1995
The Kray twins were organized crime leaders who were active in London's East End during the 1950s and 1960s. Both were sentenced to life imprisonment.

174

Harry Roberts

In 1966 Roberts (1936-) murdered three policemen on Braybrook Street, London. After a three-month long manhunt, Roberts was captured and sentenced to life imprisonment.

184

John Gotti

Gotti (1940-2002) was the boss of the Gambino crime family based in New York. In 1992 he was arrested and sentenced to life imprisonment.

194

Baader-Meinhof

Meinhof: 1934-1976
Baader: 1943-1977
Baader and Meinhof were founders of the Red Army Faction that formed in West Germany. Both Baader and Meinhof were arrested in 1972. Eventually Meinhof, Baader, and were jointly charged with four counts of murder, 54 of attempted murder, and a single count of forming a criminal association.

196

John Wayne Gacy

Gacy (1942-1949) was convicted of rape and the murders of 33 boys between 1972 and 1978. He was executed at Statesville Correctional Center on May 10, 1994 by lethal injection.

198

Charles Manson

Manson (1934-) was head of the hippie commune known as "The Family" in California during the 1960s. He was found guilty of conspiracy in the Sharon Tate/LaBianca murders. He and the other perpetrators were sentenced to death in 1971. A year later, however, the death penalty was abolished in California so all five are now serving life sentences.

200

Ted Bundy
Bundy (1946-1989) was a serial killer who confessed to 30 murders between 1974 and 1978. Bundy was executed on January 24, 1989 at Florida State Prison by electric chair.

204

Lord Lucan
Lord Richard Bingham, the 7th Earl of Lucan (1934-), disappeared the night his children's nanny was found murdered. An inquest into Sandra Rivett's death in 1975 declared Lucan as her murderer. He has never been apprehended.

206

Patty Hearst
Hearst (1954-) was a newspaper heiress who was abducted by the Symbionese Liberation Army and was subsequently imprisoned for her part in a bank heist. She was released after President Carter commuted her sentence.

212

Mayfair Bank robbery
In 1975 six armed men used a duplicate key to break into a Mayfair bank and made away with over £1,000,000 of cash and jewellery. Frank Maple, who masterminded the crime, escaped justice. He left Britain shortly after the robbery and is believed to be in Morocco, which has no extradition treaty with the UK.

214

Donald Neilson
Neilson (1936-), 'The Black Panther', was a British serial killer who was sentenced to life imprisonment for the murder of Lesley Whittle.

216

Peter Sutcliffe
Sutcliffe (1946-), 'The Yorkshire Ripper', terrorised the Yorkshire area during the 1970s. After claiming 13 female victims, he was finally captured and sentenced to life imprisonment.

224

Australia's trial of the century
In 1980 Lindy Chamberlain and her family were holidaying near Ayers Rock in Australia when Chamberlain claimed that a dingo had taken and killed her baby, Azaria. In October 1982 she was found guilty of murder and given a life sentence. In 1986 new evidence led to her release and the Chamberlains were declared completely innocent two years later.

236

Wayne Williams
Williams (1958-) was thought to be the perpetrator of the child killings in Atlanta between 1979 and 1981. He was found guilty of the murder of two adult men and sentenced to two terms of life imprisonment.

238

Jeffrey Dahmer
Dahmer (1960-1994) was an American serial killer and sex offender who murdered 17 men between 1978 and 1991. He was sentenced to 15 life terms but was murdered in prison by inmate Christopher Scarver.

242

Brinks-Mat robbery
In 1983 a gang of robbers stole £8 million from the Brinks Mat warehouse near Heathrow airport. Micky McAvoy and Brian Robinson were both jailed for 25 years in December 1984 for their part in the heist. Kenneth Noye served 14 years for handling some of the stolen gold.

244

Dennis Nilsen
Nilsen (1945-) was a British serial killer who confessed to killing 15 people between 1978 and 1983. He was sentenced to life imprisonment with a recommendation that he serve at least 25 years.

248

Michael Ryan
Ryan (1960-1987) was responsible for a massacre in Hungerford, England, in 1987. He claimed 14 lives during an unmotivated rampage, his own mother being one of them. The incident ended when Ryan turned the gun on himself.

256

O.J Simpson murder case
Simpson (1947-) was charged with the murder of his ex-wife in 1994. Following a high profile trial he was found not guilty of the murder.

262

The Wests
Fred (1941-1995), and his wife Rosemary (1953-), murdered 12 people, mostly in their own home. Included in this number was their own daughter, Heather. Fred West took his own life at Winson Green Prison on January 1, 1995. Rosemary West was convicted on 10 counts of murder and sentenced to life imprisonment.

268

Harold Shipman
Shipman (1946-2004) was a family doctor and serial killer who murdered more than 215 of his patients. He was given 15 life sentences to run concurrently for the murders. He hanged himself on January 13, 2004 at Wakefield Prison.

276

Bibliography

Organised Crime
Paul Lunde
Dorling Kindersley, 2004

Crime Investigation
John D. Wright
Parragon, 2007

Illustrated True Crime
A Photographic Record
Edited by Colin Wilson and Damon Wilson
Parragon, 2002

Masterpieces of Murder
Edited by Jonathan Goodman
Constable and Robinson Ltd, 1992

The World's Worst Criminals
An A-Z of Evil Men and Women
Charlotte Greig
Arcturus, 2007

In the Minds of Murderers
The Inside Story of Criminal Profiling
Paul Roland
Chartwell Books, 2008

The World's Most Evil Psychopaths
Horrifying True-Life Cases
John Marlowe
Arcturus, 2007

More Infamous Crimes that Shocked the World
Macdonald and Co, 1990

The World's Greatest Crimes
Murder, Robbery and Mayhem from 1900
W. Barrington Keith
Hamlyn Publishing Group, 1990

Killers
The Most Barbaric Murderers of Our Times
Nigel Cawthorne
MFJ Books, 2006

Crimes Of Passion
Colin Wilson and Damon Wilson
Carlton, 2006

Criminal Masterminds
Evil Geniuses of the Underworld
Charlotte Greig
Arcturus, 2005

Crimes of the Century
Alan J Whiticker
New Holland, 2006

The A-Z Encyclopedia of Serial Killers
Harold Schechter and David Everitt
Pocket Books, 1996

The Mammoth Book of True Crime
Colin Wilson
Constable & Robinson, 1998
Chronicle Of Murder - Brian Lane
Constable & Robinson, 2004

Mammoth Book of Murder and Science
Edited by Roger Wilkes
Robinson, 2006

Great Unsolved Crimes
Rodney Castleden
Futura, 2007

Couples Who Kill
Carol Anne Davis
Allison & Busby, 2006

Wicked Beyond Belief
Michael Bilton
Harper Collins, 2003

The Cromwell Street Murders: The Detective's Story
John Bennett and Graham Gardner
Sutton, 2005

Encyclopedia of London Crime and Vice
Fergus Linnane
Sutton, 2003

Poisoned Lives: English Poisoners And Their Victims
Katherine Watson
Hambledon & London, 2004

Acknowledgements

The photographs in this book are from the archives of the *Daily Mail*. Particular thanks to Steve Torrington and Alan Pinnock. Without their invaluable help this book would not have been possible.

Additional photographs courtesy © Gettyimages: pages: 24,25 top and bottom,26,27, 236.

Thanks also to Alice Hill for her detailed editorial work, Marie Clayton for additional text, Gordon Mills, Mark Brown, Lisa Wight, Alison Gauntlett, Jane Benn, Frances Hill, Wendy Toole, John Dunne, Cliff Salter and Mel Cox.